Springer Series on Cultural Computing

Cultural Computing is an exciting, emerging field of Human Computer Interaction, which covers the cultural impact of computing and the technological influences and requirements for the support of cultural innovation. Using support technologies such as artificial intelligence, machine learning, location-based systems, mixed/virtual/augmented reality, cloud computing, pervasive technologies and human-data interaction, researchers can explore the differences across a variety of cultures and cultural production to provide the knowledge and skills necessary to overcome cultural issues and expand human creativity.

This series presents monographs, edited collections and advanced textbooks on the current research and knowledge of a broad range of topics including creativity support systems, creative computing, digital communities, the interactive arts, cultural heritage, digital culture and intercultural collaboration.

This Series is abstracted/indexed in Scopus.

James Hutson

Art History in the Age of Artificial Intelligence

Springer

James Hutson
Department of Art History, AI, and Visual
Culture
Lindenwood University
St. Charles, MO, USA

ISSN 2195-9056 ISSN 2195-9064 (electronic)
Springer Series on Cultural Computing
ISBN 978-3-032-02919-5 ISBN 978-3-032-02920-1 (eBook)
https://doi.org/10.1007/978-3-032-02920-1

This Springer imprint is published by the registered company Springer Nature Switzerland AG
The registered company address is: Gewerbestrasse 11, 6330 Cham, Switzerland

I dedicate this manuscript to my family, whose love, curiosity, and insights have fundamentally shaped my work and life. To my wife, Piper, I am deeply grateful for your unwavering encouragement and for the neuroscience expertise you so generously shared; your perspectives on sensemaking and aesthetics have profoundly informed my understanding of artificial intelligence and its relationship to human creativity. To my son, Bishop, whose passion for designing video game characters with art generators continually reminds me of the rich, playful potential at the intersection of human imagination and generative technology—your creativity inspires me to envision futures where digital and artistic expression are interwoven. To my daughter, Aurora, who delights in making AI videos of mermaids, you are already preparing for a world in which visual storytelling becomes a dialogical process between human and machine, an ongoing, iterative creation of meaning and wonder. To my father, Jim Hutson, thank you for introducing me to art and for nurturing the curiosity that set me on this path. To all my family, friends, and loved ones—your patience, inspiration, and belief have made this project possible. I acknowledge the sacrifices you have made and the understanding you have shown as I pursued these scholarly endeavors. This manuscript stands as a testament to your support, and with heartfelt appreciation, I dedicate this work to you.

Acknowledgments

I would like to extend my sincere gratitude to the individuals and institutions who have contributed to the creation of this book and supported me throughout this journey.

I am immensely grateful to Dr. Kathi Vosevich, Dean of the College of Arts and Humanities, for her unwavering support and encouragement of the research that has culminated in this text. Her guidance and belief in my scholarly pursuits have been instrumental in shaping this book.

I wish to thank my research team, whose dedication made the completion of this manuscript possible, as well as the colleagues and coauthors on other projects whose insight and collaborative spirit directly and indirectly contributed to this volume. In particular, I would like to thank Dr. Trent Olsen, whose commitment to adapting pedagogy—from gamified curriculum to immersive digital experiences—ensures that students engage meaningfully with cultural heritage and art history in new ways. My gratitude also goes to Dr. Steven Cody at Purdue Fort Wayne for his rapid integration of AI tools into research and Renaissance Art pedagogy, and to Prof. Joe Weber, whose leadership demonstrates how administrative functions in the arts can be streamlined and improved through generative technologies. Dr. Piper Hutson's extensive work on museum inclusivity and the thoughtful integration of technology for diverse neurotypes has profoundly influenced my own approach. I am also thankful to graduate game design student Tiffani Barner, whose work on the Da Vinci AI tutor system—offering students a model for art history tutoring delivered by a digital Leonardo da Vinci—signals the exciting future of personalized learning.

Finally, I would like to thank Dr. Leda Cempellin at South Dakota State University for her nascent scholarship in art history and AI and for helping me clarify what art historians truly value, especially as distinct from priorities in STEM disciplines.

I am deeply grateful as well to my colleagues and fellow researchers who have shared their insights and provided constructive feedback throughout the course of this project. Their contributions have enriched this work and helped shape the ideas presented in this book.

Contents

About the Author

James Hutson is a leading authority at the convergence of artificial intelligence and art history, serving as a professor and department head of Art History, AI, and Visual Culture at Lindenwood University, where he also serves as the lead XR disruptor and oversees the Human-Centered AI and Interactive Technology Hub. Holding doctorates in both Art History (University of Maryland) and Artificial Intelligence (Capitol Technology University), Dr. Hutson's career bridges rigorous art historical scholarship with advanced computational and immersive technologies. He has pioneered the integration of generative intelligence, extended reality, and neuroaesthetics into both research and pedagogy, designing innovative curricula and spearheading interdisciplinary degree programs. With additional master's degrees in Leadership and Game Design, Dr. Hutson has contributed to national and international projects on digital cultural heritage, AI-driven accessibility, and the future of creative education. Recognized for both scholarly impact and educational innovation, he has authored numerous books and articles on computational art analysis and AI-enhanced learning, such as *Creative Convergence: The AI Renaissance in Art and Design* (2023) and *Inclusive Smart Museums: Engaging Neurodiverse Audiences and Enhancing Cultural Heritage* (2024).

List of Figures

List of Tables

Chapter 1
Introduction

Abstract In a discipline defined by its dialogue with images, methods, and cultural shifts, the introduction to this volume locates art history at a pivotal threshold: the emergence of intelligent technologies as both mirror and motor of disciplinary transformation. From the copperplate engravings in Winckelmann's *Monumenti antichi inediti* to the brushstroke analytics enabled by contemporary machine learning, art history has long been animated by a restless engagement with the evolving tools that mediate perception, analysis, and dissemination. Today, generative platforms and computational systems extend this lineage, unsettling familiar habits while opening interpretive horizons. Yet, such technologies also surface anxieties—about the erosion of subjective interpretation, the authority of human judgment, and the ethics of data-driven knowledge—echoing earlier debates ignited by photography or the magic lantern. This introduction charts the evolution of art historical practice as a continuum of experimental adaptation, attentive to how cross-disciplinary currents from neuroscience to media studies have continually reshaped research, pedagogy, and public engagement. It offers a critical inventory of the assumptions, ambitions, and challenges that accompany this new technological inflection, foregrounding ethical stewardship and epistemological rigor as the guiding imperatives for the chapters that follow. In doing so, it invites art historians to view the computational turn not as rupture, but as the next dialogic stage in a tradition of methodological ingenuity, interpretive depth, and cultural responsibility.

1.1 Situating Art History in the Age of Intelligent Technologies

Art historians have consistently embraced emergent technologies to interrogate, visualize, and disseminate knowledge, marking the field as uniquely poised at the crossroads of several intellectual traditions. The very formation of the discipline is inseparable from the visual technologies that have mediated its core questions, from the analyses of Johann Joachim Winckelmann (1717–1768) of classical antiquity in *Monumenti antichi inediti* (1767), with its copperplate engravings

J. Hutson, *Art History in the Age of Artificial Intelligence*, Springer Series on Cultural Computing, https://doi.org/10.1007/978-3-032-02920-1_1

(Fig. 1.1) that depicted newly excavated finds from Pompeii and Herculaneum, to the photographic archives and digitized corpora populating research databases today (Harloe 2013; Late et al. 2024). The evolution of art history in nineteenth-century Berlin and Vienna was informed by cross-disciplinary borrowings from archeology, philology, aesthetics, anthropology, and natural sciences, foregrounding a methodological eclecticism that made technological innovation essential (Preziosi 2009; Stafford 1988). Technologies beyond the printed word became necessary not only for recording and reproducing individual objects but also for enabling comparative visual analysis, mapping stylistic development, and disseminating new findings. This technological trajectory migrated to American contexts in the late nineteenth and early twentieth centuries, where institutions such as Harvard and Princeton leveraged photographic archives and lantern-slide collections to reinforce the reliance of the discipline on visual evidence and facilitate novel forms of public engagement (Harris 2024; Nelson 2000).

Successive technological adoption by art historians has systematically expanded the reach, precision, and impact of visual scholarship. For instance, the advent of the magic lantern (Fig. 1.2) in the nineteenth century brought the moving image into the lecture hall, transforming static descriptions into vibrant visual narratives to the ever-broadening pedagogical arsenal (Dellmann and Kessler 2020; Holly 1996). Photographic slides and carousel projectors enabled rapid, dynamic comparison of artworks across temporal and spatial divides, thus deepening methodological rigor and fostering a more critical, dialogic approach to visual analysis (Belting

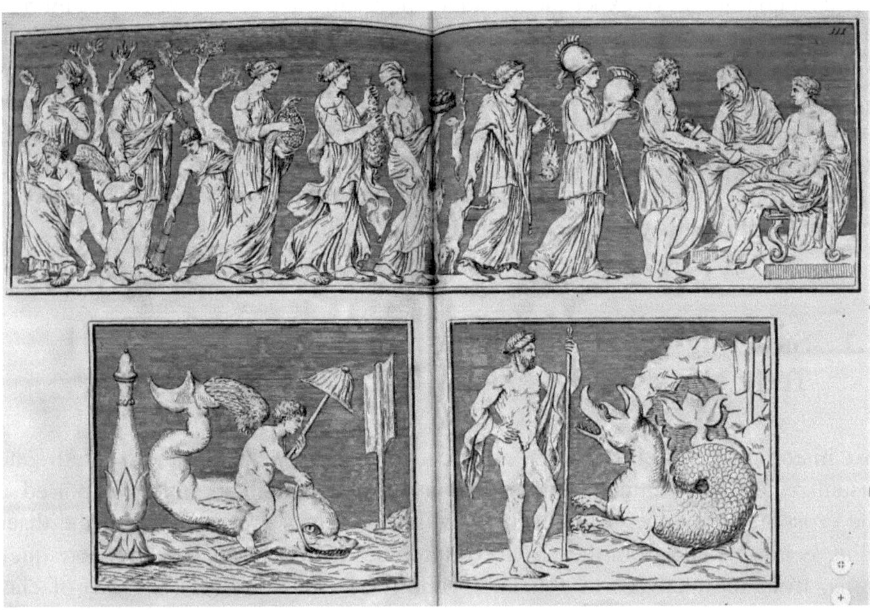

Fig. 1.1 Johann Joachim Winckelmann, *Monumenti antichi inediti*, 1767 (Roma: A spese dell'autore) (CC O, public domain)

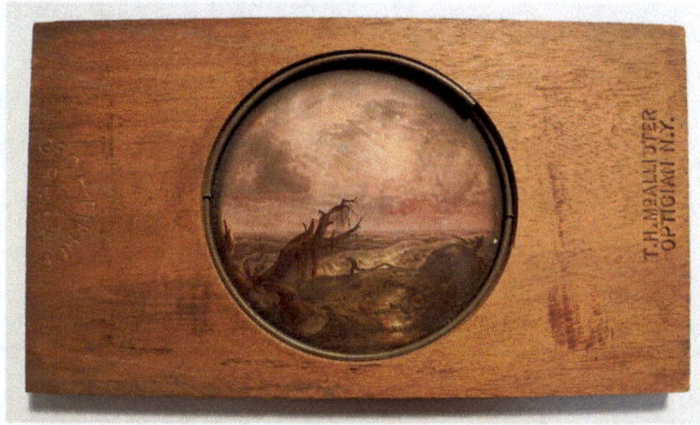

Fig. 1.2 Magic lantern slide with a wooden frame and geological topic, late nineteenth century (CC O, public domain dedication)

2003). Digital overhead projectors, emerging later in the twentieth century, further extended these visual dialogues by allowing instructors to juxtapose and manipulate multiple images interactively, making classroom engagement increasingly participatory. Today, computational techniques—computer vision, large-scale pattern recognition, and neural network-based analytics—equip researchers to discern formal continuities, quantify stylistic change across time and between artists, and analyze immense corpora of images, all at a scale previously unimaginable (Manovich 2020). Generative systems and machine learning (ML) then do not disrupt this lineage but continue it, affording scholars new means for contextualizing, analyzing, and interpreting visual culture in both depth and breadth.

Such recognition situates these emergent technologies not as alien incursions but as the latest chapter in the ongoing narrative of adaptation and ingenuity in art history. Each technological innovation has functioned as an extension of, rather than a replacement for, the interpretive skill and judgment that define the discipline. From the engraved volumes of Winckelmann to the photographic *Musée imaginaire* of André Malraux (1901–1976)—a concept developed in response to the rise of mechanical reproduction, where photography enabled individuals to curate their own personal, virtual "museum" from images of artworks previously inaccessible (like early modern "picture galleries" (Fig. 1.3)—through to the proliferation of interactive databases and generative platforms, technological adoption has proven fundamental to art historical inquiry (Darzins 1957). These tools continually renew and expand the possibilities for scholarship, teaching, and public dissemination. Generative media, far from representing a break with tradition, are best understood as sophisticated enhancements—tools that sustain the commitment of art history to interpretive richness, visual acuity, and critical dialogue, as related by Gombrich (1960). The adoption of a stance of methodological openness rooted in disciplinary tradition positions art historians to deepen and diversify field engagement with visual culture for a new era.

Yet, the long arc of technological adoption in art history is tempered by a prevailing attitude of cautious deliberation rather than uncritical enthusiasm. Historically, the field has rarely stood at the forefront of early adoption when compared with disciplines such as archeology or computer science; instead, art historians have often

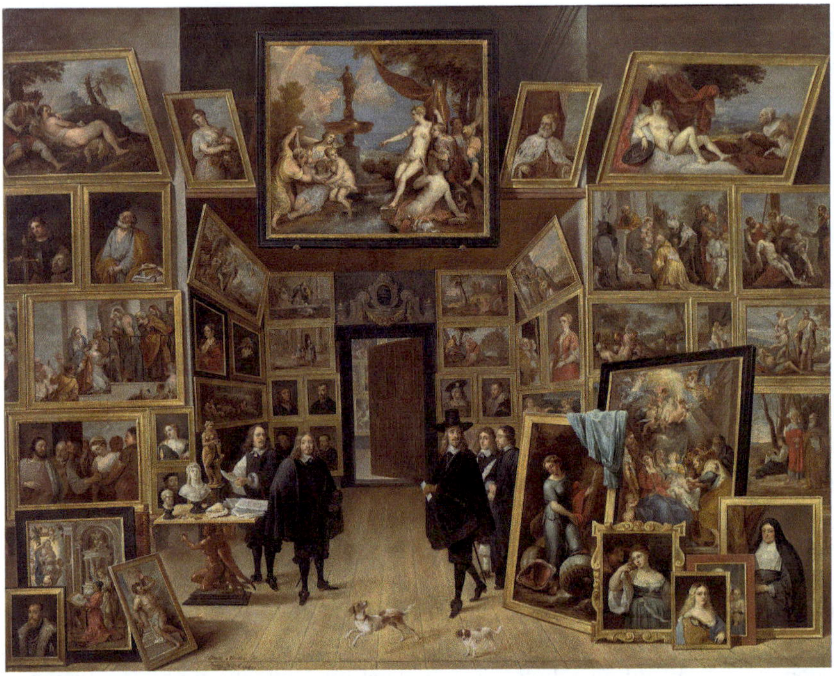

Fig. 1.3 David Teniers the Younger, *Archduke Leopold William in his picture gallery*, c. 1647, Madrid, Prado Museum (CC O, public domain)

followed a more measured path, carefully weighing the implications of new tools before widespread integration (Hutson 2024). This prudence is rooted in a deeply ingrained tradition of connoisseurship and close visual analysis (Fig. 1.4)—practices that valorize the cultivated eye and sustained engagement with material objects sans technological intermediaries (Ginzburg 2023; Kemp 1990). As a result, innovations that promise to expedite or automate aspects of interpretation are frequently met with skepticism, as faculty question whether such advances may undermine the interpretive rigor and disciplinary integrity that define the field (Drucker 2013). Recent surveys of digital art history echo this reluctance, documenting the persistent unease with which many senior scholars regard digital or generative methodologies, often associating them with a perceived threat to established expertise and the sanctity of the visual encounter (Zorich 2012; Zapata 2024).

This wariness toward digital tools and platforms is not a recent development, but echoes recurring patterns in art historical pedagogical and institutional evolution. The introduction of new teaching technologies, regardless of their subsequent ubiquity, has often been met with suspicion and resistance. The chalkboard, introduced into classrooms in the early nineteenth century, was initially seen as a disruptive device; students and instructors alike resisted its call for active participation, as it threatened established norms of memorization and oral recitation (Hennington 1978). Magic

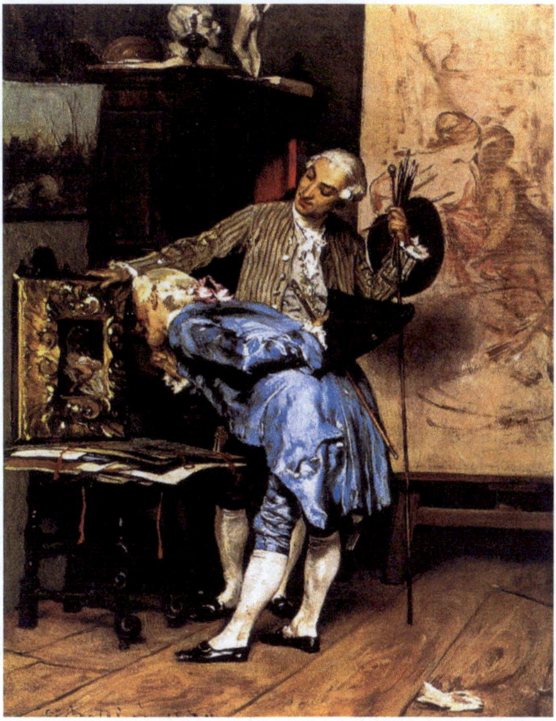

Fig. 1.4 Giovanni Boldini, *The Connoisseur*, 1870. Oil on panel. Private collection (CC O, public domain)

lanterns—later lauded for their capacity to animate lectures with projected images—were at first dismissed as little more than distractions or amusements, with faculty questioning their seriousness as pedagogical aids (Holly 1996). Even the widespread adoption of photographic slides, now taken for granted in art historical instruction, required decades of negotiation and adaptation before becoming standard practice (Nelson 2000). For those active in the field at the turn of the millennium, Howerton (2004) recounts the widespread concern over converting analog slide collections to digital formats, as well as the transition from slide carousels to PowerPoint presentations on digital projectors—a process that many experienced as both disruptive and transformative. These episodes underscore a recurrent cycle: skepticism, debate, gradual experimentation, and—if the tool proves valuable—eventual acceptance.

Such historical precedent serves as a reminder that initial resistance is not a barrier to progress but a necessary phase in the engagement with new methodologies. In fact, the measured skepticism of art historians has often served as a crucible for refining and improving the technologies embraced by the field. When deployed thoughtfully, technologies initially viewed with suspicion—whether chalkboards, lantern slides, or digital databases—have become foundational to research, teaching, and public engagement. Contemporary computational tools, including pattern-recognition algorithms and interactive databases, now hold the potential to join this lineage of once-contested, now-indispensable technologies. Recognizing the persistence of critical reflection and cautious adoption as central to this ethos may empower current and future art historians to navigate technological change more confidently and creatively, ensuring that advances serve the ideals of the field.

At the same time, and alongside the historically measured approach to innovation seen in the field, dynamic interplay has emerged in recent decades between art historians and computer scientists, reshaping the boundaries of both fields. Wryly, Wasielewski (2023) insightfully describes computer scientists as "rogue art historians," pointing to a phenomenon where data scientists and engineers, often unintentionally, adopt art historical methods—such as formal analysis, stylistic classification, and pattern recognition—in their own research and development. At the same time, art historians, particularly those situated within digital humanities centers or interdisciplinary laboratories, have long repurposed informatic tools—ranging from vast image databases and sophisticated metadata schemas to powerful pattern recognition algorithms—to address complex iconographic questions and to decipher stylistic trajectories within large image corpora (Drucker 2013; Luther 2020). This bidirectional exchange is emblematic of a larger experimental ethos that has animated art history since its formation: a willingness to adapt, retool, and reimagine methodologies in pursuit of deeper visual and contextual understanding.

Historically, such cross-fertilization occurred primarily in specialized research environments, where collaborative teams brought together expertise in data science, software engineering, and humanistic inquiry. Initiatives such as the Getty Provenance Index, the Stanford Digital Humanities Lab, and Europeana exemplify this confluence, enabling complex analyses of provenance, attribution, and reception through algorithmic means (Luther 2020). Until recently, however, meaningful engagement with data-driven techniques demanded not only significant institutional resources but also advanced technical proficiency, and these factors limited participation to a relatively small segment of the field (Zorich 2012). For example, early digital humanities projects often required dedicated servers or high-powered workstations that could cost tens of thousands of dollars, along with proprietary software licenses and ongoing IT support. Moreover, researchers were typically expected to possess coding skills in languages such as Python, R, or Java, or to collaborate closely with computer scientists capable of writing custom scripts and managing databases (Wachowiak 2022).

This technological and financial barrier stood in stark contrast to the comparatively low-cost, widely accessible nature of earlier tools like the lantern slide or the overhead projector, which required only basic equipment and minimal technical skill. The recent proliferation of affordable laptops, cloud-based solutions, and intuitive visual analytics platforms—many of which are accessible without specialized coding knowledge—has enabled a dramatic democratization of machine-based and algorithmic approaches in art historical research. No longer confined to well-funded digital humanities centers, these resources are now within reach of faculty, students, and independent scholars across a variety of institutional settings (Benilous 2025; Robinson 2014). The advent of user-friendly generative platforms such as OpenAI's ChatGPT (https://chat.openai.com), Anthropic's Claude (https://claude.ai), and Google's Gemini (https://gemini.google.com) has profoundly reshaped this landscape, offering accessible interfaces that allow for sophisticated data visualization, pattern recognition, and automated text analysis with little more than a web browser and a modest hardware investment. Today, entry-level participation in digital and data-driven scholarship may require only a standard laptop and a stable Internet connection, eliminating the need for extensive software purchases or advanced programming skills. This shift has been particularly significant for smaller institutions, under-resourced departments, and international scholars, all of whom can now engage analytic and synthetic methods without prohibitive upfront costs. The rise of such accessible tools marks a watershed moment for the field, as digital and machine-assisted research practices move from the periphery to the center of art historical inquiry, becoming common resources for a far broader and more diverse scholarly community.

The tangible impact of this shift is readily visible in the changing research methods and outputs of art historians. Photogrammetric modeling, for example, now enables rapid reconstruction of architectural spaces and mural programs, drastically reducing the time and resources once required for such undertakings (Muralidhar and Bhardwaj 2024; Remondino and El-Hakim 2006). Neural networks, trained on thousands of digitized paintings, have begun to reveal minute brushstroke patterns or compositional similarities, facilitating more accurate attribution and even the detection of workshop collaborations previously obscured in manual analysis (Li 2025; Strezoski and Worring 2017). These iterative computational processes—akin to the debugging cycles familiar in software engineering—embody a blend of analytical precision and creative exploration, yielding both new findings and new questions. Projects using deep learning algorithms have successfully tracked artistic migrations, workshop relationships, and stylistic diffusion across vast geographical and temporal spans, making possible the kind of synthetic art historical narratives once imagined but rarely realized (Santos et al. 2021).

Importantly, data-driven methodologies must be recognized as extensions—not replacements—of the interpretive traditions native to the discipline. Rather than diminishing the value of close looking, iconographic study, or historical context, these new tools serve as amplifiers, enriching the capacity of practitioners to interrogate visual phenomena and construct compelling arguments. Generative platforms and digital analytics offer additional lenses, revealing patterns and connections otherwise invisible to the unaided eye, yet the ultimate work of interpretation—situating images within cultural, political, and intellectual frameworks—remains a profoundly human endeavor (Onyejelem and Aondover 2024; Grosz 2017). Through the positioning of these new approaches within this lineage of methodological innovation, art history reaffirms its identity as an adaptable and experimentally robust field. Equipping both established scholars and the next generation with these hybrid skill sets ensures a richer, more dynamic engagement with the complexities of visual culture, sustaining disciplinary relevance and intellectual vitality in a rapidly evolving scholarly landscape.

Moreover, this technological evolution now reverberates through the three core functions central to art history since Winckelmann: teaching and learning, scholarly research and dissemination, and administrative frameworks. Within educational contexts, generative tools have enabled students—from advanced placement (AP) through graduate coursework—to produce sophisticated formal analyses and interpretive essays at unprecedented speeds. Digital platforms allow for instant reverse image searches and metadata retrieval, helping students swiftly identify works, attributions, and contextual information that once demanded laborious study and visual memory (Babić 2016; Khan et al. 2025). Such technologies undoubtedly democratize access, expand technical proficiency, and broaden engagement with visual material. Yet, their rise provokes deep concern among instructors steeped in the tradition of careful, phenomenological seeing and interpretive rigor outlined by Elkins (1997). Many faculty worry that computational shortcuts risk bypassing the essential, contemplative process of direct visual engagement, which is widely regarded as the foundation of true art historical understanding. While computational approaches may enhance technical polish, they also threaten to erode the habits of reflective observation and critical interpretation that define the pedagogical core of art history (Preziosi 2009; Nelson 2000).

This tension mirrors widespread anxieties across the humanities, where educators—concerned about the rise of tools like ChatGPT—seek to preserve the centrality of "writing as thinking," a practice that Royer (2024) warns is increasingly under threat. Writing in this context is valued not simply as a measure of academic mastery, but as a marker of subjective, affective, and intellectual engagement with course material (Barnett 2009). Within art history, instructors desire carefully crafted analytical essays not only for their sophistication or accuracy but as evidence of authentic engagement and thoughtful reflection on the experiential meaning of the artwork itself (Carpino and Hutson 2024). The key challenge for contemporary educators is reconciling the undeniable strengths of computational tools—clarity, efficiency, and speed—with the enduring commitment to nuanced, phenomenological interpretation and sustained critical analysis (Asad et al. 2024; Drucker 2013). Addressing these concerns productively requires nuanced conversation and pedagogical innovation: assignments that leverage generative technologies as supports for, not substitutes for, the practices of careful looking and thoughtful writing (Hutson 2025). Strategies such as assignment scaffolding, collaborative inquiry, and iterative peer review can help maintain the centrality of experiential engagement and reflective argumentation, even as digital tools transform the means of production and evaluation, which, Holly and Moxey (2002) relates, are not new for the field. Only by directly engaging these issues can art historians ensure that computational approaches genuinely enrich the pedagogical foundations of the field.

Comparable anxieties extend into the realm of scholarly research, fundamentally challenging traditional practices and values. Advances in computational analytics now permit rapid identification of stylistic shifts, workshop affiliations, and iconographic patterns across vast datasets—processes that once required years of painstaking, manual comparison (Manovich 2020). Multimodal language platforms and translation engines expand research horizons, making archival and epigraphic materials accessible to a much broader range of scholars and students (Sanderson 2024). The emergence of hybrid analytical models—combining visual generators with advanced reasoning systems—enables researchers to contextualize works of art within complex social, political, and religious frameworks, sometimes with greater speed and depth than ever before. However, this rapid acceleration prompts an epistemological reckoning: If machines can replicate or exceed human analytic capacities, what becomes of the uniquely subjective engagement and interpretive originality that have long been privileged in art historical scholarship espoused by Freedberg (2013)? Such developments probe the heart of the discipline, exposing the enduring tension between computational efficiency and the phenomenological encounter.

At the same time, the field stands in stark contrast to the epistemic norms of STEM disciplines. While empirical sciences value replicability, verification, and quantitative certainty, art history champions the interpretive encounter—privileging what a scholar sees, feels, and thinks as the core of disciplinary discourse (Didi-Huberman 2005). Documentation and evidence remain vital, but the persuasive articulation of critical vision and original insight lies at the center of the intellectual identity of the hybrid discipline. Many practitioners thus view algorithmic methodologies with skepticism—not because they lack rigor, but because they seem to threaten the subjective, human-centered labor of meaning-making that has always been essential to art historical knowledge. This deeply ingrained, though often unspoken, set of assumptions complicates the adoption of algorithmic methods, even when such approaches offer demonstrable gains in scope or efficiency.

For art historians to unlock the full potential of augmented scholarship, it is crucial to acknowledge and interrogate these foundational beliefs. Engaging with algorithmic analysis does not require abandoning phenomenological depth or experiential authenticity. Instead, it invites a reexamination of disciplinary priorities, evaluative criteria, and the very definition of scholarly rigor (Drucker 2013; Leib 2024). This process mirrors the existential reckoning underway in other interpretive disciplines, such as English, where Vinall and Hellmich (2025) relate that generative technologies now challenge long-standing norms of authorship and interpretation. Interdisciplinary dialogue will be essential for clarifying core values, developing new standards, and guiding responsible adoption of automation. Through active, critical engagement, art historians can shape the ethical, intellectual, and institutional contours of machine practice, ensuring it remains rooted in the most cherished ideals (Losh 2019).

Yet, it is worth noting that the adoption of computational technologies in museum visitor experiences has met with far less resistance—and often, with considerable enthusiasm (Ceccarelli et al. 2024). The drive to update institutional design, collections management, and interpretive strategies has been a hallmark of museology for decades. Museums now deploy digital wayfinding, multilingual virtual assistants, interactive recommendation engines, and augmented reality environments to broaden participation and deepen engagement (Cameron and Kenderdine 2008; Hutson and Hutson 2024). Unlike academic settings, where the fear of disciplinary erosion often prevails, museum professionals have tended to evaluate technological innovations pragmatically, assessing their effectiveness by tangible improvements in accessibility, attendance, and interpretive depth (Parry 2007). High-profile institutions, from the adoption of the Louvre of multisensory augmented reality (AR) to the use of analytics at the Van Gogh Museum to unlock hidden features of its collection, serve as models for the field (Calvi and Vermeeren 2024; Kidd 2016). Museums thus function as laboratories for experimentation, providing frameworks and models that can ultimately inform and inspire more cautious academic communities.

Administrative and academic governance offers another arena in which computational methods have been readily embraced. Predictive dashboards, demographic modeling, and intelligent analytical platforms are now widely used in museum and university management to support collection care, budgeting, audience engagement, and hiring equity (Resta and Dicuonzo 2024). These tools provide actionable insights and enhance transparency, efficiency, and accountability across institutions. Their adoption has been smooth precisely because they address organizational priorities without threatening the core interpretive and scholarly commitments that define art history. From optimizing grant applications to evaluating curricular diversity, intelligent analytics have proven their utility in supporting strategic planning and institutional alignment. The adaptability and flexibility of art historical institutions in this realm is notable, positioning the discipline to thrive in an increasingly data-driven cultural landscape.

Nonetheless, the proliferation of algorithmic and computational tools in research, administration, and public engagement raises new and urgent ethical, historiographic, and epistemological challenges. Past experiences with the introduction of photography and lantern-slide lectures reveal that technological shifts always demand a recalibration of standards and values. Algorithmic bias, privacy concerns—especially in biometric systems—and the transparency of generative outputs require critical attention (Longworth 2021). For example, as facial recognition and other data-driven systems become part of the museum experience, institutions must address issues of consent, discrimination, and data security (Rosemary 2025). Similarly, when generative reconstructions, like the digital recreation by Factum Arte of Veronese's *Wedding at Cana* (https://www.factum-arte.com/pag/38/a-facsimile-of-the-wedding-at-cana-by-paolo-veronese) (1562–63) (Fig. 1.5), are displayed, it is imperative to distinguish clearly between original and digitally inferred content, upholding scholarly trust and public confidence (Frodon 2024; Koller et al. 2010). Machine learning-based authentication and interpretation demand ongoing oversight to ensure that algorithmic decisions are transparent, subject to expert review, and never supplant curatorial judgment.

Major institutions are already grappling with these issues in real time. Both MoMA and Tate Modern have confronted the complexities of how algorithmically generated recommendations shape visitor journeys and interpretive experiences, including the risk of reinforcing bias or narrowing perspectives through hidden logics in recommendation systems (Proctor 2010; Kidd 2016). By openly addressing ethical, historiographic, and epistemological concerns, the field maintains a dynamic balance between innovation and stewardship. The history of art history's technological engagement makes clear that responsible, reflective integration—anchored in transparency, debate, and continual evaluation—does not diminish disciplinary rigor, but enriches it. As computational methodologies become ever more deeply embedded in the fabric of art historical practice, their transparent, ethical, and critical adoption will sustain the discipline's relevance, adaptability, and vitality well into the future.

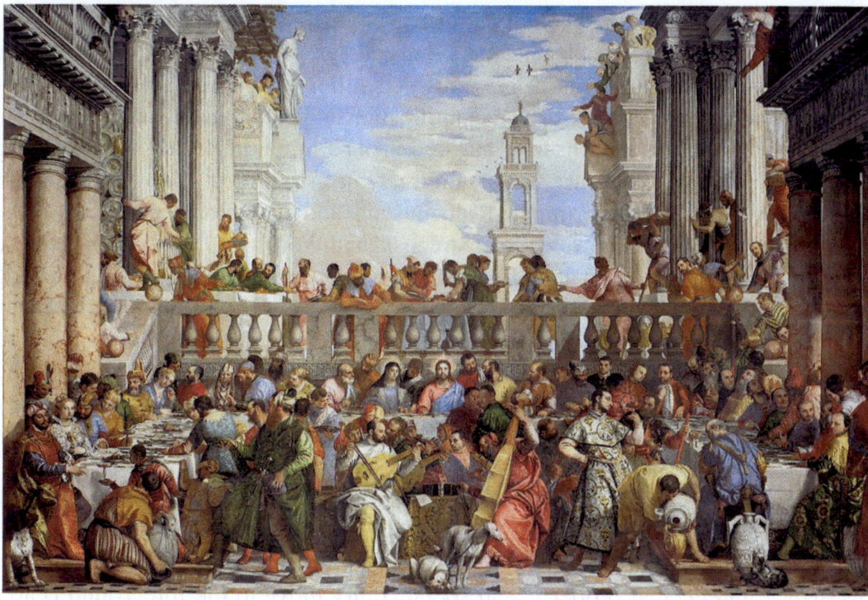

Fig. 1.5 Paolo Veronese, *The Wedding at Cana*, 1562–1563. Oil on canvas (CC O, public domain)

1.2 Scope, Structure, and Methodological Approach

The scope of this volume extends purposefully across the entire landscape of art historical practice, reflecting a recognition that computational and generative technologies are now shaping every aspect of the field. This holistic perspective is evident in the structure of the chapters, which trace the influence of these systems from the public-facing environment of museums to the often less-visible domains of research, administration, and pedagogy. Rather than treating technological innovation as an isolated phenomenon, the discussion situates intelligent systems as catalysts—agents of transformation that recalibrate established routines, expectations, and values in ways both subtle and profound (Chetry 2024; Manovich 2020; Zootzky and Pfeiffer 2024). For instance, the deployment of multilingual virtual assistants and adaptive wayfinding systems has dramatically improved accessibility and personalized engagement in institutions such as the British Museum and the Art Institute of Chicago, demonstrating how visitor experience is fundamentally reimagined through digital mediation (Cachia 2022; Kasemsarn et al. 2024; Kidd 2016). The volume is thus organized to move sequentially: beginning with museum engagement, then considering the evolving practices of research, legal governance, leadership, teaching, and finally immersive learning, culminating in an AI-powered extended-reality (XR) tutor modeled on Leonardo da Vinci.

A central methodological commitment of the volume is to ground this broad exploration in a rigorously transdisciplinary approach. The integration of computer vision—originally a domain of engineering and computer science—into art historical method has enabled large-scale analysis of visual style, composition, and attribution with a precision unimaginable to previous generations (Cheng et al. 2024). Techniques such as neural network-driven classification and automated feature extraction now support research that spans from attribution of paintings in Renaissance Florence to the analysis of contemporary visual culture, as seen in projects like the Operation Night Watch begun in 2019 from the Rijksmuseum and the digital cataloguing of the Waterhouse Pre-Raphaelite collection (Strezoski and Worring 2017). Neuroscientific research, too, has proven invaluable: studies on the neural mechanisms underlying aesthetic experience help inform museum design, accessibility policies, and interpretive programming, ensuring that technologies align with visitor perceptual and cognitive needs (Chatterjee and Vartanian 2014; Starr 2023). In tandem, the learning sciences offer evidence-based guidance for developing active and scaffolded pedagogies that can be supported and scaled through generative and immersive tools (Bransford et al. 2000; Lin and Chang 2023).

Cultural policy analysis further supplements these domains by establishing the frameworks for ethical governance and public accountability. As digital tools become deeply embedded in museum, research, and educational settings, questions of data governance, intellectual property, and social equity move to the foreground (Parry 2007; Cameron and Kenderdine (2007); Tsatsanashvili 2024). For example, the 2021 policy from the Tate on digital collections explicitly addresses the ethical use of visitor data and the responsibilities attached to digital surrogates of physical artworks (Dalal-Clayton et al. 2025). Such policy frameworks are indispensable for balancing the promise of computational innovation with the risks it introduces, ensuring that institutional practices remain transparent, inclusive, and aligned with public trust. Thus, the transdisciplinary lens adopted in this volume is not an intellectual luxury, but a methodological necessity for navigating the complexities of digital art history.

Given this rich interdisciplinarity, the methodological framework adopted here foregrounds a triad of strategies designed to maximize analytical rigor, practical impact, and ethical accountability. The first is practice-led inquiry: direct engagement with curators, educators, and administrators as they test, prototype, and refine new technologies in live institutional contexts (Engen 2021; Falk and Dierking 2016; Skains 2024). This mode of investigation surfaces not only the successes but also the challenges and limitations that come with deploying automated systems in complex organizational ecologies. The iterative approach of the Louvre to AR-based exhibition design and the collaborative process for digital interpretation of the Rijksmuseum offer instructive examples of both promise and difficulty, illustrating the necessity of adapting generic tools to discipline-specific needs. Practice-led inquiry thus ensures that the conclusions of the volume are grounded in the lived realities of art historical work, rather than abstract speculation.

Second, comparative case studies provide the analytical leverage needed to generalize from specific institutional experiences to broader disciplinary patterns. Through systematically comparing how different museums, universities, or research teams implement and adapt computational tools, the analysis surfaces patterns that transcend local context, yielding insights into best practices, scalability, and long-term impact. The contrast between the rapid, large-scale adoption of machine learning in European museum consortia and the more cautious, iterative experimentation seen in smaller North American institutions highlights how factors such as organizational culture, funding, and leadership shape the pace and nature of technological change (Parry 2007; Siri 2024). Comparative studies of curricular innovation—such as the integration of prompt engineering in graduate art history seminars versus undergraduate surveys at the Lindenwood University—further illustrate how educational traditions and institutional priorities influence the adoption and success of generative methodologies (Hutson 2024; Sharma and Bozkurt 2024).

The third methodological pillar is critical reflexivity, an explicit commitment to examining the epistemological, ethical, and political dimensions of technological adoption. This reflexivity is essential for ensuring that the enthusiasm for new tools is always tempered by sustained scrutiny of their limits, assumptions, and unintended consequences (Longworth 2021). For example, the analysis of biometric museum guides must address not only technical efficacy but also the privacy, consent, and discrimination risks attendant to their use (Kumar et al. 2024). Similarly, critical assessment of dataset provenance and bias in machine learning-based art analysis is necessary to guard against the replication of historical inequities or the uncritical elevation of computational authority over curatorial or scholarly expertise (Koller et al. 2010). Through the prioritization of reflexive analysis, the volume ensures that the integration of generative systems in art history is not merely innovative but also responsible and just.

As noted, the importance of practice-led inquiry can be further illustrated through detailed institutional studies. The codesign of the British Museum of visitor-facing digital tools with input from neurodiverse users exemplifies how iterative development processes yield both technical refinement and increased accessibility (Kidd 2016). At the Art Institute of Chicago, the collaborative deployment of an AI-driven wayfinding system required ongoing dialogue between curators, IT staff, educators, and front-line visitor services, highlighting the importance of interdisciplinary cooperation for successful implementation (Parry 2007). These examples demonstrate that technology does not merely “arrive” in art historical institutions but is shaped, contested, and remade through collaborative work and iterative feedback, underlining the value of grounded, practice-based research.

Comparative case study analysis reveals how regional, institutional, and disciplinary variations mediate the integration of computational tools. For instance, the comprehensive approach of the Rijksmuseum to computational analysis—combining neural networks, digital imaging, and open data policies—contrasts with smaller more incremental, project-based deployments of smaller institutions (Kiourexidou and Stamou 2025). Likewise, the implementation of digital archives and automated cataloguing at the Getty Provenance Index demonstrates how differences in institutional mission, funding, and governance produce divergent models for digital transformation (Luther 2020). These comparative insights not only inform best practices for technology adoption but also enrich our understanding of the broader cultural, political, and historical forces that shape art historical practice.

Critical reflexivity emerges as the linchpin for ethical and epistemological accountability, especially as algorithmic tools reshape core practices of attribution, authentication, and interpretation. As institutions such as MoMA and Tate Modern navigate the implications of algorithmically generated recommendations and visitor pathways, they confront the need for transparency about the logic and bias of computational systems (Proctor 2010). Responsible implementation entails ongoing training, rigorous evaluation, and the establishment of clear protocols for human oversight and correction. Moreover, reflexive critique must attend to the unintended consequences of digital tools, such as the potential to reinforce dominant narratives or marginalize alternative perspectives through algorithmic "black boxes" (Longworth 2021). The centering of reflexivity allows the volume to model a mode of technological adoption that is both ambitious and ethically grounded.

In sum, this volume argues that the integration of intelligent and generative technologies within art history must be guided by a comprehensive, transdisciplinary, and reflexive methodological framework. Practice-led inquiry ensures that practical relevance, comparative case studies facilitate generalization and transferability, and critical reflexivity safeguards against ethical lapses and epistemological blind spots. The result is a vision of computational art history that is rigorous, innovative, and accountable to both disciplinary traditions and the broader public good. By making explicit the assumptions, challenges, and strategies that inform this work, the volume seeks not only to document technological change but to shape its trajectory in ways that benefit the field and society at large.

The chapters that follow are structured to clearly demonstrate the transformative potential of intelligent technologies across each fundamental aspect of art historical practice, from visitor experiences in museums through scholarly research and pedagogical methodologies to administrative and leadership frameworks. Collectively, these chapters reinforce the argument that generative and computational methods represent a coherent, logical continuation of the discipline's historical engagement with innovative visual tools and interdisciplinary approaches. By systematically addressing both opportunities and challenges within each domain, the ensuing discussions provide art historians, educators, curators, and administrators with concrete models and practical insights necessary for thoughtful integration. Each chapter is briefly summarized below to orient readers, clearly delineating the progression of topics and ensuring that the narrative unfolds logically and cohesively throughout the volume.

Chapter 2 initiates the volume by examining visitor-centered intelligent technologies designed explicitly to enhance museum accessibility and create personalized interpretive experiences. Through examples ranging from multilingual virtual assistants to augmented reality applications, the chapter demonstrates how emerging tools actively support linguistic diversity, neurodiversity, and individualized museum journeys. Illustrative case studies include institutions like the Louvre and Van Gogh Museum, both of which have successfully implemented technological solutions to bridge barriers related to language, sensory perception, and cognitive engagement. Emphasis is placed on the practical outcomes of these interventions, highlighting increased visitor satisfaction, greater cultural inclusivity, and richer interpretive interactions with museum collections. Additionally, the discussion considers ethical considerations integral to deploying such technologies, particularly issues surrounding visitor privacy, informed consent, and algorithmic fairness.

Chapter 3 moves the analysis into the domain of academic research, articulating how computational tools fundamentally enhance art historical inquiry. This chapter explores advanced methodologies such as neural network-driven visual analysis, large-scale dataset aggregation, and computational pattern recognition, which collectively enable researchers to identify stylistic evolution, workshop practices, and iconographic relationships more rapidly and comprehensively than traditional methods. Examples include studies leveraging machine learning techniques to authenticate artworks or analyze compositional patterns in dispersed collections. The discussion also highlights collaborative platforms facilitated by intelligent technologies, which foster global scholarly partnerships and interdisciplinary engagement, significantly expanding the reach and depth of art historical scholarship. By foregrounding these computational methodologies, the chapter positions intelligent tools as vital enhancements rather than replacements for traditional visual analysis and scholarly interpretation.

Chapter 4 addresses critical frameworks of copyright, licensing, and fair-use guidelines that govern the responsible implementation of generative and computational tools within art historical practice. Given the rapid proliferation of AI-generated content, this chapter carefully analyzes comparative legal contexts, contrasting U.S. fair-use doctrines with European Union regulations surrounding text and data mining. Special attention is paid to ethical considerations inherent in dataset creation and usage, particularly around practices such as digital scraping, artist consent, and licensing agreements for museum collections. Concrete recommendations and best practices are provided to guide art historians, curators, and institutions in ethically and legally sound utilization of intelligent technologies. By clarifying these essential legal and ethical boundaries, the chapter ensures responsible deployment of generative content, safeguarding intellectual property rights while enabling scholarly innovation.

Chapter 5 examines how predictive analytics and automation tools streamline departmental management, institutional administration, and strategic planning within museums and universities. By deploying intelligent dashboards and data-driven decision-making systems, administrators gain critical insights into budgeting, collection care, audience development, curricular trends, and equitable hiring practices. Case studies illustrate successful institutional implementations of these technologies, demonstrating their efficacy in promoting transparency, equity, and resource efficiency. Examples include museums employing analytics to improve visitor engagement strategies and academic departments leveraging demographic data to ensure inclusive and representative curricular offerings. The discussion emphasizes that intelligent administrative solutions complement existing management practices, enhancing organizational efficiency and equity without compromising disciplinary integrity or professional judgment.

Chapter 6 introduces innovative pedagogical methodologies centered around prompt engineering, designed specifically to deepen student engagement and foster critical interpretation skills in art history courses. Prompt engineering—strategically crafting instructional prompts for generative systems—enables educators to scaffold analytical tasks, enhancing students' visual literacy, formal analysis, and contextual understanding. Concrete classroom examples, including detailed assignments analyzing Donatello's *Bronze David*, illustrate how prompt-driven interactive exercises stimulate active learning and critical reflection. Additionally, the chapter provides frameworks for assessing pedagogical effectiveness and student engagement, offering measurable outcomes that confirm the efficacy of generative media tools in achieving learning objectives. Emphasis is placed on aligning prompt-engineered methodologies with traditional art historical teaching principles, reinforcing rather than eroding core pedagogical commitments.

Chapter 7 concludes the core discussion by presenting an extended-reality educational prototype: a sophisticated virtual tutor modeled after Leonardo da Vinci, illustrating the potential for immersive, dialogic learning in art history education. Employing advanced generative systems, this AI-driven tutor interacts dynamically with students, facilitating conversational, inquiry-based learning experiences within immersive digital environments. Technical and conceptual development processes for creating such avatars are detailed, including considerations around dataset curation, interaction scripting, and pedagogical principles underpinning virtual learning. Practical classroom scenarios demonstrate the tutor's efficacy in enhancing visual analysis, interpretive dialogue, and historical contextualization. The chapter acknowledges implementation challenges, such as technical complexity and dataset integrity, while forecasting potential future developments, thus positioning extended-reality tutors as significant innovations in contemporary educational practice.

The **Conclusion** synthesizes core insights from across the volume, reflecting critically upon ethical imperatives, methodological implications, and practical strategies for sustainable adoption of intelligent technologies. Key themes are revisited—including disciplinary continuity, interdisciplinary collaboration, responsible governance, and reflective pedagogical design—underscoring the necessity of ethically informed, critically reflective engagement with generative methods. Finally, the conclusion proposes concrete pathways forward, articulating recommendations for institutions, researchers, educators, and administrators to navigate the evolving landscape of computational art history effectively. By offering a clear synthesis and proactive vision, this closing discussion ensures that intelligent tools are thoughtfully and sustainably integrated into art historical practice, shaping the discipline responsibly and innovatively into the future.

References

Asad MM, Shahzad S, Shah SHA, Sherwani F, Almusharraf NM (2024) ChatGPT as artificial intelligence-based generative multimedia for English writing pedagogy: challenges and opportunities from an educator's perspective. Int J Inf Learn Technol 41(5):490–506

Babić D (2016) Bridging the boundaries between museum and heritage studies. Musm Int 68(1–2):15–28

Barnett R (2009) Knowing and becoming in the higher education curriculum. Stud High Educ 34(4):429–440

Belting H (2003) Art history after modernism. University of Chicago Press

Benilous B (2025) Collaboration in digitisation programmes for cost efficiencies and equitable access. J Digit Media Manag 13(2):187–198

Bransford JD, Brown AL, Cocking RR (2000) How people learn, vol 11. National Academy Press, Washington, DC

Cachia A (ed) (2022) Curating access: disability art activism and creative accommodation. Taylor & Francis

Calvi L, Vermeeren AP (2024) Digitally enriched museum experiences–what technology can do. Musm Manag Curatorship 39(3):335–356

Cameron F, Kenderdine S (2008) Theorizing digital cultural heritage: a critical discourse (Media in Transition). The MIT Press

Carpino K, Hutson J (2024) A new canvas of learning: enhancing formal analysis skills in AP art history through AI-generated Islamic art. In: Forum for education studies, vol 2, no 2

Ceccarelli S, Cesta A, Cortellessa G, De Benedictis R, Fracasso F, Leopardi L, Schaerf M (2024) Evaluating visitors' experience in museum: comparing artificial intelligence and multi-partitioned analysis. Digit Appl Archaeol Cult Herit 33:e00340

Chatterjee A, Vartanian (2014) Neuroaesthetics. Trend Cogn Sci 18(7):370–375

Cheng J, Yang L, Tong S (2024) Recognition and analysis of painting styles with the help of computer vision techniques. Informatica 48(21)

Chetry KK (2024) Transforming education: how AI is revolutionizing the learning experience. Int J Res Publ Rev 5(5):6352–6356

Dalal-Clayton A, Barton H, Rutherford A, Griffin C, Gillick J, Rebernak J, Kaminska F (2025) Transforming collections: reimagining art, nation and heritage

Darzins J (1957) Malraux and the destruction of aesthetics. Yale Fr Stud 18:107–113

Dellmann S, Kessler F (eds) (2020) A million pictures: magic lantern slides in the history of learning. Indiana University Press

Didi-Huberman G (2005) Confronting images: questioning the ends of a certain history of art. Penn State Press

Drucker J (2013) Is there a "digital" art history? Vis Resour 29(1–2):5–13

Elkins J (1997) The object stares back: on the nature of seeing. Houghton Mifflin Harcourt

Engen L (2021) Practice-led research in the art museum: research on education practices led by the practitioners. Nord J Art Res 10(2)

Falk JH, Dierking LD (2016) The museum experience revisited. Routledge

Freedberg D (2013) The power of images: studies in the history and theory of response. University of Chicago Press

Frodon JM (2024) An interview with Adam Lowe: to re-produce works of art. Theory Cult Soc 41(5):113–133

Ginzburg C (2023) Morelli, Freud and Sherlock Holmes: clues and scientific method. In: Popular fiction. Routledge, pp 252–276

Gombrich EH (1960) Art and illusion: a study in the psychology of pictorial representation. Pantheon Press

Grosz E (2017) The incorporeal: ontology, ethics, and the limits of materialism. Columbia University Press

Harloe K (2013) Winckelmann and the invention of antiquity: history and aesthetics in the age of Altertumswissenschaft. OUP, Oxford
Harris L (2024) Photography, architecture, and the modern Italian landscape: primitivism and progress. Taylor & Francis
Hennington JA (1978) Innovate with the chalkboard. J Bus Educ 54(2):68–71
Holly MA (1996) Past looking: historical imagination and the rhetoric of the image. Cornell University Press
Holly MA, Moxey KP (2002) Art history, aesthetics, visual studies. Clark Art Institute
Howerton B (2004) Beyond PowerPoint: visual presentation tools for online learning. Innov J Online Educ 1(2)
Hutson J (2024) Integrating art and AI: evaluating the educational impact of AI tools in digital art history learning. In: Forum for art studies, vol 1, no 1
Hutson J (2025) Human-AI collaboration in writing: a multidimensional framework for creative and intellectual authorship. Int J Chang Educ, pp 1–10
Hutson J, Hutson P (2024) Immersive technologies. In: Inclusive smart museums: engaging neurodiverse audiences and enhancing cultural heritage. Springer Nature Switzerland, Cham, pp 153–228
Kasemsarn K, Sawadsri A, Harrison D, Nickpour F (2024) Museums for older adults and mobility-impaired people: applying inclusive design principles and digital storytelling guidelines—a review. Heritage 7(4):1893–1916
Kemp M (1990) The science of art: optical themes in western art from Brunelleschi to Seurat. Yale University Press
Khan SA, Dierickx L, Furuly JG, Vold HB, Tahseen R, Linden CG, Dang-Nguyen DT (2025) Debunking war information disorder: a case study in assessing the use of multimedia verification tools. J Assoc Inf Sci Technol 76(5):752–769
Kidd J (2016) Museums in the new mediascape: transmedia, participation, ethics. Routledge
Kiourexidou M, Stamou S (2025) Interactive heritage: the role of artificial intelligence in digital museums. Electronics 14(9):1884
Koller D, Frischer B, Humphreys G (2010) Research challenges for digital archives of 3D cultural heritage models. J Comput Cult Herit (JOCCH) 2(3):1–17
Kumar T, Bhushan S, Sharma P, Garg V (2024) Examining the vulnerabilities of biometric systems: privacy and security perspectives. In: Leveraging computer vision to biometric applications. Chapman and Hall/CRC, pp 34–67
Late E, Ruotsalainen H, Kumpulainen S (2024) Image searching in an open photograph archive: search tactics and faced barriers in historical research. Int J Dig Lib 25(4):715–728
Leib RS (2024) Beginning AI phenomenology. J Specul Philos 38(1):62–82
Li W (2025) Enhanced automated art curation using supervised modified CNN for art style classification. Sci Rep 15(1):7319
Lin MPC, Chang D (2023) CHAT-ACTS: a pedagogical framework for personalized chatbot to enhance active learning and self-regulated learning. Comput Educ Artif Intell 5:100167
Longworth J (2021) Benjamin Ruha (2019) race after technology: abolitionist tools for the new Jim code. Medford: Polity Press. Sci Technol Stud 34(2):92–94
Losh E (2019) Hashtag. Bloomsbury Publishing, USA
Luther A (2020) Digital provenance, open access, and data-driven art history. In: The Routledge companion to digital humanities and art history. Routledge, pp 448–458
Manovich L (2020) Cultural analytics. Mit Press
Muralidhar S, Bhardwaj A (2024) Preservation and archiving of historic murals using a digital non-metric camera. Eng Proc 82(1):60
Nelson RS (2000) The slide lecture, or the work of art "history" in the age of mechanical reproduction. Crit Inq 26(3):414–434
Onyejelem TE, Aondover EM (2024) Digital generative multimedia tool theory (DGMTT): a theoretical postulation in the era of artificial intelligence. Adv Mach Learn Artif Intell 5(2):1–9
Parry R (2007) Recoding the museum: digital heritage and the technologies of change. Routledge

Preziosi D (2009) The art of art history: a critical anthology. OUP, Oxford
Proctor N (2010) Digital: museum as platform, curator as champion, in the age of social media. Curator Mus J 53(1):35
Remondino F, El-Hakim S (2006) Image-based 3D modelling: a review. Photogramm Rec 21(115):269–291
Resta G, Dicuonzo F (2024) Towards a digital shift in museum visiting experience. Drafting the research agenda between academic research and practice of museum management. Arch Des Ind 4.0 609–648
Robinson P (2014) Digital humanities: is bigger, better? In: Advancing digital humanities: research, methods, theories. Palgrave Macmillan UK, London, pp 243–257
Rosemary FT (2025) Leveraging artificial intelligence and data analytics for enhancing museum experiences: exploring historical narratives, visitor engagement, and digital transformation in the age of innovation. Int Res J Mod Eng Technol Sci 7(1)
Royer C (2024) Outsourcing humanity? ChatGPT, critical thinking, and the crisis in higher education. Stud Philos Educ 43(5):479–497
Sanderson R (2024) Implementing linked art in a multi-modal database for cross-collection discovery. Open Libr Humanit 10(2)
Santos I, Castro L, Rodriguez-Fernandez N, Torrente-Patino A, Carballal A (2021) Artificial neural networks and deep learning in the visual arts: a review. Neural Comput Appl 33:121–157
Sharma RC, Bozkurt A (eds) (2024) Transforming education with generative AI: prompt engineering and synthetic content creation. IGI Global
Siri A (2024) Emerging trends and future directions in artificial intelligence for museums: a comprehensive bibliometric analysis based on Scopus (1983–2024). Geopolit Soc Secur Free J. https://doi.org/10.2478/gssfj-2024-0002
Skains RL (2024) Designing and conducting practice-based research projects: a practical guide for arts student researchers. Intellect
Stafford BM (1988) The eighteenth-century: towards an interdisciplinary model. Art Bull 70(1):6–24
Starr GG (2023) Aesthetic experience models human learning. Front Hum Neurosci 17:1146083
Strezoski G, Worring M (2017) Omniart: multi-task deep learning for artistic data analysis. arXiv preprint arXiv:1708.00684
Tsatsanashvili A (2024) Artificial intelligence in the protection of intangible cultural heritage. Eur J Transform Stud 12(1):163–178
Vinall K, Hellmich E (2025) Whose words are they? Authorship in the age of artificial intelligence. In: Rethinking writing education in the age of generative AI. Routledge, pp 57–70
Wachowiak MP (2022) The "R Vs. Python" debate in the digital humanities. Digital humanities tools and techniques I
Wasielewski A (2023) Computational formalism: art history and machine learning. MIT Press
Winckelmann JJ (1767) Monumenti antichi inediti. Aspese dell'autore
Zapata PB (2024) Computation in art history. From hype to reality, p 69
Zootzky G, Pfeiffer A (2024) Educational transformation through AI: preparing for a new era of learning. In: INTED2024 proceedings. IATED, pp 1202–1207
Zorich DM (2012) Transitioning to a digital world. In: Art history, its research centers, and digital scholarship. The Samuel H. Kress Foundation and The Roy Rosenzweig Center for History and New Media George Mason University

Chapter 2
Enhancing Inclusivity Through Visitor Experiences

Abstract This chapter investigates the potential effects of digital, algorithmic, and data-driven technologies on the contemporary museum experience, documenting the sector's shift from static repositories to dynamic, visitor-centered institutions. It demonstrates how tools such as multilingual virtual assistants, recommendation engines, and augmented reality guides have enabled museums to support linguistic and neurodiverse audiences and personalize interpretive journeys. Case studies—including implementations at the Louvre and Van Gogh Museum—illustrate how these innovations enhance cultural inclusivity, break down sensory and cognitive barriers, and deepen visitor engagement. The chapter also foregrounds the practical outcomes of these interventions, highlighting increases in visitor satisfaction and more meaningful interactions with collections. It critically examines the ethical dimensions of these technological deployments, with particular attention to privacy, informed consent, and algorithmic fairness. By situating these tools within a broader history of museum adaptation, the chapter argues for the centrality of inclusivity, transparency, and responsible design in the future of public-facing cultural heritage.

2.1 Museums in the Digital Age: From Repository to Dynamic Engagement

The history of museums traces a long arc from the princely collections, *Wunderkammern* (cabinets of wonder), and *Kunstkammern* (art chambers) (Fig. 2.1) of early modern Europe to the universal art museums that dominated the nineteenth-century cultural landscape (Findlen 1994; Bennett 2013). Originating in the private treasure rooms and eclectic assemblages of monarchs, aristocrats, and scholars, these early institutions gathered objects from distant geographies and disparate temporalities, symbolizing both the reach of personal curiosity and the expanding horizon of European exploration. The rise of the enlightenment museum transformed these once-exclusive displays into civic spaces that sought to rationalize, categorize, and democratize knowledge for broader publics. In this evolution, the Wunderkammern and Kunstkammern became both symbols of early collecting practices and enduring

J. Hutson, *Art History in the Age of Artificial Intelligence*, Springer Series on Cultural Computing, https://doi.org/10.1007/978-3-032-02920-1_2

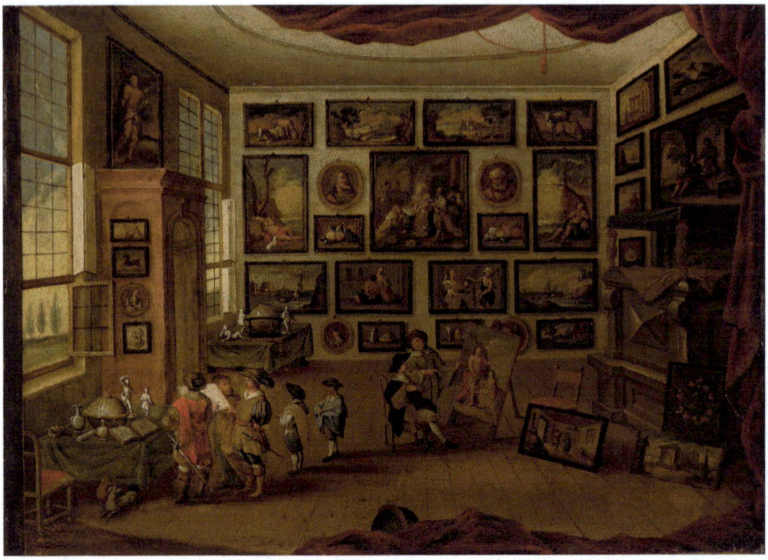

Fig. 2.1 Hans Jordaens III, *Kunstkammer*, 1660. Slovak National Gallery (CC O, public domain)

models of how objects could be marshaled to narrate histories of power, empire, and cultural identity. As the enlightenment advanced, princely collections gave way to public institutions with ambitious missions: to present the sum of human artistic achievement, to educate the citizenry, and, often, to manifest the ideological aspirations of the nation-state (Merewether 2024).

Nineteenth-century "universal" museums—such as the Louvre, the British Museum, and the Altes Museum—systematically organized their collections by chronological, geographic, and stylistic schema: beginning with ancient Egypt, progressing through Greece and Rome, and culminating in the so-called Old Masters of the Renaissance and the contemporary productions of the host nation (Duncan 2005; Macdonald 2003). These arrangements functioned as much as ideological declarations of national identity and progress as they did as aesthetic presentations; the pride of place given to French painting in the Louvre, English art at the National Gallery, or German works at the Alte Nationalgalerie in Berlin (Fig. 2.2) made clear the role of the museum as a stage for cultural self-fashioning (Pomian 1990). The very architecture of these institutions—the neoclassical facades, the grand entrance halls, the processional galleries—reinforced the message that to move through the museum was to traverse the history of civilization, arriving at the pinnacle of one's own national tradition.

Early visitor engagement with permanent collections reflected this mix of spectacle, instruction, and social order. While the first public museums were open to a select few—requiring formal attire, advance reservations, or letters of introduction—the nineteenth century saw the gradual democratization of access, culminating in crowds of varying backgrounds and decorum streaming through the Louvre, the

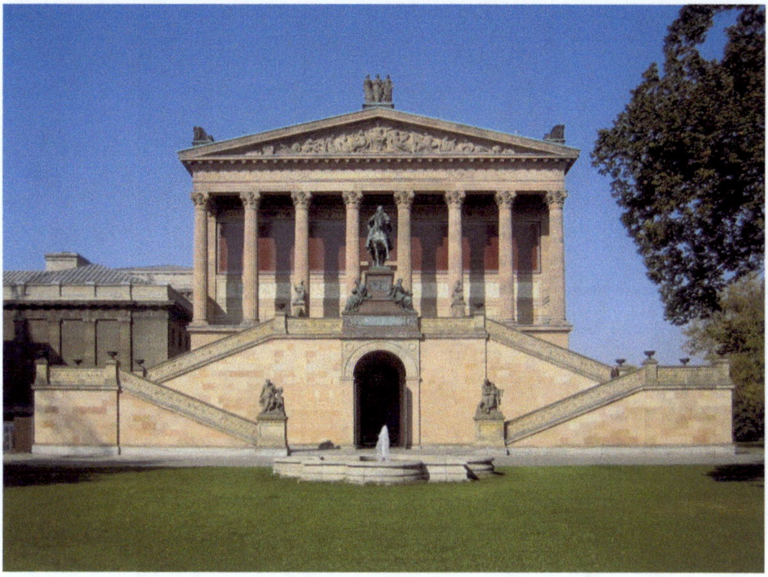

Fig. 2.2 Alte Nationalgalerie, 1866–1876. Berlin, Germany (CC O, public domain)

British Museum, and other institutions (Bennett 2013). The French Salons (Fig. 2.3), in particular, stand as emblematic examples of the evolving role of public exhibitions: held annually or biennially in Paris, these temporary displays drew thousands of visitors who jostled for space, debated works loudly, and mingled in a vibrant, if sometimes unruly, atmosphere (Crow 1985). Such gatherings fostered a culture of public critique and social engagement, foreshadowing the participatory turn that would come to define museum practice in later centuries. Yet, permanent collections in traditional galleries remained largely static, with objects arranged for optimal viewing but little direct interaction or interpretive flexibility afforded to visitors (Duncan 2005). Wall labels, catalogues, and guided tours provided some orientation, but the pedagogical authority remained largely unchallenged. Only in the late twentieth and early twenty-first centuries did a pronounced shift occur, as museums began to foreground visitor experience, community involvement, and adaptive, participatory design (Simon 2010). This new approach prioritized accessibility, interactivity, and cultural inclusivity, fundamentally transforming the social and epistemological contract between museums and their publics.

As museums evolved beyond their origins as repositories of elite or universal culture, the static, object-centered model increasingly gave way to one that prioritizes visitor participation, cocreation, and the needs of a diverse public (Black 2012; Simon 2010). This transformation reflects broader social changes: rising expectations for inclusivity, global migration, and the recognition that museums serve as sites of informal and lifelong learning, not merely guardians of national heritage. Art museums have adapted by redesigning programming, interpretive frameworks,

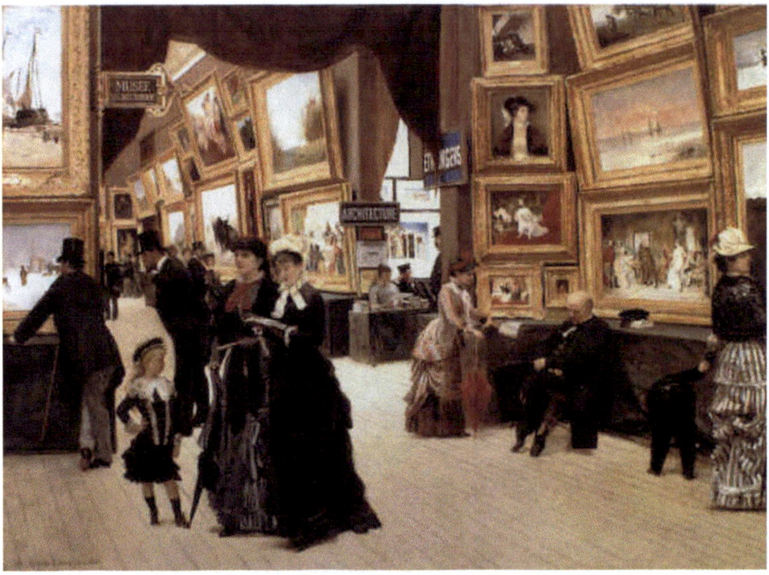

Fig. 2.3 Edouard Dantan, *Un Coin du Salon en 1880*, 1880 (CC O, public domain)

and physical spaces to address shifting demographics and expanding cultural expectations. This turn toward inclusivity responds to an audience that now encompasses not only enthusiasts of Western canonical art, but also speakers of many languages, people with physical or sensory disabilities, and neurodiverse individuals seeking multimodal engagement (Falk 2016; Wang 2024). These shifts, often driven by equity-focused policy and public advocacy, signal a conscious effort to dismantle historic barriers and ensure museums serve as open, dialogic platforms rather than exclusive temples of high culture. The American Alliance of Museums (AAM) and International Council of Museums (ICOM) have both foregrounded accessibility and equity in recent strategic plans, illustrating the global reach and urgency of these priorities (Black 2012).

Emerging digital and algorithmic technologies have dramatically expanded the ability of museums to refine visitor engagement, adapting content and navigation to individual preferences and access needs. Recommendation systems now curate pathways through exhibitions that reflect visitor interests, prior knowledge, or preferred learning styles, turning passive observation into an active, adaptive experience (Hayde et al. 2023; Varitimiadis et al. 2020). Museums increasingly employ computer vision and pattern recognition tools not only to reveal new aspects of objects—for instance, previously hidden underdrawings or material changes in paintings at the Van Gogh Museum (Musílek et al. 2024)—but also to make these discoveries accessible to a wider audience through dynamic digital interpretation. Projects like MIT's MosAIc demonstrate how algorithmic models can connect works from disparate eras and cultures, highlighting networks of global influence often overlooked in more traditional, geographically-bounded displays (Cascone 2020). At the same time, institutions like the Smithsonian use data-driven analysis to identify underrepresented stories in their collections and exhibitions, ensuring that new narratives and historically marginalized voices reach the public (Rogala et al. 2023). The pioneering use of augmented reality and multilingual digital guides at the Louvre shows how machine-driven mediation can bridge linguistic, cognitive, and cultural barriers, reinforcing the missions of the museum as truly public spaces (Brischetto et al. 2023; Neather 2024).

Crucially, these innovations are not limited to abstract or administrative functions; they are being embedded into the physical and digital infrastructure of museum experience. For example, AI-supported recommendation engines now empower educators to design exhibition pathways and thematic routes that respond to visitor interests or preferred pace, allowing for hyper-personalized and differentiated engagement (Hayde et al. 2023). At the Smithsonian National Museum of African American History and Culture, machine-driven platforms adjust interpretive content in real time, accommodating a spectrum of cultural backgrounds and familiarity with the subject matter. Such flexible models can support learners who require additional scaffolding, those seeking challenge, or visitors who benefit from alternative sensory or linguistic modes of engagement (Woodruff 2023; Filipchuk and Udych 2021). These approaches foster equitable access for visitors who might otherwise encounter significant barriers to participation, including individuals navigating physical, cognitive, or neurological challenges.

Innovations in accessibility are particularly notable in the adoption of language support, spatial guidance, and multisensory interaction tools. Natural language processing, augmented reality, and machine learning have enabled museums to clarify wayfinding, facilitate translation, and diversify interpretive delivery for audiences of different backgrounds and abilities (Capece and Chivaran 2020). At the Metropolitan Museum of Art, machine-driven chatbots can translate curatorial texts and wayfinding information into multiple languages, making the galleries more approachable for international and immigrant visitors (Eziamaka et al. 2024; Neather 2024). Haptic feedback and tactile interfaces, often informed by algorithmic analysis, support independent navigation and in-depth engagement with objects for visitors with visual or mobility impairments, providing a richer, hands-on experience (Brischetto et al. 2023). These new modalities build on previous accessibility initiatives, such as audio tours and raised-line diagrams, but bring unprecedented flexibility and adaptability to the design of inclusive spaces.

The widespread adoption of large language models (LLMs) like ChatGPT and multimodal platforms has accelerated these changes, allowing museums to deliver interactive, personalized, and dynamic content at scale (Vasic et al. 2024). Building on the foundation established by multilingual chatbots, AR tours, and machine learning-guided tactile tools, these systems now support highly adaptive learning experiences that reflect individual needs and preferences. For example, content can be tailored for different reading levels (Fig. 2.4), sensory sensitivities, or cultural perspectives, ensuring that young children, advanced scholars, and neurodiverse audiences all find

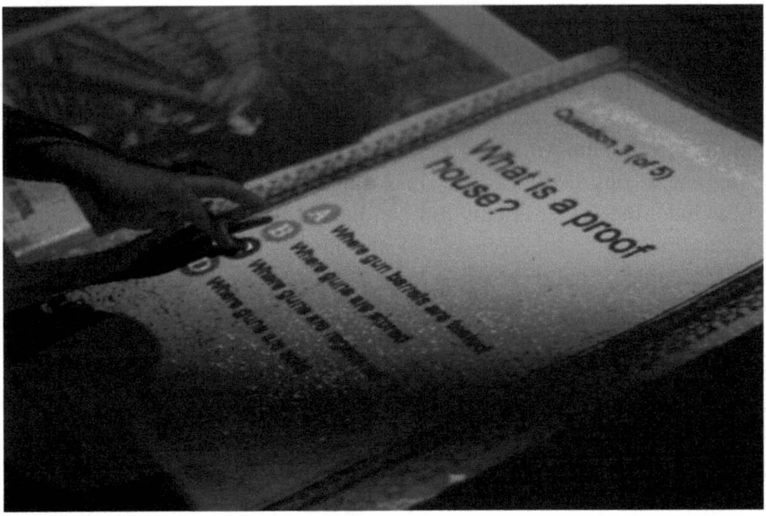

Fig. 2.4 Interactive exhibit at the London Museum, 2010 (CC 2.0)

relevant points of entry to the collection. These developments position the museum as a responsive environment, able to meet the rapidly evolving expectations of twenty-first-century publics (Simon 2010; Wang 2024).

Therefore, the transformation of the museum from a static repository to a dynamic, visitor-centered institution is inseparable from the ongoing digital and machine-based turn in art historical practice. This evolution marks not just a technological shift but a profound cultural and epistemological change—one in which institutional authority is reframed as collaborative, participatory, and dialogic rather than monolithic or didactic (Black 2012; Simon 2009). The convergence of digital strategy, equity-focused programming, and algorithmic personalization ensures that museums remain vital civic spaces where individuals from all walks of life can encounter, interpret, and contribute to the ongoing story of art. As digital innovation accelerates, museums are increasingly defined by their capacity to foster open inquiry, enable diverse narratives, and empower visitors as cocreators of meaning. The museum thus becomes a living laboratory for experimentation with new forms of access, inclusion, and interpretation—its relevance contingent upon continual responsiveness to the changing needs of its audiences. This participatory ethos, anchored in both technological potential and a renewed sense of public mission, signals a permanent reorientation of the museum's role in civic life. The following sections explore how these trends manifest in specific areas: supporting linguistic and neurodiverse visitors, creating intelligent recommendation systems, enabling multisensory engagement, and navigating the complex ethical terrain that accompanies new forms of data-driven mediation and personalization. In doing so, they reveal how the museum's digital transformation offers not only enhanced engagement, but also new opportunities for reimagining the social contract between cultural institutions and the publics they serve.

2.2 Accessibility and Supporting Linguistic and Neurodiverse Visitors

In recent decades, museums have increasingly recognized the necessity of designing environments and experiences that accommodate the wide-ranging needs of both linguistic minorities and neurodiverse visitors. Historically, museum practice assumed a "universal visitor"—one who could read and comprehend interpretive texts, move independently through galleries, and access meaning in a largely uniform manner (Falk 2016; Simon 2009). However, critical scholarship and advocacy by disability studies experts, linguists, and neurodiversity activists have challenged this paradigm, highlighting the barriers faced by individuals for whom traditional museum conventions are exclusionary (Hutson and Hutson 2024; Silverman 2009). Growing empirical research demonstrates that inclusive museum design not only expands audience reach but also enriches interpretive outcomes for all visitors, making equity and accessibility essential criteria for institutional success (Wang 2024). Major policy initiatives—such as the United Nations' Convention on the Rights of Persons with Disabilities and national legislation like the Americans with Disabilities Act (ADA)—have set legal and ethical standards that drive continuous institutional improvement (Hutson and Hutson 2023).

One of the first barriers for many visitors is language. As museums increasingly serve global and multilingual audiences, reliance on monolingual signage, catalogues, and interpretation creates substantial obstacles to access (Neather 2024). Recent studies indicate that linguistic exclusion disproportionately affects immigrant and refugee communities, as well as international tourists and heritage speakers who may possess limited proficiency in the primary language of museum texts (Black 2012). To address these gaps, institutions such as the Museum of New Zealand Te Papa Tongarewa and the Louvre (https://www.louvre.fr/en) have implemented comprehensive multilingual interpretation systems, ranging from printed guides and audio tours in over ten languages to mobile apps that instantly translate labels using natural language processing (Eziamaka et al. 2024). Such tools help dismantle barriers to participation and foster a sense of belonging among linguistically diverse visitors, affirming the museum's role as a space of welcome and encounter.

Neurodiversity presents a parallel challenge and opportunity for museums seeking to foster true inclusivity. Neurodiverse individuals—including those on the autism spectrum, with ADHD, dyslexia, or sensory processing differences—often experience traditional gallery environments as overwhelming or inaccessible, given the prevalence of bright lighting, crowded spaces, and unpredictable soundscapes (Filipchuk and Udych 2021; Brischetto et al. 2023). Scholars and practitioners have shown that even modest interventions—such as visual schedules, sensory-friendly maps (Fig. 2.5), or quiet hours—can dramatically improve accessibility and comfort for neurodiverse audiences (Wang 2024). The National Gallery of Art in Washington, DC, for example, offers sensory-friendly mornings with reduced noise, dimmed lighting, and additional staff support to ensure visitors with sensory sensitivities can engage deeply with the collection. They have also produced accessibility guides and resources (https://www.nga.gov/accessibility).

A growing number of institutions are developing specialized programs and resources to serve neurodiverse learners and their families. The Museum of Modern Art's "Create Ability" workshops (https://www.moma.org/calendar/programs/34), for instance, provide structured, multisensory activities for children and adults with cognitive disabilities, blending visual analysis with hands-on art making and movement (Woodruff 2023). These initiatives are informed by consultation with neurodiversity advocates, occupational therapists, and educators, ensuring that museum experiences are not only accessible but also genuinely engaging. Research demonstrates that such programs enhance self-expression, social interaction, and cognitive development for neurodiverse participants while offering valuable models for broader institutional practice (Simon 2009; Filipchuk and Udych 2021).

Digital innovation has accelerated the pace and scope of accessibility transformation. Machine learning and natural language processing underpin a new generation of mobile apps and gallery kiosks that translate interpretive content, provide audio description for the visually impaired, and convert curatorial texts to plain language or visual symbols (Eziamaka et al. 2024; Capece and Chivaran 2020). The British Museum's smart guide app (https://www.britishmuseum.org/visit/audio-app), for example, enables visitors to select preferred modes of engagement—visual, auditory, or tactile—while algorithmic personalization offers suggestions tailored to reading level, cognitive style, or sensory needs. These advances democratize access to knowledge, extending the reach of curatorial interpretation and facilitating deeper, more individualized learning for all audiences.

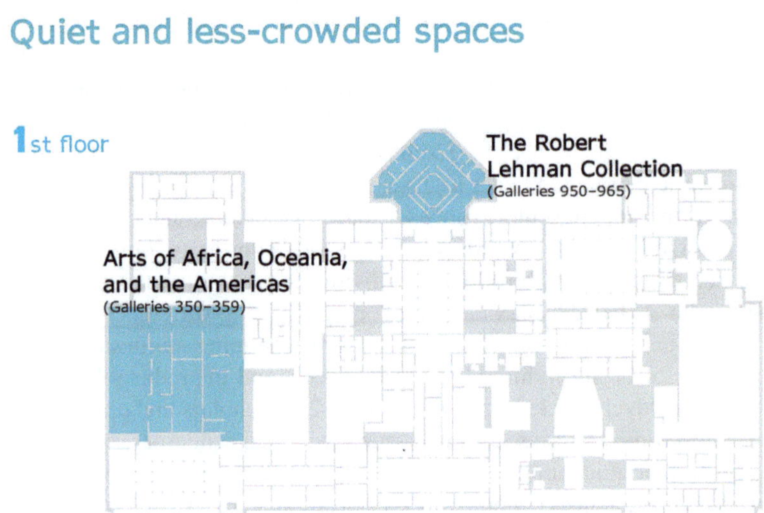

Fig. 2.5 Quiet and less-crowded spaces, sensory friendly map of the Metropolitan Museum of Art for visitors on the autism spectrum, 2015 (Courtesy of Accessibility Education, MET)

Language accessibility also extends to participatory programming and community partnerships. Museums like the Brooklyn Museum and Chicago's National Museum of Mexican Art have built relationships with local schools, community groups, and advocacy organizations to cocreate bilingual tours, translation initiatives, and heritage days celebrating linguistic diversity (Wang 2024). These collaborative projects position the museum as a forum for cross-cultural dialogue and empower underrepresented voices to contribute to institutional narratives. In doing so, museums not only fulfill their missions of public education and service but also reflect the lived realities of the communities they serve. Such initiatives frequently involve community advisors in the selection and presentation of objects, ensuring that interpretation is culturally resonant and linguistically inclusive. Through participatory translation and interpretive workshops, institutions can address historical gaps in access while fostering trust and reciprocity with multilingual audiences. These approaches move beyond tokenistic outreach to cultivate sustained relationships, making the museum a more porous, responsive, and socially relevant space. Ultimately, language accessibility initiatives signal a broader commitment to equity and cocreation that is essential for museums' future vitality and legitimacy.

Neurodiversity inclusion increasingly draws upon sensory mapping and spatial analytics to guide exhibition design and visitor flow. Tools such as quiet zones, tactile wayfinding, and immersive "chill rooms" offer respite and orientation for visitors prone to overstimulation or anxiety (Brischetto et al. 2023). The Science Museum in London's "Early Birds" program uses digital ticketing and real-time crowd monitoring to regulate capacity and reduce noise, while interactive signage and sensory backpacks equipped with noise-canceling headphones help visitors manage their own comfort. These data-driven and user-centered approaches exemplify the shift from one-size-fits-all galleries to responsive, participatory museum environments. Museums are also piloting mobile apps that allow neurodiverse visitors to customize lighting, audio, and navigation preferences, creating a personalized experience attuned to individual sensory needs. Staff training programs increasingly emphasize neurodiversity awareness, equipping museum personnel with strategies for empathetic engagement and flexible communication. Community consultations, focus groups, and feedback loops with neurodiverse audiences are now integral to exhibition planning and evaluation, ensuring that design solutions are informed by lived expertise. Collectively, these initiatives reframe accessibility as an ongoing, collaborative process—one that positions neurodiverse visitors not as exceptions, but as cocreators of the museum's public space and interpretive mission.

The implementation of augmented and virtual reality tools has further enhanced accessibility. The Louvre's AR tours (https://apps.apple.com/us/app/louvre-visit-guide/id1220004840) can be adapted for neurodiverse users, offering the ability to control visual intensity, narration speed, or content complexity based on personal preference (Neather 2024). The Metropolitan Museum of Art is piloting VR-based exploration tools that allow remote or mobility-impaired visitors to navigate the collection virtually, with customizable settings for visual contrast, font size, and pacing. Moreover, the Met 360° Project expands on this with six short videos that allow virtual visits to areas in the museum as never seen before (https://www.metmuseum.org/art/online-features/met-360-project) (Eziamaka et al. 2024). These innovations not only expand access but also redefine what it means to "visit" a museum, extending engagement far beyond physical walls. Moreover, ongoing research continues to refine these strategies. Studies published in museum education and disability studies journals consistently emphasize the importance of codesign, evaluation, and feedback from neurodiverse and multilingual users (Filipchuk and Udych 2021; Woodruff 2023). Institutions are increasingly sharing best practices and standardized evaluation tools, fostering a culture of collaboration and accountability within the global museum community. This reflexive, evidence-based approach drives continuous improvement, ensuring that accessibility remains a living priority rather than a one-time achievement.

2.3 Intelligent Recommendation Systems: Personalized Museum Journeys

The evolution of personalized engagement in art museums has progressed from early hypermedia tools to the robust, machine-based platforms that place visitor agency at the core of interpretive experience today. Initial projects, such as those by Khandelwal et al. (2004), allowed users to navigate historical narratives through curated web content, laying the groundwork for subsequent advances in interactive storytelling. Latif et al. (2021) expanded these possibilities with VisKonnect (https://vis.informatik.uni-due.de/fileadmin/migratedchairt3assets/file/VisKonnect.pdf), a platform leveraging event-based knowledge graphs and GPT-3-generated explanations to map relationships among historical figures. Similar efforts—like Haller and Rebedea's historical chatbots and Duguleană et al.'s cultural exhibit interfaces—demonstrate how natural language interactions can transform passive spectatorship into dialogic participation, allowing visitors to simulate conversations with figures from the past or engage directly with museum collections. The blending of generative neural networks and immersive XR platforms, as seen in MyHeritage AI Time Machine (https://www.myheritage.com/ai-time-machine) and Monash University's Virtual Angkor (https://www.virtualangkor.com/), now offers historically themed, context-rich explorations tailored to visitor interests and identities (Chandler and Clulow 2020). These projects mark a shift toward digital docents and interactive avatars, enabling a move from static content delivery to multisensory, participatory learning experiences.

The emergence of digital docents further exemplifies this transition. At the Genesee Country Village and Museum, Geigel et al. (2020) developed a 3D avatar—Dr. Frederick F. Backus—who guided visitors through nineteenth-century narratives using AR-enabled HoloLens experiences. These interactive, place-based vignettes encouraged visitors to analyze historical significance through critical assessment, fostering both personal connection and analytical depth. Similarly, the Hello History AI app (https://www.hellohistory.ai/) invites users to converse with thousands of simulated historical figures, leveraging neural network personality models to facilitate engaging, educational dialogue (Klee 2023). Initiatives at the University of Southern California, such as the Chinatown AR Project (https://polymathic.usc.edu/ahmanson-lab/chinatown-history-project) and the VR reconstruction of the Vatican Stanza della Segnatura (https://polymathic.usc.edu/ahmanson-lab/building-virtual-renaissance-library-julius-iis-stanza-della-segnatura), illustrate how XR democratizes access to complex cultural and historical environments through layered, individualized journeys. These examples collectively highlight the capacity for digital and XR tools to transform the museum visit into an interactive and interpretive process shaped by the visitor's own questions and context.

Museum professionals have rapidly adopted LLMs to advance personalized engagement, moving beyond conventional audio tours toward dynamic, dialogue-based experiences. Where earlier approaches required specialized hardware and limited narrative flexibility, app-based platforms now are accessible on visitor smartphones (see Fig. 2.6). QR codes or exhibit numbers embedded throughout the gallery launch web interfaces or conversational "personal curator" apps, inviting visitors to tailor the complexity and language of explanations to their needs (Neather 2024). This modularity enables a fifth-grade class to access age-appropriate content with references to contemporary culture, while seasoned scholars can pursue deeper investigations into provenance, style, and historiography (Eziamaka et al. 2024). Such adaptive customization supports inclusive learning for guests with language differences, visual or auditory challenges, and varied cognitive or sensory profiles. Notably, the Civic Art Gallery of Ascoli's use of GPT-4 to power 3D virtual tours exemplifies the potential of natural language interfaces to shape content according to a user's background and preferences (Vasic et al. 2024). CuratorAI's integration of visual analytics and natural language processing marks another advance, bridging static information delivery and dialogic, multilayered engagement (Chaudhary et al. 2023). While many current implementations rely on curated content preselected by museum staff, the next generation of LLM-powered guides aspires to real-time, holistic personalization that adapts fluidly to each visitor's learning style and engagement level.

This moves museums beyond piecemeal, object-by-object interpretation toward comprehensive, hyper-personalized narratives that span entire collections and resonate with a wide spectrum of audiences. Strategic adoption of customizable digital platforms—anchored in LLMs like GPT-4o or o1 mini—allows museums to deliver content tailored to the cultural, intellectual, and accessibility needs of visitors (Hayde et al. 2023; Varitimiadis et al. 2020). Such platforms invite guests to choose their preferred language, thematic focus, or access features upon entry, generating interpretive pathways that shift dynamically based on feedback and interaction. The democratization of LLM training tools—now requiring little or no programming background—enables even smaller institutions or individual curators to develop virtual curators and adaptive tours. By curating high-quality textual data and structuring prompts that reflect institutional mission and visitor profiles, museums can create inclusive, evolving interpretive resources without reliance on external vendors or technical specialists (Esposito 2024).

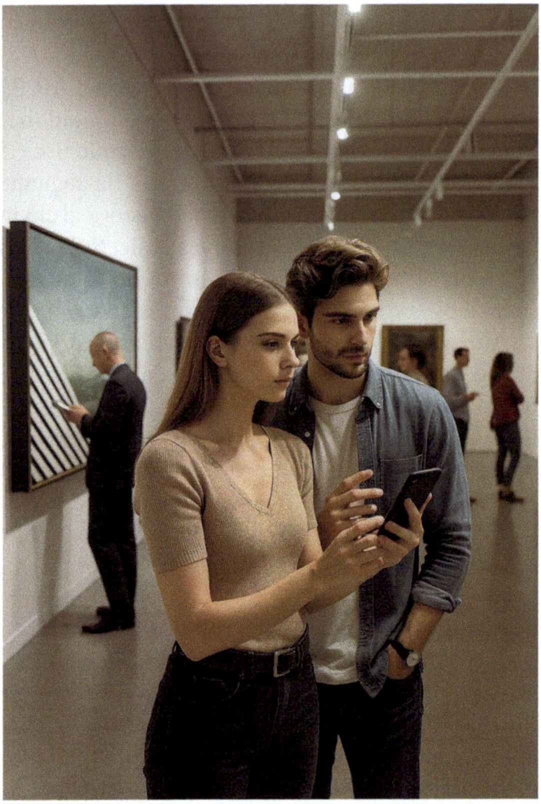

Fig. 2.6 James Hutson, museum visitors using smartphone interface with QR code, 4o (Permission of author)

A hallmark of these augmented experiences is the integration of features designed for equitable participation by visitors with diverse mobility, auditory, and linguistic needs. Multisensory systems, supported by machine learning, generate tactile renderings of artworks or auditory guides that contextualize artistic technique and cultural significance (Brischetto et al. 2023; Sheehy et al. 2019). Natural language processing supports multilingual chatbots and interpretive tools that deliver content in multiple languages or formats, including text, audio, or sign language, expanding access to those previously marginalized by monolingual or visually exclusive presentation (Capece and Chivaran 2020). Advanced speech-to-text capabilities enable responsive, multimodal guidance, ensuring that visitors who require written transcripts or audio descriptions are fully included (Woodruff 2023; Filipchuk and Udych 2021). Thematic storytelling further customizes experiences, allowing users to explore chosen topics—such as "Renaissance Portraiture" or "Modernist Abstraction"—through targeted, interactive routes that combine artifact highlights, visualizations, and contextual narrative (Varitimiadis et al. 2020). Embedding these platforms within museum operations reflects a robust commitment to universal design, supporting differentiated learning for school groups, families, scholars, and visitors with disabilities alike (Eziamaka et al. 2024).

Implementing a robust personalization strategy, especially with generative platforms, demands a careful balance of ambition and pragmatism. While major institutions like the Metropolitan Museum of Art and the Smithsonian have set benchmarks in this domain (Brischetto et al. 2023; Woodruff 2023), even small museums can initiate pilot projects to test visitor response and refine strategies incrementally. By training models on locally relevant data—curatorial texts, biographies, archival material—and shaping prompt templates for diverse audiences, curators gain unprecedented control over content delivery (Esposito 2024). New features, such as OpenAI's model customization tools, facilitate the process for nontechnical staff and allow for seamless updates as collections grow or interpretations shift. Through staged rollouts and iterative feedback, even modestly resourced institutions can sustain dynamic, personalized interpretive systems that remain in step with evolving collections and audience needs.

What sets these new systems apart is their accessibility: the threshold for creating a personalized "virtual curator" has never been lower (Table 2.1). A single curator can now define the scope of an interpretive tool by setting clear goals—enhancing accessibility, presenting deeper historical context, or supporting thematic exploration—then organizing relevant content into a structured dataset. Using an OpenAI account or similar user-friendly platform, they can upload materials, design prompts, and test responses to reflect the educational mission of institutions. Deployment is similarly straightforward: generated content can be linked to QR codes or integrated into browser-based guides, with multilingual options and adaptive features built in. Initial pilot programs with select visitor groups yield feedback that guides ongoing refinement, ensuring accuracy, resonance, and alignment with institutional priorities. As new research, audience data, and interpretive trends emerge, the system can be updated, scaled, and adapted for broader use—fostering an ever-evolving, visitor-centered museum experience.

This approach expedites the development of specialized "virtual curators" that interact with visitors in real time, continually refining their responses and thematic recommendations as they accumulate data from ongoing engagements (Capece and Chivaran 2020). Such iterative improvements highlight the dynamic, adaptive potential of algorithmic gallery experiences, enabling museum staff to optimize content for relevance, minimize misunderstandings, and construct narratives that genuinely resonate with diverse communities (Filipchuk and Udych 2021). The resultant user-centric model enriches interpretive quality while simultaneously amplifying inclusivity across linguistic, cultural, and educational boundaries (Hayde et al. 2023). As museums further integrate these machine-driven strategies, collaboration with technology vendors, academic partners, and community organizations will become increasingly important in sustaining an equitable, participatory vision for the museum environment (Neather 2024). To foster the full potential of these advances, museums must also invest in comprehensive staff training and community partnerships, empowering curators and educators to lead digital engagement and ensuring that system design and content remain rooted in institutional expertise and local relevance (Hayde et al. 2023). Workshops, peer learning, and ongoing

Table 2.1 Framework for developing AI-powered virtual curators

Step	Description	Tools/resources	Instructions
1. Identify key goals	Define the objectives for the AI-driven experience, such as enhancing accessibility, providing historical context, or offering personalized thematic tours	Strategic Foresight Toolkit (https://www.aam-us.org/programs/toolkits/strategic-foresight-toolkit/)	Utilize this toolkit to align AI initiatives with institutional goals
2. Gather collection data	Compile high-quality textual descriptions, artist biographies, and archival materials that accurately represent the museum's collection	NPS Museum Handbook (https://www.nps.gov/museum/publications/MHII/mh2ch1.pdf)	Follow guidelines for documenting and cataloguing collections
3. Set up OpenAI access	Create an OpenAI account to obtain an API key, enabling communication with GPT models	OpenAI API Quickstart Guide (https://platform.openai.com/docs/quickstart/introduction)	Follow the guide to create an account and generate an API key
4. Customize the model	Upload the curated dataset to OpenAI's platform and develop prompts that align with the museum's educational mission, ensuring clarity for diverse audiences	OpenAI Fine-Tuning Guide (https://platform.openai.com/docs/guides/fine-tuning)	Use the guide to fine-tune the model with your data and prompts
5. Develop user Interface	Integrate the GPT model into a user-friendly interface, such as a web site or mobile app, allowing visitors to interact with the virtual curator	Streamlit Web App Framework (https://streamlit.io/)	Utilize these frameworks to build the interface; refer to their documentation for implementation details
6. Pilot test and collect feedback	Launch a pilot version to a select group of users, gathering feedback on usability and content effectiveness	Museum AI Toolkit (https://themuseumsainetwork.files.wordpress.com/2020/02/20190317_museums-and-ai-toolkit_rl_web.pdf)	Apply best practices from the toolkit to evaluate and refine the virtual curator

(continued)

Table 2.1 (continued)

Step	Description	Tools/resources	Instructions
7. Refine and expand	Update the model and interface based on feedback, and consider scaling to include more collections or features	A Guide to Transforming Visitor Experiences with AI in Museums (https://completeaitraining.com/blog/a-guide-to-transforming-visitor-experiences-with-ai-in-museums/)	Consult this guide for strategies to enhance and expand AI-driven experiences
8. Maintain and evolve	Regularly review analytics to adjust the virtual curator, incorporating new data and technological advancements to keep it dynamic and relevant	AI and Museums: A Year of Transformation and a Glimpse into 2025 (https://museumobserver.com/ai-and-museums-a-year-of-transformation-and-a-glimpse-into-2025/)	Stay informed about the latest trends and advancements in AI applications within museums

collaboration with both technology specialists and user groups help build institutional capacity and maintain a feedback-rich environment, supporting the continual refinement of personalized platforms.

The field continues to evolve rapidly as researchers and technologists investigate new frontiers for machine-driven personalization. Projects currently underway seek to integrate real-time emotional analysis, gaze tracking, and adaptive pacing, so that digital guides can respond not only to visitors' stated interests but also to subtle nonverbal cues and patterns of attention (Vasic et al. 2024). In parallel, "coexperience" platforms are being piloted that connect visitors with shared backgrounds or interests, enabling collaborative interpretation and social learning within galleries. The convergence of these tools points to a near future in which museum journeys are not only individualized but also inherently dialogic and relational, leveraging technology to deepen both personal reflection and collective engagement.

As this section has demonstrated, the rise of intelligent recommendation systems and LLM-powered guides signals a transformative reimagining of what it means to visit and participate in a museum. The experience is shifting from a passive, predetermined reception of information to an open-ended, adaptive, and interactive process—one that welcomes the identities, learning styles, and aspirations of every visitor. This transformation is neither technologically deterministic nor unidirectional; rather, it is a process marked by ongoing experimentation, critical reflection, and collaborative cocreation among curators, educators, technologists, and the communities they serve. In this way, the integration of personalized digital systems stands not as a replacement for curatorial authority or historical rigor, but as an invitation to broaden the conversation and democratize the pleasures and responsibilities of interpreting art and cultural heritage.

2.4 Multisensory Engagement: Augmented Reality in Global Contexts

The global adoption of augmented reality (AR) in museums marks a new chapter in the design of visitor experiences, moving beyond strictly visual engagement to embrace truly multisensory interaction. Unlike virtual reality (VR), which, while popular for certain high-profile installations, often relies on costly, cumbersome headsets that may tether visitors in place or limit free movement, AR offers scalable solutions by leveraging the devices that most visitors already carry—smartphones and tablets (Li et al. 2024). AR overlays digital content such as images, sound, animation, and even haptic feedback directly onto physical environments, allowing visitors to interact with objects, spaces, and stories in real time and within museum galleries (Fig. 2.7). This accessibility enables museums to offer rich, layered interpretive experiences without the logistical and financial barriers associated with VR deployment, making it feasible to reach a much wider and more diverse audience (Creed et al. 2024).

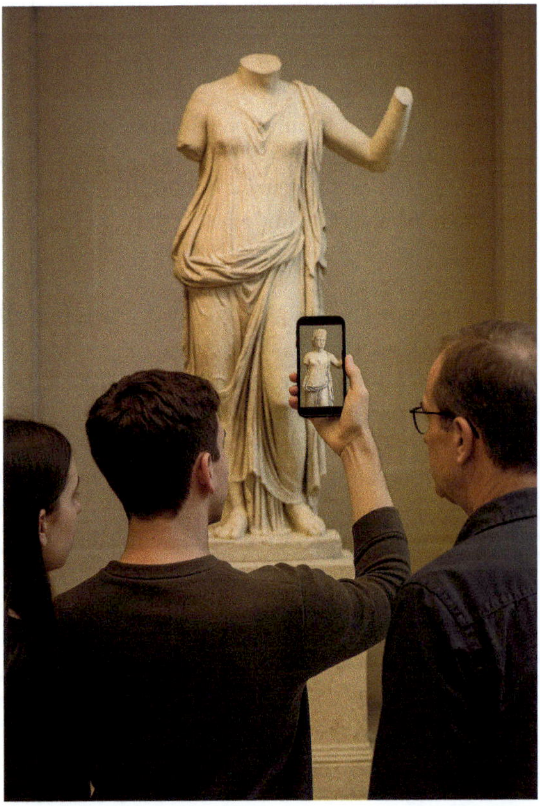

Fig. 2.7 James Hutson, museum visitors using AR with smartphone interface to reconstitute a sculpture, 4o (Permission of author)

This technology has proven especially effective in bridging the gap between static displays and dynamic interpretation, offering visitors not only new ways of seeing but also innovative ways of hearing, touching, and even moving within galleries. Museums in diverse regions, from the Louvre in Paris to the National Museum of Singapore, now leverage AR to animate historic sites, reveal lost details of artifacts, or reconstruct lost architectural spaces (El Gazi and Ibrahimi 2025; Hsieh et al. 2025). The Van Gogh Museum's Meet Vincent van Gogh Experience (https://www.vangoghmuseum.nl/en/about/news-and-press/press-releases/meet-vincent-van-gogh-experience-travels-to-south-america-for-the-first-time) uses AR to allow visitors to step inside recreated versions of the artist's studio, combining 3D visuals with tactile surfaces and audio storytelling (Brischetto et al. 2023; Prokůpek and Gombault 2024). Meanwhile, the Acropolis Museum in Athens has implemented AR apps (https://www.theacropolismuseum.gr/en/multimedia-applications) that overlay original colors and decorative elements onto ancient sculptures, enabling viewers to perceive the objects as they might have appeared in antiquity (Capece and Chivaran 2020). These projects demonstrate the potential of AR to revitalize familiar collections and broaden access for diverse audiences.

Research highlights that AR-driven, multisensory experiences not only foster curiosity but can also enhance knowledge retention, particularly for visitors with different learning styles or access needs (Kakoulidou 2024; Pietroni 2025). By engaging multiple senses, museums are able to address a wider spectrum of cognitive and sensory preferences, supporting neurodiverse and multilingual visitors who might struggle with traditional, text-heavy interpretation (Filipchuk and Udych 2021; Luo et al. 2024). Case studies at the Science Museum in London and the Smithsonian National Museum of Natural History show that AR-enhanced exhibitions encourage longer visits, more social interaction, and greater recall of key interpretive messages (Morgan 2025; McLaughlin and Coleman 2024; Woodruff 2023). The multisensory framework is especially valuable in educational programming, where immersive environments invite participants to manipulate virtual objects, solve puzzles, or cocreate digital artworks—activities that anchor learning in embodied, experiential modes. These findings align with broader shifts in museum education, where constructivist and participatory strategies increasingly supplant didactic, unidirectional instruction (Jefferies 2024). The integration of AR helps museums create environments where visitors are both learners and contributors, blurring the line between expert and audience in the coproduction of knowledge (Simon 2010).

One of the most celebrated examples of VR in heritage contexts is the Vatican's Stanza della Segnatura project, developed by the University of Southern California, which enables remote or in-person visitors to explore Raphael's frescoes in three dimensions (https://polymathic.usc.edu/ahmanson-lab/building-virtual-renaissance-library-julius-iis-stanza-della-segnatura). The experience provides layered commentary on the frescoes and has annotations of the library that would have been there. Similar approaches have been adopted in East Asia, where the Palace Museum in Beijing uses immersive experiences to reconstruct lost Ming dynasty palaces, allowing users to "walk through" ancient court life with auditory, visual, and haptic cues (Yu et al. 2024). These projects underscore the international momentum behind immersive reality as a tool for heritage conservation and interpretive renewal, illustrating how multisensory design is becoming a shared global priority.

Immersive experiences have also been instrumental in democratizing access for visitors with disabilities. Museums such as the Museum of Fine Arts, Boston, have collaborated with technology providers to develop systems that provide descriptive audio overlays (https://www.mfa.org/visit/mfa-mobile), virtual models, and customizable visual settings for visitors with low vision or sensory sensitivities (Brischetto et al. 2023). Research in inclusive design demonstrates that these features not only benefit visitors with specific impairments but also enhance the experience for all users, reflecting the principles of universal design. For example, spatialized audio offers location-based storytelling for those who learn best through sound (Wan 2024). This commitment to accessibility is reinforced by ongoing evaluation and feedback, ensuring that such initiatives evolve alongside the needs and expectations of diverse publics.

Interactive augmentation has also enabled museums to reimagine cultural storytelling, particularly for diasporic and indigenous communities. The National Museum of African American History and Culture offers various virtual experiences, including a 3D tour of the Point of Pines Slave Cabin and online exhibits that explore African American history and culture. Virtual tours and digital resources through the Smithsonian Learning Lab and National Museum of African American History and Culture Web sites (https://3d.si.edu/object/3d/cabin-point-pines-plantation-charleston-county-south-carolina%3A5879321a-d9ef-4791-a036-8413b640289d) (Rogala et al. 2023; Sodaro 2024). The National Museum of the American Indian (NMAI) integrates similar features that allow users to listen to indigenous languages (https://americanindian.si.edu/nk360/code-talkers/native-languages/), reinforcing the living, participatory nature of cultural heritage. Such projects foreground the epistemological value of sensory immersion, challenging Eurocentric conventions that privilege sight over other modes of engagement and validating the importance of memory, sound, and embodied experience in historical understanding.

In the context of temporary exhibitions and outdoor installations, immersive technologies provide unprecedented flexibility and reach. The Chinatown History Project at the University of Southern California overlays archival photos, oral histories, and historical maps onto present-day streets using AR, allowing users to experience lost neighborhoods and hear the voices of past residents (https://polymathic.usc.edu/ahmanson-lab/chinatown-history-project). This model of site-specific, multisensory interpretation has been adopted in cities from New York to Melbourne, enabling cultural organizations to activate public space and foster dialogue across generations and communities. The success of these initiatives underscores the potential of the technology not only as a tool for gallery enhancement but also as a platform for social justice, community memory, and placemaking (Verhoeff 2025).

While much attention focuses on the "wow factor" of AR and VR, sustained research reveals that the most impactful applications are those deeply integrated with curatorial strategy and visitor research. Museums that consult with educators, designers, and target user groups early in the design process report higher levels of satisfaction, inclusivity, and interpretive depth (Capece and Chivaran 2020; Filipchuk and Udych 2021). At the Canadian Museum for Human Rights (https://humanrights.ca/), various immersive experiences are used to illustrate the evolution of human rights concepts through interactive timelines and testimonies, developed in partnership with advocacy organizations and community stakeholders. This participatory, evidence-driven approach ensures that AR enriches rather than distracts from the museum's educational mission, reinforcing trust and transparency with audiences.

Museum professionals must also grapple with the logistical and ethical challenges of multisensory deployment. Issues such as device compatibility, privacy, and accessibility remain at the forefront, requiring ongoing investment in staff training and technical support (Neather 2024). Institutions like the Louvre and the Science Museum in London offer device loans and step-by-step tutorials to bridge the digital divide, while feedback mechanisms ensure that these tools remain usable, responsive, and secure. Equally important are questions of content authorship, algorithmic bias, and the protection of cultural knowledge, particularly when working with marginalized or indigenous communities. Robust governance frameworks and cocreation models are vital to mitigating these risks and fostering ethical stewardship.

Looking forward, the future of AI-driven immersive experiences in museums is shaped by rapid innovation and collaborative experimentation. Advances in real-time gesture recognition, haptic feedback, and large language models promise to make multisensory engagement more intuitive, adaptive, and participatory (Vasic et al. 2024). Pilot programs in Italy and Japan are testing "virtual docents" that respond to visitor mood, learning preferences, and cultural background, creating truly personalized, relational museum experiences (Diket 2008). As these capabilities mature, they will further blur the boundaries between physical and digital, object and story, and curator and audience. The adoption of multisensory experiences signals a paradigm shift in the ways museums fulfill their educational, social, and civic missions. Through designing environments that speak to the full range of human senses, institutions create spaces where every visitor can find a meaningful point of entry to cultural heritage. This transformation demands both technological innovation and critical reflection, ensuring that new tools reinforce core values of inclusivity, participation, and historical rigor. As we move deeper into the era of interactive, machine-enhanced interpretation, art museums stand poised to realize their potential as truly global, dialogic, and multisensory spaces for learning and connection.

2.5 Ethical Dimensions in Museum Contexts: Privacy, Consent, and Fairness

While the capability to deliver highly personalized experiences is now technologically feasible, these advancements rest on the extensive collection and processing of visitor data. The integration of algorithmic systems in museum settings thus requires a robust ethical framework, foregrounding user privacy and data security as primary concerns. As museums deploy recommendation engines, adaptive guides, and data-driven curation strategies, they collect granular information about visitor movements, preferences, identities, and sometimes even biometric markers (Rosemary 2025). Protecting this sensitive data mandates the implementation of technical safeguards—data anonymization, end-to-end encryption, and explicit privacy protocols—designed to prevent unauthorized access, breaches, or misuse (Yanamala et al. 2024). International standards, such as the General Data Protection Regulation (GDPR) in Europe, set rigorous benchmarks for data governance. In response, institutions like the British Museum and the Rijksmuseum have systematically evaluated their use of third-party tools, restricted the duration of data retention, and instituted clear consent procedures for digital initiatives (Cameron 2023). Transparent communication about data use is essential for building public trust, ensuring that visitors understand not only what information is collected but how it will be stored, analyzed, and potentially shared.

Consent, in this context, is not a mere formality but a cornerstone of ethical practice. Museums must ensure that visitors are provided with clear, accessible explanations of the benefits and risks associated with data-driven personalization, as well as meaningful opportunities to opt in or out (Foka et al. 2023). For example, the Science Museum in London and the Metropolitan Museum of Art now feature detailed signage, mobile app notifications, and digital privacy dashboards, allowing users to adjust settings and review the scope of data sharing at any point during their visit (Lewis 2024). Such practices not only align with legal mandates but also reinforce the responsibility to treat audiences as partners in the cocreation of knowledge, rather than as passive sources of behavioral data. Research underscores that when visitors feel respected and empowered, their willingness to engage with algorithmic experiences and provide feedback increases, fostering a climate of mutual benefit (Chen et al. 2025; Silverman 2009).

A persistent challenge in the adoption of AI, and automated technologies in general, is the risk of algorithmic bias—wherein the systems that power digital curation or recommendation may inadvertently perpetuate dominant cultural narratives, reinforce historical exclusions, or marginalize underrepresented groups. Museums have a unique ethical mandate to interrogate and address these risks, ensuring that automated interpretive strategies do not simply replicate the inequities of the past (Jaillant and Rees 2023). The Smithsonian's data ethics committee, for example, regularly audits exhibition content and digital outputs for evidence of bias, working with external advisors to diversify the datasets and interpretive frameworks that inform both AI training and curatorial practice (Muhammad and Orji 2024). Such efforts are increasingly regarded as best practice within the field, reflecting a growing awareness that algorithmic neutrality is an illusion and that cultural stewardship requires deliberate, reflexive intervention (Ingram and Johnson 2024).

Achieving fairness in digital curation also depends on the inclusion of a broad array of stakeholders in the design and oversight of algorithmic tools. Collaboration among technologists, curators, educators, ethicists, and community representatives creates a more comprehensive understanding of the potential pitfalls and unintended consequences of personalization (Mikhaylov et al. 2018). For instance, the Van Gogh Museum and the Louvre have convened interdisciplinary panels to assess the impact of data-driven technologies on audience diversity and the representation of minority artists or narratives (Giannini and Bowen 2024). These panels review not only technical outcomes but also the broader cultural implications of digital engagement, ensuring that the role of the museum as an interpreter of heritage is not subsumed by the logic of technological efficiency or popularity algorithms.

Transparency and explainability are central to ethical digital engagement in the museum context. Visitors and stakeholders must be able to understand, question, and critique how machine-based decisions are made, particularly when these shape the selection, sequencing, or interpretation of cultural artifacts (Pansoni et al. 2023). Museums have begun to implement open-access dashboards, interpretive panels, and online platforms that allow users to view AI-generated recommendations, review the provenance of digital datasets, and participate in ongoing research projects. These mechanisms serve both an educational and a regulatory function, inviting public scrutiny and reinforcing institutional accountability. They also contribute to intellectual transparency, making the "black box" of algorithmic curation more accessible to nonspecialists and building trust in new modes of cultural interpretation.

Ethical implementation of automated personalization further necessitates attention to accessibility and equity. AI-powered guides or recommendation systems must accommodate the full spectrum of user abilities, linguistic backgrounds, and sensory needs—otherwise, the promise of inclusivity becomes little more than rhetoric (Filipchuk and Udych 2021). For example, as noted, museums in the Netherlands and Canada have developed multilingual and sensory-friendly AI interfaces that adapt not only language but also font size, contrast, and auditory output, based on visitor feedback and user analytics (Brischetto et al. 2023). Inclusive design strategies also extend to training datasets, which should reflect the diversity of the audiences and collections, and to the curation of interpretive content, ensuring that all visitors encounter narratives that resonate with their identities and experiences. Training and professional development for museum staff play a vital role in supporting these ethical innovations. As algorithmic and machine-assisted platforms become more central to visitor experience, curators, educators, and front-line staff require the skills to oversee, troubleshoot, and refine these tools in real time. Institutions are increasingly turning to collaborative initiatives and hands-on experimentation to foster AI literacy and collective learning among staff and stakeholders. For example, the Creative Interfaces Research + Design Studio, in partnership with the Georgia Institute of Technology, recently conducted a trial run of three AI-based exhibits at the Griffin Museum of Science and Industry. This project brought together curators, educators, technologists, and designers to explore the practical challenges and ethical considerations of deploying machine-driven interpretation in a real-world museum setting, promoting shared responsibility and professional development through direct experience and cross-disciplinary dialogue (Northwestern 2024).

The evolving field of ethical AI in museums emphasizes participatory research and public consultation. Engaging local communities, advocacy groups, and external experts in the cocreation of digital policies and tools deepens institutional accountability and surfaces concerns that may otherwise be overlooked (Mikhaylov et al. 2018). Several museums now host open forums, citizen science projects, and AI ethics cafés, inviting visitors to shape the development of new interpretive strategies, assess algorithmic fairness, and contribute to ongoing evaluation. These participatory models reflect a broader shift toward transparency, responsiveness, and democratic engagement in the stewardship of cultural heritage. Thus, as museums continue to experiment with machine-based personalization and digital augmentation, they must remain vigilant about the ethical, legal, and social implications of their choices. The main themes emerging from this chapter are clear: while technological advances have expanded the horizons of engagement and inclusivity, they simultaneously demand greater responsibility and reflexivity from museums and their stakeholders. Achieving a balance between innovation and stewardship is not a static goal but an ongoing, iterative process—one that requires open dialogue, interdisciplinary expertise, and a commitment to the highest standards of privacy, consent, and fairness. In doing so, museums can fulfill their dual mandate as custodians of both cultural memory and public trust, ensuring that digital transformation is always in service to the communities they serve.

In reflection, this chapter has demonstrated that the digital transformation of museums is not simply a matter of technical enhancement but signals a fundamental reimagining of institutional purpose and public engagement. By tracing the evolution from early modern cabinets of wonder to today's algorithmically personalized, visitor-centered institutions, the chapter reveals how museums have continually renegotiated their roles as sites of knowledge production, cultural exchange, and civic participation. The case studies presented—spanning language accessibility, neurodiversity inclusion, and the deployment of intelligent recommendation systems—highlight that digital tools are most effective when embedded within ethical, dialogic frameworks that prioritize equity, agency, and responsiveness. Rather than reinforcing existing boundaries or institutional hierarchies, technology serves as a catalyst for pluralism, cocreation, and shared authority. The integration of sensory analytics, participatory programming, and real-time feedback underscores the museum's capacity to adapt to the diverse and shifting needs of contemporary publics. Ultimately, this chapter underscores the necessity of aligning innovation with inclusivity, situating technological experimentation within a broader commitment to cultural stewardship and social trust.

The main findings of the chapter reveal that meaningful digital engagement depends on intentional design and sustained community collaboration. Initiatives such as multilingual programming, sensory mapping, and adaptive mobile interfaces offer models for how museums can foster cross-cultural dialogue, support neurodiverse visitors, and democratize interpretive authority. These approaches succeed not because of technological novelty alone, but because they are developed through iterative, participatory processes that draw upon the lived expertise of local communities and user groups. The chapter also notes that addressing ethical concerns around privacy, data use, and algorithmic bias is integral to building public confidence and maintaining institutional legitimacy. Museums that prioritize transparency, open communication, and flexible governance are better positioned to respond to emerging challenges and opportunities in the digital landscape. The successful deployment of intelligent systems is thus inseparable from a broader ethos of openness, accountability, and care.

Looking ahead, the chapter calls for museums to move beyond pilot projects and isolated interventions toward the development of holistic, scalable frameworks for digital inclusion and participation. Sustained investment in community partnerships, professional development, and cross-institutional collaboration will be essential for ensuring that the gains of digital innovation are widely distributed and continually renewed. Future considerations must also include the cultivation of interdisciplinary teams capable of integrating technological, ethical, and curatorial expertise, as well as the establishment of robust feedback and evaluation mechanisms to monitor impact over time. As algorithmic systems and digital platforms continue to evolve, museums must remain vigilant to the risks of exclusion, surveillance, or technological determinism, reaffirming their commitment to equity, pluralism, and public service. The path forward lies in treating digital transformation not as a finished project, but as an ongoing, adaptive process—one that positions museums as living laboratories for participatory cultural democracy.

References

Bennett T (2013) The birth of the museum: history, theory, politics. Routledge

Black G (2012) The engaging museum: developing museums for visitor involvement. Routledge, pp 1–280

Brischetto A, Iacono E, Becchimanzi C (2023) Digital technologies in museums: critical issues and opportunities for equal access to cultural heritage. In: AHFE international, pp 32–41

Cameron HR (2023) Outdata-ed museums: creating ethical and transparent data collection processes in museums. Doctoral dissertation, University of Nottingham

Capece S, Chivaran C (2020) The sensorial dimension of the contemporary museum between design and emerging technologies. In: IOP conference series: materials science and engineering, vol 949. https://doi.org/10.1088/1757-899X/949/1/012067

Cascone S (2020) An AI algorithm developed at MIT can spot similarities between artworks made in vastly different periods of art history. Art News, 6 Aug. Retrieved from: https://news.artnet.com/art-world/mit-mosaic-ai-curator-1900193

Chandler T, Clulow A (2020) Modeling virtual Angkor: an evolutionary approach to a single urban space. IEEE Comput Graph Appl 40(3):9–16

Chaudhary A Yang K Stevens J Curator (2023) AI: enhancing art appreciation through AI-powered insights. Appl Sci 11(18):8627

Chen J, Zhang Y, Liu Z (2025) Unlocking the power of algorithmic recommendations: the effect of recommendation characteristics on users' willingness to value co-creation. Curr Psychol 1–19

Creed C, Al-Kalbani M, Theil A, Sarcar S, Williams I (2024) Inclusive AR/VR: accessibility barriers for immersive technologies. Univers Access Inf Soc 23(1):59–73

Crow TE (1985) Painters and public life in eighteenth-century Paris. Yale University Press

Diket RM (2008) The politics of education in museums. In: Political approaches to educational administration and leadership. Routledge, pp 199–213

Duncan C (2005) Civilizing rituals: inside public art museums. Routledge

El Gazi S, Ibrahimi A (2025) Immersive technologies: augmented reality (AR) and virtual reality (VR). In: E-learning and smart engineering systems (ELSES 2024). Atlantis Press, pp 580–591

Esposito F (2024) Programming large language models with azure open AI: conversational programming and prompt engineering with LLMs. Microsoft Press

Eziamaka NV, Odonkor TN, Akinsulire AA (2024) AI-driven accessibility: transformative software solutions for empowering individuals with disabilities. Int J Appl Res Soc Sci 6(8):1612–1641

Falk J (2016) Museum audiences: a visitor-centered perspective. Loisir Société/Soc Leis 39(3):357–370

Filipchuk N, Udych Z (2021) Social aspect of museum educational interaction. Aesthet Ethics Pedagog Action 23:27–42

Findlen P (1994) Possessing nature: museums, collecting, and scientific culture in early modern Italy. University of California Press

Foka A, Eklund L, Løvlie AS, Griffin G (2023) Critically assessing AI/ML for cultural heritage: potentials and challenges. In: Handbook of critical studies of artificial intelligence, pp 815–825

Geigel J, Shitut KS, Decker J, Doherty A, Jacobs G (2020) The digital docent: Xr storytelling for a living history museum. In: Proceedings of the 26th ACM symposium on virtual reality software and technology, pp 1–3

Giannini T, Bowen JP (2024) The future of arts in a computational culture. In: The arts and computational culture: real and virtual worlds. Springer Nature Switzerland, Cham, pp 685–721

Hayde D, Weiss L, Meyer JR (2023) The role of visitor studies in shaping visitor-centered museums. Curator Mus J, 68(3), pp 161–180

Hsieh TJ, Su YH, Lin LS (2025) Augmented reality art museum mobile guide for enhancing user experience. IEEE Comput Graph Appl, 68(3), pp 161–180

Hutson J, Hutson P (2023) Digital inclusion for people with autism spectrum disorders: review of the current legal models and doctrinal concepts. J Digit Technol Law 1(4):851–879

Hutson J, Hutson P (2024) Inclusive smart museums: engaging neurodiverse audiences and enhancing cultural heritage. Springer Nature

Ingram WA, Johnson SA (2024) Archives, digital search, and AI ethics. In: The Routledge companion to libraries, archives, and the digital humanities. Routledge, pp 479–492

Jaillant L, Rees A (2023) Applying AI to digital archives: trust, collaboration and shared professional ethics. Digit Sch Humanit 38(2):571–585

Jefferies L (2024) Engaged or not engaged, that is the question: the impact of duality on the participatory experience of augmented-reality interventions in cultural spaces. Mimesis J 13(2):625–640

Kakoulidou GN (2024) Dissemination of archaeological knowledge through digital technologies: the case of the multisensory museum

Khandelwal M, Kerne A, Mistrot JM (2004) Manipulating history in generative hypermedia. In: Proceedings of the fifteenth ACM conference on hypertext and hypermedia, pp 139–140

Klee M (2023) 'Historical figures' AI lets famous dead people lie to you. Rolling Stone, 20 Jan. Retrieved from: https://www.rollingstone.com/culture/culture-news/historical-figures-ai-chat-bot-lies-dead-people-1234664257/

Latif S, Agarwal S, Gottschalk S, Chrosch C, Feit F, Jahn J, Beck F (2021) Visually connecting historical figures through event knowledge graphs. In: 2021 IEEE visualization conference (VIS). IEEE, pp 156–160

Lewis R (2024) Collections as networked images: the (re)use of the science museum group collections. In: The form of digital images through social media. Doctoral dissertation, School of Advanced Study, University of London

Li J, Tu XF, Nie JW, Ye J, Lv C (2024) Visitors' acceptance of wearable AR technology in museums, vol 14, no 4. SAGE Open, p 21582440241303507

Luo D, Doucé L, Nys K (2024) Multisensory museum experience: an integrative view and future research directions. Mus Manag Curatorship:1–28

Macdonald S (2003) Museums, national, postnational and transcultural identities. Mus Soc 1(1):1–16

McLaughlin H, Coleman LE (2024) The next evolution of museum studies: museum masterclasses in augmented and virtual reality. In: Museum studies for a post-pandemic world. Routledge, pp 56–64

Merewether C (2024) From private to public collecting and museums. In: From fascination to folly: a troubled history of collecting since the 1600s. Springer Nature Singapore, Singapore, pp 89–124

Mikhaylov SJ, Esteve M, Campion A (2018) Artificial intelligence for the public sector: opportunities and challenges of cross-sector collaboration. Philos Trans R Soc A Math Phys Eng Sci 376(2128):20170357

Morgan G (2025) Science fiction: voyage to the edge of the imagination by the science museum in London. In: Cultivating futures thinking in museums. Routledge, pp 160–165

Muhammad F, Orji CM (2024) Revolutionizing education in the digital era: the role of AI in promoting inclusivity, equality, and ethical innovation. Am J Soc Sci Educ Innov 6(09):151–157

Musílek L, Čechák T, Trojek T (2024) X-ray fluorescence analysis in the study of paintings—an overview. Eff Defects Solids 179(9–10):1218–1232

Neather R (2024) Translating for museums, galleries and heritage sites. Taylor & Francis

Northwestern (2024) AI literacy at museum of science and industry. Northwestern, 20 Sept. Retreived from: https://hci.northwestern.edu/news-events/articles/2024/creative_interface_research_and_design_studio_museum_of_science_of_industry.html

Pansoni S, Tiribelli S, Paolanti M, Frontoni E, Giovanola B (2023) Design of an ethical framework for artificial intelligence in cultural heritage. In: 2023 IEEE international symposium on ethics in engineering, science, and technology (ETHICS). IEEE, pp 1–5

Pietroni E (2025) Multisensory museums, hybrid realities, narration and technological innovation: a discussion around new perspectives in experience design and sense of authenticity

Pomian K (1990) Collectors and curiosities: Paris and Venice. Polity Press, Cambridge, pp 1500–1800

Prokůpek M, Gombault A (2024) Museums and corporate partners: the case of van Gogh Museum and shell. Int J Arts Manag 27(1)

Rogala D, Averyt K, Johnson J, Lione B, Flores J, Tompkins W (2023) Innovation and adaptation at the Smithsonian Institution in response to changing times and increased need. J Inst Conserv 46(3):253–271

Rosemary FT (2025) Leveraging artificial intelligence and data analytics for enhancing museum experiences: exploring historical narratives, visitor engagement, and digital transformation in the age of innovation. Int Res J Mod Eng Technol Sci 7(1)

Sheehy K, Garcia Carrizosa H, Rix J, Seale J, Hayhoe S (2019) Inclusive museums and augmented reality. Affordances, participation, ethics and fun. Int J Incl Mus 12(4):67–85

Silverman LH (2009) The social work of museums. Routledge

Simon N (2010) The participatory museum. Museum 2.0

Sodaro A (2024) 'Feeling truth': objects, embodiment, and temporality in the National Museum of African American history and culture (Washington, DC) and the legacy museum (Montgomery, Alabama). Museums, narratives, and critical histories: narrating the past for the present and future. Walter de Gruyter, Boston, pp 25–44

Varitimiadis S, Kotis K, Skamagis A, Tzortzakakis A, Tsekouras G, Spiliotopoulos D (2020) Towards implementing an AI chatbot platform for museums. In: International conference on cultural informatics, communication & media studies, vol 1, no 1. https://doi.org/10.12681/cicms.2732

Vasic I, Fill H G, Quattrini R, Pierdicca R (2024) Llm-aided museum guide: personalized tours based on user preferences. In: International conference on extended reality. Springer Nature Switzerland, Cham, pp 249–262

Verhoeff N (2025) Urban screens: situations, practices, concepts. Amsterdam University Press

Wan YKP (2024) Accessibility of tourist signage at heritage sites: an application of the universal design principles. Tour Recreat Res 49(4):757–771

Wang Y (2024) Diversity and inclusion in art management: a comprehensive analysis of strategies and initiatives. Front Art Res 6(2)

Woodruff A (2023) Creating visitor-centered museum experiences for adults with developmental disabilities: a collaborative story. Stud Art Educ 64:359–378. https://doi.org/10.1080/00393541.2023.2220102

Yanamala AKY, Suryadevara S, Kalli VDR (2024) Balancing innovation and privacy: the intersection of data protection and artificial intelligence. Int J Mach Learn Res Cybersecur Artif Intell 15(1):1–43

Yu Z, Hongxiao C, Qingfeng Z (2024) Study on visitor experience value assessment based on multidimensional factor analysis-case study of Forbidden City Museum in Beijing, world cultural heritage site. Int J Adv Cult Technol 12(4):96–112

Chapter 3
Augmenting Art Historical Research

Abstract This section investigates the ways in which algorithmic, machine-based, and generative technologies are fundamentally reshaping art historical research, catalyzing new paradigms in both methodology and collaboration. The chapter begins by outlining how the intersection of art history and computational systems has initiated a series of profound shifts, moving beyond conventional models of visual inquiry toward data-driven and automated approaches that uncover patterns and relationships invisible to the unaided eye. It critically assesses the use of generative tools for scholarly research, from large-scale data aggregation and multimodal interpretation to automated bibliometric mapping and the creation of synthetic datasets. Through detailed case studies, the discussion foregrounds emerging methodologies in computational art analysis, such as neural network-based attribution, stylistic clustering, and automated iconographic mapping, illustrating their strengths and limitations within academic practice. The chapter also explores how smart, collaborative platforms are breaking down disciplinary silos, fostering new alliances among art historians, computer scientists, data engineers, and cultural institutions.

3.1 The Intersection of AI and Art History: Paradigm Shifts and Opportunities

The evolution of art historical research has been firmly rooted in qualitative traditions, characterized by detailed engagement with archival resources, printed catalogues, and the close study of original objects. For generations, art historians have reconstructed the provenance and broader context of artworks by examining primary documents such as artists' letters (Fig. 3.1), workshop inventories, exhibition catalogues, and collector ledgers, often preserved within the secure vaults of museum archives and cultural heritage institutions (Friedrich et al. 2017). This methodical process, which frequently involves the comparison of handwritten receipts (Fig. 3.2), curatorial annotations, and multigenerational conservation records, has provided the evidentiary foundation for tracing an object's passage through history and unraveling its social, political, and economic significance (Fuchsgruber 2019). The field has long

J. Hutson, *Art History in the Age of Artificial Intelligence*, Springer Series on Cultural Computing, https://doi.org/10.1007/978-3-032-02920-1_3

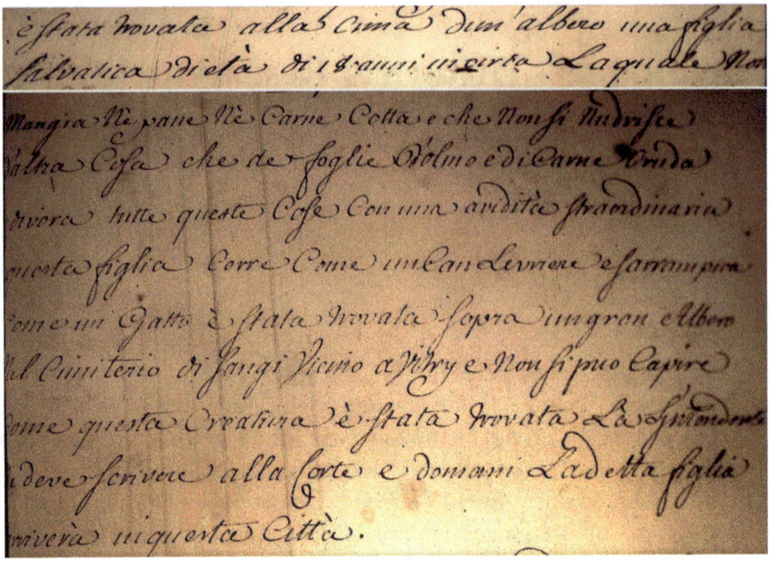

Fig. 3.1 Les Archives secrètes du Vatican offrent avec précision le lieu de capture de la fille sauvage, dont l'âge est d'environ 18 ans, 30 October, 1731 (CC O public domain)

depended on the creation of catalogues raisonnés and comprehensive museum inventories, resources that have enabled scholars to piece together patterns of artistic practice, style, and collection, even though this work traditionally required painstaking, manual cross-referencing, and years of labor. Museum archives (Fig. 3.3) have thus played a foundational role, serving as living records that document not only the material and technical features of objects but also the historical circumstances—such as exhibition history, restoration interventions, and critical reception—that shape evolving interpretations (Corrado and Sandy 2017).

Throughout the twentieth century, art historians built scholarly arguments by uniting physical observation of objects in galleries or storerooms with research conducted in library reading rooms (Fig. 3.4), gradually weaving together fragments of documentation from disparate sources. The intellectual vitality of the field has long depended on the interplay between the trained connoisseurial eye—attuned to subtle differences in facture or surface—and the archivist's resolve to corroborate findings through exhaustive primary research. Landmark collaborative initiatives, like the Getty Provenance Index (https://www.getty.edu/databases-tools-and-technologies/provenance/) and the Witt Library's photographic archive in London (https://photocollections.courtauld.ac.uk/menu-item1/witt-library), have epitomized the cumulative, networked nature of art historical inquiry, empowering new attributions, reconstructing lost collections, and even exposing instances of forgery or restitution involving looted art (Amineddoleh 2016; Clark 2018; Jauregui 1996). These successes reveal the field's long-standing commitment to interdisciplinary, empirical research grounded in a combination of visual, textual, and material evidence.

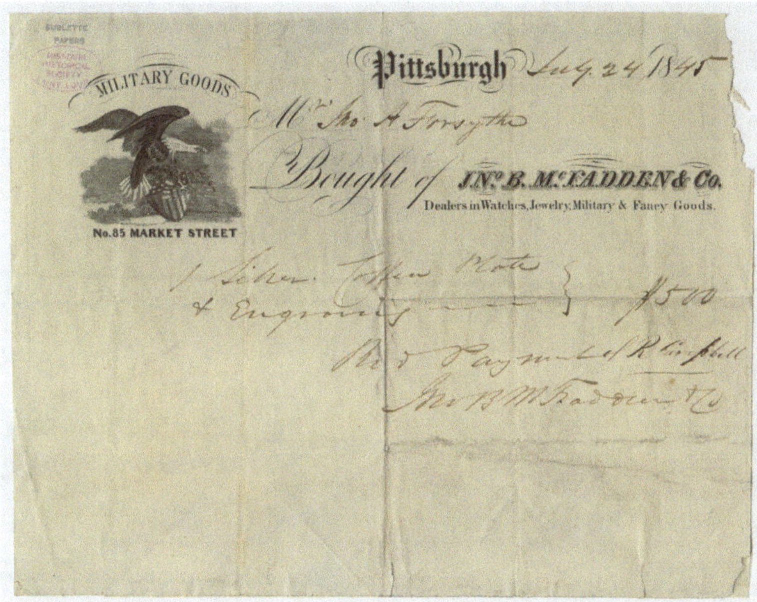

Fig. 3.2 Accounts of W.L. Sublette in St. Louis and of his widow in Pittsburgh, the latter for his leaden coffin, etc., July 1845 (CC O, public domain)

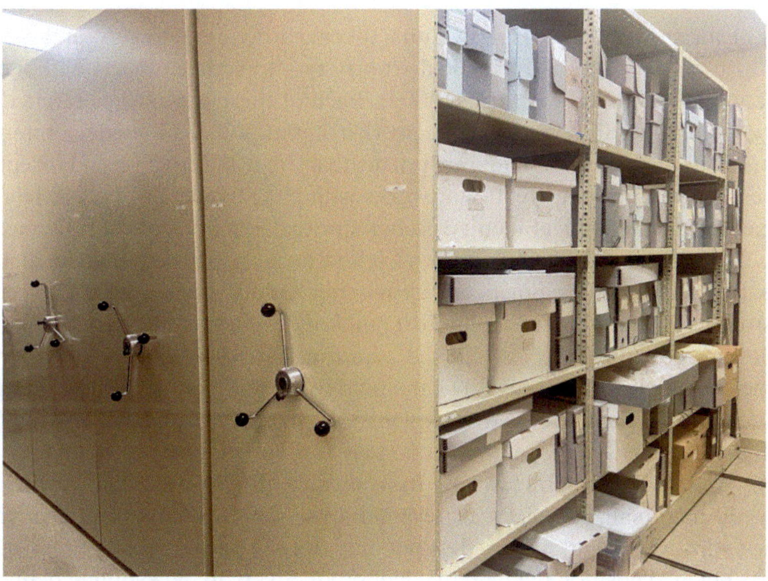

Fig. 3.3 Collections archive, St. Petersburg Museum of History, St. Petersburg, FL, 2024 (CC 2.0)

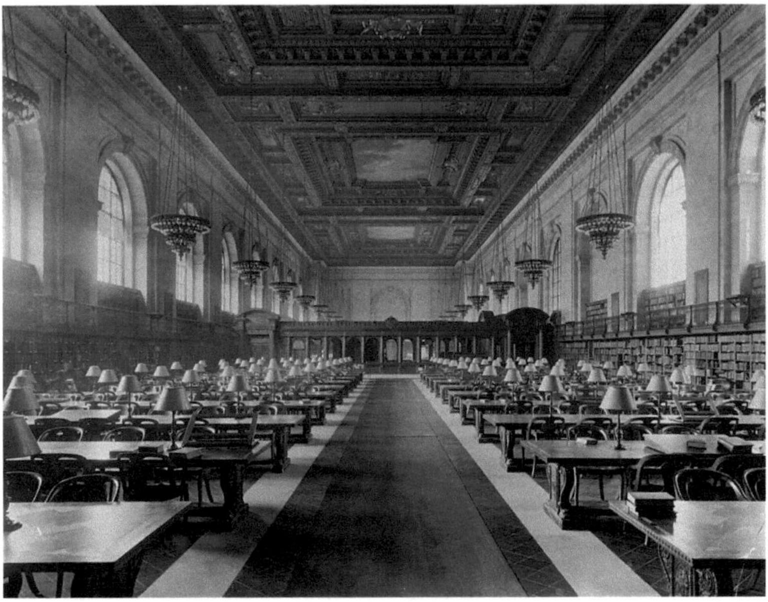

Fig. 3.4 Main reading room of the New York City Public Library on 5th Avenue, ca 1910–1920 (CC O, public domain)

Art historians have always drawn on a diverse array of methods—anthropology, social history, theology, and technical art history—to situate objects within expansive networks of meaning (Preziosi 2009). Each of these approaches offers distinct analytic tools and interpretive frameworks: anthropological models foreground rituals, social practices, and cultural systems that shape the creation and reception of art; social historians contextualize artworks within the dynamics of class, labor, and political power; theological inquiry probes spiritual symbolism and religious function; while technical art history employs scientific analysis to investigate materials, processes, and workshop practices. By moving fluidly among these perspectives, art historians have developed a pluralistic toolkit that is attentive to both the micro-histories of individual objects and the macro-narratives of collective experience. This methodological richness allows the field to embrace complexity, contingency, and ambiguity, refusing reductive explanations in favor of layered interpretation. Such flexibility has been especially important as the discipline encounters new challenges—whether interpreting works from outside the Western canon, integrating previously marginalized voices, or responding to rapid technological change. The diverse approaches of art history thus not only deepen understanding of objects and contexts but also position the field to adapt productively to the evolving demands of scholarship, curation, and public engagement.

As such, fieldwork at archeological sites (Fig. 3.5), scientific analysis of materials, and oral history interviews with artists or collectors have continuously expanded the toolkit of the art historian. At the core of these traditions are two complementary

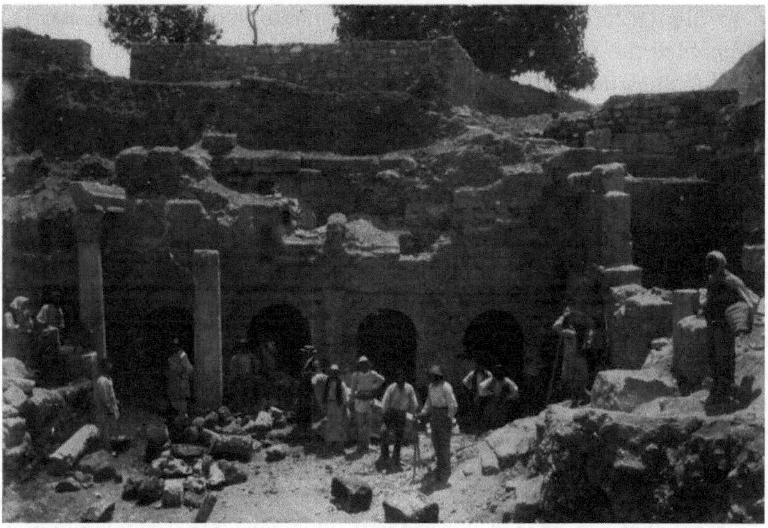

Fig. 3.5 Corinth excavation, Pirene, 1989. Archaeologists of the American School of Classical Studies at Athens (CC O, public domain)

frameworks: formal analysis, focused on visual elements like color, line, and composition; and iconographic interpretation, which decodes symbols and themes to illuminate deeper cultural, religious, or social meaning (Markey 1988; Panofsky 1962). Together, these strategies enable a nuanced approach that integrates aesthetic assessment with historical and thematic context. By synthesizing these approaches, scholars have cultivated a richly layered understanding of artworks as both aesthetic artifacts and social documents, embedded within specific cultural and historical milieus. This methodological flexibility has allowed art historians to adapt their interpretive lens as new discoveries or research paradigms have emerged.

Yet, the inherent limitations of manual research—especially the slow, labor-intensive process of collating widely dispersed sources—have constrained the scope and speed of scholarly discovery. Large-scale comparative research has often been reserved for those with access to considerable resources, institutional support, or years of travel and archival work (Crookham and Dunn 2019). The logistical demands of gathering, cross-referencing, and analyzing information from scattered archives have not only limited who can participate in ambitious art historical inquiry but have also slowed the pace at which new connections, patterns, or critical questions come to light (Barnes et al. 2018). The fragmentation of sources across countries, languages, and cataloguing conventions has also posed significant barriers to synthesis, making it challenging to develop comprehensive narratives or global perspectives.

The rise of the digital humanities in recent decades has begun to address many of these structural challenges, as museums and research consortia worldwide have worked to digitize archives, catalogues, and photographic collections. Digitization has enabled the consolidation of object data, exhibition histories, and scholarly bibliographies into searchable, centralized databases that are accessible from anywhere in the world (Corrado and Sandy 2017). High-resolution digital images, linked to rich metadata on materials, provenance, and curatorial interpretation, now allow for comparative analysis that transcends institutional and national boundaries. The development of interoperable museum databases and open-access platforms, such as Europeana (https://www.europeana.eu/en) and the Digital Public Library of America (https://dp.la/), has facilitated networked, collaborative research infrastructure, breaking down the traditional silos of archives and expanding the reach of art historical scholarship.

This shift toward digital, networked resources has amplified the scale and ambition of art historical research. Massive digital repositories, like the Internet Archive (https://archive.org/), now provide access to millions of documents, books, and images. However, scaling research to accommodate such large datasets presents new challenges, as each entry often requires detailed provenance and contextual linkage—tasks that can exceed the capacity of conventional cataloguing systems (AlNoamany et al. 2014; Reimer et al. 2023). The vastness of available data enables new forms of cross-institutional and cross-cultural analysis, but also necessitates sophisticated tools for managing, searching, and interpreting information at scale. Automated metadata generation, machine learning algorithms, and collaborative knowledge graphs are increasingly deployed to establish connections and identify patterns within these immense archives. Yet, such tools demand careful oversight to ensure data quality, transparency, and scholarly rigor, especially as errors or omissions can propagate rapidly through networked platforms. Art historians must now balance the opportunities of "big data" research with the methodological discipline of critical provenance, contextual analysis, and source evaluation. Ultimately, the promise of digital scale can only be realized through an ongoing dialogue between technological innovation and the interpretive values at the heart of the field.

Alongside the digitization of archives and records, established scholarly databases such as JSTOR (https://www.jstor.org) and Artstor (library.artstor.org) have become indispensable resources for art historians. These platforms offer centralized access to a vast array of journal articles, visual resources, and museum collections, making it possible for scholars to conduct research across multiple institutions without leaving their own desks. Artstor, in particular, has expanded access to high-resolution images and detailed metadata from collections worldwide, facilitating comparative studies, iconographic research, and global art historical inquiry (Szabo 2012). These databases not only streamline access but also enable more comprehensive, nuanced research through cross-referencing and metadata-driven exploration. At the same time, the integration of specialized databases tailored to art history has transformed the construction of scholarly narratives. Researchers can now combine images, provenance records, and exhibition histories in ways that would have been laborious or impossible using analog methods (Keeran 2013). These digital tools support robust comparative and iconographic analyses, empowering art historians to detect patterns, anomalies, and cross-cultural connections that enrich our understanding of objects and their significance. As digital resources continue to expand, they promise to further democratize the field, enabling broader participation by scholars, students, and the public.

This digital turn is also reshaping pedagogical and collaborative practices. Instructors can now design assignments that engage students with global collections, online archives, and digital visualization tools, cultivating new skills in critical analysis and research. Collaborative digital platforms facilitate interdisciplinary projects, linking art historians with computer scientists, archivists, and other specialists to address complex questions and develop innovative methodologies. As these platforms evolve, they foster an intellectual ecosystem that supports experimentation, shared discovery, and ongoing refinement of research strategies. Digital classroom environments encourage peer learning and collaborative interpretation, as students work together to annotate digital images, curate virtual exhibitions, or contribute to collective knowledge bases. Faculty development initiatives increasingly emphasize digital literacy and collaborative pedagogy, preparing educators to integrate technology thoughtfully and inclusively into their teaching. The capacity to collaborate across disciplinary and geographic boundaries also accelerates the pace of scholarly innovation, expanding the reach and impact of art historical research.

The Scholarship of Teaching and Learning (SoTL) in art history, as highlighted in the special issue of *Art History Pedagogy & Practice*, reflects a growing recognition of these challenges and the potential for significant change (Sienkewicz 2021). The evolution of SoTL in art history gained momentum at the 2015 College Art Association (CAA), where a pivotal session cochaired by Leda Cempellin and Julia A. Sienkewicz brought national attention to the empirical study of teaching and learning within the discipline. This development has fostered the integration of human subjects research and quantitative methodologies into art historical practice, representing a pioneering shift beyond the field's traditional qualitative, descriptive approaches toward methods that align more closely with those of the social sciences (Weber 2017). By welcoming empirical research designs, art historians now draw on surveys, ethnographic fieldwork, and statistical analysis to assess both teaching effectiveness and student learning outcomes. Such a shift aligns with parallel efforts in digital art history (DAH) and assessment, where SoTL serves as a bridge between scholarly research and pedagogical practice, supporting a data-informed, reflective approach to both (Spivey and McGarry 2019). This ongoing integration ensures that teaching in art history is not only rooted in deep disciplinary knowledge but also in the best practices of evidence-based education.

Moreover, the methodological pluralism championed by SoTL has encouraged art historians to engage with cognitive psychology, sociology, and education research in rethinking pedagogical strategies. Phenomenological methodologies, widely adopted in the social sciences, now inform SoTL studies that probe the lived experiences of both faculty and students, leading to a more reflective, inclusive, and evidence-driven pedagogy (Webb and Welsh 2016). Storytelling, too, has been leveraged as a strategy within SoTL to build community-driven learning environments, fostering an atmosphere of inclusivity and shared inquiry that enriches art history classrooms (Spivey et al. 2016). Such cross-pollination between fields has broadened the interpretive toolkit, helping art historians consider how best to support a range of learners and learning styles while strengthening the intellectual rigor of their courses.

Recent research also points to a discipline-wide transition from qualitative to data-driven methodologies in art historical analysis. Whereas traditional approaches relied heavily on subjective interpretation of archival documents and stylistic analysis, the adoption of quantitative methods—such as pattern-recognition algorithms and large-scale data aggregation—has introduced new empirical standards for attribution, provenance, and stylistic classification (Jari et al. 2016). For example, machine-driven analysis of brushstroke textures and color compositions enables scholars to identify trends and relationships across vast datasets, often revealing connections that manual research could not uncover. Digital image processing and computational classification, as demonstrated by Kim (2022), have facilitated the large-scale indexing of museum archives, enabling new approaches to the classification and study of artworks based on objective, repeatable criteria. While these techniques do not supplant the nuanced interpretation at the heart of the field, they offer robust means to validate findings, complementing and strengthening traditional qualitative research.

This shift in both pedagogy and methodology aligns closely with advances in writing, search, and information retrieval tools—most notably the rise of LLMs such as OpenAI's ChatGPT. Launched in November 2022, these generative models represent a new frontier for research in the humanities, allowing for the synthesis and organization of information beyond the reach of traditional search engines. Tools such as Perplexity.ai (https://www.perplexity.ai/) can search vast repositories, generate citations, and facilitate rapid cross-referencing, while digital platforms like JSTOR Beta have introduced generative search and summarization features that transform how scholars access and interact with academic content (Ojala 2023). The broad adoption of such tools has the potential to democratize access to information, bridging gaps between specialized archives and dispersed collections, and opening up new pathways for comparative analysis, historiographic study, and interdisciplinary inquiry.

With these technological and methodological advances, art historians are increasingly empowered to overcome barriers of time, geography, and cognitive load, making it possible to uncover connections and synthesize knowledge at a speed and scale previously unattainable (Persson 2024). LLMs and generative databases act as critical complements to established research practices, augmenting the ability to assemble, analyze, and interpret complex bodies of visual and written evidence. This new landscape demands ongoing critical engagement—balancing the efficiencies and opportunities of automation with the intellectual rigor and interpretive depth that remain the hallmarks of the discipline. In doing so, art history is positioned to thrive within an era defined by digital networks, computational tools, and an ever-expanding body of global cultural knowledge.

3.2 Generative Tools in Scholarly Research: Data Aggregation to Interpretation

The proliferation of generative research tools over the past half-decade has initiated a profound recalibration of art historical methodology, rendering quantitative analysis not merely a specialized practice for computationally trained scholars but an accessible and often indispensable resource for the discipline at large. Where art historians once relied almost exclusively on qualitative expertise—close visual examination, iconographic interpretation, and hermeneutic contextualization—to extract meaning from images and objects, a new generation of digital tools now affords practitioners the capacity to interrogate vast corpora of images, texts, and archival materials with unprecedented efficiency and analytical power. This democratization of computational methods marks a critical inflection point in the field: the erstwhile technical barriers to advanced data analysis—familiarity with coding languages, statistical modeling, or machine learning frameworks—have been mitigated by user-friendly platforms that foreground intuitive interfaces and workflow automation. Consequently, researchers without prior training in computer vision, machine learning, or advanced data science are newly equipped to undertake quantitative inquiry that was once the exclusive province of interdisciplinary teams or digital humanities laboratories.

This transformation is not merely procedural, but epistemological: as scholars integrate data-driven techniques into their research, the analytical landscape of art history expands to encompass questions, patterns, and interpretive possibilities that lie beyond the reach of traditional methods. Quantitative tools enable the systematic aggregation, normalization, and visualization of data—whether metadata on provenance, exhibition history, or stylistic attributes—illuminating trends, correlations, and outliers at a scope previously unimaginable (Wasielewski 2023). Such methods render visible the longue durée of stylistic evolution, the transnational diffusion of motifs, or the microhistories embedded in patronage and collection records. A paradigmatic example can be seen in the adoption of museum archiving frameworks that meld statistical analysis with digital content creation, thereby advancing both authentication and the historical appreciation of objects while supporting institutional preservation (Kim 2022). Through the visualization of robust datasets—spanning high-resolution photographs, digitized catalogues, and epistolary correspondence—scholars gain a more holistic understanding of artworks and the cultural ecologies that shaped their production and reception. Quantitative methods thus do not displace the qualitative core of the discipline; rather, they act as powerful amplifiers and complements, affording art historians new modes of pattern recognition, argumentation, and synthesis.

Among the most consequential advances enabled by generative research tools is the capacity to work with historical archives at a speed and scale unimaginable just a decade ago. Modern optical character recognition (OCR) (Fig. 3.6) and handwriting transcription platforms—such as Transkribus, OCR.space, and the AI-enhanced interfaces built into institutional repositories—allow for the rapid digitization, search,

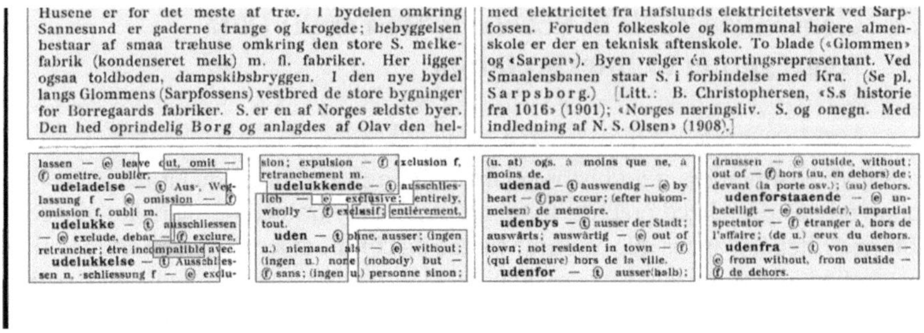

Fig. 3.6 Fragmented OCR segments, 2011 (CC O, public domain)

and annotation of handwritten letters, diaries, ledgers, and archival records. Previously, the decipherment and transcription of early modern handwriting or epistolary archives required specialized paleographic training and months of patient labor; now, AI-driven models, trained on a few pages of manuscript samples, can convert centuries-old correspondence into fully searchable, metadata-rich texts in a matter of hours. This technological leap not only democratizes archival research for those without linguistic or paleographic expertise but also supports large-scale comparative projects, such as reconstructing workshop networks, mapping provenance histories, or collating exhibition data across institutional boundaries. The result is an exponential increase in both the breadth and depth of archival scholarship: art historians can now test hypotheses, detect thematic or geographic clusters, and identify hitherto overlooked patterns by querying millions of digitized records in moments.

Parallel to advances in archival transcription, the landscape of scholarly literature review has been fundamentally reshaped by generative platforms. Tools such as Elicit, Iris.ai, Perplexity.ai, and Consensus offer automated literature discovery, citation network mapping, and evidence synthesis, thereby transforming one of the most laborious dimensions of academic inquiry. Rather than manually tracking down, reading, and summarizing dozens or hundreds of articles, scholars may now direct these platforms to aggregate and synthesize research on any topic—returning concise, source-linked overviews that include direct quotations, evidence tables, and bibliometric context. Such capabilities are not limited to STEM literature but increasingly include major art historical databases, journals, and open-access repositories, expanding the scope of literature mapping to include both canonical and marginalized voices. For early-career researchers or those working in cross-disciplinary areas, this rapid collation of the scholarly record ensures both rigor and inclusivity, while freeing time for interpretive and synthetic work.

Most consequentially, the emergence of NLP and LLMs such as ChatGPT, Claude, and Gemini, has further amplified the analytic and interpretive capacities of art historians. No longer restricted to the realm of coders or digital humanists, these generative models empower researchers to summarize archival texts, classify documents by theme or genre, identify iconographic motifs, or trace the evolution of arguments across the literature. For example, ChatGPT can ingest raw archival outputs—hundreds of digitized letters, meeting minutes, or curatorial reports—and return thematic synopses, trend analyses, or critical bibliographies in a matter of minutes (Guo 2024). Models like 4o, fine-tuned for image generation, can visualize hypothetical reconstructions or synthesize comparative illustrations, further enriching interpretive frameworks. The integration of these NLP tools enables scholars to bridge the gap between close reading and distant reading: by shifting between granular textual analysis and large-scale data aggregation, art historians can construct nuanced arguments grounded in both evidence and context.

Moreover, the methodological toolkit available to art historians has expanded dramatically in recent years, as generative and AI-powered platforms have redefined how research, data management, and archival exploration are conducted across the discipline (Table 3.1). Automated literature review tools now play a foundational role at the outset of scholarly inquiry, enabling art historians to systematically map the scholarly landscape, trace evolving debates, and identify emergent research clusters without the prohibitive bottleneck of manual searching. For instance, Elicit leverages large language models to parse more than 125 million papers, extract tables of findings, and support hypothesis generation, while Iris.ai can extract key concepts and organize reading lists by analyzing patterns across both scientific and humanistic texts.

When examining the iconography of a single motif across cultures or centuries, platforms such as Iris.ai help uncover conceptual connections and overlooked debates, while Scite's classification of over a billion citation statements empowers researchers to verify claims, trace the evolution of attribution controversies, and ensure citation compliance within the literature. Visual mapping platforms such as ResearchRabbit and Connected Papers add another dimension, displaying citation networks and thematic clusters so that scholars can visualize the intellectual genealogy of a method or follow the spread of a critical idea across subfields and eras. Semantic Scholar and Scholarcy further streamline literature discovery, employing NLP to generate summaries and citation contexts or distilling articles into easily accessible "flashcards" that expedite comprehension for both students and seasoned researchers.

Litmaps, Consensus, and Perplexity.ai take this approach even further by connecting user-supplied seed papers to dynamic networks of related studies, scanning for newly published work that fits the research footprint, and generating source-linked answers to fact-checking queries or literature synthesis tasks. These platforms automate the mapping of scholarly discourse, surfacing both canonical and emergent literature that might otherwise remain hidden in traditional search workflows. By leveraging artificial intelligence and machine learning, they enable art historians to rapidly identify gaps in the literature, trace evolving debates, and monitor the emergence of new methodologies or theoretical perspectives. The integration of real-time updates ensures that researchers remain current, continuously adjusting their inquiry as new findings and publications appear. Fact-checking and synthesis capabilities further support rigorous scholarship, allowing users to quickly verify claims and

Table 3.1 AI tools for art historical and archival research

Tool name	URL	Description	Use case for art historians
Elicit	https://elicit.com/	Automates literature reviews, data extraction, and hypothesis generation with LLMs. Parses 125M+ papers, extracts tables, supports systematic reviews	Compiling literature reviews, extracting evidence from art historical texts, and mapping research themes
Iris.ai	https://iris.ai/	AI for reading list generation, key concept extraction, and smart search. Supports mapping and deep knowledge automation across publications	Identifying debates and building concept maps for thematic research in art history
Scite	https://scite.ai/	Indexes 1B+ citation statements and classifies citations as supporting, disputing, or mentioning. Tracks claim evolution	Verifying provenance, tracing art debates, and identifying consensus or disputes in the literature
Research Rabbit	https://www.researchrabbit.ai/	Visualizes citation networks, trend mapping, and literature discovery. Suggests related papers and tracks new research	Mapping artist schools, networks, or exhibition histories through citation mapping
Connected Papers	https://www.connectedpapers.com/	Builds graph maps of academic papers using cocitation and bibliographic coupling to show research clusters and trends	Identifying clusters of research around movements, periods, or contested attributions in art history
Semantic Scholar	https://www.semanticscholar.org/	NLP-powered summaries, key figure extraction, and topic feeds from 200M+ papers. Features semantic highlights and citation context cards	Extracting summaries and key insights from a wide range of art and technical literature
Scholarcy	https://www.scholarcy.com/	Summarizes articles into flashcards, extracts findings, and builds annotated bibliographies for rapid comprehension	Creating annotated reading lists, summarizing exhibition research, or speeding up primary source review
Litmaps	https://www.litmaps.com/	Dynamic mapping of related papers, tracking new publications relevant to your footprint	Monitoring new research for provenance, technical analysis, or historiographic shifts in art scholarship

(continued)

Table 3.1 (continued)

Tool name	URL	Description	Use case for art historians
Consensus	https://consensus.app/	AI-native search engine querying 200M+ scientific docs; synthesizes evidence-backed answers with citations	Quickly synthesizing scholarly consensus or debates on art historical questions
Perplexity.ai	https://www.perplexity.ai/	Citing mode searches academic repositories, returns source-linked answers. Excels at rapid Q&A and literature lookup	On-demand research support for classroom, exhibition, or cataloguing work
Transkribus	https://transkribus.eu/	State-of-the-art HTR and OCR to transcribe archival documents (letters, ledgers, and diaries) into searchable text	Transcribing and searching handwritten correspondence or provenance documents in archives
JSTOR SeekLight	https://support.jstor.org/hc/en-us/articles/360056387854-Using-JSTOR-SeekLight	AI indexes and surfaces hidden/dark archive materials; enhances metadata and suggests subject linkages	Surfacing undercatalogued materials for provenance or exhibition research in special collections
Voyant Tools	http://voyant-tools.org/	Open-source text analysis for word frequency, KWIC, and thematic exploration of digitized texts	Rapid thematic and linguistic analysis of large corpora (catalogues, reviews, and exhibition texts)
OCR.space	https://ocr.space/	Free, cloud-based OCR that extracts text from images and PDFs using AI. Batch processes archival documents for full-text search	Digitizing and making searchable old catalogues, artist notes, or ephemera
Recogito	https://recogito.pelagios.org/	AI-assisted place-name recognition and crowdsourced annotation for geolocating archival docs	Mapping provenance, correspondence, or exhibition records spatially and temporally
ArchiveAI	https://www.clir.org/2024/10/ai-meets-archives-the-future-of-machine-learning-in-cultural-heritage/	ML-powered platform for cleaning, exploring, and visualizing large archival datasets; offers dashboards for metadata enrichment and collection analysis	Visualizing collection strengths, gaps, or historical shifts; cleaning up and enriching legacy collection data

contextualize findings within the broader field. Together, these tools ensure that art historians move beyond the labor-intensive practices of the past, instead harnessing the power of generative search and automated synthesis to support both breadth and rigor in scholarly engagement. As these technologies become more deeply embedded in research workflows, they promise to redefine not only the efficiency but also the scope and ambition of art historical inquiry. The resulting acceleration in literature discovery and synthesis paves the way for more agile, informed, and impactful scholarship across the discipline.

Digitization and automated transcription of archival sources represent another transformative area, with handwriting recognition and OCR tools reducing what was once a formidable bottleneck for those working in manuscript-rich traditions. Transkribus exemplifies this change by using state-of-the-art handwritten text recognition (HTR) and OCR to convert scans of letters, diaries, and ledgers into fully searchable digital texts after only a brief training phase with manuscript samples. For art historians reconstructing provenance histories or tracking the transmission of ideas through epistolary networks, this means that thousands of pages can be processed in hours rather than months, democratizing access to sources and facilitating new forms of large-scale comparative analysis. OCR.space, available as a free, cloud-based API, complements this by extracting text from images and PDFs in bulk, supporting the digitization of exhibition catalogues, press clippings, and even marginalia found in rare books.

When rapid thematic or linguistic analysis is required, Voyant Tools offers a lightweight web application that enables users to perform word-frequency analysis, frequency distribution plotting, and keyword-in-context exploration on digitized texts ranging from curatorial essays to nineteenth-century art criticism. JSTOR SeekLight, a digital stewardship tool, extends the power of machine learning to archival discovery by surfacing previously "dark" or poorly catalogued materials, cleaning metadata, and generating prompts that guide researchers to hidden documents within institutional collections. These advances collectively reduce the dependence on specialist training for archival research and enable art historians to batch-process, annotate, and interrogate vast archival corpora with both speed and accuracy, enhancing the evidentiary base of the discipline. Through these approaches, art historians are not only accelerating workflows but also increasing the inclusivity and comprehensiveness of archival scholarship, expanding interpretive horizons and opening new lines of inquiry across local and global contexts.

As research in art history increasingly addresses questions of circulation, mobility, and the global movement of objects, spatial and semantic annotation tools have become vital components of the digital scholar's repertoire. Recogito exemplifies the genre by integrating AI-assisted named-entity recognition (NER) and crowdsourced annotation to geolocate archival documents and map networks of correspondence, object provenance, or exhibition history. This capability allows researchers to move beyond static catalogues and develop dynamic, interactive maps that trace the dispersal of artworks, the emergence of avant-garde communities, or the shifting routes of cultural influence, offering new spatial and temporal perspectives on familiar datasets. For example, a scholar investigating the afterlife of a looted artifact might employ Recogito to visualize its trajectory from excavation to collection, drawing connections between geographic, institutional, and personal networks.

Emerging platforms such as ArchiveAI further this trend by leveraging machine learning to clean, enrich, and visualize large-scale archival datasets, including born-digital web archives, and providing researchers and curators with actionable dashboards for collection analysis, metadata enrichment, and strategic planning. These tools not only support advanced scholarly work, such as reconstructing lost collections or modeling the spread of artistic techniques, but also enhance public engagement through interactive exhibitions and digital storytelling. By integrating spatial annotation, dataset visualization, and real-time enrichment, art historians gain an unprecedented capacity to model institutional priorities, interrogate historical gaps, and tell more nuanced stories about the global movement of art. As these platforms become increasingly user-friendly and widely adopted, they promise to transform not only the speed and scope of art historical research but also its narrative complexity, fostering a practice that is at once more analytical and more accessible to broader audiences.

Recent scholarship has illustrated the increasing adoption of tools like these, such as AI-driven and OCR-based applications in humanities and art historical research, offering insights into their practical integration within digitization, transcription, and analysis of primary sources. For example, the OCRopus system, as described by Breuel (2007), was implemented to capture and recognize classical literature, enabling both the digitization of Sanskrit texts and the automated extraction of relevant linguistic features. The modular, probabilistic design of the system allowed for the addition of customized text recognition models, making it especially suitable for large multilingual corpora and historical archives. The study not only demonstrates the utility of OCR in generating searchable, machine-readable archives but also its capacity to integrate seamlessly with downstream computational linguistic and information extraction modules, making complex archival materials accessible for large-scale analysis. This approach closely parallels emerging workflows in art history, where handwritten letters, catalogues, and ledgers are digitized and analyzed *en masse* to reconstruct provenance, artist networks, or institutional histories (Friedrich et al. 2017). Such examples underscore how OCR and allied technologies now support a more systematic and data-driven approach to archival research, moving beyond the manual, document-by-document practices that dominated prior centuries. Indeed, these advances enable a shift from individualistic, anecdotal findings to more robust, reproducible insights grounded in quantitative and qualitative data. The integration of these tools reflects a maturation of digital methods in the field, bridging traditional scholarship with computational analytics.

In parallel, comparative studies of OCR toolsets have helped clarify the strengths and weaknesses of various platforms for specific historical research needs, informing their application to art historical projects. Jain and colleagues conducted a systematic comparison of open-source and proprietary OCR solutions, highlighting the significant differences in recognition accuracy, language support, and adaptability to handwritten or degraded historical documents (Jain et al. 2021). The study's findings demonstrate that open-source solutions, while flexible and cost-effective, often require considerable configuration and may underperform on heterogeneous or low-quality source material. Conversely, proprietary or specialized platforms can offer higher baseline accuracy and broader language support, which is especially critical for multilingual art historical archives. The comparative approach adopted in this study has been mirrored by art historians evaluating OCR platforms for digitizing diverse epistolary collections, exhibition catalogues, or visual culture documents, thus shaping best practices for digital conversion. Importantly, Jain et al. emphasized the ongoing need for human oversight in postprocessing, particularly when working with complex layouts or rare scripts, an observation echoed across digitization projects in museums and archives. Such studies provide a roadmap for selecting, implementing, and refining OCR tools tailored to the unique materiality of art historical archives. The incremental gains in automation and accuracy achieved by these methods facilitate more comprehensive digital archives and enable large-scale comparative analyses previously constrained by the slow pace of manual transcription.

Beyond transcription, the integration of text mining and information retrieval platforms has been transformative for literature mapping, thematic analysis, and evidence synthesis within art historical research. Medisetti et al. (2024) introduced LitAI, a multimodal platform combining generative AI and OCR for extracting, classifying, and mining information from complex scholarly documents, including text, tables, and figures. This system enabled users to construct domain-specific prompts and retrieve structured data across diverse formats, providing a foundation for systematic literature reviews and cross-document analyses. Empirical evaluations demonstrated LitAI's superior performance compared to traditional OCR and even leading generative models, particularly in complex, multimodal contexts. Although primarily tested in ecological and biological sciences, the platform's methodology—especially in automating the aggregation of literature and supporting rapid synthesis—has clear analogues in art history, where researchers must navigate heterogeneous materials from exhibition catalogues to epistolary archives. The integration of OCR, text mining, and advanced retrieval, such platforms make it feasible to assemble comprehensive thematic datasets, map citation networks, or extract patterns of influence at a scale and speed previously unattainable. This has direct implications for the future of digital art history, supporting both empirical research and broader synthetic scholarship.

Studies on the deployment of OCR and document processing platforms in business and cultural heritage have further highlighted the value of these technologies for automating data extraction and facilitating archival discovery. Calvo (2018), in a business context, chronicled the success of Cogent Labs in Japan with its Tegaki platform, which achieved over 99% accuracy in recognizing printed and handwritten Japanese texts and was rapidly adopted in financial and cultural sectors for business process automation. The collaborative, cross-functional product teams harmonized entrepreneurial and technical expertise to quickly develop and implement AI-OCR solutions, enabling rapid digitization and cataloguing of complex handwritten archives. Although the primary case centered on business process outsourcing, the implications for art history are profound: similar OCR algorithms have since been leveraged in museum collections and library digitization projects, unlocking access to previously "dark" archives and supporting provenance, curatorial, or restitution research. These studies reinforce the need for both technical innovation and interdisciplinary collaboration to realize the full benefits of digitization in the arts and humanities.

Lastly, the literature reveals the increasing importance of combining OCR-based digitization with advanced data analytics and network analysis for mapping archival provenance, citation histories, and influence patterns in art historical research. Singh et al. (2012) surveyed a wide range of OCR applications and noted that the integration of OCR with genetic algorithms and advanced segmentation has greatly improved the accuracy of text extraction from degraded or visually complex sources. These advances have made it possible to digitize and search large corpora of historical texts, from exhibition catalogues to institutional records, supporting both targeted inquiry and broad data mining. Furthermore, platforms capable of handling multilingual documents have opened new possibilities for cross-cultural research, enabling comparative studies that transcend traditional linguistic and national boundaries (Friedrich et al. 2017). The ability to automate the extraction and analysis of large-scale textual data empowers art historians to investigate patterns of influence, migration, and exchange that define the discipline's global turn. The adoption of these digital and computational tools thus signals a methodological transformation, positioning art history at the forefront of interdisciplinary, data-rich humanities research.

As such, the strategic incorporation of these generative tools ensures art historians are newly empowered to traverse the entire research arc, from literature discovery and synthesis, to rapid archival transcription and metadata extraction, to spatial annotation and visualization at scale. These innovations do not merely expedite existing workflows; they foster fundamentally new forms of analysis and argumentation, allowing scholars to uncover previously invisible patterns, trace relationships across time and space, and interrogate cultural phenomena with methodological rigor and creative agility. In practice, this means an art historian can move from identifying a research question and collating relevant literature, to digitizing and annotating primary sources, to producing interactive maps and dashboards that model historical change or cultural diffusion—all within a seamless, interconnected research environment. The adoption of these tools signals a broader methodological transformation, as qualitative interpretation and quantitative insight converge to generate more holistic, dynamic accounts of visual and material culture. For the discipline, this shift does not represent a rupture but an extension of its foundational commitment to rigor, complexity, and intellectual curiosity—ensuring that art history remains vibrant, innovative, and deeply relevant in the era of generative technology.

Crucially, the adoption of these generative and quantitative methodologies does not merely accelerate existing workflows; it invites the discipline to pose new research questions and explore novel epistemic terrains. By enabling large-scale data aggregation and interpretation, art historians may interrogate the interplay of influence, dissemination, and cultural exchange with a methodological precision that complements, rather than replaces, the qualitative traditions. As generative platforms and AI-driven tools continue to evolve—incorporating multimodal data, supporting collaborative inquiry across disciplinary boundaries, and embedding interpretive feedback loops—art history stands poised to harness a richer, more dynamic engagement with its objects, archives, and arguments. The future of the discipline thus resides not in a choice between quantitative and qualitative paradigms, but in their productive convergence: an era in which the aggregation, translation, and interpretation of data serve as catalysts for new scholarship, fresh critical insight, and a renewed commitment to the complexity of visual culture.

Therefore, new computational technologies have proven instrumental in interpreting textual corpora, providing a new dimension of thematic inquiry that complements archival research. ChatGPT, for instance, has been employed to refine keyword searches and prompt engineering techniques in order to extract subtle intellectual currents underlying an artist's oeuvre or an entire artistic movement's ideological foundations (Guo 2024). Such applications illuminate recurring motifs, narrative patterns, and cultural references that might otherwise remain obscured in vast textual repositories. By identifying these thematic threads and contextualizing them within sociopolitical or economic frameworks, advanced textual analysis enables art historians to develop more comprehensive readings that integrate visual data with archival and literary sources. This convergence of methodologies not only advances interpretative depth but also encourages cross-disciplinary scholarship that spans cultural studies, intellectual history, and other related fields. In this manner, AI reconfigures the scope of traditional research, building more robust narratives and establishing connections that transcend established disciplinary boundaries. As the possibilities for research and interpretation expand, the next section will turn from text-based methodologies to the rapidly developing field of computational visual analysis—examining the tools and techniques that now enable art historians to interrogate, classify, and interpret visual culture at an unprecedented scale and level of precision.

3.3 Computational Art Analysis: Case Studies and Emerging Methodologies

A decade ago, visual analysis in art history depended primarily on the discerning eye of the connoisseur, whose expertise in identifying brushstroke nuances or compositional quirks was honed through years of close study and direct engagement with objects. Today, that trained gaze is increasingly amplified by computational tools that allow scholars to systematically analyze visual features at a scale and level of detail previously unimaginable. Digital image processing has become a crucial element in this evolution, enabling researchers to isolate distinctive elements such as brushstroke patterns, paint textures, and chromatic distributions—features that often serve as artist-specific markers or reveal the underlying processes of artistic creation.

Rather than limiting these analyses to a select number of canonical works, feature-based methods can be applied across vast museum collections, democratizing access and inviting new voices into scholarly debates (Lang and Ommer 2021). As a result, questions of authorship, style, and artistic influence have shifted from being the exclusive domain of the individual expert to an arena where empirical data and traditional judgment coexist. Recent studies, for example, have demonstrated that such computational approaches can rapidly identify stylistic clusters and workshop collaborations among nineteenth-century European painters, shedding new light on attribution controversies and patterns of artistic migration (Kim 2022). Visualization platforms make these findings accessible, presenting complex relationships through interactive maps, networks, and timelines, which encourage both deeper analysis and public engagement. This convergence of traditional and quantitative analysis ensures that empirical rigor is never detached from the historical, material, and cultural contexts that remain central to art historical inquiry.

These shifts prompt a fundamental reconsideration of what constitutes evidence, comparison, and authority within the discipline. The acceleration of analytic tasks and the automation of stylistic evaluations allow art historians to pose new questions and pursue large-scale comparisons that were simply impractical a generation ago. However, the adoption of these tools also invites a reflexive approach: What does it mean for a machine to "see" style, and how does this computational lens reshape the narratives and arguments that scholars construct? As machine learning and digital visualization become more embedded in art historical research, critical reflection on their limitations, biases, and interpretive frameworks remains essential. The goal is not to supplant human expertise, but to create a more robust and inclusive analytical toolkit that leverages both the breadth of computational data and the depth of contextual, material knowledge. The coming discussion explores the diverse range of platforms now available for visual analysis, from systems that automate image retrieval to advanced models capable of formal and stylistic comparison.

In fact, the ecosystem of visual analysis tools now available to art historians is both expansive and remarkably diverse, reflecting a field that is moving swiftly from static catalogues and subjective comparison toward a more dynamic, data-rich paradigm. These tools can be grouped into several categories—each serving a different stage in the research process, and together enabling nuanced exploration from the individual artwork to entire institutional holdings (Table 3.2). Annotation and organization tools form one foundational layer, supporting scholars as they navigate vast personal or institutional archives. For example, Tropy has become an essential resource for those working with digitized archival photographs. By allowing users to group, tag, and annotate images, then cluster-related records with the aid of suggestion algorithms, Tropy streamlines the creation of research-ready databases. The capacity to export these annotations for integration with Omeka S and other platforms also opens new possibilities for collaborative projects and public-facing exhibitions.

Image recognition and object detection platforms represent a second crucial domain. Clarifai, for example, provides an accessible suite of computer vision tools—object detection, visual similarity search, and custom model training—enabling scholars to identify stylistic features or iconographic motifs across collections. Such

Table 3.2 Visual analysis, retrieval, and annotation tools for art historians

Tool name	URL	Description	Use case for art historians
Tropy	https://tropy.org/	Organizes photographs of archival materials into item records, applies tags, attaches notes; AI-assisted clustering of related documents; exports for Omeka S integration	Annotating and organizing image-based research, linking photos with metadata for visual archive projects
Clarifai	https://clarifai.com/	Comprehensive computer vision API with object detection, visual similarity search, and custom model training. Fine-tunes models to detect brushstrokes, motifs, clusters by compositional similarity	Identifying stylistic features, cataloguing collections, and comparing compositional styles
Google Cloud Vision	https://cloud.google.com/vision	Extracts labels, landmarks, OCR from images; web-entity detection finds visually similar artworks online; face/emotion detection for portrait studies	Cross-referencing iconography, identifying depicted locations or people, enhancing catalogue records
Microsoft Azure Computer Vision	https://azure.microsoft.com/services/cognitive-services/computer-vision/	Classifies images, generates descriptive captions, identifies color schemes and dominant objects; supports rapid indexing and comparative analyses of collections	Bulk cataloguing, analyzing color and form trends across museum holdings
IBM Watson Visual Recognition	https://www.ibm.com/cloud/watson-visual-recognition	Provides custom classifier creation, scene-text detection, keyword-based image tagging. Supports automated stylistic categorization based on user-trained datasets	Automating architectural style recognition, distinguishing between art movements, or tagging attributes
Imagga	https://imagga.com/	Auto-tagging, color extraction, visual search APIs; palette extraction supports color trend analysis, similarity search finds related works	Formal color analysis, discovering iconographic or stylistic affinities across images
iART	https://arxiv.org/abs/2108.01542	Art historical image search engine for content- and concept-based retrieval; uses deep embeddings and clustering for visual correspondences between artworks	Exploring formal or thematic connections, discovering overlooked visual parallels across eras
ICC++	https://arxiv.org/abs/2206.11115	Explainable image retrieval system; extracts compositional elements and retrieves images with similar layouts—ideal for narrative or iconographic studies	Comparing scene structure, analyzing storytelling devices in large image sets

(continued)

Table 3.2 (continued)

Tool name	URL	Description	Use case for art historians
GalleryGPT	https://github.com/steven640pixel/GalleryGPT	Multimodal model fine-tuned on paintings; generates paragraph-length formal analyses, identifies stylistic, thematic, and compositional features in images	Producing formal analyses, supporting cataloguing and didactic interpretation
SMKExplore	https://arxiv.org/html/2403.19174v1	Applies object detection to a national museum collection; enables interactive browsing by iconographic category or object, such as "skull," "horse," or "bust"	Thematic browsing, building digital exhibitions based on detected subjects or motifs
The Art Genome Project (Artsy)	https://artsy.net/theartgenomeproject	Encodes 1000+ "genes" (attributes, movements, subjects) into a taxonomic graph; queries reveal visually/thematically related works for network or comparative analysis	Mapping stylistic lineages, building comparative datasets for research or exhibition planning

functionality becomes invaluable in studies where precise tracking of recurring elements—like the evolution of a particular drapery fold or ornamental motif—may illuminate questions of workshop practice or regional style. Google Cloud Vision and Microsoft Azure Computer Vision extend these capabilities to broader audiences, with APIs that extract descriptive labels, detect landmarks, and identify compositional features such as color palettes or facial expressions. The integration of face and emotion detection, in particular, has made it possible to reexamine portraiture, not only from a formal standpoint but also with renewed attention to representation, affect, and context. IBM Watson's Visual Recognition service similarly allows for the creation of highly specific classifiers, empowering art historians to distinguish among periods, schools, or even individual hands within a tradition by automating keyword-based tagging and stylistic grouping.

Platforms that focus on advanced formal and semantic analysis are now pushing the boundaries of what visual analysis can achieve. Imagga, with its auto-tagging and color extraction functions, has proven especially useful for formal analysis, allowing scholars to quantify trends in color usage or compositional arrangement. Content- and concept-based retrieval systems, such as iART, use deep embeddings to reveal unexpected formal or thematic connections between works—connections that may have been invisible in traditional, manually constructed catalogues. ICC++ takes this a step further, employing explainable algorithms to retrieve images with similar structural layouts or compositional patterns, a powerful feature for narrative-scene analysis or comparative iconography. Large-multimodal models like GalleryGPT, trained on painting datasets, now generate formal analyses in paragraph form—identifying stylistic hallmarks and providing an interpretive bridge between machine calculation and art historical narrative.

At the institutional and networked level, new tools are facilitating interactive exploration and taxonomic mapping on a national or global scale. SMKExplore, for instance, demonstrates how object detection pipelines can be applied to entire museum collections, allowing users to search for works featuring specific objects, such as "skulls" or "horses," and thereby enabling thematic investigations that cut across traditional cataloguing categories. The Art Genome Project, behind the Artsy platform, encodes over a thousand attributes—ranging from formal properties to iconographic motifs and historical context—into a taxonomic graph. This taxonomy enables researchers to conduct comparative and network analyses with unprecedented granularity, uncovering lines of influence, thematic continuities, and divergences both within and across collections. Together, these tools are not only accelerating research and curation but also reshaping the kinds of questions art historians can ask about visual culture and its transmission through time, space, and media.

At the same time as these tools proliferate in number, a growing body of research demonstrates how computer vision and deep learning methods are reshaping art historical inquiry, making previously labor-intensive or subjective analytic processes more systematic and scalable. For instance, a research team at the Rijksmuseum used metadata analysis powered by natural language processing and visual recognition to recover provenance details for hundreds of paintings, aligning lost archival fragments and auction records in ways that had eluded earlier cataloguing efforts (Zhang et al. 2023). These technologies do not only support provenance research; they now play an integral role in iconographic analysis, as systems trained to recognize recurring motifs or compositional schemes allow scholars to categorize symbols and themes across vast visual corpora. Automated literature review tools such as Scite.ai further enhance this process, enabling scholars to situate new hypotheses about iconographic meaning within the evolving landscape of published research and providing rapid verification or refutation of traditional interpretations.

Computer vision has become central to questions of attribution as well. A well-publicized Stanford University study used deep learning to compare brushwork and pigment distribution in digitized Renaissance paintings, enabling the reattribution of several canvases after identifying characteristic variations in stroke and material that were invisible to the naked eye (Li 2025; Stork 2023). These computational approaches offer a level of precision and scalability unattainable through traditional connoisseurship, revealing patterns across large datasets that would otherwise go undetected. Likewise, advances in digital imaging have improved the field of art conservation, making it possible to generate predictive models that guide the restoration of damaged artworks by extrapolating from stylistic consistencies across an artist's oeuvre or period. Such predictive capabilities not only enhance restoration accuracy but also open new possibilities for reconstructing lost or fragmentary works. With the emergence of hybrid generative models such as 4o, researchers are also creating composite visuals to highlight stylistic features or juxtapose iconographic variants, thus enriching comparative studies that span centuries (Zhang et al. 2024). These tools allow art historians to visualize stylistic evolution, trace influences, and experiment with alternative attributions or reconstructions. The growing integration of computer vision in art history exemplifies how digital methodologies can augment—and in some cases transform—the field's fundamental practices of analysis and interpretation. As the technology matures, its implications for attribution, conservation, and comparative research are poised to become even more far-reaching.

Further examples from international museum and library collaborations reveal how machine learning and image classification are bringing new depth to the analysis and accessibility of large collections. At the Metropolitan Museum of Art, researchers applied convolutional neural networks—testing models like ResNet and Inception-ResNet-V2—to automate the classification of over 470,000 digitized works, allowing for efficient retrieval, clustering, and thematic exploration of art objects (Surapaneni et al. 2020). The project not only improved cataloguing efficiency but also made it possible to identify and address biases in existing labels, opening new pathways for multilabel and fine-grained classification of works by subject, style, or even sentiment. Similarly, face recognition and pose estimation systems, such as FACES 2.0 developed with support from the Kress Foundation by Conrad Rudolf (https://www.youtube.com/watch?v=0xTK7IYMFi0), are being used to match portraits across collections—testing the probability of shared identity and illuminating genealogies that previously depended on limited archival records or connoisseurial guesswork. At the Getty Research Institute, collaborations between computer scientists and art historians have led to the evaluation of deep learning approaches for classification and object detection on datasets comprising thousands of paintings and drawings, demonstrating that publicly available training sets can be effectively leveraged to supplement and strengthen domain-specific analyses (Bartz and Krestel 2021).

Specialized platforms designed for art and heritage research are also driving advances in iconographic and compositional analysis. For example, Peter Bell's (2018) "Into Iconography" project at Friedrich-Alexander University (https://www.frick.org/interact/miniseries/searching_seeing/peter_bell_iconography_understanding_images_pose_interaction) applies pose detection and interaction modeling to compare variations within major iconographic themes—such as the Annunciation and the Baptism of Christ—across extended periods and regions. This approach enables the study of granular differences in gesture, composition, and spatial arrangement, providing a framework for systematic iconographic comparison that moves beyond simple object recognition (Spratt 2018). Elsewhere, residual neural networks have been deployed to classify and analyze Baroque portraits, extracting features that can be used in search and retrieval systems within large online collections (Kvak 2022). The ArtPI platform, developed at Rutgers, uses models trained on more than a million images to recognize artists, styles, and formal elements in public domain collections, opening these holdings to new types of inquiry and public engagement. These developments collectively point toward a field in which computational analysis not only enhances but also redefines the scale, specificity, and critical rigor of visual interpretation.

Finally, the integration of computer vision with interactive exploration tools is reshaping curatorial and research practice. Systems such as ARIES (Art Image Exploration Space) (https://artimageexplorationspace.com/) enable researchers to manipulate, compare, and overlay digital images in a manner analogous to the use of physical light boxes in traditional curatorial work, but with the added benefit of computational feature matching and dynamic clustering (Deutch 2021). Such platforms support both close reading and "distant viewing," allowing patterns, anomalies, and lines of influence to emerge in ways not possible through manual methods alone (Van Noord 2022). These tools have begun to bridge the long-standing divide between the precision of quantitative methods and the interpretive depth of humanistic analysis. As a result, the discipline stands at the threshold of a new era, one in which collaboration between art historians and technologists becomes essential to fully realize the interpretive and educational potential of digitized visual culture.

Taken together, the rapid integration of visual analysis tools has propelled art history into a new phase of methodological pluralism and interpretive depth. The ability to automate formal and iconographic analysis, visualize stylistic relationships across time and geography, and engage with large-scale collections in dynamic new ways has fundamentally expanded the scope and ambition of scholarly inquiry. Rather than replacing the foundational skills of close looking, historical contextualization, and critical interpretation, these computational platforms serve as powerful extensions—bridging the gap between human expertise and the complexity of today's digitized visual archives. This synthesis invites both established and emerging scholars to revisit old debates with new evidence, discover patterns invisible to the unaided eye, and foster collaborative ventures across disciplinary and institutional boundaries. Crucially, these innovations help democratize access to cultural heritage, supporting more inclusive narratives and diverse research agendas. As art historians continue to adopt and adapt these tools, the discipline is not only better equipped to address enduring questions, but is also poised to articulate its value within a broader landscape of digital scholarship. With this in mind, the next section turns to the collaborative platforms and project environments that are reshaping how research teams, collections, and communities work together—further enhancing the field's capacity for shared discovery and creative engagement.

3.4 Facilitating Interdisciplinary Collaborations Through Smart Platforms

Along with new abilities in analysis of writing and visual imagery, the rapid expansion of these computational tools has ushered in a new era of interdisciplinary collaboration within art historical research. Automation has transformed routine cataloguing and data management, allowing curators, historians, and technical experts to focus on higher-level analysis and creative interpretation. Machine learning systems now cluster stylistic features, categorize iconographic motifs, and cross-reference provenance data with a speed and precision that far outpaces manual methods. These advances have led to major improvements in collection management, as AI-driven platforms can automatically tag and classify thousands of artworks, simplifying access and enabling researchers to unearth overlooked relationships and patterns (Fernández-Castrillo 2023). The capacity to synthesize vast troves of metadata not only accelerates research but also provides a foundation for richer, more nuanced studies of artistic transmission, influence, and adaptation. In provenance research, for example, computational models have revealed previously undocumented histories by connecting disparate archival traces and standardizing descriptive conventions across institutions (Glinka and Müller-Birn 2023). What was once a painstaking, artifact-by-artifact process now happens at scale, offering a more holistic understanding of the movement and meaning of objects within and beyond museum walls.

Crucially, these technological developments have also created new opportunities for collaboration between art historians, computer scientists, conservators, and museum professionals. Teams with diverse backgrounds can work together within shared digital environments, using platforms like ChatGPT to develop common research vocabularies and coordinate analytical strategies. In one recent project, art historians joined forces with data scientists to investigate how periods of political upheaval in the nineteenth century affected artistic iconography, combining computer vision with thematic text analysis to map the interplay of visual and historical change (Zhang et al. 2023). This interdisciplinary approach illuminated the ways shifting social conditions were encoded in the language of images—insights that might have remained invisible without the combined force of humanistic inquiry and computational analysis. The result is a more agile, adaptive field in which collaborative teams are empowered to ask larger questions, draw on a broader range of evidence, and navigate the complexities of cultural heritage in an increasingly interconnected world.

One of the most significant advances in research has been the development of new document storage and assessment tools, which have transformed how art historians—and researchers across many fields—organize, annotate, and share their materials (Table 3.3). While digital solutions like Google Notebook have been well-trodden, they paved the way for a new generation of platforms that support collaborative, multimodal scholarship. Google Notebook's core features—real-time sharing, full-text search, and flexible organization of clippings, PDFs, and notes—anticipated the integrated workflows now standard in digital research environments. Today, open-source platforms like Zotero are widely adopted across the humanities for managing references, PDFs, and online materials. Zotero's strengths include not just full-text search and tagging but also group libraries and seamless citation integration with word processors, enabling teams to build and annotate shared bibliographies for collective projects or exhibition catalogues.

Mendeley, a staple for many researchers, offers similar functionality with the addition of automated metadata extraction and "smart folders" that organize documents by customizable criteria—making it especially useful for large, evolving projects. For Mac users, DEVONthink stands out with its hierarchical database structure and AI-driven classification features, helping researchers surface hidden connections through "See Also" recommendations and topic clustering. Obsidian, meanwhile, has found a loyal following among scholars who value personal knowledge management and networked thinking. Its markdown-based system supports not only bidirectional links between notes but also graph visualizations, plugins for PDF annotation, and Dataview queries that collate insights across an entire research vault.

Table 3.3 Collaborative and document management tools for art historians

Tool name	URL	Description	Use case for art historians
Google Notebook	https://www.google.com/notebook/ (archived)	Early web-based notebook for clipping text, images, links; searchable, shareable, and annotatable. Now discontinued, but legacy influences remain	Aggregating web and PDF sources, collaborating on shared bibliographies or thematic project folders
Zotero	https://www.zotero.org/	Open-source reference manager for PDFs, notes, tags, collections, and full-text search; supports shared group libraries and word-processor integration	Building annotated bibliographies, organizing research, and collaborating on group exhibition research
Mendeley	https://www.mendeley.com/	PDF/library management for desktop/web; auto-imports metadata, supports collaborative shared libraries, tagging, and citation tools	Managing digital archives, sharing articles and catalogues, cowriting with citation management
DEVONthink	https://www.devontechnologies.com/apps/devonthink	AI-driven document database (macOS) with robust search, auto-filing, topic clustering, and full PDF/web capture support	Surface hidden connections in large archives, cluster-related works, or automate project filing
Obsidian	https://obsidian.md/	Markdown-based knowledge manager, with PDF embedding/indexing, bidirectional linking, visual graph view, and plugin support for research workflows	Building linked note vaults, visualizing thematic connections, and annotating exhibition or project data
Polar	https://getpolarized.io/	Research assistant and PDF reader with automatic extraction of highlights and annotations, global search, and study guide export	Annotating and extracting key ideas from exhibition catalogues, articles, and digitized archival documents
Read Cube Papers	https://www.readcube.com/papers/	Cloud-synced PDF library with discovery, annotation, citation, one-click metadata lookup, and reading metrics	Collaborative library for exhibition teams, tracking article impact and integrating with reference workflows
Qiqqa	https://www.qiqqa.com/	Free PDF organizer for windows, supports mind-maps, citation, tagging, and smart project folders	Mapping research topics, brainstorming, and managing citations for catalogue essays or grant applications

(continued)

Table 3.3 (continued)

Tool name	URL	Description	Use case for art historians
Connected Papers	https://www.connectedpapers.com/	Builds graph maps of literature linked to your own PDFs, showing semantic and citation relationships	Exploring scholarly networks, visualizing art historical debates, and connecting primary/secondary sources
Tropy	https://tropy.org/	Organizes archival photos and PDFs into items with notes, tags, and metadata; supports structured export for further analysis or sharing	Structuring digital photo archives, annotating fieldwork, and exporting research datasets for Omeka or exhibits

Other platforms cater to more specialized needs or preferences in reading and data extraction. Polar automatically extracts highlights and annotations from PDFs and articles, letting researchers build collections and export structured study guides for deeper engagement with their materials. ReadCube Papers combines a cloud-synced PDF library with powerful annotation and discovery tools—including metrics on document usage—while Qiqqa, a free desktop app for Windows, supports mind mapping, advanced search, and citation management within large project libraries. For those interested in mapping research networks, Connected Papers visualizes literature connections in "graph maps," helping users see how uploaded PDFs relate to broader research trends or clusters. Finally, Tropy has become invaluable for organizing photographs of archival materials, providing robust metadata, tagging, and item-level search capabilities, and enabling export for further structured analysis. Collectively, these tools offer art historians unprecedented flexibility to manage, explore, and share the wide range of digital documents and images that define contemporary research—enabling deeper collaboration and insight across disciplines and institutions.

The arrival of deeply integrated collaborative platforms has fundamentally altered the landscape for art historians seeking to work with colleagues in other disciplines, institutions, and even time zones (Table 3.4). For example, the seamless connectivity offered by ChatGPT and Gemini AI assistants means that research teams can query vast collections of documents, extract metadata, or generate draft summaries directly within cloud-based environments like Office 365 and Google Workspace. This kind of integration is especially powerful for multiinstitutional projects—such as cataloguing shared collections, preparing exhibition checklists, or assembling digital humanities corpora—because it allows all contributors to access, analyze, and annotate files in real time without duplicating effort or risking version confusion. Researchers can quickly synthesize notes from team meetings, generate literature reviews that incorporate materials uploaded by any team member, or build consensus on emerging research questions by collaboratively reviewing primary source documents in a single, centralized workspace. Crucially, these platforms maintain existing access controls and audit trails, which is essential for collaborative work involving sensitive or proprietary data.

Beyond these AI-driven assistants, art historians now benefit from an expanding toolkit of specialized project management and knowledge-sharing platforms. Notion, for example, functions as a flexible "second brain" for research teams: PDFs, images,

Table 3.4 Collaborative project platforms

Tool name	URL	Description	Use case for art historians
Notion	https://www.notion.com/	All-in-one collaborative workspace: upload/share PDFs, images, notes, full-text search, coediting, Kanban boards, and more	Coordinating group projects, maintaining digital object inventories, coauthoring research or catalogues
Overleaf	https://www.overleaf.com/	Cloud-based LaTeX editor for real-time collaborative writing, PDF upload, annotation, and version tracking	Coauthoring scholarly articles, catalogues raisonnés, or digital exhibition guides with images/figures
Slack	https://slack.com/	Real-time messaging with channels, file sharing, integrations (Google Drive, Notion, Asana), and persistent conversation logs	Discussing research, sharing drafts, and managing digitization tasks or team meetings asynchronously
Microsoft Teams	https://www.microsoft.com/en-us/microsoft-teams/	Channels with built-in document coauthoring, shared OneNote notebooks, and video meetings; integrated with Office 365/OneDrive	Reviewing high-res scans, coauthoring reports, and managing exhibition planning across departments
Airtable	https://www.airtable.com/	Spreadsheet-database hybrid for uploading PDFs, images, and metadata; rich field types and permissions for team research	Tracking provenance, managing exhibition lists, or coordinating collaborative grant proposals
Asana	https://asana.com/	Task/project management with boards, timelines, file attachments, comments, and AI-powered project tracking	Managing research workflows, peer review cycles, or cataloguing with clear dependencies and milestones
Trello	https://trello.com/	Kanban-style boards and cards with attachments, checklists, and collaborative notes	Coordinating fieldwork, digital photo projects, or publication sprints in a visual, intuitive workspace
Miro	https://miro.com/	Infinite-canvas whiteboard for PDF/image uploads, sticky notes, and mapping relationships in real time	Visualizing research questions, mapping iconographic themes, or brainstorming with teams remotely

and links can be organized into collaborative databases, exhibition object lists, or annotated timelines. Real-time editing and customizable templates support everything from syllabus planning to image catalogue development, while full-text search ensures that no critical detail goes overlooked. Overleaf provides a collaborative environment for writing and editing LaTeX-based documents, such as scholarly articles or complex exhibition catalogues that require consistent formatting, embedded figures, and transparent version control—features particularly valued in cross-disciplinary projects where curators, historians, and scientists must coauthor technical appendices or detailed methodological notes. Communication platforms such as Slack and Microsoft Teams further streamline interdisciplinary work, enabling researchers to share files, annotate images, and organize conversations around specific projects or collections. These tools support both spontaneous exchanges and carefully documented project workflows, accommodating everything from urgent conservation questions to long-term planning for grant-funded initiatives.

The possibilities extend even further when teams leverage project management and visual collaboration tools tailored for complex research environments. Airtable, for instance, offers database functionality that can be customized for provenance research, condition reporting, or loan tracking, with built-in permissions for granular collaboration among archivists, conservators, and outside scholars. Asana and Trello facilitate the assignment and monitoring of research tasks—whether cataloguing a newly digitized photo archive or coordinating the writing of a multiauthor monograph—by providing clear visual timelines, task dependencies, and communication threads. Miro, with its infinite whiteboard and high-resolution image support, enables teams to visually map relationships among artists, brainstorm digital exhibition layouts, or prototype new interpretive models in a shared, interactive space. These platforms not only support internal project management, but also serve as bridges to colleagues in media studies, computer science, anthropology, or education—helping art historians harness cross-disciplinary expertise for richer, more contextualized research outcomes. Ultimately, the convergence of document management, real-time communication, and flexible project planning tools allows today's art historians to form agile, interdisciplinary teams capable of tackling the methodological and interpretive challenges that define contemporary scholarship.

AI-driven technologies have opened new avenues for interdisciplinary research by bridging art history with fields like digital humanities, conservation science, and computational analysis. For example, collaborative platforms now support virtual coauthorship, where scholars from different backgrounds can contribute to shared projects regardless of location or institutional affiliation (Zhang and Candy 2006). The AI for digital humanities project highlights this dynamic, using media analysis, pattern recognition, and computer vision to tackle research questions that exceed the scope of any single discipline (Stark et al. 2022). These collaborations introduce a diversity of methods and perspectives, enriching art historical research by drawing on data science, technical conservation, and museum practice. Through such partnerships, AI acts as a catalyst for innovation—helping scholars cluster stylistic motifs, automate cataloguing, and cross-reference records in ways previously impossible. The result is a broader, more nuanced field that welcomes both new questions and novel analytical frameworks. As methods continue to advance, these collaborations promise not just greater efficiency, but more meaningful, multilayered interpretations of art and its contexts.

The rise of platforms like Humanities Commons further demonstrates how technology can enhance interdisciplinary dialogue and knowledge-sharing. Leveraging AI, Humanities Commons connects researchers based on themes or projects, making it easier to share data, coauthor papers, and publish collaboratively (Nordström et al. 2023). This model has encouraged partnerships among art historians, computer scientists, and conservators, allowing large projects—such as multilingual catalogue raisonné compilations or digital epigraphy—to proceed more efficiently. AI-powered translation tools, for instance, enable the collaborative study of texts and inscriptions across languages and cultures, breaking down barriers that once limited global art historical research (Glinka and Müller-Birn 2023). The democratizing effect of these platforms is significant: they allow emerging scholars and practitioners from diverse backgrounds to participate in research, while promoting broader dissemination and engagement with cultural heritage. This interconnected research environment not only enhances the rigor of scholarship but also supports a more inclusive, globally integrated art history.

New models for creative and scholarly collaboration are also emerging from projects that blend curatorial, technological, and artistic expertise. The Botto Project is a notable example, bringing together curators and machine learning specialists to cocreate blockchain-based digital artworks—a process that challenges conventional boundaries of authorship and artistic value (Fernández-Castrillo 2023). The COSTART initiative has similarly fostered partnerships between artists and technologists, revealing how intelligent systems and coding frameworks can support and expand creative practice (Zhang and Candy 2006). Meanwhile, advances in computer vision have enabled large-scale, automated classification of visual datasets, supporting critical reflection and collaborative interpretation of complex image archives (Stark et al. 2022; Glinka and Müller-Birn 2023). While these platforms offer unprecedented power and flexibility, they also require ongoing attention to ethical and methodological questions—including data bias, the interpretability of results, and the distinct contributions of human and machine collaborators (Nordström et al. 2023). By proactively engaging with these challenges, the field can ensure that new technologies serve not as a replacement for humanistic values and expertise, but as an extension and enrichment of them. This collaborative ethos, supported by smart platforms and interdisciplinary networks, will continue to drive both innovation and critical reflection in the evolving landscape of art historical research.

3.5 Future Trajectories in AI-Assisted Art Historical Research

The next decade promises a dramatic lowering of barriers to quantitative research in art history, as new computational platforms and smart technologies rapidly become more intuitive and accessible. Recent studies underscore the expanding influence of data-driven tools in cultural heritage—enabling scholars to cluster visual patterns, reconstruct damaged works, manage metadata, and visualize entire museum collections with a precision that would have been unthinkable just a few years ago (Harisanty et al. 2024). Where once the mastery of coding or advanced statistics acted as a gatekeeper, intuitive interfaces and automated processes now allow researchers from diverse backgrounds to participate in computational analysis. As immersive media, robotics, and sensor technologies gain ground, future research will increasingly move beyond digitization and classification toward the creation of shared, interactive experiences in both virtual and physical environments (Harisanty et al. 2024; Pappa and Makropoulos 2021). These trajectories point to a field in which art historians are no longer limited by the mechanics of tool use but are instead free to pose more ambitious questions about networks of influence, transmission of style, and patterns of cultural memory.

The direction of these developments also suggests that advanced visual and quantitative analysis will become standard components of the art historical methodological toolkit. Studies have shown that deep learning and pattern-recognition systems can reliably identify stylistic trends, distinguish between hands in workshop production, and even generate predictive models for virtual restoration (Castellano and Vessio 2021; Folino et al. 2024). As these tools are more seamlessly integrated into digital collection management systems, they not only streamline cataloguing and conservation but also facilitate new forms of public engagement through interactive exhibits and digital storytelling. These changes underscore a shift toward research outputs that are dynamic and collaborative, with scholars, institutions, and communities working together to interpret and present cultural heritage.

As these capabilities mature, so too will the types of questions scholars bring to their research are shifting in tandem. Workflows that once required months of manual labor—such as tracing provenance, comparing motifs, or analyzing the spread of iconography—can now be handled in days or even hours through automated clustering, visual search, or multilingual data extraction (Castellano and Vessio 2021; Shen 2024). This offloading of routine and repetitive analysis frees researchers to focus on the interpretive heart of the discipline: making sense of objects produced by humans and for humans, and reconstructing how these works would have been seen, used, and valued in their own historical contexts. Methodological output is also evolving—moving from static catalogues or single-author monographs to dynamic, interactive databases, network visualizations, and public-facing digital exhibits. The very shape of art historical argument is becoming more collaborative, more responsive to new evidence, and more attentive to the intersections of social, political, and material histories.

The discipline is also being shaped by the increasing integration of immersive and interactive technologies. Research on the use of XR, including augmented and virtual reality, indicates that these modalities are not only changing how art and heritage are preserved but also how they are experienced and studied (Pappa and Makropoulos 2021). Virtual exhibitions, digital reconstructions, and remote collaborations now make it possible to bring objects, environments, and scholarly communities together across geographical divides. The implications are profound: new forms of access and public engagement are possible, challenging traditional notions of authority, expertise, and audience in art historical practice. These technologies foster multisensory and participatory encounters that invite audiences to explore artworks and historical sites in ways that are both personally meaningful and academically rigorous. As a result, the boundaries between researcher, curator, and visitor become more fluid, encouraging collaborative knowledge creation and shared stewardship of cultural heritage.

Ethical questions inevitably follow these methodological innovations. Scholars like Tiribelli et al. (2024) have emphasized the need for frameworks that address interpretive bias, data provenance, and questions of authenticity and authorship as computational tools are woven into the discipline's fabric. Open-access governance, responsible stewardship of data, and robust dialogue with communities of origin are not simply technical issues but fundamental to the ongoing credibility and inclusivity of the discipline. Concerns about equity remain pressing, as the cost and complexity of certain commercial platforms may limit participation by under-resourced scholars or institutions. Addressing these issues will require ongoing investment in open, adaptable tools designed with the workflows of art historians in mind, as well as a renewed emphasis on transparency and critical reflection at every stage of the research process (Ba'ai and Aris 2024).

The scope of what constitutes "heritage" is also expanding, as researchers document and interpret intangible assets such as oral traditions, social practices, and ritual knowledge. Ba'ai and Aris (2024) demonstrate how computational and language tools make it possible to archive and analyze nonmaterial culture, enabling global audiences to access, search, and contribute to living archives. This broadening is critical for a more inclusive, globally representative field, as it supports collaborative stewardship and engagement with communities whose histories have often been marginalized in traditional scholarship. As these projects grow, art history becomes more participatory and reflective of diverse cultural values. For example, recent initiatives in digital storytelling platforms have allowed communities to curate their own histories, contributing audio recordings and contextual narratives that are woven into museum and university databases. Such efforts not only ensure the preservation of intangible heritage but also facilitate dialogic exchanges, where community voices shape both the interpretation and future curation of cultural memory.

At the same time, as research platforms become increasingly open and modular, calls for investment in domain-specific, community-governed tools grow louder. Shen (2024) highlights the effectiveness of automated classification and interactive curatorial systems in enhancing both scholarly workflows and public experiences, but cautions that over-reliance on proprietary commercial platforms may exacerbate inequities in access. The future depends on supporting open, transparent, and interoperable solutions that are responsive to the diverse needs of scholars, curators, and audiences worldwide. These directions suggest a field where technological and humanistic rigor evolve hand in hand. For instance, the development of open-source platforms for digital cataloguing—codesigned by academic and museum partners—has already begun to address challenges in language localization, accessibility, and data sovereignty. By prioritizing community input and collaborative governance, such tools foster more equitable participation in both the production and dissemination of art historical knowledge.

One especially promising trend is the integration of these tools into collaborative, community-based research and the preservation of intangible cultural heritage. New systems now make it possible to document, translate, and share oral histories, ritual knowledge, and ephemeral cultural practices at a global scale, breaking down long-standing barriers of language and access. Social robots, virtual assistants, and interactive platforms are enriching both the research process and the visitor experience, helping to build archives that are not only more inclusive but also more engaging for diverse audiences (Shen 2024; Sheng 2024). For example, projects that pair interactive kiosks in museums with cloud-based translation and transcription services now enable visitors to record personal stories or contribute traditional songs, instantly making these contributions available to researchers and other community members worldwide. By making it easier to bring global voices and perspectives into dialogue, these developments reinforce the potential of the field as a platform for public history and shared cultural stewardship, cultivating a sense of ownership and participation that strengthens the relevance of art historical research.

Importantly, as routine analytical tasks become more automated, the unique interpretive role of the art historian comes even more clearly into focus. While machines can rapidly sort, classify, and visualize patterns in vast troves of data, it is the art historian's expertise that transforms these findings into meaningful narratives—connecting artifacts to the complex social, religious, and political dynamics that shaped their creation and reception (Sheng 2024). The challenge of reconstructing historical context, uncovering layers of symbolic meaning, and understanding how objects have functioned as carriers of identity, memory, or dissent cannot be delegated to algorithms alone. Indeed, the act of interpretation requires a capacity for critical reflection, ethical judgment, and empathy—skills honed through rigorous engagement with theory, primary sources, and the lived realities of communities past and present. As art history moves forward, the field's value will increasingly reside in its practitioners' ability to bridge data-driven insight with deep contextual knowledge, continually asking not just what objects are, but why they mattered to those who made, used, and viewed them.

This human interpretive work will also be central to addressing ambiguity, contradiction, and gaps in the historical record—areas where computational systems may struggle or risk reinforcing biases. Scholars will need to remain vigilant in questioning the assumptions embedded within both their datasets and their tools, ensuring that their analyses remain attentive to complexity, contingency, and the possibility of multiple readings. As digital methods multiply what can be seen or measured, it will be the reflective questioning, critical synthesis, and imaginative engagement of the art historian that shape how the past is understood and communicated. The next era of research will not be defined by automation alone, but by the creative and ethical capacities of those who interpret what machines reveal, ensuring that art history remains a profoundly humanistic discipline at its core.

Therefore, the field stands at a pivotal juncture. As quantitative methods become increasingly integrated into mainstream practice, the discipline gains power to ask new questions, visualize knowledge in innovative forms, and open participation to a broader range of collaborators. The greatest advances will not simply be technical but will stem from the creative and critical interplay between digital innovation and human interpretation. Responsible stewardship, inclusivity, and reflexivity will remain essential as art historians navigate the opportunities and challenges of this rapidly changing landscape. The discipline's enduring value will rest on its ability to unite analytical rigor with contextual insight, ensuring that as tools evolve, the core mission of understanding art in all its complexity is never lost.

Upon reflection, this chapter has illuminated how computational and algorithmic methods are fundamentally reshaping the landscape of art historical research. The survey of digital repositories, large-scale dataset aggregation, and the rapid development of computer vision has demonstrated that art history now operates at unprecedented scale, breadth, and analytical sophistication. The integration of artificial intelligence—through tools like Litmaps, Consensus, and Perplexity.ai—has accelerated literature discovery, enabled real-time synthesis of scholarly debates, and supported more agile, data-driven research processes. Notably, advances in computer vision and deep learning have moved questions of attribution and conservation into new empirical territory, allowing for the detection of patterns invisible to the naked eye and the development of predictive models for restoration. These technologies do not supplant traditional connoisseurship or historical contextualization; rather, they enrich interpretive frameworks by surfacing latent relationships and expanding the evidentiary base of the field. Collaborative digital platforms have also facilitated new modes of interdisciplinary research, bringing together art historians, data scientists, conservators, and technical specialists to tackle complex questions. Throughout, the chapter has shown that the most robust research emerges from a dynamic interplay of human judgment, technological capability, and critical scrutiny.

Key takeaways here emphasize that digital methods are most effective when paired with rigorous, reflective scholarship. The promise of "big data" and automated analysis comes with the responsibility to ensure data quality, provenance, and transparency at every stage of inquiry. Successful digital art historical research draws on the field's long-standing pluralism—blending anthropological, social, theological, and technical methods—while integrating new forms of algorithmic analysis and visualization. The chapter cautions against technological determinism and calls for ongoing attention to the epistemological limits, potential biases, and ethical implications of computational models. It also foregrounds the necessity of digital literacy and methodological agility, not just among specialists but across the discipline, as scholars and students alike must learn to navigate, curate, and critically interpret networked resources. The capacity for interdisciplinary collaboration, continuous feedback, and open knowledge-sharing has become a central professional competency in the digital age.

Looking forward, this section urges the field to invest in sustainable, open infrastructures for digital research—developing shared benchmarks, collaborative datasets, and transparent tools that can be adapted as technology evolves. There is a clear call for more inclusive and participatory forms of data curation, involving diverse voices in the construction, annotation, and critical evaluation of digital archives and analytic frameworks. As computational art history becomes more central to the discipline, future research should focus on developing hybrid methodologies that foreground both humanistic interpretation and machine-driven discovery, ensuring that scale never comes at the expense of depth or context. Institutions are encouraged to foster environments that support ongoing professional development, critical experimentation, and dialogue between the arts and sciences. Ultimately, the future of art historical research will depend on the discipline's ability to maintain a balance between innovation and intellectual rigor—harnessing the power of technology while remaining grounded in the interpretive values and social responsibilities that define the field.

References

AlNoamany Y, AlSum A, Weigle MC, Nelson ML (2014) Who and what links to the internet archive. Int J Digit Libr 14:101–115

Amineddoleh LA (2016) Are you faux real: an examination of art forgery and the legal tools protecting art collectors. Cardozo Arts Entertain Law J 34:59

Ba'ai N, Aris A (2024) AI and cultural heritage: preserving and promoting global cultures through technology. Nanotechnology perceptions. https://doiorg/1062441/nano-ntpvi3454

Barnes CM, Dang CT, Leavitt K, Guarana CL, Uhlmann EL (2018) Archival data in micro-organizational research: a toolkit for moving to a broader set of topics. J Manag 44:1453–1478

Bartz C, Krestel R (2021) Deep learning for computer vision in the art domain: proceedings of the master seminar on practical introduction to deep learning for computer vision. HPI WS 20/21. Universitätsverlag Potsdam

Breuel TM (2007) Applying the OCRopus OCR system to scholarly Sanskrit literature. In: International Sanskrit computational linguistics symposium. Springer, Berlin, pp 391–402

Calvo P (2018) The cordial economy, Ethics, recognition and reciprocity, Springer. https://doi.org/10.1007/978-3-319-90784-0

Castellano G, Vessio G (2021) Understanding art with AI: our research experience. DP@ AI* IA, pp 92–98

Clark LR (2018) Collecting art in the Italian renaissance court: objects and exchanges. Cambridge University Press, pp 1–320

Corrado EM, Sandy HM (2017) Digital preservation for libraries, archives, and museums. Rowman & Littlefield, pp 1–292

Crookham A, Dunn S (2019) Reframing art: opening up art dealers' archives to multi-disciplinary research. Vis Resour 35:180–183. https://doi.org/10.1080/01973762.2019.1553447

Deutch S (2021) ARt image exploration space (ARIES): a response to the image needs of art library patrons. Art Libr J 46(1):7–12

Fernández-Castrillo C (2023) The AI work of art in the age of its co-creation. Magazén 4:357–383

Folino F, Foresta MF, Maurmo D, Ruga T, Zumpano E, Vocaturo E (2024) AI image-based systems for enhancing the cultural tourism experience. In: 2024 IEEE international conference on big data (BigData), pp 4720–4726
Friedrich M, Müller P, Riordan M (2017) Practices of historical research in archives and libraries from the eighteenth to the nineteenth century. Hist Humanit 2:3–13
Fuchsgruber L (2019) Museum photo archives and the history of the art market: a digital approach. In: Arts, vol 8, no 3. MDPI, p 93
Glinka K, Müller-Birn C (2023) Critical-reflective human-AI collaboration: exploring computational tools for art historical image retrieval. Proc ACM Hum-Comput Interact 7:1–33
Guo Q (2024) Prompting change: ChatGPT's impact on digital humanities pedagogy—a case study in art history. Int J Humanit Arts Comput 18:58–78
Harisanty D, Obille KLB, Anna NEV, Purwanti E, Retrialisca F (2024) Cultural heritage preservation in the digital age, harnessing artificial intelligence for the future: a bibliometric analysis. Digit Libr Perspect 40(4):609–630
Jari J, Saliu A, Gyegwe A (2016) Qualitative and quantitative methods in computer application to painting: an art historical perspective. Arts Des Stud 43:50–65
Jain H, Padmanabhan B, Pavlou PA, Raghu TS (2021) Editorial for the special section on humans, Algorithms and augmented intelligence: The future of work, organizations, and society. Information Systems Research, 32(3), pp 675–687. https://doi.org/10.1287/isre.2021.1046
Jauregui R (1996) Rembrandt portraits: economic negligence in art attribution. UCLA Law Rev 44:1947
Keeran P (2013) Art and art history. In: Information literacy instruction that works: a guide to teaching by discipline and student population, pp 125–143
Kim M (2022) New method for museum archiving: quantitative analysis meets art history. ACM J Comput Cult Herit 15:1–17. https://doi.org/10.1145/3531018
Kvak D (2022) Leveraging computer vision application in visual arts: a case study on the use of residual neural network to classify and analyze baroque paintings. arXiv preprint arXiv:2210.15300
Lang S, Ommer B (2021) Transforming information into knowledge: how computational methods reshape art history. DHQ Digit Humanit Q 15:3
Li W (2025) Enhanced automated art curation using supervised modified CNN for art style classification. Sci Rep 15(1):7319
Markey K (1988) Access to iconographical research collections. Libr Trends 37:1–12
Medisetti G, Compson Z, Fan H, Yang H, Feng Y (2024, August) LitAI: Enhancing multimodal literature understanding and mining with generative AI. In 2024 IEEE 7th International Conference on Multimedia Information Processing and Retrieval (MIPR) pp. 471–476. IEEE.
Nordström P, Lundman R, Hautala J (2023) Evolving coagency between artists and AI in the spatial cocreative process of artmaking. Ann Am Assoc Geogr 113:2203–2218
Ojala M (2023) AI-powered research assistants. Comput Libr 43:43–45
Panofsky E (1962) Studies in iconology, p 198
Pappa D, Makropoulos C (2021) Novel ways of discovering, capturing and experiencing cultural heritage: a review of current state-of-the-art, challenges and future directions. IntechOpen
Persson A (2024) Cognition and the machine: exploring human-AI interaction via predictive processing. Doctoral dissertation. Acta Universitatis Upsaliensis, pp 1–230
Preziosi D (2009) The art of art history, a critical anthology, OUP Oxford
Reimer JH, Schmidt S, Fröbe M, Gienapp L, Scells H, Stein B, Potthast M (2023) The archive query log: mining millions of search result pages of hundreds of search engines from 25 years of web archives. In: Proceedings of the 46th international ACM SIGIR conference on research and development in information retrieval, pp 2848–2860
Shen J (2024) The investigation of artificial intelligence in cultural relics protection. Science and Technology of Engineering, Chemistry and Environmental Protection. https://doi.org/10.61173/hhpeyy15

Sheng Y (2024) AI-assisted curatorial research. Int J Soc Sci Public Adm. https://doi.org/10.62051/ijsspa.v4n3.18
Sienkewicz JA (2021) Guest editor introduction: cultivating our field through SoTL practice: teaching and learning the art history of the United States. Art Hist Pedagog Pract 6:1
Spivey V, McGarry R (2019) Bridging the research/teaching divide with DAH and SoTL-AH. Vis Resour 35:34–51
Spivey V, Fisher M, Shelby K, McGarry R, Giuntini P, Wentrack K, Hohensee N (2016) Storytelling as strategy: building support for SoTL in art history
Spratt E (2018) The Frick collection and Frick art reference library. Searching through seeing: optimizing computer vision technology
Stark M, Thielen E, Holtmann C et al (2022) XR art and culture: successful collaborations in interdisciplinary development processes. i-com 21:123–138
Stork DG (2023) Pixels & paintings: foundations of computer-assisted connoisseurship. Wiley
Surapaneni S, Syed S, Lee LY (2020) Exploring themes and bias in art using machine learning image analysis. In: 2020 systems and information engineering design symposium (SIEDS). IEEE, pp 1–6
Szabo V (2012) Transforming art history research with database analytics: visualizing art markets. Art Doc J Art Libr Soc N Am 31:158–175
Tiribelli S, Pansoni S, Frontoni E, Giovanola B (2024) Ethics of artificial intelligence for cultural heritage: opportunities and challenges. IEEE Trans Technol Soc 5(3):293–305
Van Noord N (2022) A survey of computational methods for iconic image analysis. Digit Sch Humanit 37(4):1316–1338
Wasielewski A (2023) Computational formalism: art history and machine learning. MIT Press, pp 1–240
Webb A, Welsh A (2016) SoTL stories: phenomenology as a methodology for SoTL research
Weber M (2017) Methodology of social sciences. Routledge, pp 1–230
Zhang Y, Candy L (2006) Investigating collaboration in art and technology. CoDesign 2:239–248
Zhang H, Wu C, Xie J, Lyu Y, Cai J, Carroll JM (2023) Redefining qualitative analysis in the AI era: utilizing ChatGPT for efficient thematic analysis. arXiv preprint arXiv:2309.10771
Zhang W, Kam-Kwai W, Chen Y, Jia A, Wang L, Zhang JW, Chen W (2024) Scrolltimes: tracing the provenance of paintings as a window into history. IEEE Trans Vis Comput Graph 1–12

Chapter 4
Copyright and Legal Frameworks in Art and Scholarship

Abstract This section provides a critical examination of the complex copyright and legal frameworks now shaping art historical research and publication, as well as museum practice in an era increasingly defined by generative content creation. The chapter begins by analyzing the evolving challenges to authorship and originality presented by digital and automated outputs, highlighting the blurred boundaries between human and machine agency in creative and scholarly work. It then offers a comparative analysis of legal frameworks, contrasting U.S. fair-use doctrines with European Union policies on text and data mining and discussing the implications for researchers, curators, and artists operating across jurisdictions. The chapter further explores practical strategies for protecting intellectual property, offering guidelines for museums and individual scholars navigating rapidly changing legal environments. Concluding with a synthesis of best practices, the discussion equips art historians and cultural professionals with critical tools for ethically and legally responsible engagement with synthetic and generative technologies, ensuring both innovation and compliance in the pursuit of new knowledge.

4.1 AI-Generated Content and the Challenges to Authorship and Originality

There is no doubt that from the summer of 2022, starting with art generators, AI has disrupted creative industries more quickly than any previous emergent technology, providing tools that enable unprecedented levels of content generation and artistic creation. For instance, ChatGPT, launched by OpenAI in late 2022, quickly set a record as the fastest-adopted technology in history by reaching one million users in just five days, followed by over 100 million monthly active users by February 2023 (Gordon 2023). From generating music and visual art to drafting written content, generative technologies like Claude, Stable Diffusion, and Runway have expanded the creative landscape, offering both opportunities and legal challenges. Such technologies work by employing machine learning models that produce new content based on patterns learned from vast datasets (Feuerriegel et al. 2024). Unlike more

J. Hutson, *Art History in the Age of Artificial Intelligence*, Springer Series on Cultural Computing, https://doi.org/10.1007/978-3-032-02920-1_4

traditional tools like cameras or Photoshop, which require direct human input to capture or edit existing content, visual models are trained on extensive datasets, often containing text, images, and other media, to learn structures, styles, and elements within these media. As such, the "generative" in AI refers to the ability of the model to create entirely new content by combining learned elements in ways that simulate human creativity, rather than simply modifying existing content (Epstein et al. 2023).

For example, Stable Diffusion and Runway generate images by using neural networks trained on large collections of images, where they learn to reproduce certain visual patterns. Given a textual description or prompt, these models can generate new images that match the specifications of a prompt. This process, based on diffusion models or transformers, synthesizes new visual or textual content that may convincingly resemble human-made works but is derived from algorithmic understanding rather than human-originated design or manipulation (Moreno et al. 2023). At the same time, creators can leverage prompt engineering to align AI-generated output more closely with their intentions, but the degree of human involvement varies significantly compared to traditional creative tools. Unlike cameras or Photoshop, which serve as direct extensions of human creativity by capturing or modifying real-world elements, GAI can operate without a direct creative act from the user, synthesizing novel content autonomously (Aaland 2006; Kelby 2020). Tools like cameras and image editing software require human decisions—such as framing, lighting, or post-production modifications—to shape the final work, emphasizing a continuum of human intervention (Moreno et al. 2023). GAI, by contrast, shifts this paradigm, functioning as both a powerful tool for artistic expansion and a disruptor of established notions of originality and authorship (Feuerriegel et al. 2024).

The levels of human involvement in the creation of generative outputs remain highly contested, as the technology is seen to autonomously interpret prompts and produce algorithmically generated content without directly replicating specific training data (Risi and Togelius 2020). This capability to generate novel content, often indistinguishable from human-made works, presents both opportunities for rapid content production and challenges for copyright law, which historically emphasizes human originality and intentional creativity as prerequisites for protection (Abdikhakimov 2023; Ploman and Hamilton 2024). The U.S. Copyright Office, in particular, has clarified that works lacking "human authorship" are ineligible for copyright, a standard consistently applied in notable cases. For example, in *Allen v. U.S. Copyright Office* (2024) (Fig. 4.1), the Office rejected the claim of Jason Allen for his AI-assisted and award-winning artwork *Théâtre D'opéra Spatial* (2022), created with Midjourney. Despite the argument on the part of the artist that prompt engineering constituted a creative act, the Office determined that copyright requires direct human creativity, not simply guiding an algorithm (Brittain 2024). This decision reinforces the principle that human authorship must involve more than indirect input to qualify for copyright protection.

Similarly, in *Thaler v. Perlmutter*, the court ruled against granting copyright for *A Recent Entrance to Paradise* (2012) (Fig. 4.2), an image created autonomously by the Creativity Machine of the computer scientist Stephen Thaler, further emphasizing the necessity of human authorship. The assertion by Thaler that his ownership of the

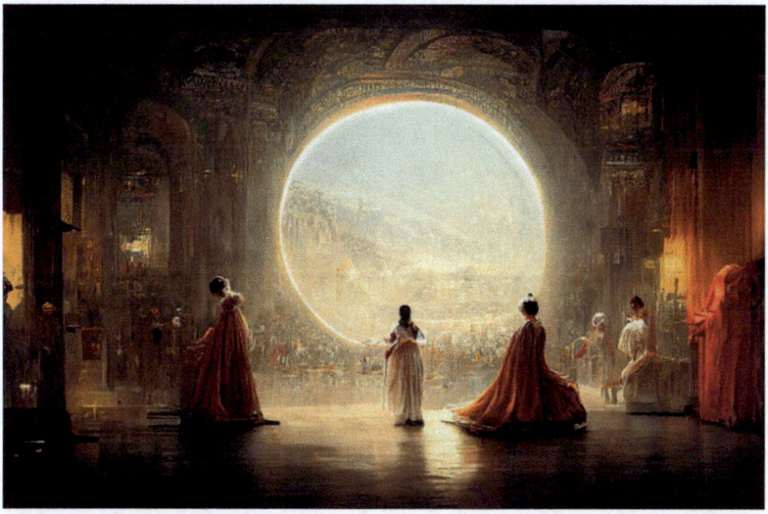

Fig. 4.1 Jason M. Allen, *Théâtre D'opéra Spatial*, 2022. Midjourney (CC O, public domain)

device should establish copyright eligibility was rejected, as the work lacked human intentionality and creative decision-making (Mathur 2023). These rulings demonstrate the difficulty of applying traditional copyright frameworks to AI-generated works, which often operate through data-driven algorithms rather than human intent. Cases like *Andersen* et al. *v. Stability AI Ltd.,* which address the use of copyrighted materials in AI training datasets, further complicate the landscape, as courts must navigate whether such practices constitute infringement or fall under "fair use" (Spica 2024). Together, these cases underscore the urgent need for updated legal frameworks that define the boundaries of human involvement in assistive creations and establish clear standards for copyright eligibility in this new age.

For art historians, understanding the implications of generative technologies within copyright law is vital, as it directly influences both professional responsibilities and academic practices. The transformative impact of these tools not only redefines the production and ownership of creative works but also reshapes methodologies for researching, curating, and teaching art. Art historians, who frequently rely on digital tools for cataloguing and analyzing artworks, must address the ethical and legal considerations associated with AI-generated content (Zhitomirsky-Geffet et al. 2023). Researchers require clarity regarding what can be copyrighted and what cannot, particularly for the publication and use of imagery in scholarship. Similarly, museum professionals must evaluate the implications of "fair use" for training datasets, particularly when ensuring that artists have the option to opt out of having their work displayed on sites potentially used for model training (Hanna and Khan 2023). These challenges demand a nuanced understanding of copyright and fair use, enabling art historians to address legal concerns proactively and advocate for balanced frameworks that respect the contributions of both humans and technology

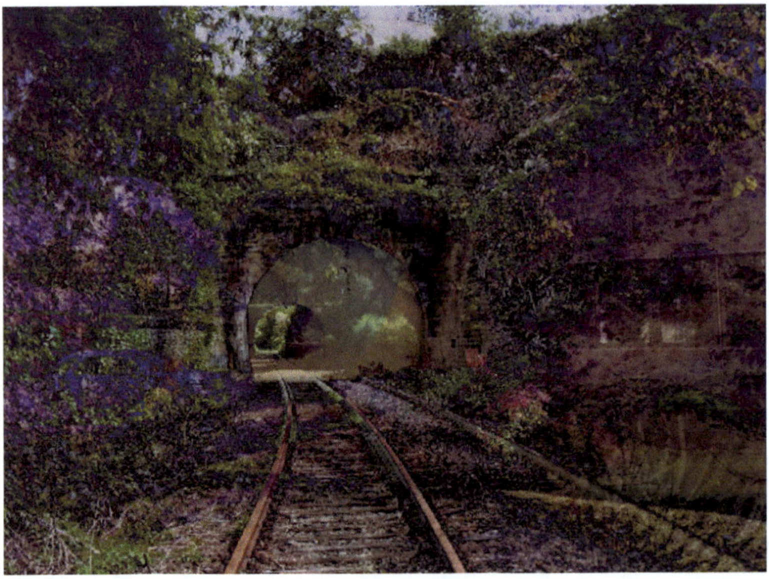

Fig. 4.2 Stephen Thaler, *A Recent Entrance to Paradise*, 2012. Creativity Machine (CC O, public domain)

in the arts. As the technology continues to evolve, art historians will remain pivotal in shaping the discourse surrounding creativity, authorship, and the ethical integration of generative technologies.

At the same time, the debates seen today over whether an artform should be granted copyright protection should recall a similar one in the nineteenth century with the emergence of photography. Critics, including poet-critic Charles Baudelaire (1821–1867), dismissed photography as a mechanical process devoid of creativity, arguing that the camera merely replicated reality without artistic intervention (Rexer 2019). The critic claimed that photography lacked the "soul" of the artist reflected a broader skepticism that it was a technical craft rather than a creative pursuit. Because photographs appeared to be direct copies of nature, they challenged traditional notions of originality, raising doubts about whether photographers could be considered authors. This controversy highlighted a fundamental tension in visual culture—how new technologies reshape artistic authorship. The question of whether photography merited copyright protection was at the core of this debate, as skeptics viewed the role of the camera as passive and automatic (Price and Wells 2021). However, defenders of photography argued that the choices of the photographer—such as composition, lighting, and subject arrangement—played a crucial role in shaping the final image (Krages 2012). This dispute remains significant for art historians, as it reflects ongoing challenges in defining creativity in technologically mediated artistic practices.

The U.S. Supreme Court addressed this debate in *Burrow-Giles Lithographic Co. v. Sarony* (1884), a case that ultimately affirmed photography's artistic legitimacy.

The defendants argued that photographs were not authored works but mere mechanical reproductions of reality and, therefore, ineligible for copyright (Allen 1986). The Court, however, ruled that photography could involve intellectual authorship, comparable to painting or engraving. The case centered on the portrait of Oscar Wilde (Fig. 4.3) by Napoleon Sarony (1821–1896), which the justices deemed an original creation due to the artistic decisions of Sarony, such as posing, lighting, and costume arrangement. The acknowledgement of the role of the photographer in shaping the artistic and expressive qualities of an image by the Court established that photographs could reflect creativity and personal vision. The ability of the photographer to construct a composition through deliberate stylistic choices demonstrated that photography was not merely mechanical but could convey artistic intent. The decision set a crucial precedent by affirming that copyright law protects works that embody the intellectual conception of an artist, even when created through a technological medium. This ruling significantly influenced the acceptance of photography as an art form, reinforcing the idea that artistic originality does not depend on the physical act of painting or sculpting but on creative input and authorship.

The struggle to define artistic authorship and protect creative works predates photography and can be traced back to the Renaissance, when printmaking first raised questions of ownership. Albrecht Dürer (1471–1528), a leading printmaker of his time, faced rampant unauthorized copying of his engravings, prompting him to seek an Imperial Privilege from Emperor Maximilian I (1459–1519)—an early form of copyright-like protection (Cooper 2021). This privilege functioned as a bespoke contract, granting Dürer legal recognition as the owner of his designs, much like modern copyright laws. His monogram, "AD," (Fig. 4.4) became one of the first artist trademarks, signaling authenticity and discouraging forgery (Karapapa 2022). Giorgio Vasari (1511–1574) later documented that Dürer pursued legal action against Marcantonio Raimondi (ca. 1470–1482—ca. 1527–1534), an engraver who replicated his works line-for-line. While the Venetian court ruled that Raimondi could copy the German artist's compositions, he was forbidden from reproducing his monogram, marking an early legal acknowledgment of artist authorship (Mulevičiūtė 2018). Although Renaissance courts did not establish comprehensive copyright laws, these precedents reflected the evolving recognition of artist intellectual ownership. The case of Dürer represents a critical shift from medieval workshop traditions, where art was seen as a collective guild product, toward an individualized notion of artistic genius.

The development of early copyright concepts was further propelled by the emergence of the art market and print publishers in the sixteenth and seventeenth centuries. Print sellers often profited from reproducing successful artworks, prompting artists to seek ways to retain control over their images (Barron 2020). In the absence of formal copyright statutes, tailored agreements—similar to the privilege extended to Dürer—became a primary means of establishing ownership. Artists and patrons increasingly relied on detailed contracts to specify rights over designs and reproductions, functioning as an early licensing system (Burke 2018). These agreements laid the foundation for later copyright doctrines by demonstrating that artistic originality and commercial rights were intertwined. As the biographies of Vasari exalted the

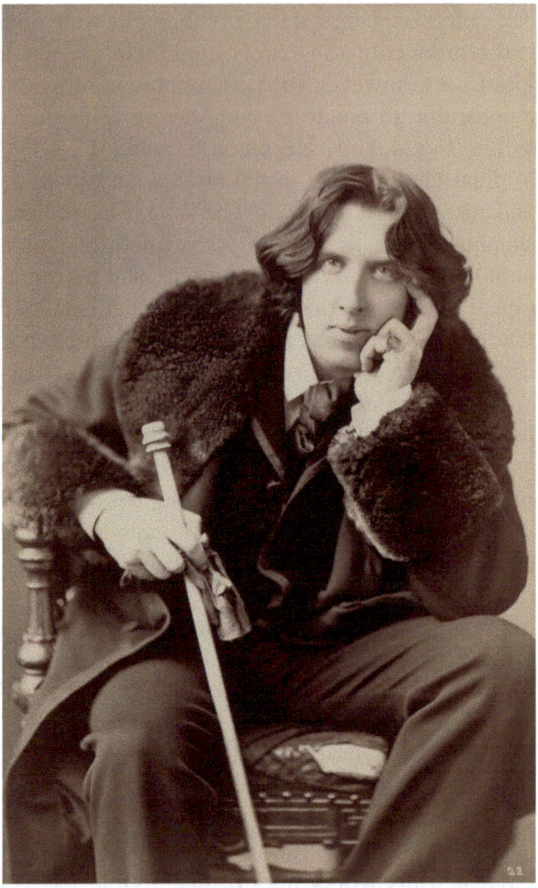

Fig. 4.3 Napoleon Sarony, *Oscar Wilde*, 1882. Albumen print on card mount (CC O, public domain)

individuality of Renaissance artists, legal recognition of their authorship followed suit, reinforcing the idea that visual works originated from a singular creative mind rather than a collective tradition (Marvin 2013). This period illustrates how legal and artistic notions of authorship coevolved, shaping the trajectory of intellectual property in art.

By the twentieth century, the conceptual art movement further challenged traditional notions of authorship and ownership. Conceptual artists, valuing the idea over the physical execution, introduced Certificates of Authenticity as contractual proof of authorship and ownership (Said 2015). Artists such as Sol LeWitt (1928–2007) and Yves Klein (1928–1962) used these certificates to define their artworks, ensuring that the legitimacy of a piece rested on legal documentation rather than physical form (Burke 2018). Collectors came to recognize these certificates as essential components of artwork provenance—without them, the authenticity of the piece could be disputed. The practice demonstrated that legal frameworks could be embedded into

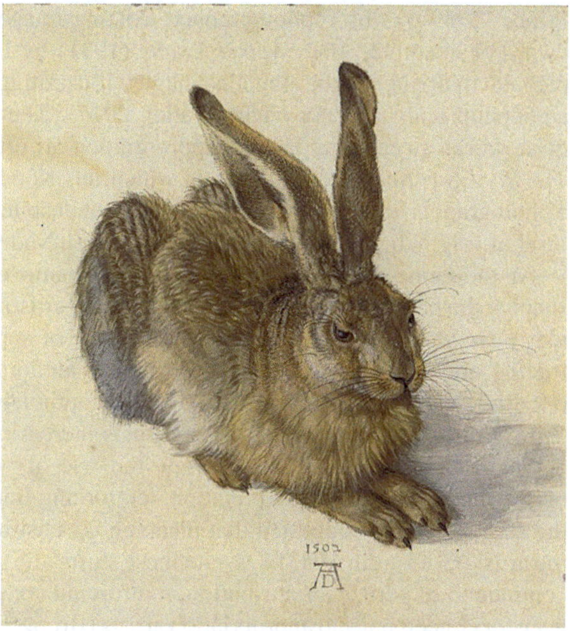

Fig. 4.4 Albrecht Dürer, *Feldhase*, 1502 (CC O, public domain)

artistic expression itself, blurring the line between art and contract law. Art historians have since recognized that conceptual art radically expanded the definition of what an artwork is, shifting the emphasis from tangible objects to documented ideas. The interplay between legal conventions and artistic practice has continued into contemporary art, where copyright laws often struggle to accommodate new artistic forms. While traditional copyright protects painting, sculpture, and photography, it has been less effective in addressing nontraditional works such as performance and digital art (Karapapa 2022). Some artists deliberately play with legal frameworks, appropriating contracts, trademarks, and property rights into their work as a critique of commodification (Barron 2020). For example, conceptual artists use certificates not only to validate ownership but also to highlight the bureaucratic structures that govern art circulation (Burke 2018).

While conceptual artists challenged and expanded notions of artistic authorship, perhaps no figure is more influential in this shift than Marcel Duchamp (1887–1968). His 1917 submission of *Fountain* (Fig. 4.5), a mass-produced urinal signed "R. Mutt," questioned whether authorship lay in the physical act of creation or the intellectual act of designation (Vella Rago 2015). His readymades—ordinary objects presented as art—radically redefined artistic creativity as conceptual rather than technical (Lombardo 2010). His intent was to shift art from a "retinal" focus on visual pleasure to an intellectual engagement with meaning (Cousijn 2016). *Fountain* was never copyrighted since Duchamp refused to disclose his identity as its author, further complicating the legal understanding of artistic ownership (Pelcher 2019). His legacy directly influenced later artists such as Sherrie Levine (1947–) and Richard

Prince (1949–), who rephotographed existing images and presented them as their own. For example, *After Walker Evans* (1981) by Levine critiqued originality by recontextualizing public domain images, illustrating the tensions between artistic authorship and legal copyright (Bailey 2017). The art world may have accepted these works as new, but legally, appropriation art often ran afoul of copyright law. The *Rogers v. Koons* case (1992), in which Jeff Koons was found liable for copying a photographer's composition, reinforced that despite conceptual reimagining, some level of originality remained legally necessary (Nodelman 2008).

At the same time, the influence of Duchamp extended beyond readymades, shaping the broader debate over originality and artistic ownership. His works, particularly *Fountain*, remain central to discussions of appropriation and conceptual art, forcing art historians to reconsider whether authorship is material or intellectual (Housefield 2002). His challenge to artistic authorship anticipated the postmodern shift in the 1960s and 1970s, where artists increasingly questioned the role of the author (Seamon 2001). This era saw the rise of works that blurred distinctions between creation and reinterpretation, reinforcing Barthesian notion of the "death of the author," which suggested that meaning is constructed by the viewer rather than the artist (Goldsmith 1983). Despite these shifts, the art market and legal institutions continue to require clear attribution, reinforcing conventional notions of authorship even for conceptual and appropriation artists (Brough 1997). The impact of Duchamp extends into contemporary copyright debates, particularly regarding whether purely conceptual works qualify for the same protection as traditional, handcrafted art. His artistic strategies also laid the groundwork for Pop artists like Warhol (1928–1987),

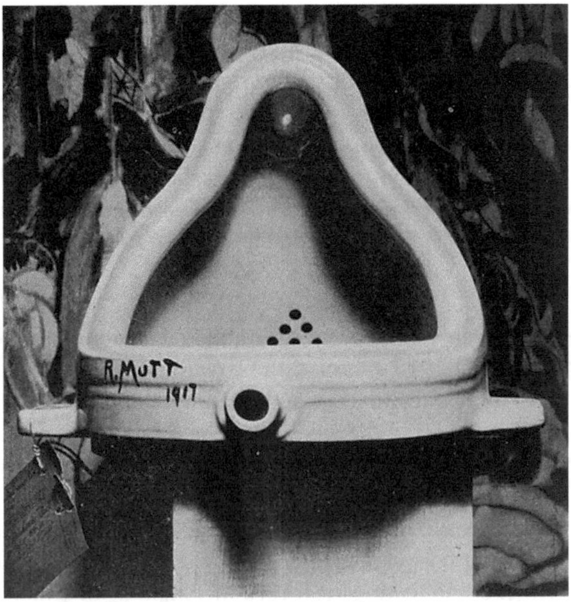

Fig. 4.5 Marcel Duchamp, *Fountain*, 1917 (CC O, public domain)

who further blurred the line between mass production and artistic expression (Bailey 2017).

The challenge of authorship is further complicated by the inherently collaborative nature of many artistic practices. Large-scale projects, from architecture to installations, involve multiple contributors, breaking away from the traditional idea of the singular artist (Cousijn 2016). Graphic design theorist Michael Rock argued that most contemporary design is created in a collaborative setting, making it difficult to attribute authorship to a single individual (Pelcher 2019). His essay, "The Designer as Author," (1996) emphasized the role of the audience and process in shaping meaning, echoing postmodern theories of authorship. This shift parallels historical precedents in art workshops, where pieces were often cocreated under the name of a master artist. However, copyright law remains structured around individual ownership, posing challenges for artworks created through collective processes (Housefield 2002). This mismatch highlights the ongoing friction between legal and artistic understandings of authorship, necessitating interdisciplinary dialogue between art historians and legal scholars. Without clearer legal frameworks, contemporary artists working in collaborative or appropriation-based modes risk facing legal uncertainties when asserting ownership over their work (Bailey 2017).

The legal system has often struggled to address the complexities of conceptual and appropriation art, as traditional copyright laws prioritize tangible works, making it difficult to apply protections to conceptual or performative pieces (Seamon 2001). The challenge is evident in *Fountain*, which raises questions about whether legal authorship resides in the conceptual act of selecting the object or in its physical production (Goldsmith 1983). Contemporary debates surrounding artificial intelligence-generated art mirror these challenges, as courts and copyright offices determine whether AI-generated works qualify for copyright if a human artist was involved in their creation (Bailey 2017). Much like photography in the nineteenth century, generative art tests existing copyright frameworks by raising questions about human intent, authorship, and originality. The radical redefinition of authorship found in readymades continues to inform discussions on emerging technologies in art, providing art historians with a framework for navigating contemporary debates on authorship in digital and generated art. Beyond *Fountain* and the readymades, this approach redefined the role of the artist, transforming authorship into an intellectual and legal construct rather than a purely material act (Nodelman 2008). While courts continue to require a demonstrable level of originality, readymades challenged the idea that originality must be tied to an artist's direct craftsmanship (Bailey 2017).

These historical precedents reveal that copyright law evolves in response to artistic innovation, yet it consistently lags behind the conceptual advances of creators and the realities of new media. As AI-generated art and algorithmic practices proliferate, art historians and legal scholars alike must grapple with the persistent ambiguity at the intersection of human intent, technological mediation, and legal recognition. The readymade's legacy suggests that legal frameworks must accommodate forms of authorship rooted in creative decision-making, selection, and curation, not just manual execution. This ongoing tension between legal standards and artistic experimentation underscores the need for flexible, adaptive copyright policies capable of addressing the shifting landscape of art production. In the contemporary context, debates over AI-generated works echo—and, in some cases, amplify—the controversies ignited by Duchamp and his contemporaries. As art continues to test and expand the boundaries of originality and authorship, legal interpretations will need to be guided by both historical insight and a willingness to rethink established categories. Only by engaging critically with these precedents can the field develop copyright regimes that honor both creative autonomy and the collaborative, evolving nature of artistic practice.

4.2 Comparative Legal Perspectives: U.S. Fair Use Versus EU Text and Data Mining

The evolving landscape of digital scholarship and computational creativity has exposed significant differences in how copyright frameworks approach the balance between access, innovation, and protection across global contexts. In particular, the United States and the European Union have developed distinct legal doctrines to address the challenges posed by large-scale digitization, text and data mining, and the reuse of copyrighted materials in research and art. U.S. copyright law centers on the doctrine of fair use, which provides a flexible, case-by-case mechanism for determining when unauthorized uses may nonetheless serve the public interest. In contrast, the European Union has adopted a more prescriptive approach, enacting explicit exceptions for text and data mining (TDM) that are embedded within broader regulatory efforts to harmonize copyright across member states. These divergent strategies reflect not only differing legal traditions but also contrasting cultural attitudes toward originality, authorship, and the social value of information. As courts, institutions, and creators navigate these frameworks, the boundaries of what constitutes lawful and ethical practice continue to evolve, shaping both the opportunities and constraints for digital humanities research and generative art. Before examining specific court cases and recent controversies, it is essential to understand the foundational principles that guide each system and the implications they hold for contemporary scholarship.

In the United States, copyright law is fundamentally anchored in the principle of human authorship, a standard articulated under *17 U.S.C. § 102*. This requirement—that a work originate from human creativity—applies regardless of whether the medium is analog or digital and serves as a cornerstone for claims of ownership and protection. The statutory framework is premised on incentivizing human creators, whose originality and personal input are understood as prerequisites for legal recognition. Recent litigation, such as *Allen v. U.S. Copyright Office*, has exposed the complexities inherent in applying this doctrine to works generated by generative systems; in these cases, courts have consistently ruled that works created solely by automated processes do not meet the threshold of human authorship required for copyright (Kasap 2021; Bridy 2016). This position is reinforced by a persistent emphasis on the "human touch," which mandates that a work must contain independently-conceived and original elements contributed by a human agent—a concept that remains central even as creative tools become more technologically advanced.

Judicial precedents further clarify this requirement for meaningful human intervention in digital contexts. *Bridgeman Art Library v. Corel Corp.* and *Meshwerks, Inc. v. Toyota Motor Sales, U.S.A., Inc.* are particularly illustrative. In *Bridgeman v. Corel*, the court determined that photographic reproductions of public domain artworks, lacking any creative deviation from the originals, were ineligible for copyright protection (Kasap 2021). Meshwerks similarly involved digital wireframe models of Toyota vehicles, produced for marketing purposes; the court concluded that, because these models merely replicated existing objects without introducing creative decisions or originality, they could not be protected under copyright law. The significance of *Meshwerks* is especially pronounced for digital artists and those employing generative tools, as it draws a clear line: technical skill and faithful reproduction, without additional human creativity, are insufficient for copyright eligibility (Burylo 2022). Together, these cases highlight that digital and generative outputs require substantial human input to satisfy the legal standard of originality.

Eligibility for copyright protection in the visual arts depends on meeting two statutory criteria: originality and fixation. The requirement for originality demands independent creation and at least a minimal degree of creativity, while fixation requires that the work be embodied in a tangible medium—be it a digital file or a physical print (*17 U.S.C. § 102(a)*). The decision of the U.S. Supreme Court in *Feist Publications, Inc. v. Rural Telephone Service Co.* clarified that "minimal creativity" is needed, but that works produced through mere mechanical or automated means do not qualify (Yu 2017). This standard poses particular challenges for generative outputs, where the role of the human operator may be limited to entering prompts or reviewing results. In these circumstances, works that lack substantial human creative input are unlikely to meet the originality or fixation requirements for copyright protection (Hedrick 2018).

It is worth emphasizing that, under U.S. law, fixation in a tangible medium—digital or physical—is a necessary but not sufficient condition for copyright. The key consideration remains the demonstration of creative input from a human actor. Where humans use generative tools for ideation but substantially modify, curate, or arrange the resulting materials, courts and the Copyright Office have indicated that the final work may be recognized as a product of human authorship. The U.S. Copyright Office Compendium provides that, where a human "selected or arranged the elements in a sufficiently creative way," the resulting work may be eligible for copyright protection (*Compendium, § 906.1*). Thus, copyright law in the United States accommodates works created with the assistance of generative tools, provided that there is substantial and creative human contribution. Courts have held that protection may extend to human-authored portions—such as prompt design, selection, curation, and postprocessing—while excluding purely automated content. Landmark decisions like *Feist* further underscore that copyright requires not only technical skill but a modicum of creative judgment, such as the arrangement or selection of factual data (Kasap 2021).

In practical terms, the mere application of a filter or reliance on an automated effect is unlikely to suffice; instead, creative decisions regarding composition, structure, and expression remain the touchstone for copyrightable originality (Burylo 2022). This emphasis on human creativity is further reinforced by decisions such as *Mannion v. Coors Brewing Co.*, which articulated that copyright hinges on "distinctive creative choices" reflecting personal authorship. In the context of AI-assisted works, such choices might include not only the initial design of prompts, but also the iterative refinement, curation, or substantial transformation of the generated content—activities now explicitly recognized in the latest U.S. Copyright Office guidelines (Horzyk 2023). These guidelines make clear that, while protection may extend to works involving generative tools, it does not cover parts created without significant human-led decisions.

The case of *Zarya of the Dawn* (2022) (Fig. 4.6) serves as a critical example of the current approach of U.S. copyright law toward AI-assisted creative works and the necessity of human authorship for legal protection. In this matter, artist Kris Kashtanova created an AI-assisted graphic novel, combining images generated using the MidJourney platform with a narrative and overall structure authored by the artist themself. The U.S. Copyright Office initially denied registration for the images themselves, ruling that the visual elements—created predominantly through prompts input into generative software—lacked the requisite degree of human creativity to qualify as original works under *17 U.S.C. § 102*. However, copyright was granted for the human-written text and the narrative arrangement of the comic, recognizing the creative decisions of the artist in organizing, sequencing, and contextualizing the visual and textual content.

The reasoning for granting rights to the text and not the imagery clarified that copyright eligibility rests on "original authorship," requiring discernible creative choices made by a human contributor at some stage in the process. In its decision, the Office reiterated that images produced by automated systems, without significant human modification or intervention, cannot be protected, while components reflecting human storytelling, structure, or editorial vision may still qualify for copyright (Klukosky and Kohel 2024). This outcome highlights the current commitment to preserving the centrality of human input in copyright law and draws a clear boundary between works that are merely facilitated by technology and those where human creativity plays a decisive role.

At the same time, it is important to recognize that the United States represents only one approach to copyright in the age of generative technologies. International disparities are now a central concern for scholars and practitioners, especially as creative production and research increasingly operate across borders. The text and data mining (TDM) exception of the European Union stands in stark contrast to the U.S. model, permitting the use of copyrighted materials for noncommercial research and machine learning training provided that rights holders have not opted out (Kretschmer et al. 2024). This regulatory difference compels institutions and art historians to consider

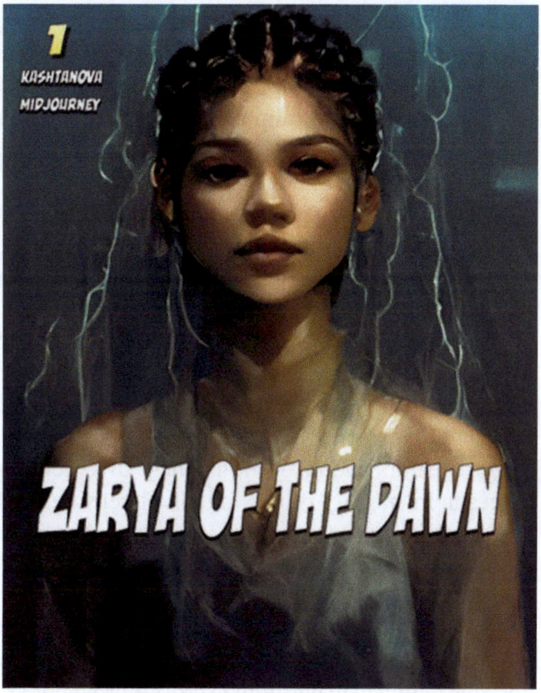

Fig. 4.6 Kris Kashtanova, *Zarya of the Dawn*, Cover, Comic Book, 2022 (CC O, public domain)

the legal frameworks of all relevant jurisdictions when developing or sharing AI-trained models and digital archives. Practical steps, such as embedding robust metadata into digital files, are gaining traction—metadata can signal licensing terms and permissions, providing an automated means for systems to respect legal boundaries and help prevent unauthorized use (Pellegrini 2023).

Within the EU, the TDM exception is rooted in the Directive on Copyright in the Digital Single Market, reflecting a deliberate policy choice to encourage research and innovation while maintaining respect for intellectual property rights. Under this framework, copyrighted works may be used for computational analysis without explicit permission, so long as the purpose is noncommercial and rights holders have not registered an opt-out (Sobel 2021). This approach is fundamentally different from the American reliance on fair use, which offers flexibility but less predictability, especially for automated analysis and large-scale data mining. The clarity of the European model gives researchers greater confidence when building collaborative, cross-border projects, but also places a burden on rights holders to manage their preferences actively.

Ongoing litigation and legislative debate are likely to shape future global norms. High-profile cases, such as *Andersen v. Stability AI*, may clarify whether explicit licenses are required for training data, or whether broad fair-use defenses will prevail in the U.S. context. A ruling that demands explicit licensing could impose new costs and logistical hurdles, potentially limiting access to data and slowing progress in generative fields. Conversely, upholding fair use might undermine creators' economic interests, intensifying concern over uncompensated and unlicensed exploitation of their works (McCann 2021). Scholars have proposed various solutions, including new licensing regimes for training datasets, clearer rules for derivative works, and updates to fair use or fair dealing doctrines that address the unique realities of computational content generation (Elkin-Koren et al. 2023).

The United Kingdom, meanwhile, has charted a middle path. It continues to follow a fair dealing regime rather than the more flexible U.S. fair-use model. Recent debates have suggested a move toward policies akin to the TDM exception of the EU, aiming to provide a predictable legal environment for innovation while ensuring the protection of creator rights (Ploman and Hamilton 2024). This would bring the United Kingdom into closer alignment with European practices, expanding opportunities for research and cross-border data use while establishing limits that preserve the interests of content creators and rights holders.

For creators and institutions, these divergent legal regimes create persistent challenges in managing, protecting, and licensing works globally. Content may be well-protected in one jurisdiction yet exposed to unlicensed use in another, making it difficult to enforce rights or receive fair compensation. As a result, some are turning to technological solutions such as blockchain to track and verify the provenance and licensing of digital assets internationally (Mia et al. 2023). The potential of blockchain to record immutable, time-stamped ownership and usage rights offers a possible pathway to harmonize cross-border copyright management, but current legal systems must adapt before widespread adoption is feasible (Bonnet and Teuteberg 2023).

The complexities of international copyright enforcement underscore the importance of clear, accessible tools and standards for rights management. For example, metadata tagging—long a standard in digital publishing and photography—now serves as a vital tool for communicating usage rights, facilitating automated permissions checks, and providing greater transparency in how digital works may be used or shared (Pellegrini 2023). As these practices become more widespread, they can help bridge the legal gaps between jurisdictions and support both creators and researchers in respecting diverse copyright standards. Looking ahead, policymakers face the dual challenge of supporting rapid innovation in computational technologies while safeguarding the interests and moral rights of creators. This balancing act is evident in the ongoing policy reforms and consultations in the United States, EU, and United Kingdom, each seeking a framework that can evolve with the pace of technological change. Successful reform will require international cooperation, transparency, and adaptive policy mechanisms—ensuring that copyright protections are meaningful, enforceable, and relevant in a global digital landscape. In this way, the future of copyright law will be shaped not just by legal doctrine, but by the practical needs of creators, researchers, and audiences operating in an increasingly interconnected world.

4.3 Dataset Ethics: Scraping, Licensing, and Artist Consent

As legal and policy debates over copyright and ownership swirl around generative models, it becomes essential to understand not only what these systems produce but how they actually function—and why this represents a departure from earlier digital tools. The controversy over dataset ethics, scraping, and artist consent arises largely from the mechanisms by which these new models are trained. Unlike text-based large language models such as ChatGPT, which are primarily trained on text scraped from web sources, digital archives, and open datasets with clear textual structure, generative image models like Stable Diffusion are trained on vast, often uncurated datasets of images and associated metadata (Feuerriegel et al. 2024). The process of collecting and curating such visual data raises unique legal and ethical questions, especially regarding the provenance of training materials and the degree to which artists, photographers, or rights holders have given explicit consent. In this section, the focus shifts from the regulatory landscape to the technical realities underpinning generative systems, comparing their dataset construction and learning approaches to those of previous digital tools like cameras, Photoshop, and even text-based generative models. Understanding these mechanisms is critical for evaluating the legitimacy, transparency, and social impact of contemporary creative technologies.

Generative image models, such as Stable Diffusion, Runway, and DALL-E, employ neural networks trained on extensive image datasets compiled from the Internet and public or private archives. These datasets often contain millions—or even billions—of images, sometimes paired with descriptive text or metadata to facilitate prompt-based generation. Unlike digital imaging software, which relies on direct user input and manipulation, generative systems learn the distribution of visual features, composition, and style across a dataset, ultimately synthesizing new images based on probabilistic models rather than direct reproduction or manual editing (Epstein et al. 2023). Stable Diffusion (Fig. 4.7), for instance, utilizes a diffusion process in which random noise is iteratively transformed into coherent images, guided by the statistical patterns it has learned during training. The end result is a model capable of producing outputs that can convincingly mimic the aesthetics of existing art, photography, or design, even though no specific original is directly copied. This "sampling from learned distributions" fundamentally differs from how a photographer or digital artist works, complicating questions of authorship and originality.

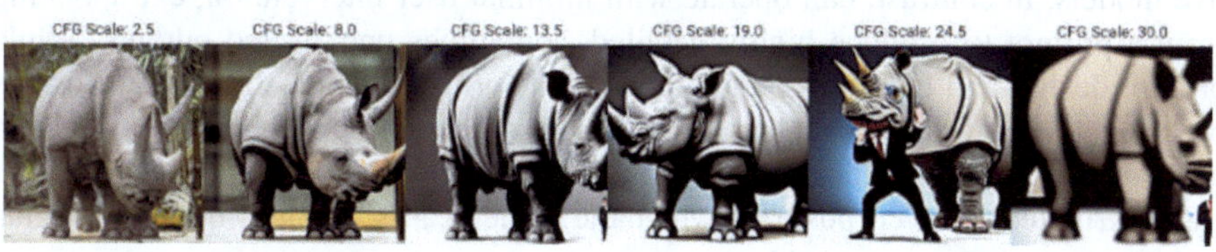

Fig. 4.7 Rhino XY plot with different CFG scale, stable diffusion. December 12, 2022 (CC O, public domain)

The mechanics of diffusion models further set them apart from both conventional tools and earlier forms of machine learning. These models operate by training on pairs of images and noise, gradually learning to "denoise" random inputs into recognizable forms. Over many training iterations, they internalize not just superficial appearances but also deeper stylistic and compositional structures, enabling the system to recombine elements in innovative ways (Moreno et al. 2023). Prompt engineering—the art of crafting textual or multimodal prompts to guide the model—becomes a new form of creative authorship, though the capacity of the system to surprise or diverge from user expectations underscores its relative autonomy. As users submit increasingly specific or imaginative prompts, the model generates visual outputs that reflect both learned conventions and the underlying variability of its training set. This process, while highly flexible, also exposes the model to the risk of unintentionally replicating copyrighted material or artistic styles, since it is trained on works that may not always have been included with explicit permission.

Hybrid models, such as ChatGPT-4o, signal another shift in generative technology, blurring the boundaries between text, image, and even audio synthesis. Unlike purely text-based or image-based systems, hybrid architectures are trained on multimodal datasets—combinations of text, images, sounds, and sometimes video—which enable them to respond to prompts across a range of modalities. For example, 4o can generate a written description from an image, create an image from a textual prompt, or even synthesize new visual or audio outputs based on a complex interplay of inputs. These systems require large, cross-referenced training sets, frequently built by scraping both public web content and curated proprietary archives, further raising concerns about provenance, rights management, and consent. The technical feat is impressive, but the ethical stakes are raised: whereas Photoshop or a traditional language model might be governed by clear lines of input and output, hybrid models can remix, reinterpret, and regenerate content across forms, making the tracing of creative contribution—and responsibility—ever more complex (Feuerriegel et al. 2024).

A crucial distinction between earlier creative tools and generative systems is the locus of agency and authorship. Traditional digital tools, such as cameras and Photoshop (Fig. 4.8), function primarily as extensions of the user's intent, requiring direct creative action at every stage. The photographer selects the subject, frames the shot, and determines exposure; the digital artist manipulates, edits, and assembles images based on aesthetic and conceptual decisions (Aaland 2006; Kelby 2020). Generative models, in contrast, can operate with minimal user intervention, extrapolating from a prompt to produce highly detailed, sometimes unexpected outputs. While prompt design and curation remain significant forms of input, the heavy lifting is performed by algorithms that learn from—and sometimes appropriate—the creative labor of many others. This shift foregrounds the importance of dataset ethics: who has contributed to the corpus from which the model learns, and how have their rights and intentions been respected?

The process of dataset construction for generative models is itself a source of ongoing controversy and litigation. Large image datasets, such as LAION-5B, are often compiled by web scraping and may include images from social media,

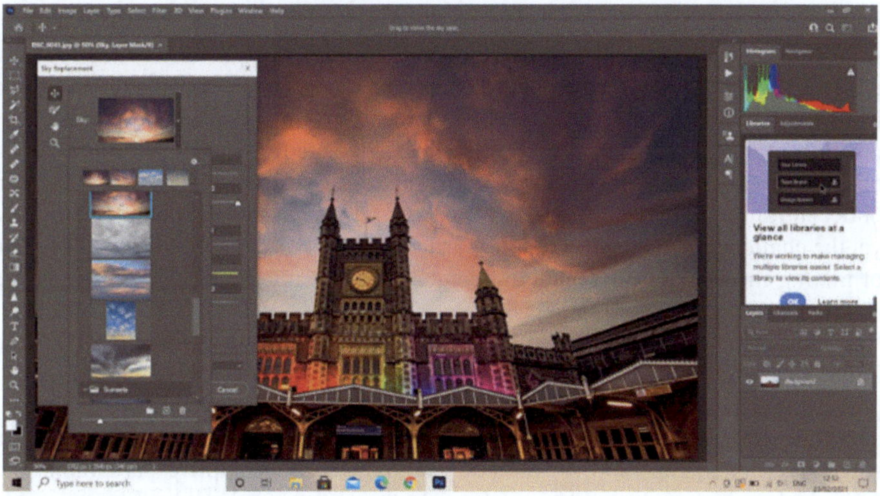

Fig. 4.8 Adobe Photoshop, 2021 (CC O, public domain)

stock photo sites, museum archives, and artist portfolios—sometimes with explicit licensing, but often without the knowledge or consent of creators. As a result, models may absorb stylistic signatures, watermark patterns, or even fragments of identifiable works, raising difficult questions about copyright infringement, plagiarism, and fair compensation (Kretschmer et al. 2024; Pellegrini 2023). Legal battles, such as those concerning Stability AI and Getty Images, highlight the lack of consensus about whether the use of such material constitutes transformative fair use, infringement, or a new species of derivative work. In this contested landscape, some institutions and artists have begun to develop opt-out protocols or technical solutions for flagging or restricting the inclusion of their work in future datasets.

Ethical concerns are not limited to questions of licensing or compensation; they also include the broader issue of artistic consent. The majority of creators whose works populate training datasets have not been asked whether they wish to participate in the development of generative tools. This absence of consent undermines trust and can alienate artists, particularly when outputs closely mimic their personal style or reproduce elements of their work in ways they never intended. Emerging technical and policy responses include embedding robust metadata in digital files, leveraging digital watermarks, and developing industry-wide registries for works that should not be used in dataset construction (Pellegrini 2023). These tools, while promising, require widespread adoption and legal recognition to be truly effective, suggesting that the resolution of dataset ethics will require both technological and institutional cooperation.

The difference between generative models and conventional software is also apparent in how they handle attribution and provenance. Photoshop preserves a history of edits in project files; a camera embeds metadata about capture conditions;

both rely on the direct manipulation of the user and leave a clear trail of authorship. Generative systems, by contrast, operate through opaque, distributed learning processes: once trained, the model can produce outputs that are statistically informed by the entire dataset, but not directly attributable to any individual image or artist. This opacity complicates efforts to trace influences, give credit, or resolve disputes about originality. Legal scholars and technologists alike are exploring the use of blockchain or decentralized ledgers to record training data provenance and track model outputs, yet the challenge remains formidable, particularly as hybrid models become capable of mixing modalities and generating content from composite or abstracted sources (Bonnet and Teuteberg 2023).

Finally, the rapid evolution of hybrid and multimodal models like ChatGPT-4o introduces a new set of ethical and practical dilemmas. These systems can ingest, process, and generate across text, image, audio, and even video, rendering traditional copyright categories and authorship models increasingly obsolete. For instance, a single prompt might yield a synthetic photograph, a descriptive paragraph, and a musical score—each constructed from learned patterns that blend innumerable sources. This versatility expands creative possibilities but also exacerbates the challenges of attribution, licensing, and user consent. As these systems become more sophisticated, it will be imperative for policymakers, scholars, and creators to work collaboratively in developing transparent frameworks for dataset construction, output attribution, and ethical deployment.

As such, the transition from traditional tools like Photoshop and cameras to generative and hybrid models represents a seismic shift in how creative works are produced, valued, and regulated. The fundamental difference lies not only in the technologies themselves, but in the dynamics of authorship, consent, and ethical stewardship they introduce. As the field moves forward, careful attention to dataset ethics, licensing, and artist consent will be necessary to ensure that generative technologies support, rather than undermine, the rights and contributions of human creators. Ongoing legal debates, technological innovation, and institutional leadership will together shape a future where new forms of creative collaboration and cultural production can thrive—without sacrificing the trust, equity, and integrity that define the arts.

4.4 Protecting Intellectual Property: Strategies for Museums and Researchers

Museums, libraries, and archives occupy a unique position as stewards of cultural heritage and as institutions navigating the shifting landscape of copyright, digital reproduction, and generative tools. The need to balance accessibility with protection has never been more urgent: on one hand, there is a clear mandate to make collections available for research, education, and innovation; on the other, there is a growing imperative to respect the rights and wishes of artists, donors, and the public (Mia et al. 2023). Institutions are increasingly experimenting with layered or tiered access—granting broader use for scholarly purposes while limiting commercial exploitation—through open-access frameworks and negotiated licenses. Some, such as the Rijksmuseum, have pioneered controlled digital releases, where high-resolution images are provided for educational and scholarly use but subject to digital watermarks or metadata restrictions to deter unauthorized reuse (Jaillant et al. 2025). These policies not only preserve institutional trust but also support a culture of consent, signaling to users and creators alike that rights are being taken seriously in the digital age. The broader adoption of such approaches will shape the field's reputation, public engagement, and legal exposure for decades to come.

For art historians, an informed engagement with copyright law is now essential, especially as litigation intensifies around the use of digital content for generative model training. Cases like *Andersen v. Stability AI* have foregrounded the dilemma of unlicensed content scraping, where artists allege infringement when their works appear in training datasets without consent (Samuelson 2023a, b). Researchers and authors using images or datasets sourced from online repositories must carefully assess whether permissions are needed, particularly if their work will be used in future model training, commercial publication, or mass distribution. An additional challenge lies in the increasing use of "opt-out" mechanisms, whereby artists and rights holders proactively indicate their preference to exclude works from data harvesting. Museums and academic publishers, in turn, must establish clear guidelines to communicate how such preferences are honored in their digital policies and in licensing agreements for their online materials (Jaillant et al. 2025; Lucchi 2023).

The backbone of many generative systems is the vast dataset—often built with little transparency about its provenance, licensing, or the inclusion of copyrighted works. This reliance on scraped or aggregated digital archives has sparked controversy and led to calls for more robust legal standards and documentation practices (Lucchi 2023). Some museums have started developing explicit digital content policies, specifying under what terms their collections may be used for computational training or creative reuse. Others are investing in digital watermarking and metadata infrastructure to make it easier for automated systems to recognize, respect, and enforce copyright restrictions (Pellegrini 2023). For researchers, this means an added layer of due diligence: when preparing datasets for scholarly analysis or machine learning, careful attention must be paid to the licensing status of each image or text, with explicit tracking of permissions, attributions, and any relevant "no scrape" or "no AI use" directives.

The question of fair use continues to be debated in the United States, where courts are only beginning to address whether the use of copyrighted images in training datasets is transformative or simply derivative. Proponents of fair use argue that using works for the purposes of training a model—especially in noncommercial, research-driven contexts—may be permissible, but this interpretation remains unsettled in the absence of definitive legal rulings (Torrance and Tomlinson 2023). Recent scholarship has highlighted the risks of overreliance on fair use, noting that models sometimes replicate distinctive stylistic elements or even generate close copies of training images, potentially crossing the line into infringement (Samuelson 2023a, b). In response, some technology firms and museums have begun negotiating blanket licensing agreements for training datasets, creating revenue streams for rights holders while providing legal clarity for model developers. This trend toward licensing signals a move toward more predictable, regulated data use in the cultural heritage sector, though smaller institutions may face resource constraints in following suit.

Internationally, derivative work doctrines are of particular importance in the context of AI-assisted creativity. Under *17 U.S.C. § 101*, a derivative work is defined as one that is based on or transforms existing content, thus extending copyright protection to new, original contributions layered atop preexisting material. In practical terms, when a human modifies, collages, or meaningfully alters the output of a generative model, this adaptation may itself be copyrightable, provided it meets the originality threshold (Gervais 2022). Recent research in the EU has echoed these concerns, noting that derivative works produced in collaboration with machine-generated content can qualify for protection so long as human authorship is substantial and creative (Kretschmer et al. 2024). For art historians and curators, this means that the act of curating, arranging, or editorializing model-generated material is not only intellectually significant but legally meaningful.

Defining what constitutes originality in derivative works has always been a challenge, but it is further complicated in the age of generative models. The U.S. Supreme Court's decision in *Feist Publications, Inc. v. Rural Telephone Service Co.* remains the touchstone, requiring "a minimal degree of creativity" to distinguish new works from mechanical reproductions (Wagh et al. 2023). In AI-assisted research, this might involve the selection of outputs, the creative modification of generated content, or the combination of model outputs with new material to convey a distinct message or viewpoint. The originality standard is a bulwark against the proliferation of unmodified, algorithmically produced outputs that lack a human creative stamp. Museums and researchers are thus encouraged to document their creative interventions and decisions, both to support copyright claims and to clarify intellectual lineage in their outputs.

Transparency and documentation are critical as museums and researchers chart a path through the evolving landscape of copyright and generative tools. Leading institutions are implementing policies that require rigorous record-keeping of dataset sources, explicit permissions, and detailed logs of human modification and curation. Recent research advocates for blockchain-based provenance tracking as a means of recording the usage rights, creation dates, and chain of custody for digital artworks and dataset elements (Bonnet and Teuteberg 2023). This technology, while not yet universally adopted, promises to make the flow of cultural content more visible, traceable, and legally defensible. By documenting the creative process at every stage—from data acquisition to publication—institutions can strengthen both their legal position and their credibility with artists and stakeholders.

A further strategic consideration involves the development of collaborative frameworks with creators and rights holders. Museums are increasingly working with living artists, estates, and donor communities to craft policies that honor legacy, respect intent, and provide avenues for input into how works are presented, licensed, or repurposed in new media contexts (Pellegrini 2023). Some museums now offer opt-in or opt-out systems, allowing artists to dictate whether and how their works are included in digital or generative datasets. These frameworks may be supported by community advisory boards or digital stewardship committees, which can help balance institutional goals with individual and collective rights. By foregrounding dialogue and cocreation, museums and researchers can foster relationships of trust, shared authority, and ethical stewardship in the digital realm.

Emerging scholarship also points to the growing use of standardized metadata and DRM tools. These systems allow for the automatic signaling of permissions, restrictions, and licensing terms to both human users and generative models. For example, the adoption of Creative Commons licenses, machine-readable metadata, and digital watermarking is enabling institutions to communicate usage terms at scale (Pellegrini 2023). At the same time, policy researchers caution that DRM must not become overly restrictive, lest it undermine access and scholarly innovation. The challenge lies in building interoperable, adaptable frameworks that are sensitive to context, technology, and the needs of multiple user groups.

Finally, as the debate continues to evolve, museum professionals and art historians are increasingly called upon to participate in policy formation at both institutional and governmental levels. Many are now engaging with international working groups, consortia, and standard-setting bodies to advocate for balanced frameworks that reflect the unique needs of the cultural heritage sector. Recent initiatives have included efforts to harmonize metadata standards across museums and archives, to share best practices in licensing and attribution, and to articulate principles of responsible innovation in the use of generative tools (Bonnet and Teuteberg 2023; Kretschmer et al. 2024). Through these collaborative efforts, museums and researchers can help shape the future of copyright, ensuring that the cultural record remains both vibrant and protected in an age of rapid technological change.

Ergo, protecting intellectual property in the digital age requires an ongoing commitment to flexibility, transparency, and collaboration among museums, researchers, artists, and policymakers. The complexities of generative models, open-access expectations, and evolving copyright standards demand that institutions adopt proactive strategies for consent, licensing, provenance, and documentation—approaches that must be responsive to both legal requirements and ethical imperatives. As the cultural sector navigates these shifting currents, the most resilient museums and research communities will be those that embrace adaptive governance, foster sustained dialogue with creators and publics, and invest in robust technological infrastructure for rights management and tracking. Importantly, this is not simply a matter of compliance; it is a chance to model leadership, trust, and creativity in shaping the next chapter of digital stewardship. The future will belong to institutions that can balance the need for open, equitable access to cultural heritage with the equally vital necessity of honoring the agency and contributions of artists, rights holders, and source communities. Art historians and cultural professionals, by foregrounding ethical best practices and remaining vigilant to new legal developments, can help ensure that the circulation, transformation, and creation of digital art continue to serve both the public good and the integrity of cultural heritage. In this way, the strategies developed today will not only mitigate risk but also lay the groundwork for sustainable, innovative, and responsible practices in the decades ahead. The challenge, and the opportunity, is to lead the conversation—proactively shaping policy and practice to safeguard the future of artistic creativity and historical inquiry.

4.5 Best Practices for Art Historians Working with AI

The landscape for copyright and AI-generated content has shifted dramatically with the 2025 addendum from the U.S. Copyright Office, which clarifies the eligibility of works produced with intelligent systems (Table 4.1). For the first time, the Office has outlined a framework in which copyright protection can extend to AI-generated content—so long as there is a demonstrable element of human authorship. The guidance makes clear that content created by machines is not, by default, excluded from protection, provided that the final output reflects direct human input and creative control that goes beyond the mere formulation of prompts or commands (U.S. Copyright Office 2025). This development signals a practical recognition that generative tools are now woven into the fabric of creative practice and scholarship, and that their outputs, when shaped by human agency, can meet the originality standard necessary for copyright. For art historians and museum professionals, this means that thoughtful, intentional engagement with these systems is not only permissible but, in some cases, may yield works that are protected under current law.

The new Copyright Office guidance addresses long-standing uncertainties about authorship and originality in the context of generative models like Midjourney, Stable Diffusion, and ChatGPT-4o. The report emphasizes that copyrightable works must bear the imprint of "human creativity"—requiring, for example, substantial editorial decisions, unique selection or arrangement of AI outputs, or interpretive transformations that transcend the output of the model alone. In practical terms, an image automatically generated by a diffusion model is not sufficient to claim authorship; however, when an art historian modifies, curates, or creatively arranges such content, copyright protection may be conferred on the resulting composite (Mathur 2023). This interpretation is a significant shift from earlier, more restrictive stances, reflecting the increasing acceptance of hybrid workflows in art history and related fields.

Importantly, the 2025 report acknowledges that the distinction between machine and human authorship will continue to evolve as generative technologies become more sophisticated. Art historians and researchers are advised to document the stages at which creative decisions are made, highlighting the unique contributions of human agency in selecting, interpreting, and refining AI-generated content. For instance, projects that combine outputs from multiple models or integrate AI-generated visual material with traditional research commentary are more likely to meet the threshold for protection, provided the human intervention is clear and meaningful (U.S. Copyright Office 2025). This documentation is not only good practice for asserting intellectual property rights but also serves the broader goal of transparency in scholarly communication. The report further recommends that the scholarly community

Table 4.1 Landmark legal precedents shaping copyright law for art

Case name and year	Central issue	Significance for copyright development
Burrow-Giles Lithographic Co. v. Sarony (1884)	Whether photography constitutes authorship and is eligible for copyright protection	Established that photographs can reflect original authorship and are copyrightable if they embody the creative choices of the artist (Allen 1986)
Dürer's Imperial Privilege (ca. 1512–1520)	Protection of artist's engravings from unauthorized copying	Early legal recognition of individual artist ownership and proto-copyright, leading to artist monograms and privileges (Cooper 2021; Mulevičiūtė 2018)
Venetian Court Ruling: Dürer v. Raimondi (ca. 1511–1520)	Whether Marcantonio Raimondi could reproduce Dürer's engravings	Allowed reproduction of compositions but forbade copying Dürer's monogram, signaling early differentiation between design and authorship (Karapapa 2022)
Bridgeman Art Library v. Corel Corp. (1999)	Whether photographic reproductions of public domain artworks are copyrightable	Ruled that exact reproductions lacking creative deviation are not copyrightable, clarifying that originality is essential for digital and analog works (Kasap 2021)
Meshwerks, Inc. v. Toyota Motor Sales, U.S.A., Inc. (2008)	Whether digital wireframe models of cars, faithfully representing originals, are copyrightable	Affirmed that technical skill alone is not enough for copyright; human originality and creative input are required (Burylo 2022)
Feist Publications, Inc. v. Rural Telephone Service Co. (1991)	Whether the selection and arrangement of factual data meets the threshold for copyright protection	Confirmed that a minimal degree of creativity is required, reinforcing the originality standard in U.S. copyright (Yu 2017)
Thaler v. Perlmutter (2022)	Whether a computer-generated image lacking human authorship is eligible for copyright	Ruled that works must be created by a human to be copyrightable, excluding fully autonomous outputs from protection (Mathur 2023)
Allen v. U.S. Copyright Office (2024)	Whether prompt engineering and AI-assisted art are sufficient for copyright	Upheld the requirement for direct human creativity; prompt engineering alone is not enough for copyright eligibility (Brittain 2024)

(continued)

Table 4.1 (continued)

Case name and year	Central issue	Significance for copyright development
Zarya of the Dawn (2022)	Whether AI-generated images with human-authored narrative and arrangement can be copyrighted	Copyright was granted for human elements (text, arrangement) but denied for AI-generated imagery, highlighting the threshold of "original authorship" (Klukosky and Kohel 2024)
Andersen et al. v. Stability AI Ltd. (Ongoing)	Whether use of copyrighted materials in AI training datasets constitutes infringement or fair use	Expected to clarify standards for data use in generative model training and influence global licensing and fair-use debates (Spica 2024)

remains vigilant in assessing the technological evolution of these tools. As AI models advance, they may allow for greater degrees of human control, enabling new modes of collaboration between the user and the system. It is conceivable that, as models become more interactive or offer real-time cocreation, the line between prompt and product will blur, further complicating the criteria for authorship (Majumdar et al. 2023). In this environment, best practices will require art historians to continually assess the degree of creative input and maintain thorough records of their editorial and curatorial processes.

Specifically, the report advises implementing standardized templates or digital logs to capture every substantive human intervention—whether it involves curating model outputs, revising AI-generated text, or assembling composite works from multiple generative sources. By distinguishing between the raw outputs of an algorithm and the editorial strategies employed by a researcher, scholars can better articulate how meaning, selection, and originality are infused into the creative process. This has direct implications for peer review, publication, and the defense of rights in cases of infringement or contestation. The report notes that courts and copyright offices are likely to look for evidence of human judgment—such as notes, drafts, or recorded prompts—when evaluating claims of originality in AI-assisted works. It further suggests that as collaborative tools enable more dialogic forms of cocreation (e.g., interactive installations or iterative image editing in response to real-time input), institutions may need to update authorship policies, consent forms, and attribution standards. Ultimately, such vigilance and record-keeping will not only clarify the allocation of rights but will also strengthen the legitimacy of scholarly contributions in an era of increasingly hybrid creativity. As the landscape of generative art continues to shift, these practices will empower art historians to advocate for their agency, assert their intellectual property, and model transparency in both research and public engagement.

Adapting to these new realities calls for more than just compliance with evolving legal frameworks. Art historians must embrace an active role in shaping ethical standards, advocating for mechanisms such as opt-in and opt-out protocols for dataset use, and developing community-driven guidelines for the responsible deployment of generative tools. Recent scholarship has highlighted the potential for Creative Commons-style licensing regimes that empower artists and rights holders while facilitating innovation and scholarly use (Majumdar et al. 2023). By participating in these conversations, art historians help ensure that the rights and interests of creators are respected as the boundaries of authorship and originality continue to expand. As such, collaboration remains central to meeting the challenges and opportunities presented by generative media. Art historians should foster partnerships with technologists, legal scholars, and cultural heritage professionals to articulate best practices for the use, attribution, and curation of AI-assisted works. Such collaborations are essential in developing standards for metadata, provenance, and attribution that keep pace with rapid technical change (Gervais 2022). The ability to work across disciplinary boundaries also strengthens advocacy efforts for fair and effective copyright policy that is responsive to the evolving needs of the scholarly and creative communities.

Crucially, the 2025 Copyright Office report advises a case-by-case approach to assessing the copyrightability of AI-assisted works. This reflects the reality that each project may involve different levels of human involvement, creative decision-making, and technological mediation. Art historians, therefore, are encouraged to approach each new work with an evaluative framework that takes into account the originality, transformation, and context of its creation (U.S. Copyright Office 2025). This approach not only aligns with legal standards but also upholds the tradition of rigorous historical and critical analysis. Therefore, as automated content creation platforms become the norm, the art historical field must adapt its research methodologies, teaching practices, and ethical commitments. There is an urgent need for curricula and professional development programs that educate scholars on intellectual property law, dataset ethics, and the practicalities of working with generative models. In doing so, the discipline can continue to provide leadership in debates over originality, attribution, and the preservation of cultural memory in an era of digital abundance (Samuelson 2023a, b). Ensuring that students and emerging scholars are equipped to navigate these complexities is an investment in the long-term relevance and integrity of the field.

Looking ahead, the proliferation of generative content is unlikely to reverse course. Rather than resisting these technologies, the field is well served by integrating them thoughtfully—updating professional norms, research protocols, and public engagement strategies to reflect a landscape where hybrid creative practice is standard. This means not only accepting but embracing generative content as a regular feature of scholarship, curation, and exhibition, provided that the foundational values of transparency, attribution, and respect for creator rights remain paramount (Elkin-Koren et al. 2023). The evolving legal and ethical frameworks will require flexibility, but also a sustained commitment to the principles that have long defined art history as a discipline.

Reflecting on the chapter's analysis, it is clear that the legal and ethical terrain surrounding copyright and generative technologies in art history is both dynamic and increasingly consequential. The discussion has highlighted how long-standing debates over authorship, originality, and intellectual property have been reanimated and redefined by the rise of algorithmic tools and digital practices. The 2025 U.S. Copyright Office guidance—affirming that AI-generated works may be protected if meaningful human creativity is involved—signals a pivotal moment, bridging historical precedents such as the readymade and conceptual art with the complexities of computational creativity. Legal frameworks are catching up to new realities, but they require active interpretation and adaptation by practitioners who understand both the nuances of artistic production and the technological infrastructures that now shape research and curation. Museums, researchers, and artists must negotiate an evolving ecosystem in which rights, permissions, and documentation are as vital as innovation itself.

The key takeaways emphasize that informed, proactive engagement is essential at every level of practice. Art historians and museum professionals are encouraged to develop rigorous strategies for documenting creative input, curating collaborative workflows, and communicating clearly with both rights holders and the public. Best practices now include maintaining detailed records of human interventions in AI-assisted work, using standardized templates for consent and attribution, and participating in the design of institutional policies that reflect emerging legal and ethical standards. Collaborative engagement across legal, technical, and curatorial domains has become a professional necessity, ensuring that decisions around copyright are grounded in both legal expertise and disciplinary values. The field must also invest in continuous professional development, remaining agile as both legislation and technology evolve. Transparency and accountability are not merely compliance measures; they are foundational to building trust and authority in a rapidly changing digital landscape. By foregrounding these practices, art historians help shape the standards by which creativity, stewardship, and public good will be defined.

Looking to the future, the chapter urges the field to remain vigilant, flexible, and forward-thinking in the stewardship of visual culture. New developments in AI, machine learning, and digital collaboration will continue to challenge established boundaries and prompt fresh debates about what constitutes authorship, originality, and value. The discipline's ongoing engagement with policymakers, legal scholars, and technical experts will be crucial in shaping copyright law that serves both creators and the public interest. Institutions must advocate for fair, adaptable policies that balance openness with protection, and researchers must model ethical, well-documented approaches to the use of generative tools. As digital and algorithmic systems grow ever more sophisticated, art history stands at the threshold of unprecedented creative and scholarly possibilities—possibilities that will be fully realized only through a commitment to rigor, equity, and ethical innovation. The coming years will demand not only legal and technical literacy but also courage and imagination, as the field reimagines its relationship to creativity, collaboration, and cultural stewardship.

References

Aaland M (2006) Photoshop elements 3 solutions: the art of digital photography. Wiley
Abdikhakimov I (2023) Unraveling the copyright conundrum: exploring AI-generated content and its implications for intellectual property rights. In: International conference on legal sciences, vol 1, no 5, pp 18–32
Allen W (1986) Legal tests of photography-as-art: Sarony and others. Hist Photogr 10(3):221–228
Bailey B (2017) Before, during, and beyond the Brillo box: the impact of pop on the 1964 edition of Duchamp's readymades. Vis Resour 34(4):347–363
Barron A (2020) Copyright law and the claims of art. SSRN Electron J. https://doi.org/10.2139/ssrn.346361
Bonnet S, Teuteberg F (2023) Impact of blockchain and distributed ledger technology for the management of the intellectual property life cycle: a multiple case study analysis. Comput Ind 144:103789
Bridy A (2016) The evolution of authorship: work made by code. C J Law Arts 39:395–401. https://doi.org/10.7916/D8CV4J6W
Brittain B (2024) Artist sues after US rejects copyright for AI-generated image. Reuters, 26 Sept. Retrieved from: https://www.reuters.com/legal/litigation/artist-sues-after-us-rejects-copyright-ai-generated-image-2024-09-26/
Brough JB (1997) Image and artistic value
Burke S (2018) Copyright and conceptual art. In: Non-conventional copyright. Edward Elgar Publishing, pp 44–61
Burylo Y (2022) AI generated works and copyright protection. Entrep Econ Law 3:7–13
Cooper E (2021) Art and modern copyright: the contested image. Cambridge University Press, p 47
Cousijn M (2016) Marcel Duchamp and the art of exhibition making. RELIEF-Rev Électronique Littérature Française 10(2):143–149
Elkin-Koren N, Hacohen U, Livni R, Moran S (2023) Can copyright be reduced to privacy? arXiv, abs/2305.14822. https://doi.org/10.48550/arXiv.2305.14822
Epstein Z, Hertzmann A, Investigators of Human Creativity, Akten M, Farid H, Fjeld J, Smith A (2023) Art and the science of generative AI. Science 380(6650):1110–1111
Feuerriegel S, Hartmann J, Janiesch C, Zschech P (2024) Generative AI. Bus Inf Syst Eng 66(1):111–126
Gervais D (2022) AI derivatives: the application to the derivative work right to literary and artistic productions of AI machines. SSRN Electron J. https://doi.org/10.2139/ssrn.4022665
Goldsmith S (1983) The readymades of Marcel Duchamp: the ambiguities of aesthetic revolution. J Aesthet Art Criticism 42(2):197
Gordon C (2023) ChatGPT is the fastest growing app in the history of web applications. Forbes, 2 Feb. Retrieved from: https://www.forbes.com/sites/cindygordon/2023/02/02/chatgpt-is-the-fastest-growing-ap-in-the-history-of-web-applications/
Hanna A, Khan M (2023) The subjects and stages of AI dataset development: A framework for dataset accountability. Ohio State Technology Law Journal. Lombardo V (2010). Duchamp's Audience
Hedrick SF (2018) I think, therefore I create: claiming copyright in the outputs of algorithms. NYU J Intellect Prop Entertain Law 8:324
Horzyk A (2023) How AI affects our understanding of musical works that should be protected by copyright. In: 2023 international joint conference on neural networks (IJCNN), pp 1–8. https://doi.org/10.1109/IJCNN54540.2023.10191524
Housefield J (2002) Marcel Duchamp's art and the geography of modern Paris. Geographical Review, 92(4): 477–502
Jaillant L, Warwick C, Gooding P, Aske K, Layne-Worthey G, Downie JS (2025) Navigating artificial intelligence for cultural heritage organisations
Karapapa S (2022) Art and modern copyright: the contested image. J Legal Hist 43:116–117

Kasap A (2021) Copyright and creative artificial intelligence (AI) systems: a twenty-first century approach to authorship of AI-generated works in the United States. Wake For Intellect Prop Law J 19:335

Kelby S (2020) The digital photography book, vol 1. Rocky Nook, Inc.

Klukosky FP, Kohel MD (2024) An update on the state of play with generative artificial intelligence and intellectual property issues. Intellect Prop Litig 34(1):10–17

Krages B (2012) Photography: the art of composition. Simon and Schuster

Kretschmer M, Margoni T, Oruç P (2024) Copyright law and the lifecycle of machine learning models. IIC-Int Rev Intellect Prop Compet Law 55(1):110–138

Lucchi N (2023) ChatGPT: a case study on copyright challenges for generative artificial intelligence systems. Eur J Risk Regul. https://doi.org/10.1017/err.2023.59

Majumdar S, Paul S, Paul D, Bandyopadhyay A, Chattopadhyay S, Das PP, Majumder P (2023) Generative AI for software metadata: overview of the information retrieval in software engineering track at fire 2023. arXiv preprint arXiv:2311.03374

Mathur A (2023) Case review: Thaler v. Perlmutter (2023). Center for Art Law. https://itsartlaw.org/2023/12/11/case-summary-and-review-thaler-v-perlmutter/

McCann S (2021) Copyright throughout a creative AI pipeline. SSRN Electron J. https://doi.org/10.2139/ssrn.3893972

Mia M, Wessels J, Adam S (2023) The use of Blockchain technology to improve transfer-pricing compliance and administration in South Africa. In: ICABR conference. Springer Nature Switzerland, pp 357–378

Moreno H, Gómez A, Altares-López S, Ribeiro A, Andújar D (2023) Analysis of stable diffusion-derived fake weeds performance for training convolutional neural networks. Comput Electron Agric 214:108324

Mulevičiūtė J (2018) To whom does art belong? On the origins of copyright law in Lithuania. Menotyra 25(4)

Nodelman S (2008) Hanging the work of art: love and death in the Duchampian readymades. Interstices J Arch Relat Arts 3(1):41–44

Pelcher B (2023) "We Need Only Take Scissors", Dada and/as Photographic Image. In Dada's Subject and Structure: Performing Ideology Poorly. Springer International Publishing: Cham, pp 107–157

Pellegrini T (2023) Digital rights management–technologies, application areas, and governance. In: Handbook of media and communication economics: a European perspective. Springer Fachmedien Wiesbaden, pp 1–17

Ploman EW, Hamilton LC (2024) Copyright: intellectual property in the information age. Taylor & Francis

Price D, Wells L (2021) Thinking about photography: debates, historically and now. In: Photography. Routledge, pp 11–82

Rexer R (2019) Baudelaire's bodies, or redressing the wrongs of nude photography. Word & Image 35(2):126–140

Risi S, Togelius J (2020) Increasing generality in machine learning through procedural content generation. Nat Mach Intell 2(8):428–436

Said ZK (2015) Copyright's illogical exclusion of conceptual art. C J Law Arts 39:335–354

Samuelson P (2023a) Ongoing lawsuits could affect everyone who uses generative AI. Science 381:6654

Samuelson P (2023b) Generative AI meets copyright. Science 381:158–161. https://doi.org/10.1126/science.adi0656

Seamon R (2001) The conceptual dimension in art and the modern theory of artistic value. The Journal of aesthetics and art criticism. 59(2): 139–151

Sobel B (2021) A taxonomy of training data. Artificial intelligence and intellectual property. https://doi.org/10.1093/oso/9780198870944.003.0011

Spica E (2024) Public interest, the true soul: copyright's fair use doctrine and the use of copyrighted works to train generative AI tools. Tex Intellect Prop Law J 33(1)

Torrance A, Tomlinson B (2023) Training is everything: artificial intelligence, copyright, and fair training. ArXiv, abs/2305.03720. https://doi.org/10.48550/arXiv.2305.03720

U.S. Copyright Office (2025) Copyright and artificial intelligence, part 2: Copyrightability. U.S. Copyright Office. https://www.copyright.gov/ai

Vella Rago M (2015) Marcel Duchamp, art and the ethical signifi cance of a renewed relationship with the object

Wagh S, Peerzada D, Rote P (2023) AI and copyright. Uijin Jishu/J Propuls Technol. https://doi org/1052783/tjjptv44i32053

Yu R (2017) The machine author: what level of copyright protection is appropriate for fully independent computer-generated works? Univ Pa Law Rev 165:1245

Zhitomirsky-Geffet M, Kizhner I, Minster S (2023) What do they make us see, a comparative study of cultural bias in online databases of two large museums, Journal of Documentation, 79(2): 320–340

Chapter 5
Administrative Leadership and Strategic Management

Abstract This section explores the implications of machine-based technologies for administrative leadership and strategic management within art history departments and cultural institutions. The chapter opens by examining the evolving responsibilities of the art historian as administrator, tracing the shift from traditional, intuition-driven leadership to roles increasingly defined by data stewardship, technological literacy, and collaborative decision-making. It investigates how algorithmic tools and automated platforms can streamline curriculum planning, program assessment, and resource allocation, equipping leaders with actionable insights to enhance institutional effectiveness. Attention is given to the deployment of data-driven analytics for institutional excellence, illustrating how dashboards and predictive models inform everything from enrollment forecasting to audience development and staffing decisions. The discussion critically addresses the ethical imperatives of privacy and compliance, reviewing best practices for responsible data governance, consent, and regulatory adherence in both academic and museum contexts.

5.1 The Evolving Role of the Art Historian as Administrator

Art history departments face a dual challenge: on one hand, they must manage an increasing volume of administrative responsibilities, and on the other, they must maintain strategic leadership capacities to support faculty development, sustain institutional relevance, and strengthen community connections. These administrative duties—such as scheduling, program assessments, and curriculum planning—are not only labor-intensive but also fiscally burdensome, consuming valuable time that might otherwise be devoted to pedagogical advancement or scholarly mentorship (Mohan 2023). Studies indicate that, in some cases, administrators spend nearly an hour per day on routine tasks, diverting their attention away from strategic initiatives and critical activities that further departmental long-term vitality (Martin et al. 2024).

J. Hutson, *Art History in the Age of Artificial Intelligence*, Springer Series on Cultural Computing, https://doi.org/10.1007/978-3-032-02920-1_5

Such operational imperatives, while necessary for institutional oversight, risk overshadowing the leadership roles that ensure cohesive faculty support, robust student engagement, and meaningful alignment with institutional values (Heck et al. 2000).

The most effective administrators are those who balance these dual demands—fulfilling basic departmental obligations while simultaneously fostering intellectual innovation, shaping departmental identity, and advocating for needed resources and policies that enable sustainable growth. Striking this balance requires a recalibration of priorities and the adoption of forward-looking strategies that allow art history leaders to address both operational pressures and leadership responsibilities in a more integrated manner. Consequently, identifying tools that can streamline routine tasks without compromising departmental integrity or the quality of academic offerings has become an urgent priority (Burden et al. 2012). In light of this urgency, administrators are increasingly turning to new technologies, including the tools discussed so far, in search of approaches that enhance both efficiency and strategic vision.

New tools like LLMs offer a suite of capabilities—ranging from data analysis and natural language processing to automated reporting and advanced trend forecasting—that hold the potential to reconfigure the administrative landscape in art history departments. Through expediting tasks such as curricular mapping, market analyses, communication flows, and evaluation protocols, generativebled tools can liberate administrator time and energy for the mentoring, advocacy, and diplomatic functions that strengthen departmental resilience (Herd et al. 2023). While the promise of such tools is considerable, their implementation is not without limitations and risks, particularly in terms of data privacy, ethical considerations, and compliance with regulatory frameworks like the Family Educational Rights and Privacy Act (FERPA). Indeed, the legal and ethical implications of incorporating these technologies remain pressing concerns that must be thoughtfully addressed, ensuring that deployments respect the rights and identities of all stakeholders, including underrepresented groups.

The role of these new computational tools in academic administration extends beyond automating routine tasks; it serves as an essential tool for optimizing core administrative functions such as professional communication, curriculum development, assessment, and institutional reporting. NLP tools facilitate efficient and context-aware communication, allowing administrators to draft emails, faculty meeting agendas, and departmental policy updates with improved clarity and responsiveness. Similarly, assistive curriculum development harnesses large datasets, including enrollment trends, student feedback, and shifting disciplinary priorities, to recommend course structures that reflect institutional goals and contemporary academic demands. In assessment and reporting, predictive analytics enable administrators to track student learning outcomes (SLOs) and program-level outcomes (PLOs), streamlining accreditation processes while providing actionable insights into pedagogical effectiveness. By focusing on these key administrative areas, this chapter demonstrates how these tools can be systematically integrated into art history administration to alleviate operational burdens while reinforcing academic leadership.

However, adopting computational tools in administration requires more than technological adoption—it demands a shift in leadership mindset. Traditionally, administrative roles in art history have centered on procedural oversight, ensuring compliance with institutional policies, managing faculty workloads, and addressing logistical concerns. With the introduction of widely available LLMs, administrators must transition (as in their role as researchers) from being task managers to strategic decision-makers who leverage the technology to enhance efficiency and data-informed planning. In the same way, authors are now editors who review outputs from these models and, with their expertise, decide what to include, revise, or throw out. This shift necessitates developing "AI literacy," cultivating a critical understanding of how insights are generated from these models, and maintaining a balance between automated recommendations and human expertise and oversight. For instance, enrollment forecasting can help identify potential course expansions or contractions, but administrators must contextualize these projections within broader institutional and disciplinary trends. Similarly, assistive hiring models can analyze applicant pools for diversity metrics and subject-area expertise, yet final decisions must remain grounded in human judgment to uphold academic integrity and departmental vision. In simple terms, administrators should offload tasks that are easily automatable—making agendas for departmental meetings or formatting minutes taken—and retain control over those that require critical evaluation. In such a way, the embracing of these tools for augmenting administrative acumen rather than merely expediting tasks, art history administrators can refine their leadership approach, making more informed, strategic decisions that align with both institutional objectives and the evolving landscape of the humanities.

As such, this chapter thus aims to examine such applications within art history administration, acknowledging both its potential and the constraints that must be navigated to employ it responsibly. By doing so, the analysis emphasizes a balanced perspective, encouraging art history administrators to view generative systems not as a panacea, but as a tool for thoughtful innovation that upholds academic values. Through case studies and evidence-based guidelines, the chapter will review strategies for integrating these systems into everyday administrative practices, enhancing efficiency while reinforcing ethical standards and preserving the core mission of art history departments. This exploration situates these intelligent systems as a strategic asset—one that, if harnessed judiciously, can invigorate the leadership dimensions of art history administration and secure the sustainability of the discipline within contemporary academic environments.

For instance, the emergence of natural language models has brought about a significant transformation in academic administration, enabling art history departments to automate a broad array of operational tasks. Rather than simply accelerating scheduling or reporting, these systems synthesize and interpret heterogeneous datasets—such as faculty workload data, curricular trends, and student feedback—to provide evidence-driven support for departmental decision-making (Khadangi et al. 2025). In practice, integrating LLMs into workload management allows department leaders to allocate teaching and service more transparently and equitably, supporting both faculty satisfaction and institutional goals. Tools like Claude, Gemini, and

ChatGPT now draft preliminary communications or policy documents, allowing administrators to devote more time to strategic priorities, and knowing initial drafts can be quickly generated and then tailored for tone or nuance (Snyder et al. 2024). At the same time, automated summarization of accreditation reports or annual assessments reduces cognitive overhead, enabling leaders to concentrate on forward-looking goals. The overall result is an administrative culture less encumbered by repetitive tasks and more attuned to holistic, data-informed leadership. These technologies are not just accelerators; they also act as interpreters, making it possible to identify underlying trends or emerging challenges early. As these systems continue to evolve, their impact on the time and focus of academic leadership will only deepen.

Art historians bring distinctive intellectual strengths—critical analysis, contextual reasoning, and visual literacy—that can be productively paired with generated outputs. Rather than treating technology as a rigid authority, scholars use these outputs as the basis for creative dialogue and adaptive problem-solving. For example, in curriculum design, department leaders can blend data-driven recommendations from language models with qualitative feedback from students, alumni, and faculty, ensuring reforms are both innovative and contextually grounded (Khadangi et al. 2025). Automated models can identify gaps in course coverage or highlight new disciplinary trends, but it is the academic leader who ensures curricular changes reflect local values and strategic vision. When reviewing feedback, art historians are adept at distinguishing between signal and noise—recognizing which themes warrant immediate action and which call for further discussion or investigation. In this way, LLMs serve as springboards for interpretation rather than deterministic engines. The most effective departments will cultivate a culture where faculty expertise and digital insight complement one another, resulting in richer and more responsive academic programs. The aim is not to replace scholarly judgment, but to enhance it.

Instructors also benefit from technology-assisted evaluations that streamline labor while preserving the value of professional judgment. These tools can aggregate teaching evaluations and generate longitudinal reports, giving administrators a high-level overview of strengths and weaknesses while freeing up time for in-depth peer review or mentorship (Shaikh et al. 2023). Faculty can access insights into classroom trends, patterns of student satisfaction, or recurring issues, all without combing through endless spreadsheets or open-ended comments. When it comes to high-stakes decisions—such as promotions or curriculum renewal—department heads can use this data as a starting point, supplementing it with qualitative observation and faculty input. These efficiencies create space for meaningful conversations about pedagogy and student engagement. Academic leaders thus move from reactive, task-oriented oversight to proactive, reflective planning. In effect, technology becomes a catalyst for elevating the role of human expertise, helping to ensure that decisions are grounded in evidence but interpreted through the lens of disciplinary values. This synergy is key to maintaining academic rigor as automation becomes routine.

There is clear evidence that these computational tools can enhance strategic leadership at the institutional level. Predictive analytics, powered by these models, help universities anticipate enrollment fluctuations and changing student interests, supporting targeted investments in faculty development or course offerings (Snyder et al. 2024). Interactive dashboards generated by LLMs provide real-time insights into faculty research output, grant activity, or teaching effectiveness, giving department heads accessible, actionable intelligence. These tools also facilitate compliance and accreditation by automatically compiling documentation, highlighting compliance gaps, and generating draft self-assessment narratives for review (Yuan and Hu 2024). Human administrators then refine these documents, ensuring they accurately represent departmental strengths and address areas for improvement. Strategic planning is further enhanced by the capacity to model multiple scenarios based on changing enrollment, funding, or policy contexts. As a result, leaders are better equipped to make adaptive, data-informed decisions. By marrying automated insight with reflective leadership, departments can thrive in rapidly evolving academic landscapes. These practices are already redefining the role of the department chair in many institutions.

Communication has also been profoundly changed by advances in natural language processing. Administrators can now use them to standardize messaging, draft tailored emails, or produce concise summaries of complex policies or institutional reports (Snyder et al. 2024). This reduces miscommunication and ensures that messages are consistent across different audiences. However, while automation streamlines these processes, it is not a substitute for the empathy and sensitivity required for delicate topics—such as faculty evaluations or restructuring (Perkins 2023). Human oversight remains essential, as only a department leader can appropriately frame difficult news or respond to unique concerns. Institutions are developing protocols to ensure automated drafts are always reviewed and refined by faculty or administrative leaders. The best communication practices now blend the efficiency of automation with the nuance of human judgment. This approach ensures that digital tools serve as aids to, rather than replacements for, the interpersonal skills central to effective academic leadership.

A growing body of research highlights the value of generative models for promoting equity and inclusion within academic departments. By analyzing patterns in faculty assignments, teaching evaluations, and student achievement, automated systems can surface systemic inequities that might otherwise remain hidden (Shaikh et al. 2023). For example, they can detect gender or race-based disparities in course assignments or identify when certain faculty are overburdened with service roles. Department chairs can then use this information to implement fairer workload policies or targeted support programs. However, these gains must be balanced against the risk of perpetuating algorithmic biases embedded in training data (Kim and Vajravelu 2023). Regular audits and human review are essential to ensure that automated recommendations do not inadvertently reinforce existing disparities. Transparency in data collection and model selection is critical to building trust with faculty and students. The goal should be to use technology as a tool for progress, guided at every stage by a commitment to justice and inclusivity.

Resource allocation and strategic planning also benefit from computational analytics. By generating enrollment forecasts and mapping shifts in student interest, academic leaders can proactively adjust course offerings and invest in new areas of research or instruction (Sohail and Zhang 2025). These models can identify under-enrolled courses or growing fields that warrant additional investment, helping departments remain nimble in the face of demographic or disciplinary change. When preparing for accreditation or program review, these models facilitate the assembly and synthesis of complex documentation, allowing faculty to focus on articulating strengths and addressing concerns rather than compiling paperwork (Yuan and Hu 2024). The result is a planning process that is both more responsive and more strategic. This capability is especially valuable for smaller programs with limited administrative support. As these tools mature, departments that integrate them thoughtfully will be better positioned to secure institutional support and advocate for their continued relevance.

In institutional research and compliance, intelligent systems automate the collection and initial analysis of student learning outcomes, assessment data, and annual reviews. By providing quick summaries and flagging gaps, these systems enable departments to respond rapidly to external audits and accreditation requests (Kim and Vajravelu 2023). Importantly, automation frees leaders to focus on data interpretation and continuous improvement, not just compliance. Departments that document (where appropriate) both their use of AI tools and their human oversight processes demonstrate a commitment to transparency and accountability. This documentation is increasingly important as external reviewers expect evidence of data-informed decision-making. The most successful departments will make compliance an ongoing process, integrated into daily operations rather than an annual hurdle. In doing so, they foster a culture of reflection and quality enhancement. LLMs become not just tools of efficiency, but instruments for institutional learning and growth.

The adoption of these technologies requires intentional investment in digital literacy and professional development. Art history administrators must understand both the strengths and the limitations of the models, ensuring they are used in ways that align with the mission and values of the department (Sohail and Zhang 2025). Workshops, seminars, and collaborative exchanges with IT professionals are essential for building the capacity to evaluate, select, and integrate new tools. Leaders must also cultivate a critical awareness of the ethical, legal, and practical constraints of automation in academic contexts. This means remaining engaged with ongoing research, participating in policy discussions, and advocating for the responsible use of digital solutions in higher education. Only through continuous learning and critical reflection can departments remain at the forefront of innovation. Digital tools are not a replacement for thoughtful leadership, but a means to enhance its reach and impact.

The responsible use of language models and automated tools marks a profound shift in academic culture, not just in technical processes. By combining computational efficiency with human judgment and sensitivity, art history administrators can foster innovation, equity, and resilience across their departments. Leaders who embrace these tools thoughtfully—while remaining vigilant about ethical risks and the need for human oversight—will be best positioned to advance the mission of art history in a rapidly evolving educational landscape. The path forward lies in the synthesis of tradition and technology, of evidence and interpretation, and of efficiency and care.

By navigating this balance, academic leaders ensure that generative technologies become strategic assets in the ongoing evolution of higher education.

In this context, the strategic adoption of AI and automated systems does not diminish the centrality of human expertise; rather, it amplifies the administrator's role as a steward of academic values, collaborative culture, and institutional vision. The success of these initiatives depends on transparent governance, inclusive policy-making, and ongoing dialogue among faculty, staff, and students—ensuring that innovation is grounded in the needs and aspirations of the academic community. As art history departments chart their digital futures, administrators must cultivate adaptability, continuous learning, and ethical reflection as core competencies. The chapter's insights affirm that technological advancement, when harmonized with reflective leadership and a commitment to equity, can transform challenges into opportunities for growth and renewal. The anchoring of AI implementation within the discipline's tradition of critical inquiry and public service allows academic leaders sustain both the rigor and relevance of art historical education for generations to come.

5.1.1 Efficient Curriculum Planning and Program Assessment

The accelerating integration of data analytics and AI-powered tools is reshaping the landscape of curriculum planning and program assessment in art history and the humanities. No longer limited to static course schedules and retrospective evaluations, academic leaders now have access to real-time dashboards, predictive modeling, and automated feedback systems that support evidence-based decision-making at every stage. These technologies promise not only to streamline administrative workflows but also to enhance curricular responsiveness, align program outcomes with institutional goals, and identify emerging trends in student learning and engagement. Yet, the adoption of such tools also raises critical questions about data quality, privacy, equity, and the preservation of academic autonomy. As departments consider the opportunities and risks associated with automated planning and assessment, it becomes essential to frame these discussions within the broader values of transparency, inclusivity, and academic freedom. This section explores the practical, ethical, and strategic dimensions of AI-driven curriculum management, highlighting best practices for harnessing technology in ways that support both innovation and the core mission of higher education. By foregrounding the intersection of digital efficiency and human judgment, the following discussion offers a roadmap for academic leaders seeking to navigate the evolving challenges of program development and evaluation.

Digital platforms powered by computational models are revolutionizing curriculum development, offering a wealth of capabilities for art history departments seeking to remain current and inclusive. Through the integration of enrollment data, student surveys, and broader academic trends, these systems help educators refine course offerings, assess learning outcomes, and tailor instructional strategies to reflect evolving cultural priorities (Hill 2003). For example, when an art history department aims to diversify its curriculum, such platforms can surface global artists, noncanonical movements, and underrepresented voices that may otherwise be overlooked. They can also recommend multimedia resources, comparative modules, or case studies that expand student visual literacy and cultural understanding (Walker 1970). Notably, interactive dashboards and feedback tools provide educators with ongoing insights into student engagement and learning preferences, supporting real-time curricular adjustments (Rice-Crenshaw and Howard 2003). This dynamic approach ensures that academic programs can adapt swiftly to changes in student interest or institutional mission. However, faculty may struggle with the technical demands of these tools—such as prompt design or data interpretation—necessitating targeted professional development or collaboration with specialists. To maximize impact, departments should foster an environment of continuous learning and interdisciplinary exchange. With that being said, a historical perspective will best frame the discussion with each of these considerations.

For instance, traditional curriculum planning in higher education typically centers on the establishment of structured, discipline-specific courses designed to transmit foundational knowledge and skills within a given academic field. In this model, curriculum committees composed of faculty members determine course objectives, sequencing, and assessment strategies, often guided by departmental traditions, accreditation requirements, and external benchmarks (Kabara 1972). The curriculum is organized as a series of discrete courses, each with its own learning outcomes, content, and methods, emphasizing mastery of canonical texts, core competencies, and established theoretical frameworks. Assessment mechanisms—such as exams, essays, and presentations—are standardized within the department and serve to evaluate student progress against predetermined criteria (Rush et al. 1976). Planning is generally top-down, with faculty and academic administrators leading the process and students having limited input into course design or content (Harvey and Denby 1970). This approach is meant to emphasize stability, academic rigor, and fidelity to disciplinary knowledge, with periodic review cycles scheduled to update or revise content as needed. The primary aim is to ensure coherence, academic depth, and the gradual accumulation of expertise within a particular field. While this structure has been successful in the past in maintaining academic standards, it is plagued by rigidity and slow responsiveness to changes in disciplinary or societal needs (de Moraes Abrahão et al. 2024).

A defining feature of traditional curriculum planning is the reliance on content-based models, in which subject-matter expertise and established canons guide both the selection of course topics and instructional materials (Kelly 1986). Faculty members, drawing on their disciplinary training, set learning goals and decide on course prerequisites, major requirements, and elective offerings, aiming to provide a comprehensive and sequential educational experience. The process tends to prioritize breadth and depth of knowledge over interdisciplinary integration or practical application, reflecting a view of higher education as primarily a vehicle for intellectual formation and scholarly inquiry (Linden et al. 2015). Curriculum reviews are often prompted by accreditation cycles or administrative mandates, with changes debated and implemented incrementally. Program assessment focuses on academic achievement within the discipline, measured by grades, retention rates, and completion of required coursework. Opportunities for student involvement in curriculum development are minimal, with student feedback typically gathered through end-of-course evaluations rather than incorporated into initial planning (Garner and Acklen 1979). Faculty authority remains paramount, and curricular change is often a slow, consensus-driven process that seeks to preserve the integrity of the academic tradition. This method has been described as stable but resistant to innovation or cross-disciplinary collaboration (Farooq 2024).

The traditional approach is further characterized by its limited responsiveness to external influences and its emphasis on maintaining boundaries between disciplines. Although periodic reviews may address issues such as changing accreditation standards, job market trends, or societal shifts, these are typically accommodated through the addition of new electives or minor updates to existing courses rather than fundamental redesign (Parkay et al. 1999). The compartmentalization of knowledge—where subjects such as history, literature, or science are taught in isolation—reflects a belief in the autonomy and integrity of academic disciplines (Feng-hua 2008). Efforts to introduce interdisciplinary perspectives, experiential learning, or student-centered pedagogies often encounter resistance, as traditional planning processes are geared toward reinforcing established curricular structures (Lawton and Barnes 1998). While this approach provides clear academic pathways and a strong grounding in disciplinary methods, critics argue that it can marginalize innovative teaching methods, limit adaptability, and underprepare students for the complexities of contemporary professional and civic life (Kabara 1972).

Shifting from the traditional approach, which often relied on insular, discipline-specific planning, departments now have access to tools and methodologies that make collaborative curriculum review and external benchmarking both practical and impactful. Where once course mapping and revision were the exclusive purview of a small committee, the newest generation of digital platforms enables all faculty to engage meaningfully with curricular data, student outcomes, and peer comparisons. These systems synthesize information from institutional research, enrollment statistics, and even anonymized peer institution syllabi, empowering both administrators and faculty to make decisions informed by real-time trends and external standards (Dhillon 2018). For example, rather than updating courses in isolation, a department can now systematically review how its offerings compare to those at leading R1 universities, regional teaching institutions, or community colleges—taking into account differences in mission, accreditation, and local community needs. As an example, the following provides a sample prompt that can be pasted into an LLM of choosing:

Prompt for Comparative Table Generation: Create a comparative table of leading R1 universities in the United States that offer undergraduate courses specifically focused on global art history. For each institution, include the following columns:

- Institution name

- Regional accreditation
- Course title(s) related to global art history
- Brief course description(s)
- Whether the course is required or elective
- Diversity/global requirement status (yes/no)
- Integration of non-Western, Indigenous, or underrepresented art (yes/no or examples)
- Credit hours
- Year last reviewed/updated
- Any unique features (such as practicum, digital curation, or community engagement).

Use recent institutional catalogues, public syllabi, or department Web sites to complete the table. If possible, indicate the semester or academic year when the information was last verified.

For best results when generating a comparative table of global art history offerings at R1 institutions, administrators should ensure that the language model or research assistant has access to current web search capabilities and can query up-to-date institutional catalogues and department Web sites. Activating the web search function allows the system to retrieve the latest course listings, descriptions, and accreditation details, minimizing reliance on outdated or incomplete information. It is also advisable to specify a recent academic year for verification, clarify data privacy requirements (avoiding confidential internal documents), and request that sources for each data point are cited where possible. Providing clear column headers and expectations for detail—such as diversity content or experiential components—will further improve the quality and relevance of the generated comparison. Regularly reviewing and updating the prompt as institutional offerings evolve will help maintain the accuracy and utility of the table.

Additionally, the process of horizon scanning is increasingly accessible, moving from sporadic conference conversations to structured, ongoing inquiry. Departments can now analyze not only which topics are trending globally in art history curricula, but also which competencies or methodological approaches are gaining traction—such as digital curation, public history, or decolonial methodologies. These tools allow departments to anticipate student interests, emerging scholarly discourses, and shifting accreditation requirements, ensuring program relevance and institutional competitiveness (Dhillon 2018; Kabara 1972). Moreover, such platforms can flag gaps in social justice themes, helping humanities programs ensure their syllabi reflect stated values as well as contemporary conversations around equity and access. Such a sample prompt to use is as follows:

Example Horizon Scanning Prompt for Art History Administration:

Prompt: Conduct a horizon scan of global trends in art history curricula and pedagogy for [weekly/monthly/semesterly] reporting. Aggregate and analyze data from the following sources:

- Recent course catalogues and syllabi from leading R1 universities, teaching institutions, and community colleges
- Academic conference programs and calls for papers
- Major art history journals and digital scholarship platforms

- News from professional organizations (e.g., CAA, AAH, ICOM)
- Museum and gallery programming schedules
- Publicly available course syllabi and department news feeds.

For each report, provide:

- A summary of the top 5 trending topics, competencies, or methodologies in global art history teaching (e.g., digital curation, public history, decolonial approaches, and global/underrepresented artists)
- Notable curricular changes, emerging areas of student interest, or new accreditation requirements
- Recurring gaps or opportunities in social justice, equity, or interdisciplinary content
- Any recommended pedagogical resources or recent scholarship faculty may find useful
- Citation of major sources for transparency and follow-up.

Schedule this scan as a [weekly/monthly/semesterly] automated report. Output should be delivered as a brief summary with links to relevant syllabi, articles, or events for easy reference by curriculum committees, faculty, and department leaders.

For best results, administrators should first ensure that live web search and access to up-to-date institutional, professional, and open educational sources are enabled in their platform of choice. This connectivity allows the system to draw from current course catalogues, syllabi, professional organization announcements, and global academic news. Next, it is important to specify the relevant time frame for each scan—such as the current academic year or the past six months—to ensure that recommendations reflect the latest developments and not outdated content. When comparing programs or pedagogical approaches, region or institution-type filters (like community college, teaching institution, or R1 university) should be set, allowing for targeted benchmarking against specific accreditation standards or peer groups. By setting up these parameters in advance and automating recurring scans (weekly, monthly, or per semester), departments can proactively identify trending topics, emerging competencies, and gaps in equity or social justice content. The results are delivered in the form of a succinct report, highlighting actionable insights for curriculum committees and faculty development teams. An example of such a report is as follows from ChatGPT 4.1:

Example Horizon Scan Report (*Based on a hypothetical scan with recommended parameters activated*)

Time Frame: Last 6 months (Spring–Summer 2024)

Region: North America, R1 universities, Teaching Institutions, Community Colleges

Summary of Top Trends:

- Increasing adoption of global survey courses integrating African, Asian, Indigenous, and Latin American art traditions, with 74% of reviewed R1 programs now requiring at least one non-Western art history course.
- Notable rise in digital curation and computational methods as required competencies, with multiple institutions piloting courses in digital heritage, 3D imaging, and virtual exhibition design.
- Emphasis on decolonial methodologies and social justice themes; new modules address restitution debates, anti-racist curation, and community-based art history projects.

- Assessment moving toward portfolio-based evaluation and experiential learning, with growth in museum internships and fieldwork as part of graduation requirements.
- Peer institutions increasingly sharing syllabi and assessment rubrics online, enabling easier benchmarking for faculty development and curriculum committees.

Emerging Opportunities and Gaps:

- Many programs lag in integrating job market forecasting or interdisciplinary connections (e.g., art + data science).
- Several reviewed syllabi reflect gaps in Indigenous and Pacific art coverage, especially at community colleges.
- Faculty development resources remain limited in prompt engineering and computational art analysis skills, highlighting a need for targeted professional development.

Recommended Actions:

- Pilot new modules in digital curation and social justice art history; benchmark against R1 leaders with recently updated syllabi.
- Offer faculty workshops in prompt engineering and comparative syllabus analysis.
- Review current curriculum for underrepresented geographic/cultural content and add resources to close coverage gaps.
- Continue quarterly horizon scans to monitor shifts in accreditation requirements and scholarly discourse.

A critical transformation is the newfound ability for faculty and administrators to incorporate job market forecasts and employer expectations into curriculum planning. Traditionally, humanities departments—art history included—have often resisted explicit engagement with labor market data, instead emphasizing academic freedom and the pursuit of knowledge for its own sake. Yet, as higher education comes under greater scrutiny for graduate outcomes and employability, professionals can no longer ignore the practical realities students face upon graduation (Linden et al. 2015). Modern curriculum tools now allow a department chair to quickly compare graduate career trajectories with curricular content, adjust course offerings in light of regional accreditation standards, and align learning outcomes with the demands of a diverse job market. Whether at a community college with a focus on transferability, a teaching institution prioritizing workforce skills, or an R1 university with research-intensive programs, these new approaches enable nuanced, evidence-driven adaptation.

In practice, this might mean comparing how peer institutions structure their survey courses, integrate global art histories, or scaffold research methods across the major. For example, a curriculum committee can now systematically benchmark its program against accredited institutions in different regions—considering variables such as diversity requirements, digital literacy components, and practicum experiences. In so doing, departments not only ensure their programs are competitive and responsive, but also reaffirm their commitment to student success and academic integrity (Lawton and Barnes 1998). As a result, every higher education professional—from junior faculty to deans—has both the obligation and the tools to participate in a continuous process of review, horizon scanning, and strategic improvement. For example, here is a prompt that administrators can use with their chosen computational platform or language model to generate recurring reports on job market trends and actionable curriculum recommendations for art history departments:

Example Job Market Alignment Prompt for Art History Administration:

Prompt: Conduct a periodic scan (weekly, monthly, or semesterly) of current job market trends, in-demand skills, and employer expectations relevant to graduates of art history programs. Aggregate and analyze data from:

- National and regional job boards (e.g., HigherEdJobs, Indeed, LinkedIn, Chronicle of Higher Education)
- Reports and forecasts from professional associations (e.g., College Art Association, American Alliance of Museums, and National Endowment for the Arts)
- Internship postings and practicum opportunities at museums, galleries, and heritage organizations
- Skills requirements in recent art history, museum studies, and digital humanities job postings
- Industry news, employer surveys, and governmental labor statistics

For each report, provide:

- A summary of the top 5 trending jobs or career paths for art history graduates
- Key technical and transferable skills (e.g., digital curation, project management, data visualization, and grant writing) sought by employers
- Notable shifts in employer expectations (e.g., preference for interdisciplinary training, public history, DEI experience, or technology fluency)
- Examples of innovative curricular elements (such as internships, certificates, or workshops) adopted by peer institutions to address market needs
- Actionable recommendations for course or program modifications (e.g., integrating digital curation modules, adding job market workshops, and updating diversity requirements)

To ensure actionable, data-driven curriculum alignment, administrators setting up periodic job market scans must take several steps for best results. First, it is essential to enable live web search or API access for real-time labor market data, ensuring that scans reflect current trends rather than outdated information. Administrators should specify the relevant region, institution type (such as community college, teaching university, or R1 research institution), and time frame—weekly, monthly, or per semester—to tailor insights to their unique context. For transparency and follow-up, all data sources should be cited, and direct links to critical job postings, reports, or employer surveys provided. The reporting process should also highlight market trends as they pertain to different institution types, allowing for nuanced recommendations: for example, a community college may prioritize skills in art handling and museum education, while an R1 might emphasize digital research methods or interdisciplinary scholarship. In order to illustrate what the output might be, the following is from 4.1 again:

Sample Job Market Horizon Scan Report for Art History Administration

Time Frame: Last 6 months (Spring–Summer 2024)

Region: United States, R1 Universities, Teaching Institutions, Community Colleges

Summary of Top Job Market Trends:

1. Increased demand for graduates with experience in digital curation, including online exhibition design and collections management. Recent postings at leading museums and cultural nonprofits specify requirements for familiarity with digital asset management systems and basic coding skills.
2. A surge in job listings for public history, community engagement, and diversity, equity, and inclusion (DEI) coordinators in museums and university galleries. Employers highlight the importance of experience with inclusive programming and outreach to underrepresented communities.
3. Growth in interdisciplinary roles combining art history with technology—such as digital archivist, heritage data analyst, and museum educator with digital content creation responsibilities.
4. Museum studies and art history graduates with certificates or coursework in grant writing, project management, or digital storytelling are increasingly favored for entry-level and advancement positions.
5. Regional teaching institutions are piloting micro-credential programs in art handling, museum education, and art market analytics to meet demand from smaller museums and nonprofit organizations.

Notable Employer Expectations and Recommendations:

- Employers now routinely require digital portfolios as part of applications for curatorial and research roles. Departments should encourage students to create e-portfolios documenting coursework, internships, and research projects.
- Community colleges may consider integrating modules on museum education, art handling, and collections management, as job postings show growth in these entry-level areas.
- R1 institutions should ensure students have access to digital research labs and encourage interdisciplinary collaboration with computer science or public history.
- All institution types should strengthen relationships with local museums and galleries for practicum placements and fieldwork experience, as these are highly valued by employers.

Key Sources:

- HigherEdJobs Art History listings: HigherEdJobs
- American Alliance of Museums (AAM) JobHQ: AAM JobHQ
- College Art Association (CAA) Career Center: CAA Jobs
- LinkedIn Jobs: "Digital Curator," "Museum Educator," "Heritage Data Analyst"
- Museum Studies Internship Listings: Smithsonian Opportunities

Tailored Recommendations:

- Benchmark curricula against peer institutions offering digital curation or public history certificates, updating syllabi to include emerging skills and competencies.
- Host faculty workshops on digital storytelling, grant writing, and portfolio development.
- Establish regular (semesterly) scans to track how job descriptions and required skills are evolving in the sector.

Beyond generating content suggestions, language processing models serve as robust analytical engines for curriculum planning. By synthesizing historical enrollment figures, retention statistics, and student evaluation feedback, these systems can highlight successful courses and diagnose areas of declining interest. Such analysis helps program coordinators identify content gaps, assess the long-term viability of electives, and prioritize investments in innovative courses. These models can also scan disciplinary journals and conference proceedings for emerging research themes (see above), alerting educators to new methodologies or theoretical approaches worth integrating into their syllabi (Cammarata 2016). Importantly, these insights extend beyond internal academic data; computational models can process labor market reports, museum exhibition calendars, and grant opportunities, revealing skillsets or knowledge domains that are increasingly sought after outside academia (Markowitz 2015). For instance, a sudden increase in funding for digital heritage projects may prompt a department to develop new courses in computational art history or digital curation. Such proactive curriculum alignment not only benefits students but also enhances departmental competitiveness in an evolving educational landscape. The continuous interplay between automated insight and faculty expertise thus yields programs that are both innovative and market-responsive.

Contextualizing these advances, computational models now allow for the incorporation of external variables into curriculum planning. By tracking cultural trends, funding streams, and policy shifts, these systems reveal opportunities for new partnerships and course offerings. For example, analysis of international research collaborations or museum initiatives might suggest new directions for coursework on indigenous art conservation or global art markets (Hill 2003). Departments can leverage such insights to create programs that are not only academically robust but also aligned with funding priorities and societal needs. Additionally, if data shows a growing demand for data literacy in museum and gallery settings, art history curricula can be revised to include computational methods, thereby equipping students with relevant skills. These strategies ensure academic offerings remain responsive to shifting external pressures. By embedding external market intelligence into curriculum planning, departments prepare graduates for a broad range of career pathways. The end result is a curriculum that serves both disciplinary traditions and contemporary professional realities.

Despite these benefits, effective use of computational models in curriculum design requires careful human oversight. While systems can identify content trends or recommend new modules, faculty must ensure that curricular changes genuinely enhance learning and reflect institutional values. For example, a model might flag the underrepresentation of Asian or African artists in a modern art survey, but it is the responsibility of the academic team to integrate these voices meaningfully rather than simply fulfilling a diversity metric (Walker 1970). In another instance, automated recommendations based on student completion rates might call for revising course prerequisites or instructional methods, yet faculty must weigh such changes against broader pedagogical goals and departmental identity. The art historian's interpretive acumen is essential in assessing when and how to implement these data-driven suggestions. This symbiotic relationship ensures that curriculum development is not reduced to algorithmic optimization but remains an intellectually and ethically rigorous process. Critical faculty engagement transforms automated outputs into curricula that are both analytically informed and contextually grounded.

At the same time, using large-scale data in curriculum design and assessment introduces important risks. These systems often process sensitive information, including student demographics and faculty activity metrics, which raises questions about data privacy, security, and equity (Hill 2003). Poorly managed data or unchecked algorithms can reinforce existing disparities, especially if they perpetuate biases in course access or resource allocation. For example, if a model identifies low enrollment in a course on indigenous art and recommends its removal, the department must carefully consider the broader implications for diversity and cultural representation. Faculty must remain vigilant in safeguarding confidential information and ensuring that recommendations do not inadvertently disadvantage marginalized groups. Strong data anonymization protocols, periodic model audits, and robust encryption are essential safeguards. In this way, academic leaders protect both individual rights and institutional commitments to equity and inclusion. The aim is to leverage computational efficiency without compromising the values at the heart of higher education.

To address these challenges, universities must implement a multipronged strategy for responsible technology integration. Anonymizing student and faculty data, encrypting sensitive records, and conducting regular audits to identify and correct algorithmic bias are critical first steps (Rice-Crenshaw and Howard 2003). Institutions must also ensure transparency in how recommendations are generated and make it clear that faculty retain ultimate control over curricular decisions. When automated tools suggest changes that risk reducing curricular breadth or marginalizing underrepresented perspectives, departments must intervene to rebalance priorities. Institutions should support ongoing faculty development in data literacy and model interpretation, empowering educators to critically evaluate and contextualize system outputs. By institutionalizing these safeguards, universities ensure that curriculum development remains both data-driven and ethically responsible. Departments that adopt this balanced approach are better positioned to adapt to changing academic and professional environments while maintaining their mission.

In curriculum assessment and reporting, digital tools streamline processes that have long been labor-intensive and inconsistent. Automated systems can aggregate student achievement data, generate standardized performance metrics, and track program-level outcomes across cohorts and years (Markowitz 2015). For example, comprehensive frameworks such as METRICS allow for uniform evaluation, which can be readily implemented through advanced computational models (Hill 2003). These efficiencies enable department heads to shift attention from compiling reports to analyzing trends and developing targeted interventions for at-risk students or underperforming courses. Automated feedback loops can further support individualized student guidance and continuous curriculum improvement. In turn, faculty have more time for meaningful mentorship and pedagogical innovation. These practices promote both accountability and agility, helping departments demonstrate their impact to accreditors and stakeholders.

The increasing complexity of curriculum assessment and institutional reporting has long challenged art history departments and academic units, often consuming significant faculty and administrative time. As the expectations for accountability and program review have grown—driven by accrediting agencies and internal stakeholders—departments have sought ways to both improve the reliability of assessment data and reduce the burden of annual reporting. Digital platforms and advanced computational models now offer a solution by automating the aggregation, analysis, and presentation of student learning outcomes (SLOs). By embedding SLOs within learning management systems such as Blackboard or Canvas, linking them directly to course assignments and rubrics, and using automated tools to collect and analyze performance data, departments can transform a labor-intensive process into an efficient, strategic workflow. This section outlines best practices for leveraging these digital tools to simplify annual assessment, ensure compliance, and provide actionable insights for program improvement.

Best Practices for Streamlined Annual Assessment Reporting

1. **Embed Student Learning Outcomes (SLOs) in Key Assignments**:
   At the start of each academic year, ensure that SLOs are explicitly mapped to core assignments, exams, and projects within your department's LMS (such as Blackboard or Canvas). Each SLO should be linked to at least one "artifact" (e.g., research paper, exam, and portfolio submission) that is used for both grading and assessment purposes.
2. **Attach SLOs to Grading Rubrics**:
   Instructors should use LMS-integrated rubrics where each criterion corresponds to a specific SLO. This allows SLO performance to be automatically recorded as part of grading, avoiding double entry or extra paperwork.
3. **Automate SLO Data Collection**:
   At the end of each term or year, run built-in LMS reports (such as Blackboard Outcomes or Canvas Learning Mastery reports) to aggregate SLO achievement data across all relevant courses and sections. Export these reports as Excel spreadsheets for further analysis.
4. **Leverage Large Language Models for Analysis**:
   Upload the exported SLO spreadsheet to a computational platform or language model (e.g., ChatGPT, Gemini, Claude, or an institutional analytics tool). Ask the model to:

   a. Tally the number and percentage of students who met, fell below, or exceeded each benchmarked SLO.
   b. Generate comparative tables or charts illustrating performance by course, instructor, or cohort.
   c. Identify notable increases or decreases in outcomes compared to previous annual reports.

5. **Year-Over-Year Comparison and Trend Analysis**:
   Upload both the current and prior year's SLO reports. Instruct the model to perform a side-by-side comparison, highlighting which outcomes saw improvement, stagnation, or decline. The system can output summary tables and graphs suitable for institutional reporting or accreditation documentation.

6. **Automated Recommendations for Continuous Improvement**:
   Prompt the model to review the data and suggest actionable recommendations. For example, it might flag SLOs where performance declined and recommend targeted interventions (e.g., curriculum review, supplemental instruction, and faculty development). Ask the model to summarize strengths, weaknesses, and opportunities, formatted in brief narrative and tabular form for inclusion in assessment reports.
7. **Integration with Institutional Reporting**:
   Copy or export the tables, graphs, and summary recommendations directly into annual program assessment reports or accreditation self-studies, saving hours of manual compilation and analysis.

Example Prompt for LLM-Driven Reporting:

"Analyze the attached Excel spreadsheet of SLO achievement for Art History majors for academic year 2023–2024. For each SLO, report the percentage of students who exceeded, met, or fell below the benchmark. Compare this to the 2022–2023 data and summarize areas of improvement or concern. Generate tables suitable for an institutional report and recommend targeted actions for any outcomes with a downward trend."

Looking beyond efficiency, the adoption of automated assessment and reporting workflows enables department chairs and faculty to focus on the core mission of academic leadership—mentoring students, innovating pedagogy, and advancing scholarship. By freeing up time and resources previously devoted to manual data compilation and reporting, administrators are better positioned to interpret trends, develop targeted interventions for at-risk students or underperforming courses, and foster a culture of continuous improvement. Importantly, these streamlined processes also support transparency and data-driven decision-making, making it easier to demonstrate program impact to accreditors, senior leadership, and external partners. In this way, digital tools not only optimize annual reporting but also empower departments to sustain excellence and adaptability in a rapidly changing higher education landscape.

Still, the integration of automation into assessment and reporting must not obscure the complexity of academic work. Quantitative measures alone may fail to capture the depth of faculty contributions or the transformative impact of certain courses on student development (Cammarata 2016). For instance, while dashboards can highlight shifts in student engagement or course evaluations, only faculty can interpret these changes in light of departmental culture, teaching philosophy, and broader social contexts. Automated compliance reporting simplifies interactions with external agencies but should always be supplemented by qualitative review and faculty commentary. The art of academic assessment thus remains fundamentally collaborative, bringing together computational efficiency and human discernment. The best outcomes arise when faculty use data to inform, rather than dictate, their decisions.

The responsible use of computational models in curriculum and program assessment also depends on adherence to ethical and legal frameworks. In the United States, this includes compliance with regulations such as the FERPA, which mandates strict controls on student data access and use (Rice-Crenshaw and Howard 2003). Faculty and administrators must be vigilant in maintaining these standards, as improper handling of sensitive information can expose institutions to reputational and legal risks. Best practices include data anonymization, access controls, and regular security audits, alongside ongoing training for staff on privacy obligations. By maintaining high standards, institutions foster stakeholder trust and ensure that curriculum development remains both innovative and responsible.

As technology continues to reshape higher education, a key lesson is that the best curricular and assessment practices are those that foster collaboration between faculty expertise and computational power. Whether developing new courses, assessing learning outcomes, or responding to shifting external demands, academic leaders must balance efficiency with interpretive depth, data with context, and innovation with tradition. Interdisciplinary teams—bringing together technologists, data scientists, and humanities scholars—are increasingly necessary to navigate this evolving landscape (Walker 1970; Cammarata 2016). The ultimate goal is to ensure that program development and assessment remain both analytically rigorous and deeply responsive to the values and mission of art history education.

5.1.2 Data-Driven Decision-Making: Analytics for Institutional Excellence

As the complexity and pace of change in higher education accelerate, data-driven decision-making has become indispensable for achieving institutional excellence and sustaining competitive advantage. In art history and museum administration, analytics platforms now inform every aspect of operations—from enrollment forecasting and resource allocation to diversity initiatives and alumni engagement. The proliferation of dashboards, predictive models, and visualization tools empowers administrators to move beyond intuition and tradition, grounding strategy in granular, real-time evidence. However, this data-centric culture also introduces new responsibilities regarding data governance, ethical use, and the contextual interpretation of analytics. Institutional leaders must ensure that data collection and analysis are transparent, inclusive, and aligned with the values of equity and shared governance. As departments and museums deploy increasingly sophisticated tools to monitor outcomes and measure impact, the challenge lies in translating quantitative insights into meaningful, mission-driven action. This section examines the promise and limitations of analytics for institutional planning, highlighting the ways in which art history professionals can leverage data to foster continuous improvement, informed stewardship, and a culture of accountability. By placing analytics in service of the broader academic and civic mission, administrators can unlock new opportunities for excellence while safeguarding the field's core commitments.

The adoption of data-driven decision-making in higher education marks a pivotal shift toward institutional excellence, with increasing emphasis on analytics for continuous improvement. Recent research shows that, when implemented thoughtfully, analytics enable leaders to move beyond intuition and anecdotal evidence, using patterns and trends in student data, faculty activity, and external benchmarks to inform strategy at every level (Bouwma-Gearhart and Collins 2015). This approach is especially valuable in curriculum planning, where historical data, enrollment patterns, and course evaluations are synthesized to optimize offerings and anticipate shifts in student interest. Tools such as predictive analytics, dashboards, and automated reporting are now standard in many institutions, reducing administrative burden while enhancing transparency. In art history, the ability to integrate disparate data streams—such as course performance, diversity metrics, and peer benchmarking—supports more responsive and inclusive programming. Institutional decision-makers are increasingly leveraging analytics not just for compliance or accreditation, but for targeted interventions that directly impact student success and retention (Caspari-Sadeghi 2022). However, realizing these benefits requires a culture shift toward collaboration, data literacy, and robust data governance. When local context and stakeholder input are honored alongside system-wide insights, analytics become a catalyst for shared institutional goals.

Curriculum design is one area where analytics can dramatically enhance effectiveness and relevance. For example, Chang et al. (2016) outline a data-driven framework where departmental curriculum planning draws upon real-time dashboards aggregating student outcomes, enrollment trends, and faculty performance. This system supports not only annual review, but also iterative updates in response to shifting accreditation standards or labor market demands. When departments regularly benchmark their syllabi and learning outcomes against peer institutions, they can identify gaps—such as the absence of global art coverage, digital skills, or practicum experiences—and act proactively to address them. The inclusion of data from employer surveys and alumni career trajectories adds a vital external perspective, ensuring that curricular offerings align with both disciplinary standards and workforce needs. Such systematic, analytics-informed review is quickly becoming the new norm in higher education, facilitating continuous improvement and curricular agility (Chang et al. 2016). Importantly, these processes support both academic rigor and responsiveness to evolving external realities, helping departments maintain competitiveness and institutional relevance. As digital infrastructure matures, this type of proactive, data-informed curriculum design will increasingly define best practice.

Data analytics also play a transformative role in assessment and program review, allowing for timely and targeted interventions. As Sima Caspari-Sadeghi (2022) demonstrates, learning analytics systems can now monitor student progress, flag at-risk individuals, and generate automated feedback tailored to individual needs. These systems support four key assessment functions: ongoing monitoring, feedback delivery, prediction and prevention of academic difficulties, and the development of new assessment models. For art history administrators, such analytics enable early detection of students struggling with particular learning outcomes, providing a foundation for customized support or curricular adjustment. The result is a shift from reactive to proactive support, with data guiding resource allocation and teaching innovation. Faculty can use these systems to identify patterns in student achievement, guiding both mentorship and pedagogical development. Moreover, automated analysis of SLO data simplifies institutional reporting, freeing faculty time for higher-order assessment tasks. Adoption of such analytics-driven assessment processes helps institutions demonstrate accountability, promote equity, and foster student success.

One challenge in data-driven transformation is ensuring that analytics systems are designed with stakeholder needs and local realities in mind. Research by Bouwma-Gearhart and Collins (2015) stresses that, for analytics to drive meaningful institutional change, data must be salient to decision-makers and accessible to all relevant actors. Departments should prioritize the integration of systems that provide transparent, actionable insights—such as customizable dashboards and peer benchmarking tools—rather than opaque or overly technical solutions. Formalizing data collection, management, and access protocols ensures reliability and fosters a culture of collaboration. Successful implementation also hinges on regular training and development to build data literacy and analytics capacity among faculty and administrators (Bouwma-Gearhart and Collins 2015). Without such groundwork, the potential for bias, misinterpretation, or technocratic overreach increases. Participatory models that engage local stakeholders and respect disciplinary expertise produce the most effective outcomes. Institutions that align analytics implementation with local needs and values see greater buy-in and more sustainable improvement.

The evolution of analytics tools is also enabling more granular, targeted interventions in business process improvement, a trend with clear parallels for higher education. Tiwari (2024) highlights the ability of data mining, predictive analytics, and machine learning to identify operational inefficiencies, optimize resource allocation, and support strategic planning. In the context of academic departments, similar analytics can highlight under-enrolled courses, reveal imbalances in faculty workload, and pinpoint gaps in student support services. Institutions adopting data-driven approaches report not only increased efficiency, but also enhanced agility in responding to changing demands and stakeholder expectations. These systems are particularly effective when paired with strong leadership support, robust technical infrastructure, and a commitment to iterative improvement (Tiwari 2024). The lesson for art history and the broader humanities is clear: integrating analytics with traditional decision-making offers a powerful path to operational and academic excellence. By harnessing these insights, departments can allocate resources more effectively and demonstrate their value in clear, quantifiable terms.

While the benefits of analytics are substantial, their implementation must address ethical, privacy, and equity concerns. Recent studies emphasize the importance of data anonymization, strong encryption protocols, and regular audits to safeguard sensitive student and faculty information (Caspari-Sadeghi 2022). Institutions should also pay close attention to potential algorithmic bias, ensuring that analytics systems are regularly reviewed for equity in access, opportunity, and outcomes. As more data is integrated into decision-making, faculty must retain agency over interpretation and final decision-making authority, preventing undue reliance on quantitative metrics at the expense of qualitative or contextual judgment. Regular training in data ethics and responsible analytics use is increasingly seen as a necessary part of faculty development (Caspari-Sadeghi 2022). Furthermore, open communication about how data is used builds trust and encourages broad engagement with analytics initiatives. Only through intentional safeguards can analytics become a tool for fairness and inclusion. Institutions that maintain transparency and human oversight are best positioned to harness the benefits of data-driven decision-making.

Recent innovations in analytics also enable a more holistic approach to program evaluation and continuous improvement. Yang et al. (2024) present a data-driven framework using graph theory to map correlations between program modules and student outcomes, allowing departments to pinpoint curricular strengths and weaknesses with precision. This quantitative approach complements traditional review methods, providing empirical evidence for targeted interventions and curricular redesign. Applied to art history, such models can identify courses that drive student success, reveal misalignments between intended and delivered curriculum, and highlight opportunities for interdisciplinary integration. These analytics are particularly useful in transnational or multicampus programs, where coherence and consistency can be challenging to maintain. By linking intended outcomes to actual performance, departments can make informed, strategic adjustments that support excellence and innovation. The integration of advanced analytics into program review processes thus enhances both accountability and adaptability. As technology continues to evolve, these methodologies will play an ever-larger role in academic quality assurance.

Finally, the broader impact of analytics-based decision-making is the fostering of a culture of evidence-based improvement and strategic agility. Studies by Bhushan et al. (2024) and Abdul-Azeez et al. (2024) highlight the transformative power of analytics in driving organizational performance, innovation, and growth. In higher education, this means moving beyond compliance-driven reporting to embrace analytics as a source of competitive advantage and institutional learning. The embedding of analytics in every stage of planning, assessment, and strategy allows institutions to respond more effectively to emerging challenges, anticipate opportunities, and maintain excellence in a rapidly changing environment. This cultural transformation requires not just investment in tools, but a sustained commitment to leadership, collaboration, and the ethical use of data. In the context of art history and the humanities, it signals a move toward greater relevance, adaptability, and resilience. When used responsibly, analytics empower departments to make informed decisions that benefit students, faculty, and the institution as a whole.

5.1.3 Ensuring Privacy and Compliance: Ethical Use of Data in Administration

As the reliance on data analytics and AI-powered systems expands within academic and museum administration, safeguarding privacy and ensuring compliance with ethical and legal standards has become an urgent priority. The collection and analysis of student, faculty, and visitor data—ranging from enrollment records to behavioral analytics—present significant opportunities for institutional improvement, but also introduce risks related to data security, consent, and potential misuse. Administrators must navigate a complex regulatory environment shaped by frameworks such as FERPA, GDPR, and evolving local policies, while also responding to heightened public expectations for transparency and accountability. The ethical use of data requires clear protocols for access, storage, and sharing, as well as mechanisms for obtaining informed consent and addressing stakeholder concerns. Moreover, privacy considerations are inseparable from broader commitments to equity and trust: marginalized communities may be especially vulnerable to surveillance or unintentional bias embedded in algorithmic systems. This section explores best practices for designing and maintaining data governance policies that balance innovation with responsibility, highlighting the need for regular audits, stakeholder consultation, and continuous professional development. By foregrounding privacy and compliance as foundational to digital transformation, art history and museum leaders can build resilient, trustworthy institutions that earn the confidence of their communities while advancing the mission of education and cultural stewardship.

In an era defined by escalating administrative complexities and the imperative for strategic leadership, computational tools emerge as a catalytic force reshaping the landscape of art history administration. Automation of routine reporting, data integration, and digital communication platforms allows academic leaders to focus more intensively on mentorship, advocacy, and the cultivation of programmatic missions (Ghosh et al. 2024). In curriculum design and student assessment, these systems support more inclusive, culturally responsive, and evidence-based teaching, revitalizing the relevance of the humanities in the contemporary university. However, realizing these benefits requires professional development, interdisciplinary collaboration, and systematic efforts to build data and technology literacy among faculty and administrators (Doneva et al. 2021). Equally critical is the ethical use of data: institutions must institute rigorous compliance regimes, enforce best practices for data stewardship, and remain vigilant against algorithmic biases that might perpetuate inequities or erode trust. Art history administrators, in particular, face the dual challenge of leveraging data-driven innovation while safeguarding privacy and academic freedom—a balance that will define institutional resilience in the years ahead.

Given the rapid adoption of computational tools and analytics in academic administration, universities must develop robust governance policies for responsible technology use. Best practices in AI governance include establishing protocols for data security, system transparency, and algorithmic fairness, supported by multidisciplinary oversight committees (Bouwma-Gearhart and Collins 2015). As digital systems increasingly inform high-stakes decisions—such as faculty reviews or student progress tracking—universities must ensure these technologies are transparent, regularly audited, and subject to meaningful human oversight (Caspari-Sadeghi 2022). Clear delineation of responsibility is vital: faculty committees, IT specialists, and administrators should share joint authority for approving, monitoring, and updating digital systems. Regular training in data ethics and responsible system use must become a core component of professional development. Such structures not only support compliance but also reinforce a culture of informed, intentional technology use. Without governance frameworks, institutions risk deploying automation in ways that diminish accountability or introduce new forms of bias. Embedding technology governance in university administration is thus foundational for maintaining integrity and public trust.

Data privacy and compliance are not just technical concerns but also central to institutional ethics and reputation. With the proliferation of analytics platforms, universities must strictly observe regulations such as the FERPA and the GDPR, ensuring that student and faculty data are collected, processed, and stored securely (Radway et al. 2024). This involves robust encryption, routine data anonymization, and granular access controls, minimizing the risk of unauthorized disclosure or misuse (Mollakuqe and Dimitrova, 2024). Regular system audits and vulnerability assessments help detect and correct weaknesses, while clear data use agreements delineate what information is collected, for what purpose, and who is authorized to access it. Transparency in data practices not only ensures compliance but also builds trust among stakeholders, encouraging broad participation in data-driven initiatives. Violations of privacy or data misuse can have significant consequences, including legal penalties, reputational damage, and diminished stakeholder engagement. Art history departments—often dealing with sensitive cultural content and personal narratives—must be especially vigilant in aligning practices with the highest standards of privacy and stewardship.

A major ethical concern with analytics and intelligent systems is the risk of algorithmic bias—particularly as these platforms are used to inform hiring, promotion, and admissions decisions. Recent research underscores the need for periodic bias audits, diverse and representative training datasets, and ongoing review by multidisciplinary teams (Rananga and Venter 2024). Universities should create mechanisms for stakeholders to appeal or challenge algorithmically generated decisions, ensuring that human oversight remains a fundamental safeguard. Additionally, system designers should document and disclose the logic, limitations, and assumptions underlying their algorithms. By taking a transparent, iterative approach to system development and evaluation, institutions can detect and address potential sources of inequity before they become embedded in decision-making processes (Wang et al. 2024). These principles are particularly salient in the humanities, where questions of representation, inclusion, and context are deeply entwined with curricular and hiring practices. The goal must be not only technical robustness but also ethical sensitivity and adaptability.

The future of digital decision-making in higher education will depend on the ability of institutions to evolve in response to changing legal, technical, and social environments. As systems become more autonomous and influential, administrators must ensure that governance and compliance structures are updated regularly to reflect advances in technology and changes in law (Akpobome 2024). For instance, with the increasing use of predictive analytics in enrollment management and resource allocation, it is essential to develop guidelines for ethical data use, risk mitigation, and stakeholder consultation. Art history departments should remain actively engaged in these conversations, advocating for standards that reflect the values of the discipline and the needs of their diverse constituencies. Ongoing dialogue with legal counsel, data privacy officers, and external partners will be crucial for maintaining compliance and institutional integrity. Regular review cycles, open communication, and a willingness to adjust policy in response to new challenges are the hallmarks of resilient academic governance. As technology evolves, so too must the frameworks that guide its use.

Opportunities for interdisciplinary innovation abound when universities embed ethical data use and compliance into the culture of academic leadership. Art history, with its tradition of critical inquiry and reflexivity, is well-positioned to take a leading role in modeling best practices for responsible analytics. Departments can pilot transparency initiatives—such as publishing anonymized data use cases, convening public forums on ethical system design, or partnering with other humanities units to study algorithmic bias (Tiwari 2024). Such efforts not only enhance the quality of academic programs but also position the humanities as key contributors to institutional conversations about digital transformation. By sharing lessons learned and collaborating across disciplines, art history programs can help set standards that benefit the entire academic community. Engaging students in these projects, for example, through digital humanities courses or research labs, further democratizes data literacy and empowers the next generation of academic leaders. These strategies support both innovation and stewardship in a rapidly changing landscape.

Effective ethical stewardship of digital tools also demands ongoing investment in capacity building. Universities should prioritize ongoing professional development in data ethics, privacy, and analytics, ensuring that all academic leaders have the skills to manage evolving risks and opportunities (Mpofu and Chasokela 2025). Training should not be limited to technical topics but also address broader questions of equity, consent, and accountability. Faculty and administrators should be encouraged to participate in interdisciplinary seminars, certification programs, or national workshops on responsible analytics. Partnerships with external organizations, such as privacy advocacy groups or data ethics institutes, can further enhance institutional expertise and legitimacy. A culture of continuous learning and ethical reflexivity will be vital for sustaining trust and resilience as technologies advance. By making capacity building a core priority, universities can ensure that ethical principles remain central to institutional strategy.

Therefore, the role of computational tools in art history administration is best understood as one of augmentation rather than replacement. As research consistently shows, the most effective use of analytics and automation comes when they are used to support—not supplant—human expertise, critical thinking, and disciplinary values (George et al. 2024). Academic leaders must remain vigilant in maintaining agency over decision-making, interpreting data in light of local context, and fostering a culture of transparency and accountability. The path forward lies in strategic partnership: embracing digital innovation while upholding the core tenets of academic freedom, equity, and stewardship. By prioritizing transparency, governance, and continuous ethical learning, universities can realize the promise of analytics for institutional excellence without sacrificing the trust and integrity that are foundational to higher education.

5.1.4 Case Studies: Successful Integration in Departmental Leadership

Case studies from a range of disciplines underscore both the promise and the complexities of integrating advanced computational tools into curriculum planning and departmental leadership. In the context of art history, the adoption of analytics-driven approaches can enhance inclusivity, facilitate interdisciplinary dialogue, and support continuous programmatic improvement. Pan (2024) provides a compelling example: by incorporating data-informed ethical frameworks into curriculum development, departments were able to map gaps in cultural representation and align course offerings with evolving social justice goals. The study emphasizes that recommendations generated by computational systems must be filtered through principles of fairness, transparency, and historical context to ensure relevance to disciplinary identity. This aligns with broader research suggesting that ethical oversight and iterative review processes are crucial for preventing algorithmic drift or the marginalization of foundational knowledge (Shukla 2024). Departments that have piloted such systems report improved faculty engagement, as digital tools free time for strategic planning and mentorship while empowering faculty to guide technology adoption. By using computational assistants not as mere aggregators but as collaborators, art history units can leverage data-driven insights without sacrificing humanistic rigor or pedagogical depth (Ghosh et al. 2024). The resulting balance supports both institutional accountability and disciplinary autonomy.

Lim (2023) offer a detailed multiple-case analysis of ethical issues in data-driven curriculum structuring. Their findings reveal that algorithmically personalized recommendations can both expand access and create risks—especially when market-driven course content is emphasized at the expense of foundational critical inquiry. While these tools supported curricular alignment with industry needs and provided real-time feedback on student engagement, the risk of eroding core academic values was evident. Park and Bae recommend a dual-layered oversight model: automated systems should generate draft recommendations, but these should be reviewed and, where necessary, amended by faculty committees to preserve disciplinary coherence. This model supports both agility and integrity, allowing departments to adapt quickly to external shifts while maintaining intellectual mission and continuity. Institutions that formalize regular review cycles and foster a culture of shared governance are better equipped to harness technology's advantages while mitigating its risks (Caspari-Sadeghi 2022). Transparent communication with stakeholders further builds trust, especially when changes in program structure or assessment protocols are anticipated. Such transparency can also preempt concerns over data privacy, equity, and academic freedom.

The ethical integration of digital frameworks into course design requires more than algorithmic transparency; it demands institutional accountability and clear protocols for human oversight. Vakkuri et al. (2019) identify three pillars for successful implementation: (1) transparent documentation of how and why recommendations are generated, (2) formalized institutional responsibility for review and approval, and

(3) active accountability mechanisms to correct biases or unintended consequences. These pillars are echoed in more recent work by Doneva et al. (2021), which highlights the value of faculty-led committees tasked with system evaluation and iterative improvement. When departments invest in regular audit cycles and include a diverse range of disciplinary perspectives, digital assistants can augment curriculum planning without reducing academic innovation to a technical exercise. This approach is particularly relevant in art history, where context, narrative, and critical reflection are central to both content and method. The combination of robust oversight and transparent methodology ensures that digital systems serve institutional goals, rather than drive them unchecked. Such governance models are increasingly recognized as hallmarks of ethical and effective technology integration.

Successful deployments of advanced decision-support systems in academia are invariably characterized by robust governance and faculty development. Shukla (2024) reports that universities with established digital governance frameworks—encompassing data privacy, bias mitigation, and system audit protocols—achieved both improved student outcomes and greater faculty confidence in technology adoption. Key features of these frameworks include clear data stewardship guidelines, interdisciplinary oversight committees, and mandated training in responsible analytics use. Notably, Shukla's multiinstitutional study found that departments with formalized digital governance policies were able to respond more flexibly to emerging trends and external demands without sacrificing core academic values. Ongoing faculty professional development, especially around digital literacy and ethics, was cited as a critical success factor. These findings suggest that art history departments must invest not only in technology but also in people and processes to realize sustainable benefits. The willingness to adapt and iterate—both in governance and curriculum—emerged as a recurring theme in successful case studies. Structured feedback loops between faculty, students, and administrators support continuous learning and responsive leadership.

To address the AI literacy gap among art historians, universities and cultural institutions must adopt targeted strategies that integrate training into both formal education and professional development. Based on the case studies examined, the following strategies are recommended:

1. **Interdisciplinary AI Workshops**: Art history departments should collaborate with data science and digital humanities scholars to develop workshops that introduce faculty and students to AI concepts, including machine learning, natural language processing, and data visualization. This approach mirrors AI literacy initiatives in health and education, where professionals are trained to apply AI in domain-specific contexts (Adegboye 2024).

2. **AI-Integrated Curriculum Development**: Institutions should embed AI literacy modules within existing art history courses, allowing students to engage with AI-assisted research methodologies. For example, computational tools for art historical image retrieval and stylistic analysis could be incorporated into coursework, fostering familiarity with digital research methodologies (Glinka and Müller-Birn 2023).
3. **Cross-Departmental Collaborations**: Encouraging partnerships between art history faculty and computer science departments can create opportunities for team-teaching and joint research projects. Studies have shown that integrating AI education into non-STEM disciplines enhances critical engagement with technology while preserving the field's core analytical strengths (Scopa 2003).
4. **Professional Development Programs**: Museums, archives, and academic institutions should provide ongoing training in AI applications for art history professionals. Initiatives such as AI boot camps for scholars and digital skills certification programs can ensure that art historians remain proficient in emerging technologies and their ethical implications.

Such strategies allow for art history departments to foster AI literacy while maintaining the commitment of the discipline to humanistic inquiry. Ensuring that scholars and educators have the tools to critically engage with AI will allow them to harness its potential for research, teaching, and academic administration while safeguarding disciplinary integrity.

As these technologies become more deeply embedded in academic administration, a major challenge remains: the widespread lack of computational literacy in the humanities. Mpofu and Chasokela (2025) argue that, for data-informed decision-making to be effective, art historians must develop both technical fluency and critical understanding of how digital systems shape interpretation. Their research demonstrates that interdisciplinary collaborations—such as partnerships with data scientists or participation in cross-departmental analytics workshops—significantly improve both the uptake and the impact of digital tools. Art history departments that embed digital literacy modules into core courses or faculty development sessions report greater confidence in interpreting analytics and advocating for responsible system use. Importantly, these programs also foster a culture of critical engagement, encouraging faculty and students alike to interrogate the assumptions and biases embedded in data systems (George et al. 2024). By foregrounding interpretive skills and ethical reflection, such initiatives preserve the distinctive intellectual traditions of the humanities while embracing technological innovation.

Concrete examples highlight the efficacy of integrated, cross-disciplinary curriculum development. Sarkar and Johnson (2023) document how liberal arts colleges have built interdisciplinary frameworks that weave data analysis and computational thinking into the fabric of humanities education. Their study finds that structured exposure to data analysis in art history or literature courses enhances both content mastery and the ability to evaluate algorithmic recommendations. These programs typically combine introductory workshops, collaborative research projects, and ongoing faculty mentoring to ensure that digital integration does not occur in a vacuum. Peer institutions have adopted similar approaches in preservice teacher training, where future educators learn to interpret and critique automated content generation tools, preparing them for digital teaching and research environments (Mayo 2024). The success of these programs lies in their iterative design: feedback from faculty and students drives curricular adjustments, supporting continuous improvement. Departments that embrace this cycle of experimentation and reflection are better positioned to maintain disciplinary relevance and foster innovation.

Recent research also demonstrates the potential for data-driven technologies to support the assessment of critical thinking and interpretive skill in the humanities. Poce (2024) explores how digital analysis of collaborative writing and art interpretation can be used to track student engagement, argumentation, and problem-solving ability. The study finds that when computational tools are employed in conjunction with faculty-guided discussion, students develop both stronger analytical skills and a more nuanced understanding of course content. Automated feedback loops support formative assessment and enable faculty to intervene early when students encounter difficulty. Importantly, these systems do not replace human evaluation, but rather supplement it, providing new insights and freeing up time for deeper engagement. As Poce notes, the key is to use analytics as a means to enhance—not supplant—critical pedagogy and dialogic learning. This approach aligns with broader calls for a hybrid model of assessment that combines quantitative and qualitative evidence. Departments adopting such hybrid systems report both improved student outcomes and higher levels of faculty satisfaction.

Another strand of case-based research emphasizes the strategic advantage of incorporating data governance and privacy frameworks alongside curricular analytics. Mollakuqe and Dimitrova (2024) conducted a comparative analysis of access control and identity management practices in public and private universities, highlighting the necessity of robust authorization policies for any department using student data in curriculum or program assessment. Their findings indicate that clear protocols for data access, regular system audits, and transparent communication of privacy policies are essential for maintaining stakeholder trust. Art history departments engaging with digital assessment or analytics tools should ensure that all systems comply with institutional and legal standards, such as FERPA or GDPR, to mitigate the risk of data breaches or misuse. By foregrounding privacy and access as foundational elements of technology integration, departments can sustain both innovation and accountability. These case studies illustrate that technical capacity and ethical stewardship must go hand in hand.

Lastly, the role of ongoing evaluation and adaptation is a recurring theme across successful case studies of digital integration in the humanities. As Radway et al. (2024) demonstrate, continuous review of system performance, privacy practices, and user satisfaction is vital for sustaining the benefits of analytics-driven administration. Regularly scheduled audits, stakeholder surveys, and transparent reporting ensure that systems remain responsive to departmental needs and evolving external requirements. Art history departments that institutionalize this cycle of reflection, feedback, and improvement are best positioned to harness digital tools for program growth, scholarly innovation, and student success. The cumulative lesson of these case studies is clear: while computational systems can catalyze new forms of leadership and decision-making, their effectiveness depends on human interpretation, ethical vigilance, and a commitment to the core values of academic inquiry.

This chapter demonstrates that the thoughtful integration of computational tools and data-driven systems is rapidly redefining the landscape of art history administration. Through case studies and current research, we have seen how digital platforms enhance curriculum planning, streamline assessment, support evidence-based decision-making, and foster institutional excellence. The most successful departments are those that embrace a hybrid model—pairing the analytical power of modern tools with the disciplinary insight and critical judgment of faculty. Essential to this success is the establishment of robust governance policies: clear protocols for data privacy, security, and bias mitigation; collaborative review structures; and regular professional development in digital and data literacy. The importance of transparency, ethical stewardship, and human oversight is paramount—ensuring that technology serves to amplify rather than replace the humanistic values at the heart of art historical practice (Caspari-Sadeghi 2022; Mpofu and Chasokela 2025).

Key takeaways for art history administrators include the need for strategic leadership in adopting these systems: building interdisciplinary partnerships, fostering a culture of continuous improvement, and foregrounding inclusivity and accountability in all decision-making. Tools such as predictive analytics, automated assessment reporting, and horizon scanning now empower departments to remain competitive, responsive to evolving student needs, and aligned with contemporary scholarly and workforce trends. However, the transformative promise of these technologies can only be fully realized when implemented with intentional oversight, ongoing evaluation, and a commitment to academic integrity. As art history programs continue to navigate an era of technological disruption, the enduring role of administrators will be to balance innovation with tradition, leveraging the strengths of both to ensure sustainable growth and continued relevance in a changing academic landscape.

References

Abdul-Azeez O, Ihechere AO, Idemudia C (2024) Enhancing business performance: the role of data-driven analytics in strategic decision-making. Int J Manage Entrep Res

Adegboye M (2024) Impact of artificial intelligence on health information literacy: guidance for healthcare professionals. Libr Hi Tech News. https://doi.org/10.1108/lhtn-03-2024-0048

Akpobome O (2024) The impact of emerging technologies on legal frameworks: a model for adaptive regulation. Int J Res Publ Rev 5(10):5046–5060

Bhushan AV, Lakshmi G, Devi SD, Sameer SS, Usman AK, Assisstant Professor (2024) Data-driven decision-making: leveraging analytics for performance improvement. J Informat Educ Res

Bouwma-Gearhart J, Collins J (2015) What we know about data-driven decision making in higher education: informing educational policy and practice. Proc Int Acad Conf (No. 2805154). Int Inst Soc Econ Sci

Burden B, Canon D, Mayer K, Moynihan D (2012) The effect of administrative burden on bureaucratic perception of policies: evidence from election administration. Public Admin Rev 72:741–751. https://doi.org/10.1111/J.1540-6210.2012.02600.X

Cammarata L (2016) Content-based foreign language teaching. Routledge

Caspari-Sadeghi S (2022) Learning assessment in the age of big data: learning analytics in higher education. Cogent Educ

Chang JK, Tsao NL, Kuo C, Hsu HH (2016) Curriculum design—a data-driven approach. 2016 5th IIAI Int Congr Adv Appl Informatics 492–496

de Moraes Abrahão V, Vaquero-Diego M, Móstoles RC (2024) University social responsibility: the role of teachers. J Inn Know 9(1):100464

Dhillon J (2018) Curriculum design and development in higher education

Doneva R, Gaftandzhieva SN, Bandeva S (2021) Data analytics tools in higher education

Farooq N (2024) Cross-disciplinary collaboration in higher education: preparing students for a complex world. Front Inter Edu Meth 1(03):127–136

Feng-hua X (2008) Reflections on traditional curriculum concept in process philosophy. J Ningbo Univ

Garner A, Acklen LM (1979) Involving students in curriculum planning. Clearing House 53:36–39

George AS, Baskar T, Srikaanth PB (2024) The erosion of cognitive skills in the technological age: how reliance on technology impacts critical thinking, problem-solving, and creativity. Partners Univ Innov Res Publ 2(3):147–163

Ghosh D, Tiwari RK, Gundalwar PR (2024) enhancing education 4.0 with artificial intelligence. 2024 5th international conference recent trends computer science technology, pp 558–563

Glinka K, Müller-Birn C (2023) Critical-reflective human-AI collaboration: exploring computational tools for art historical image retrieval. Proc ACM Hum Comput Interact 7(CSCW2):1–33

Harvey RC, Denby RV (1970) Ncteeric summaries and sources: a reference shelf for curriculum planning, Part I: perspectives. Engl J 59:1177

Heck R, Johnsrud L, Rosser V (2000) Administrative effectiveness in higher education: improving assessment procedures. Res Higher Educ 41:663–684. https://doi.org/10.1023/A:1007096803784

Herd P, Hoynes H, Michener J, Moynihan D (2023) Introduction: administrative burden as a mechanism of inequality in policy implementation. RSF J Soc Sci 9(4):1–30

Hill C (2003) Integrating digital tools into a culturally diverse curriculum: an assessment model for the pacesetter program. Teach Coll Rec 105:278–296

Kabara JJ (1972) What is a spiral curriculum? J Med Educ 47(4):314–316

Kelly A (1986) Knowledge and curriculum planning

Khadangi A, Sartipi A, Tchappi I, Fridgen G (2025) Cognartive: large language models for automating art analysis and decoding aesthetic elements. arXiv preprint arXiv:2502.04353

Kim J, Vajravelu BN (2023) Assessing the current limitations of large language models in advancing health care education. JMIR Form Res 9

Lim LA (2023) Aligning learning analytics and learning design for personalized feedback: A multiple-case study in higher education. Educ. Sci. 13(11):1114. https://doi.org/10.3390/educsci13111114

Lawton S, Barnes RE (1998) Developing distance learning courses in a traditional university. Qual Assur Educ 6:106–111

Linden J, Annala J, Mäkinen M (2015) The role of disciplinary knowledge in higher education curriculum practices. In: Society for research into higher education annual conference

Markowitz MW (2015) Meaningful general education reform: integrating core curricula and institutional values. World Acad Sci Eng Technol Int J Soc Behav Educ Econ Bus Ind Eng 9:1560–1564

Martin L, Delaney L, Doyle O (2024) Everyday administrative burdens and inequality. Public Admin Rev 84(4):660–673

Mayo S (2024) Co-creating with AI in art education: on the precipice of the next terrain. Educ J 13(3):124–132

Mohan R (2023) Measurement, evaluation and assessment in education. PHI Learning Pvt. Ltd

Mollakuqe E, Dimitrova V (2024) Comparative analysis of identity management, access control, and authorization practices in public and private universities. Open Res Eur 4:23

Mpofu S, Chasokela D (2025) Data-informed decision-making: using analytics to drive strategic management in higher education. In: Building organizational capacity and strategic management in academia. IGI Global Science Publication, pp 103–138

Pan K (2024) Ethics in the age of AI: research of the intersection of technology, morality, and society. Lect Notes Educ Psychol Public Media 40:260–262

Parkay FW, Anctil E, Hass G (1999) Curriculum planning: a contemporary approach

Perkins M (2023) Academic integrity considerations of AI large language models in the post-pandemic era: chatgpt and beyond. J Univ Teach Learn Pract

Poce A (2024, June) Using AI for critical thinking assessment: A digital humanities education experience. In: The Learning Ideas Conference. Springer Nature Switzerland Cham: pp 94–102

Radway S, Quintanilla K, Ludden C, Votipka D (2024) An investigation of us universities implementation of FERPA student directory policies and student privacy preferences. Proceeding of the 2024 CHI conference human factors in computing system, pp 1–35

Rananga N, Venter HS (2024) A comprehensive review of machine learning applications in cybersecurity: identifying gaps and advocating for cybersecurity auditing

Rice-Crenshaw M, Howard WC (2003) Curriculum alignment and assessment: an adaptable model. The Rur Educ 25(1):36

Rush DE, Lawter WL, Thomason J, Atkisson L (1976) Essential components for effective curriculum development. Peabody J Educ 53:296–298

Sarkar S, Johnson N (2023) Empowering small liberal arts institutions: designing an in-depth curriculum for integrating AI and ML education with pedagogical considerations. Int J Integr Technol Educ. https://doi.org/10.5121/ijite.2023.12301

Scopa K (2003) The development of strategies for interdisciplinary collaboration from within the visual arts (doctoral dissertation)

Shaikh S, Daudpota SM, Yayilgan Yildirim S, Sindhu S (2023) Exploring the potential of large-language models (LLMS) for student feedback sentiment analysis. 2023 International conference on frontiers of information technology (FIT), pp 214–219

Shukla S (2024) Principles governing ethical development and deployment of AI. J Artif Intell Ethics 7(1):45–60

Snyder T, Childs RJ, White P (2024) Large language models in business case research methodology: reflections and considerations for scholar practitioners. Adv in Onl Edu: A Peer-Rev J 3(2):121–133

Sohail A, Zhang L (2025) Using large language models to facilitate academic work in the psychological sciences. Curr Psych 1–9

Tiwari V (2024) Role of data analytics in business decision making. Knowl Res Multidiscip J

Vakkuri V, Kemell KK, Abrahamsson P (2019) Implementing ethics in AI: initial results of an industrial multiple case study. In: International conference product-focused software process improvement. Springer International Publication, pp 331–338

Walker DF (1970) Toward more effective curriculum development projects in art. Stud in Art Edu 11(2):3–13

Wang Z, Wang J, Yang Q, Bai Y, Li X, Chen L, Wu F (2024) Towards next-generation logic synthesis: a scalable neural circuit generation framework. Adv Neural Inf Process Syst 37:99202–99231

Yuan B, Hu J (2024) An exploration of higher education course evaluation by large language models. ArXiv

Yang B, Gharebhaygloo M, Rondi HR, Hortis E, Lostalo EZ, Huang X, Ercal G (2024) Comparative analysis of course prerequisite networks for five Midwestern public institutions. Appl. Netw. Sci. 9(25). https://doi.org/10.1007/s41109-024-00637-z

Chapter 6
Digital Art History Pedagogy: Prompt Engineering

Abstract This section investigates the role of prompt engineering, digital pedagogy, and automated instructional strategies in the teaching and learning of art history. The chapter begins by establishing the theoretical foundations for how carefully designed prompts and multimodal interfaces enhance learning, arguing that prompt engineering fosters deeper engagement, metacognitive awareness, and transfer of critical skills. It explores a range of multimodal approaches for teaching formal analysis, demonstrating how digital platforms can scaffold visual literacy, contextual interpretation, and comparative reasoning across diverse student populations. Through a detailed case studies, the discussion illustrates how scaffolded assignments and interactive prompts can guide students through complex analytic and creative processes, leveraging generative tools to support authentic inquiry. The chapter further examines methods for cultivating critical thinking, highlighting the value of dialogic, interactive techniques that combine algorithmic feedback with reflective self-assessment. Finally, it presents evidence-based frameworks for evaluating pedagogical outcomes and student engagement, offering practical guidelines for instructors adopting prompt-driven, machine-assisted strategies.

6.1 Theoretical Foundations: How Prompt Engineering Enhances Learning

Traditional art history pedagogy has long been anchored in lecture-based formats, with faculty delivering slide lectures and students passively absorbing knowledge through note-taking and rote memorization. Standard survey courses are often organized around iconic works of art, either chronologically or thematically, thereby constructing a shared visual lexicon for students (Nelson 2000). While this approach is effective for foundational knowledge transmission, it prioritizes retention over analysis and may restrict opportunities for creative exploration or student-led inquiry (Cason 1998). Assignments such as formal analyses and research papers, though essential for developing discipline-specific writing and research skills, often reinforce established methodologies and do not always nurture the interpretive agility required

J. Hutson, *Art History in the Age of Artificial Intelligence*, Springer Series on Cultural Computing, https://doi.org/10.1007/978-3-032-02920-1_6

for nuanced critical inquiry (Gadsden 2008). Research suggests these practices can foster a sense of academic distance, potentially limiting deeper cognitive engagement or interdisciplinary connections (Bekova and Jou-Yi 2024). Many students report that such courses, while thorough, do not always equip them to critically interrogate visual culture or apply knowledge flexibly in new contexts (Viola 2023). Moreover, traditional models frequently undervalue collaborative and experiential learning, both of which are increasingly recognized as vital to higher education (Cammarata 2016). As a result, calls for pedagogical reform in art history are mounting, seeking to balance foundational learning with opportunities for analytical rigor and creative experimentation.

The proliferation of digital and multimedia tools has begun to address these limitations, enriching art history pedagogy with new forms of accessibility and engagement. Immersive experiences, 3D modeling, and interactive platforms now allow students to manipulate visual elements—such as light, scale, and spatial relationships—to deepen their understanding of technique and historical context (Alkholy 2010; Finch 2015). These technologies provide opportunities for active learning and visual experimentation, breaking the mold of passive information reception. Recent innovations have also facilitated collaborative learning, as students can now cocreate digital exhibitions, engage in virtual fieldwork, or analyze high-resolution images as a group (Choi-Lundberg et al. 2023). The integration of creative digital tools is shown to foster not only higher engagement, but also the development of critical digital literacy skills needed in contemporary professional environments (Yefimenko et al. 2021). Despite these advantages, digital initiatives often require substantial investment in infrastructure and ongoing faculty development, posing barriers to widespread adoption—especially in resource-constrained settings (Viola 2023). As institutions grapple with these challenges, many are investing in dedicated technology support units to scaffold faculty learning and promote sustainable, interdisciplinary innovation (Koh et al. 2021). The future of art history pedagogy will likely be shaped by the balance struck between digital opportunity and the realities of institutional capacity.

Considering these limitations, a scalable and accessible entry point for art history instructors aiming to integrate digital methodologies into their teaching is the practice of prompt engineering—the careful design of text-based instructions that guide language models and generative tools to yield meaningful, contextually aware responses. Unlike high-cost digital labs or advanced 3D infrastructure, prompt engineering is software-based, requiring little more than access to a multimodal LLM such as ChatGPT or Claude. This approach allows instructors at any institution to create iterative, inquiry-driven learning activities that go far beyond passive digital resources. Prompt engineering democratizes the process: instructors can design exercises that have students analyze artistic styles, compare interpretations, critique scholarship, or simulate the role of a curator, all within a chat or digital workspace. A key advantage is adaptability—prompt patterns can be shared, modified, and tailored for any teaching context, making advanced digital pedagogy portable across course levels and institution types (Sreedhar 2024; Rathod 2024).

Research consistently demonstrates that prompt engineering cultivates critical thinking and digital fluency in students, even where material resources are limited. In a case study by Guo (2024), undergraduates in a digital humanities course learned to iteratively refine prompts and interpret AI-generated responses, gaining confidence in both digital research and humanistic inquiry. Similarly, recent intervention studies found that brief workshops in prompt design measurably improved student self-efficacy, knowledge of digital tools, and analytical writing abilities—benefits sustained even after the instructional period ended (Woo et al. 2024). Prompt engineering is not merely technical; it fosters reflective questioning, helps students articulate arguments more precisely, and exposes them to a diversity of scholarly voices through simulated dialogues and counterarguments (Lazovsky et al. 2024). With careful scaffolding, instructors can align prompts with Bloom's taxonomy or other learning objectives, supporting personalized learning while reinforcing discipline-specific skills (Cain 2024; Hu and Lee 2024).

In practical terms, prompt engineering can be incorporated into everyday assignments: students might be tasked with generating AI-assisted formal analyses, comparing historiographical trends, or critiquing interpretations of a single artwork across time periods. Instructors can encourage students to use LLMs as research partners, asking them to draft, revise, and reflect on their process—thus merging traditional essay writing with digital collaboration. Visual prompt engineering, in which students instruct text-to-image models to generate artistic variations, expands the method further, making digital interpretation and creative practice available in the same classroom (Fareed et al. 2024; Oppenlaender 2024). Peer-reviewed bibliometric reviews show that such assignments not only boost engagement but also help students develop strategies for evaluating digital sources and outputs, a crucial skill in the era of multimodal misinformation (Fatawi et al. 2024). The potential for collaborative, peer-reviewed, and even plug-and-play prompt patterns means that art history faculty can share best practices, refine instructional designs, and scale innovation across programs with minimal cost or technical barrier (Schmidt et al. 2023).

Recent literature stresses that prompt engineering is a form of digital competence essential for educators across all disciplines, including the humanities and arts. Studies emphasize the need for faculty to build foundational skills in prompt construction, error analysis, and bias detection in order to use these tools responsibly (Korzyński et al. 2023). Educators can begin with structured professional development—using open-access tutorials, collaborative workshops, and institutional guides to build a prompt library tailored to their curriculum. As proficiency grows, instructors can experiment with advanced techniques such as chain-of-thought or persona prompting, supporting more complex analyses and interdisciplinary learning. Integrating prompt engineering into regular coursework not only prepares students for contemporary art historical research but also develops market-ready skills increasingly valued in academic and creative sectors (Cain 2024). Faculty collaboration in prompt design fosters a community of practice, making digital transformation more sustainable and responsive to local needs.

A further benefit is that prompt engineering allows for rapid and low-cost experimentation. Faculty can pilot new assignments, gather student feedback, and iterate designs with minimal institutional investment or technical risk (PAS 2024). Automated or plug-and-play prompt systems, such as PAS, lower the learning curve, making it possible for instructors with little digital background to achieve state-of-the-art results. Studies of plug-and-play prompt augmentation systems demonstrate their effectiveness in diverse settings, enabling instructors to adopt and adapt best practices from peer institutions (Zheng et al. 2024). When shared across departments or through public repositories, these resources can level the playing field for under-resourced programs, ensuring equitable access to digital innovation (Hu and Lee 2024). Therefore, prompt engineering stands out as a flexible, affordable, and inclusive entry point into digital art history pedagogy.

Importantly, this exercise in engaging with natural language is also associated with enhanced student autonomy and metacognitive growth. Mixed-methods research shows that self-paced prompt training increases student ability to independently navigate, evaluate, and use language models for research, writing, and creative tasks (Mzwri and Turcsányi-Szabó 2025). As students learn to critique, refine, and adapt prompts, they not only deepen their engagement with course material but also develop lifelong skills in digital inquiry and information literacy (Knoth et al. 2024). In other words, they learn what to do when confronted with something that they do not know or cannot do, as well as devising strategies to identify what questions to ask in order to move ahead. This approach supports differentiation—students can pursue personalized lines of inquiry, revisiting prompts and outputs as their interests evolve. Instructors can monitor student progress through prompt logs, reflective journals, or digital portfolios, making assessment both efficient and meaningful. Crucially, however, learning prompting must be iterative, reflexive, and continuous in order to be effective; merely copying a prompt and taking what comes out of a model will be as ineffective as doing the same with Google. As such, this blend of guided and independent practice is particularly powerful in art history, where visual literacy and interpretive depth are paramount and ambiguity is seen as a primer for continuous inquiry into a subject that has no "right answer."

Finally, as the field evolves, the relevance to the discipline under discussion is but one of many that has seen gains. In fact, a brief history of prompt engineering reveals its demonstrable impact across domains, from coding and legal analysis to creative arts and education (Leung 2024; Muktadir 2023; Murray 2024; Oppenlaender et al. 2024; Pornprasit and Tantithamthavorn 2024). Ongoing bibliometric reviews argue for the integration of prompt engineering into curricular frameworks at all educational levels and call for open-access sharing of effective patterns and assessment tools (Fatawi et al. 2024). The future of digital art history pedagogy lies in harnessing the agility, adaptability, and equity made possible by prompt engineering—moving from isolated digital initiatives to scalable, collaborative, and critically engaged teaching practice. In this landscape, every instructor—regardless of resources—can become an innovator, equipping students for both traditional scholarly rigor and the demands of a changing digital culture.

These targeted instructions leverage the technical capabilities of intelligent systems while aligning with the methodological rigor of art history, bridging the divide between emerging technologies and traditional academic practices. However, it is crucial to recognize that there is no singular "correct" approach to prompt engineering; rather, the process is inherently iterative, inviting both instructors and students to refine, test, and adapt prompts in pursuit of specific pedagogical outcomes (Cain 2024; Hu and Lee 2024). In fact, the very variability of output is why teaching prompting is so valuable: students must learn to critically evaluate AI outputs and question their own assumptions and frameworks. Building from this, best practices emphasize designing prompts that are clear, contextually relevant, and open-ended enough to encourage critical engagement, yet these should be developed in collaboration with students to foster both technical fluency and disciplinary insight (Woo et al. 2024; Lazovsky et al. 2024). In doing so, faculty can scaffold the process by modeling how to break down complex interpretive tasks, anticipate varied responses, and analyze both the strengths and limitations of generative tools. This collaborative approach transforms prompt engineering from a mechanical exercise into a dynamic, inquiry-based learning strategy that develops digital literacy, research skills, and historical analysis in tandem (Guo 2024).

For instructors who are hesitant to integrate these systems, building foundational knowledge of how language models function is becoming indispensable. Not only does this understanding enable educators to support students in their inquiries, but it also helps maintain responsible and informed use within the boundaries of academic and disciplinary standards (Korzyński et al. 2023). Educators must be prepared to discuss ethical considerations, such as data bias, authorship, and originality, ensuring that students recognize the importance of academic integrity even in digitally mediated work (Knoth et al. 2024). By openly discussing the affordances and constraints of prompt-driven systems, faculty can dispel misconceptions and foster a classroom culture rooted in curiosity, skepticism, and reflective practice. Demystifying generative tools empowers both instructors and students to treat them not as infallible authorities, but as dynamic partners in the process of scholarly inquiry. In this way, art history pedagogy can advance toward a hybrid model—one that celebrates the interpretive traditions of the discipline while embracing the creative potential of digital innovation.

To put these principles into action, this next section introduces practical exercises and customizable prompt templates designed specifically for art history classrooms, enabling instructors and students to engage directly with prompt engineering as an integral part of interpretive and analytical learning. Rafting effective prompts is an essential skill for leveraging generative systems in educational contexts, particularly within art history (Table 6.1). Prompts serve as the foundation for guiding automated responses, ensuring they align with the objectives of complex academic tasks. The instruction is the central component of any prompt, offering a clear directive that outlines the specific task or desired response. Precision in crafting this directive is critical, as vague or overly broad instructions can lead to outputs that lack focus or relevance. For example, a prompt might instruct the intelligent system to "analyze" a Renaissance painting, explicitly requesting an exploration of symbolic meanings or stylistic elements. An example of such a prompt put into an LLM could be:

> Analyze Jan van Eyck's *Arnolfini Portrait* (1434), focusing on its symbolic elements, artistic techniques, and historical context. Your analysis should address the following: (1) identify key symbols within the painting, such as the dog, the mirror, and the chandelier, and explain their potential meanings in the context of 15th-century Flemish society; (2) describe the artist's use of oil painting techniques, including detailed rendering and light effects, and discuss how these contribute to the overall composition and realism; and (3) situate the artwork within its historical and cultural framework, considering themes of wealth, status, and marriage. Limit your response to 500 words and structure it into three paragraphs corresponding to these points. Cite any historical sources referenced in your response for accuracy and depth.

Framing the instruction with clarity is fundamental to successful prompt engineering, as it ensures that both educators and students provide the model with precise guidance, ultimately shaping the quality of the generated response. Clear, well-articulated prompts minimize ambiguity and reduce the potential for the model to misinterpret the task or produce off-topic outputs. For educators, this means providing a structured roadmap—specifying the scope of analysis, desired depth, and any contextual information needed for nuanced interpretation. For students, receiving concise and unambiguous instructions enables them to engage more thoughtfully with the outputs, critically evaluating their relevance, accuracy, and alignment with the learning objectives. This clarity not only fosters analytical rigor by prompting students to interrogate the outputs against disciplinary standards but also cultivates methodological consistency across assignments. Furthermore, explicit framing helps set expectations for both process and outcome, empowering students to iterate on their prompts and refine their analytical strategies.

Table 6.1 Anatomy of an effective prompt and best practices

Component	Description	Best Practices
Instruction	A clear directive outlining the desired task or response	Use precise and unambiguous language to define the task
Context	Background information that situates the task, aiding the AI's understanding	Provide relevant background details to guide contextually appropriate responses
Input data	Specific text or data the AI should consider when generating its response	Include examples or specific datasets that align with the task's goals
Output format	Guidance on the preferred structure or style of the AI's response	Specify the format or structure required for the response (e.g., essay, list)
Constraints	Any limitations or specifications, such as length or focus areas, that the response should adhere to	Clearly define constraints such as word limits, focus areas, or prohibited topics

6.2 Multimodal Approaches: Teaching Formal Analysis

The creation and evaluation of art have always been inextricably linked to the technological means available at any given historical moment. From the earliest cave paintings to the rise of photography and now digital platforms, the tools of representation and observation have continually shaped both artistic production and critical interpretation. This dynamic is evident not only in the material form of artworks but also in the evolving strategies used to convey their meaning and presence to distant audiences. Ancient writers, such as the fourth-century Greek rhetorician Libanius, crafted descriptions for readers who had not seen a particular work in person, employing language that reimagined static images as vivid, unfolding scenes. In his celebrated account of a painting in the Council House at Antioch, Libanius did not merely enumerate details or record the artist's technical skill; he recreated the event for the reader, transforming visual analysis into a kind of narrative witnessing.

> There was a countryside and houses of a kind appropriate to peasant country-people—some larger, some smaller. Near the cottages were straight-standing cypress trees. It was not possible to see the whole of these trees, for the houses got in the way, but their tops could be seen rising above the roofs. These trees, I dare say, offered the peasant a resting-place, with the shade of their boughs and the voices of the birds joyfully perched in them. Four men were running out of the houses, one of them calling to a lad standing near—for his right hand showed this, as if giving some instructions. Another man was turned towards the first one, as if listening to the voice of a chief. A fourth, coming a little forward from the door, holding his right hand out and carrying a stick in the other, appeared to shout something to other men toiling about a wagon. For just at that moment a wagon, fully-loaded, I cannot say whether with straw or some other burden, had left the field and was in the middle of a lane. It seemed the load had not been properly tied down. But two men were trying rather carelessly to keep it in place—one on this side, one on the other: the first was naked except for a cloth round his loins and was propping up the load with a staff; of the second one saw only the head and part of his chest, but it looked from his face as if he was holding on to the load with his hands, even though the rest of him was hidden by the cart. And as for the cart, it was not a four-wheeled one of the kind Homer spoke of, but had only two wheels: and for that reason the load was jolting about and the two dark red oxen, well-nourished and thick-necked, were much in need of helpers. A belt girded the drover's tunic to the knee and he grasped the reins in his right hand, pulling at them, and in his left hand he held a switch or stick. But he had no need to use it to make the oxen willing. He raised his voice, though, saying something encouraging to the oxen, something of a kind an ox would understand. The drover had a dog too, so as to be able to sleep himself and yet still have a sentinel. And there the dog was, running beside the oxen. This approaching wagon was near a temple: for columns indicated this, peeping over the trees… (Preziosi 2009).

This mode of description operates by recounting the subject matter of the picture as if it were an unfolding reality—translating the painted scene into a vivid, almost cinematic narrative for the reader. Rather than focusing on compositional structure or formal elements, the writer adopts a natural, immersive approach, inviting readers to visualize the depicted world with immediacy and clarity. Such descriptive strategies are less abstract and analytical than those that emphasize "firm design" or formal arrangement, yet they remain fundamental to how we communicate about representational images. *Ekphrasis*, the literary genre exemplified here, excels at evoking the emotional atmosphere, movement, and lived experience within a work of art, serving to bridge the gap between distant viewer and absent artwork (Preziosi 2009).

This tradition of vivid, narrative art description continued into the Renaissance, most notably in the writings of Giorgio Vasari, whose *Lives of the Artists* employed ekphrastic passages to convey the spirit and particulars of works located in cities and villages far from his audience. Vasari's descriptions were not limited to the formal qualities of the artworks but expanded to situate them within a broader context of story, place, and lived experience, ensuring that the reader could "see" the work in the mind's eye even when they could not witness it firsthand. For instance, in his life of Cimabue, Vasari recounts:

> The name of Cimabue becoming widely known by these labours, he was invited to Assisi, a city of Umbria, where, in company with certain Greek masters, he painted a portion of the vaulted roof in the lower church of San Franceso...In these works he greatly surpassed those Greek masters, and encouraged by this, he began alone to paint the upper church in fresco. In the apsis of the church, beyond the choir, he painted certain passages from the history of the Virgin, in four compartments, -her death, when her soul is borne by Christ to Heaven upon a throne of clouds, -and her coronation, when he places the crown on her head in the midst of a choir of angels; numerous saints, male and female, standing below; works now nearly obliterated by time and dust. In the vaults of the roof, which are five, Cimabue depicted various historical scenes in like manner. In the first, over the choir, he placed the four Evangelists, larger than life, and so well done, that even in our days they are admitted to possess much merit, the freshness of colouring in the flesh-tints proving that painting in fresco was, thanks to the labours of Cimabue, beginning to make important advances... (Vasari 1910).

This practice highlights a fundamental reality for art historians: formal analysis, whether achieved through evocative verbal description, close visual study, or the use of digital tools, has always served as a bridge across distances—connecting audiences to artworks they may never encounter firsthand. Vasari's vivid narration of Cimabue's frescoes, with its attention to spatial arrangement, color, iconography, and the emotional tenor of the scenes, transforms a distant, partially vanished work into a palpable visual experience for the reader (Vasari 1910). This method not only contextualizes the art within its architectural and liturgical setting, but also invites the reader to imagine the process, presence, and atmosphere of the original viewing. Today, as new modalities—from high-resolution imaging to immersive virtual environments—reshape how we encounter and interpret works of art, the essential pedagogical function remains unchanged: formal analysis mediates between artwork and observer, making distant, destroyed, or otherwise inaccessible objects newly present. Teaching formal analysis in the twenty-first century thus requires approaches that honor these historical precedents while leveraging the expanding digital toolkit available to students and scholars. In this way, the discipline remains both rooted in tradition and adaptable to evolving forms of seeing, describing, and understanding.

As art history continues to engage with emerging technologies, the foundational work of bridging the gap between the object and its interpretation persists, ensuring that the art of making the visual verbal remains a vital, living practice. This enduring concern with transforming images into language underpins not only ancient and Renaissance approaches but also the evolution of art history pedagogy in the modern era. With the institutionalization of the discipline in universities and museums, teaching formal analysis and close looking has become a cornerstone for cultivating deep visual literacy and fostering an appreciation for the complexity of artistic production. This method prioritizes a rigorous, detailed observation of works of art, tasking students with articulating visual elements such as color, composition, line, and spatial relationships, which are the bedrock of formal analysis.

Walton (2020) underscores the challenge and importance of precise description, noting that the ability to find the right words to capture visual phenomena is a core art historical skill. Gasper-Hulvat (2017a, b) further situates formal analysis as both the entry point for art historical inquiry and the scaffolding for more complex interpretive methods. Through formal analysis, students hone their powers of close looking, systematically considering how artists across different periods and media construct meaning visually. Assignments designed to foreground these skills—including visual analysis essays and comparison papers—direct student attention to what is present in the work itself before layering in contextual or theoretical frameworks (Avci et al. 2020). This pedagogy, while traditional, is not static; contemporary research advocates for a dynamic, multimodal approach that uses both digital and analog resources to extend the classroom beyond static images and passive observation. As such, formal analysis remains central to art historical pedagogy, serving as a gateway to both academic rigor and creative interpretation.

A range of assignments now supports the cultivation of these analytical abilities. In visual analysis essays, students are guided to concentrate on close looking and direct description, intentionally minimizing the use of secondary scholarship to foreground their own interpretive skills (Elgammal et al. 2018). Comparison essays and more comprehensive research projects, by contrast, require students to integrate formal analysis with contextual evidence, such as historical documents, artist statements, and critical literature (Avci et al. 2020). The ability to shift between these modalities—moving from close description to contextual synthesis—is vital for developing robust art historical arguments. Freedman (2003) notes that successful navigation of such tasks depends not only on skill in observation, but also on a clear comprehension of assignment structure and the expectations set by the instructor. This underscores the necessity of explicit instruction and assignment scaffolding, ensuring students understand both what is required and why these methods matter. Moreover, multimodal tools—such as high-resolution image viewers, collaborative annotation platforms, and interactive discussion forums—are increasingly incorporated to deepen student engagement and enhance accessibility (Kutis 2020). These innovations help bridge the gap between traditional practices and the digital realities of contemporary higher education.

A survey of formal analysis scholarship reveals both the enduring value and the evolving methodologies of this approach. Olin (2017) traces its historical development, highlighting the nineteenth-century scientific influences on art historical method and the way formal analysis became synonymous with disciplinary authority. While initially regarded as a detached or even mechanical process, later scholarship has interrogated this reputation, showing that formal analysis has always existed in dialogue with questions of style, cultural meaning, and the expressive power of visual form. The distinction Prown (1980) makes between "formal analysis" and "stylistic analysis" clarifies that the former is primarily concerned with describing the configuration of an object, while the latter connects those formal properties to questions of artistic manner and cultural expression. Moreover, the research into collaborations between art historians and scientists Olin has made, especially during the Great War, demonstrates how formal analysis has borrowed from and contributed to fields like comparative anatomy and anthropology. These cross-disciplinary influences highlight the intellectual flexibility of formal analysis, which can be used both as a tool of classification and as a lens for exploring broader cultural dynamics. As such, contemporary approaches to formal analysis often integrate it with critical theory, social history, or material culture studies, reflecting the expanding scope of art history as a discipline.

Recent empirical research has explored how training in formal analysis impacts student perception and judgment of artworks. Locher et al. (2015) demonstrated that students with formal art training not only analyze compositional elements more deeply but also develop more nuanced aesthetic judgments, especially regarding balance and symmetry. Nelson (2000), in turn, has illustrated the pedagogical utility of visual thinking strategies (VTS) (https://vtshome.org/)—an inquiry-based approach that invites students to describe, interpret, and respond to works of art in a collaborative setting. Developed by Housen and Yenawine, VTS is credited with enhancing critical thinking, communication, and observation skills and has been adapted to both museum and classroom contexts. Nelson's case studies show that VTS connect formal analysis to broader research and information literacy skills, equipping students to transfer these competencies across academic contexts. Together, these studies indicate that formal analysis is not merely a rote method, but a dynamic practice that fosters intellectual curiosity, collaborative learning, and the capacity to generate new insights. As a result, art history educators are encouraged to embed structured visual inquiry and active learning throughout their curricula, leveraging both traditional and innovative techniques.

Effective teaching of formal analysis depends on a carefully sequenced curriculum that scaffolds observation, interpretation, and communication. Dolšina (2015) emphasizes the foundational nature of teaching students to "see"—to attend closely to the elements of art and principles of design, and to articulate these observations in clear, precise language. This process not only builds visual literacy but also supports students in gaining historical perspective and cultural awareness. Research shows that such skills are transferable, helping students to interpret artworks across media and historical periods and to communicate persuasively about art in both academic and public contexts. In response to the shift toward online learning, best practices increasingly include breaking formal analysis assignments into smaller, scaffolded tasks, using LMS platforms like Canvas to provide timely feedback and opportunities for revision. These micro-assignments give students repeated practice and promote self-regulated learning, which is crucial for success in digital and remote environments (Kutis 2020). Scaffolding also benefits diverse learners, enabling instructors to identify and support students who may struggle with foundational skills. This approach aligns with contemporary emphasis on formative assessment and differentiated instruction, ensuring equitable access to the core practices of art historical inquiry.

Digital transformation is reshaping formal analysis through the integration of multimodal approaches, especially text-to-image and prompt engineering. Mazzone and Elgammal (2019) note that while these tools have often been explored for creative production, their use in formal analysis teaching remains at the frontier of pedagogical innovation. Text-to-image platforms such as DALL-E and Stable Diffusion allow students to translate verbal prompts into original artworks, encouraging experimentation with style, medium, and iconography. Dehouche and Dehouche (2023) analyzed tens of thousands of Stable Diffusion prompts, demonstrating that such tools can expand student visual vocabulary, foster imaginative engagement, and simulate historical artistic processes at scale. These platforms are cost-effective and democratizing, enabling institutions with limited resources to provide cutting-edge creative opportunities to their students. However, the use of AI-generated images in the classroom raises important questions of authorship, authenticity, and the ethical use of digital content (Jiang et al. 2023). Instructors must guide students in critically evaluating AI outputs, considering both their creative potential and their limitations as art historical evidence. This dialogic approach turns digital tools into springboards for formal analysis, rather than replacements for human insight.

Prompt engineering emerges as a particularly potent methodology within this digital ecosystem. As Gu et al. (2023a, b) explain, prompt engineering involves crafting textual instructions that shape the output of large pretrained models, adapting them for a range of art historical and visual analysis tasks. When paired with text-to-image generators or multimodal platforms, prompt engineering allows students to simulate curatorial decisions, reconstruct historical styles, or analyze iconographic evolution—all through iterative engagement with the model's outputs. These exercises cultivate not only digital fluency, but also critical reflection, as students must continually refine their instructions to elicit meaningful, accurate, and contextually relevant results. As the research of Gu et al. (2023a, b) and Dehouche and Dehouche (2023) suggests, the real pedagogical value lies in treating prompt engineering as an iterative, collaborative process, wherein students and instructors jointly interrogate both the outputs and the logic of the systems themselves. This aligns with current scholarship advocating for hybrid approaches that integrate human judgment, ethical awareness, and the creative possibilities of digital tools.

The introduction of text-to-image and prompt engineering into the art history classroom also invites critical reflection on the changing boundaries between creator, interpreter, and audience. Hutson and Harper-Nichols (2023) caution that while these technologies offer opportunities for expanded expression, they may also risk narrowing the range of student output or reinforcing certain stylistic conventions. Yet, when used thoughtfully, generators can deepen student appreciation for the complexities of style, method, and historical context, allowing them to experiment with multiple approaches to the same art historical problem. Such assignments foster creative risk-taking, encourage debate over artistic intention, and sharpen student skills in both producing and analyzing images. The use of these technologies, therefore, should not be framed as a replacement for traditional close looking, but as a complement that expands the possibilities of formal analysis and critical interpretation. Through an embracing of multimodal, critically reflective pedagogy, art history educators can prepare students to navigate both the enduring questions of the discipline and the novel challenges of the digital age.

As these new methodologies take root, they challenge educators to reconsider what it means to "see" and to "analyze" in art history. The future of teaching formal analysis will likely be characterized by increasing hybridity, as traditional close looking is integrated with digital simulation, visual experimentation, and collaborative inquiry. Multimodal approaches offer a dynamic toolkit for developing observational acuity, aesthetic judgment, and critical analysis, equipping students for lifelong engagement with visual culture (Kutis 2020; Locher et al. 2015). However, success in this evolving landscape requires ongoing assessment, adaptation, and dialogue among faculty, students, and technology specialists. Institutions that invest in both technical infrastructure and sustained faculty development will be best positioned to realize the pedagogical potential of these innovations. Above all, art history classrooms must remain spaces for curiosity, debate, and the cultivation of both traditional and emergent skills, ensuring that students graduate prepared to interpret, critique, and contribute to an increasingly complex world of images.

Building on these principles, the following section presents practical strategies, sample assignments, and adaptable activities that art history instructors can implement to bridge formal analysis with digital experimentation—empowering students to engage critically and creatively with both traditional works and new visual technologies. First, it is important to note that models such as Claude, Gemini, and ChatGPT are all multimodal, meaning they can generate outputs across various formats, including text, imagery, and data visualizations. These models also function inversely, allowing users to input an image to generate text or input text to produce an image. For art historians, this multimodal capability is particularly valuable, as it enables students to practice formal analysis by either describing an image in writing or comparing their description to a generated visual representation. For example, uploading an image of the *Arnolfini Portrait* (1434) by Flemish painter Jan van Eyck (Fig. 6.1) with the prompt, "Perform a formal analysis on this image," yields:

> The composition skillfully balances the figures centrally against a richly detailed interior, drawing the viewer's gaze directly to the interaction of the central characters, who are positioned slightly off-center to allow the room's architecture and furnishings to frame them. The detailed execution of the floor tiles leads the eye inward, enhancing the depth of the space and highlighting the painting's perspective accuracy. The standing figures are depicted in opulent clothing, their garments rendered with meticulous attention to the textures and folds, exemplifying the artist's mastery in portraying intricate fabrics and surfaces.
>
> Lighting plays a crucial role in creating atmosphere and dimensionality. Soft, diffused light enters from the left, illuminating the interior and casting subtle shadows that give form and volume to the objects and figures. This lighting technique not only enhances the realism of the scene but also emphasizes the luxurious materials and the variegated textures of the garments and furnishings.

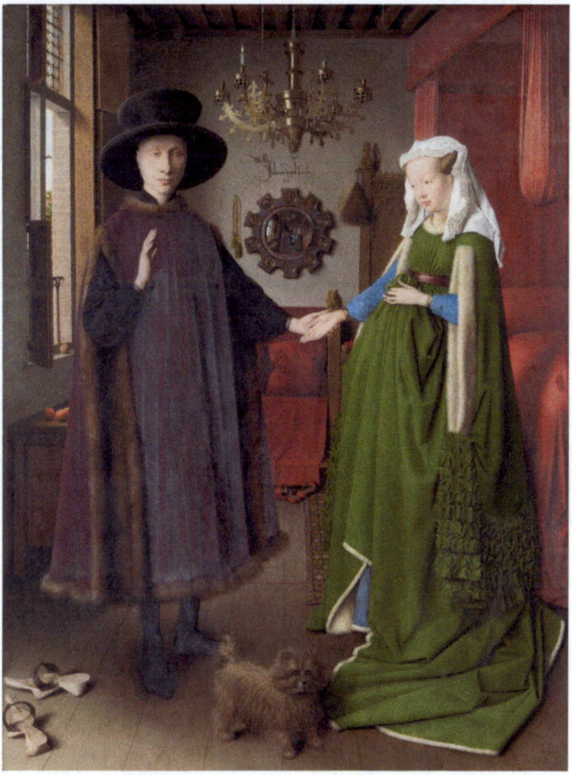

Fig. 6.1 Jan van Eyck, *Arnolfini Portrait*, 1434. (CC O, public domain)

Symbolic elements are integrated seamlessly into the visual narrative, with objects such as the chandelier, the mirror, and the small dog each contributing layers of meaning to the scene. The dog at the feet of the figures symbolizes loyalty and fidelity, while the single lit candle in the ornate chandelier above could be interpreted as a symbol of divine presence or vigilance. The mirror, surrounded by tiny detailed scenes, not only reflects the room and its occupants but also serves as a symbolic portal, echoing themes of surveillance and reflection both literal and spiritual.

The color palette is rich yet restrained, dominated by deep greens and reds that contrast with the more subdued tones of the background and flooring. This use of color not only highlights the figures by setting them against a cooler backdrop but also contributes to the overall solemnity and formality of the scene. The precision in the depiction of elements like the ornate Oriental rug and the intricate carvings on the furniture speaks to a high level of observational skill and the ability to render materials with lifelike accuracy and detail.

This dual-direction functionality enhances teaching and learning by seamlessly bridging textual and visual interpretation, allowing students to move fluidly between close written analysis and dynamic image-based inquiry. This iterative exchange encourages students to refine their descriptive precision and to test the interpretive clarity of their observations, while also exploring how digital systems perceive or represent key elements such as the convex mirror, the gestures of the figures, or the play of reflected light. As a result, students are empowered not only to interpret canonical artworks with new depth but also to interrogate and expand the boundaries of art historical method itself—cultivating skills essential for navigating an ever-evolving visual world.

Continuing with these instructions, providing context supplies the background information the model needs to situate its response within a specific framework. Context deepens the understanding of the task by anchoring it in relevant historical, cultural, or thematic details, thereby guiding the model toward more meaningful and accurate outputs. For example, when prompting an analysis of Italian renaissance sculptor Donatello and his *David* (1420s–1440s) (Fig. 6.2), including details about the political and artistic climate of fifteenth-century Florence encourages the tool to generate insights that are attuned to this particular context. Through specifying such background, the instructor helps ensure that the response addresses not just the formal qualities of the sculpture, but also its significance within the broader dynamics of Florentine society, patronage, and Renaissance artistic innovation. This approach enables students to explore the intersection of visual analysis and contextual interpretation, fostering more sophisticated art historical arguments. In practical terms, embedding context within prompts trains students to ask richer, more nuanced questions and to anticipate how historical circumstances shape both the production and interpretation of artworks.

> Analyze Donatello's *David* (c. 1440s), focusing on its political and artistic significance within the context of 15th-century Florence. Your analysis should address the following: (1) examine the sculpture's representation of David as a symbol of civic virtue and Florence's political identity, particularly in relation to the city's conflicts with rival states; (2) describe Donatello's use of bronze casting and contrapposto stance, discussing how these techniques contribute to the sculpture's naturalism and expressiveness; and (3) explore the role of the Medici family in commissioning and displaying the sculpture, considering how their patronage reflects broader themes of power, art, and propaganda. Structure your response into three paragraphs corresponding to these points, and limit the analysis to 500 words. Reference any relevant historical or artistic sources to substantiate your points.

Including such information ensures that the output is not only accurate but also deeply connected to the objectives of the task. This component helps bridge the gap between abstract instructions and the disciplinary specificity required for robust academic inquiry. In turn, students can engage more meaningfully with generated outputs, as these responses reflect the complexity and depth of the contextual framework. Context thus plays a pivotal role in making prompts more comprehensive and aligned with educational goals.

To further refine outputs, the input data specifies the materials the tool should consider during the task. Input data might include textual descriptions, visual content, or links to primary sources, ensuring that the LLM operates within a well-defined scope. A clear delineation of what should be analyzed minimizes irrelevant or tangential responses and helps students develop a more structured approach to inquiry. For example, a prompt might ask students to examine a passage from Giorgio Vasari's *Lives of the Artists* (1550/1568) and critique its historical reliability in light of more contemporary art historical scholarship. The prompt that compares the early modern perspective with the contemporary allows students to engage in historiographical

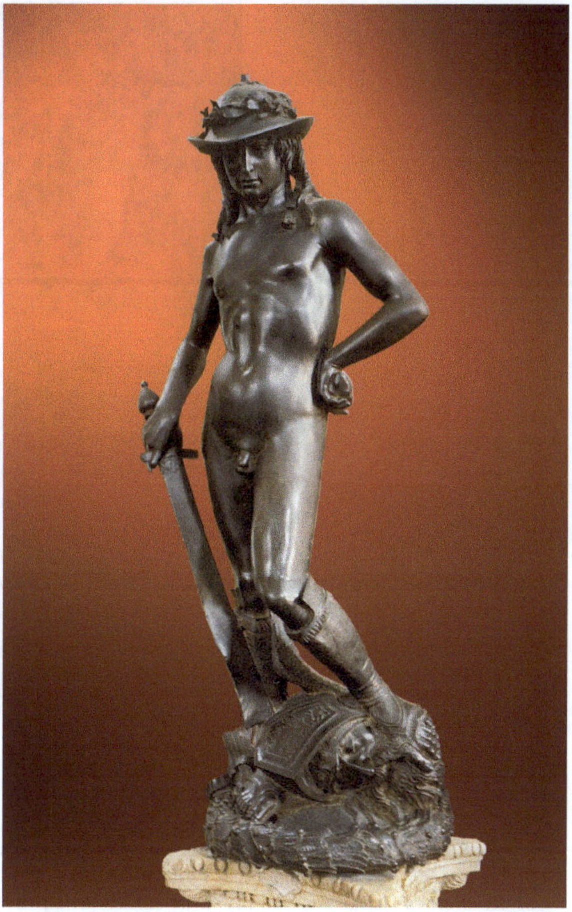

Fig. 6.2 Donatello, *David*, 1420 s–1440 s. (CC O, public domain)

analysis, questioning assumptions about artistic genius, patronage, and the canonization of certain styles. When students supply tailored input data, they not only refine the focus for the model but also practice curating and contextualizing evidence—a vital skill in academic research. This component fosters transparency in how tools process information, equipping students with a better understanding of the mechanics behind generative interpretations and how different types of evidence shape art historical narratives.

Guidance on the output format provides structure to the response, ensuring that it meets the desired style and organizational standards. Whether requesting a comparative analysis, a historiographical critique, or an essay addressing shifts in scholarly interpretations, this component frames the expected outcome. For instance, a prompt might instruct students to contrast interpretations of Artemisia Gentileschi's *Judith Slaying Holofernes* (1611–1612) (Fig. 6.3), considering feminist readings versus traditional iconographic analyses. Such a response from GPT 4.1 yields:

Fig. 6.3 Artemisia Gentileschi, *Judith Slaying Holofernes*, 1611–1612. (CC O, public domain)

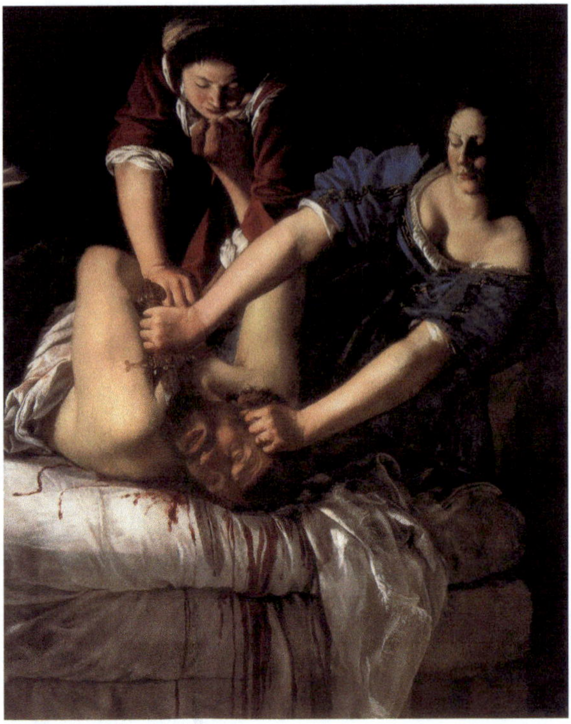

A feminist interpretation of Artemisia Gentileschi's *Judith Slaying Holofernes* foregrounds the artist's biography and the context of her experiences as a woman in seventeenth-century Italy, emphasizing themes of female agency, resistance, and empowerment. Scholars highlight how Gentileschi's depiction of Judith—strong, determined, and active in the beheading of Holofernes—contrasts sharply with earlier, often more passive portrayals of female biblical figures, suggesting a deliberate subversion of gender norms and patriarchal expectations. Feminist readings also consider Gentileschi's personal history, including her experience with sexual violence and her participation in a highly publicized trial, to interpret the painting as both a self-assertion and a visual act of reclamation. In this framework, the work is read not only as a biblical narrative but as an assertion of women's power and autonomy.

By contrast, a traditional iconographic analysis approaches the painting through formal composition, symbolism, and the established conventions of Baroque religious art. This reading examines how Gentileschi employs dramatic lighting, compositional diagonals, and expressive gestures to intensify the scene's violence and emotional impact. Attention is given to recurring motifs—such as the sword, the red drapery, and the expressions of both Judith and Holofernes—as elements that link the painting to broader biblical iconography and artistic traditions. This method situates Gentileschi's work within the lineage of artists such as Caravaggio, comparing her compositional choices and use of tenebrism to those of her male contemporaries. Traditional iconographic analysis also considers patronage, religious context, and narrative fidelity, focusing on the ways Gentileschi adapts and transforms familiar visual tropes.

The explicitly structured format encourages students to critically engage with differing scholarly viewpoints, highlighting how argumentation and evidence shape the understanding of an artwork. Additionally, clear format directives encourage a collaborative, iterative learning process, where students can refine their prompts based on initial outputs, compare their own biases with generated perspectives, and reassess their conclusions.

Constraints further refine the scope and focus of generated responses, promoting both academic rigor and analytical depth. These boundaries might include word limits, thematic requirements, or the expectation that students engage directly with specific scholarly perspectives or types of evidence. For example, a prompt could instruct students to compose a 500-word analysis of the drip paintings of Jackson Pollock, requiring reference to at least one primary and one secondary source when discussing the critical reception of the work. Such targeted limitations encourage students to think critically about the evolution of art historical debates and to reflect on how their own analytical positions align with or diverge from established interpretations. Clear intellectual boundaries help prompt metacognitive reflection, enabling students to recognize the assumptions they bring to their analyses and to see how structured inquiry can lead to more nuanced critical engagement with art historical discourse. Integrating these elements—such as input data, output format, and well-defined constraints—guides students toward producing precise and focused responses while deepening their self-awareness as interpreters. This approach transforms prompt design into an active pedagogical strategy that sharpens analytical reasoning, supports effective historical argumentation, and cultivates a more reflective and methodologically rigorous engagement with art history.

Building on this foundation, it becomes clear that constraining assignments with clear parameters not only clarifies expectations but also scaffolds deeper learning outcomes—especially when paired with the unique capabilities of multimodal models. Instructors can harness these systems most effectively by encouraging students to engage with both textual and visual modes, requiring them to translate careful formal analysis into structured prompts and then to evaluate and refine the results iteratively. In order to demonstrate the viability of these models to assist students in improving their formal analysis skills, a study was undertaken with graduate and undergraduate students in an Ancient Art History course (Hutson 2024). The assignment they were given, AI Art History Assignment: Formal Analysis (Table 6.2), students were challenged to apply their close-looking skills and art historical vocabulary to prompt an image generator—crafting descriptions that omit easy identifiers and instead rely on detailed observation of line, color, composition, and iconography. The closer the resultant image generated came to the work under investigation, the higher the student would score as demonstration of their grasp of the relationship between description and interpretation, as every choice in wording can shift the generated outcome.

The iterative assignment process of the study—requiring students to generate, revise, and document prompts as well as reflect on their experience—encouraged a more nuanced understanding of how art historical interpretation and digital creation can intersect. Engaging with multimodal tools, students became attuned to the ways in which description, visual analysis, and image synthesis could support or challenge one another. As students navigated the technology, they confronted both the strengths

Table 6.2 AI art history assignment: formal analysis

Component	Description
Assignment name	AI art history assignment
Objective 1	Demonstrate understanding of a historical artwork through detailed formal analysis
Objective 2	Apply prompt engineering skills to recreate the artwork using an AI art generator
Objective 3	Reflect on the intersection of art history and digital image generation in the creation and study of art
Step 1: select artwork	Choose a piece of art covered in class (any period discussed) that resonates with you
Step 2: AI art generators	Select and explore at least one of the following AI art generators: midjourney (https://www.midjourney.com/home) Stable diffusion (https://stability.ai/stable-diffusion/) Craiyon (https://www.craiyon.com/) DALL·E 2 (https://openai.com/dall-e-2) ChatGPT-4 with DALL·E 3 (https://openai.com/blog/chatgpt)
Step 3: formal analysis	Write a detailed visual description of your chosen artwork, focusing on formal elements such as material, composition, subject matter, lighting, line, form, and structure. Do not use the title, region, or style in your prompt
Step 4: create AI artwork	Use your formal analysis to craft prompts for the AI generator, iterating as needed to recreate the artwork as closely as possible. Document the evolution of your prompts
Step 5: reflective essay	Compose a 750–1000 word essay reflecting on the process of translating formal analysis into prompts, the challenges of digital recreation, insights into the artwork, and your perspective on digital tools in art history
Submission requirements	Submit your best AI-generated image, the reflective essay, and screenshots or descriptions of your prompt iterations

and limits of digital models: some found prompt-based recreation of complex or highly specific works to be difficult, while others observed that digital outputs, even when visually convincing, often fell short of capturing the subtle emotional resonance or distinctive features of the originals. The challenge of crafting effective prompts was a recurring theme, with several students noting that precise, descriptive language required careful iteration and creative problem-solving. Logistical considerations—including access to free platforms and technical quirks such as awkward figure rendering—also shaped students' experiences and outcomes.

Survey results provided further insight into the classroom dynamic. Of the eight participants, most had never used art generators prior to the course, making the project a first opportunity to experiment with this technology in an academic context. Tool choice varied: Craiyon proved most popular, while Midjourney and ChatGPT-4 with DALL·E 3, as well as a few other options, were also explored. The majority found the process relatively intuitive, describing it as very or somewhat easy, while only a small number reported challenges. Students' views on the impact of these tools were mixed; some saw value in using digital generators to deepen their understanding of historical art, while others felt the exercise helped with engagement but less so with overall comprehension. Notably, free-response feedback highlighted a range of responses to the creative process—citing everything from the inability of generators to fully capture complex works to the challenge of producing naturalistic human forms.

Reflective essays and open-ended feedback revealed both enthusiasm and skepticism about the educational value of these methods. While several students described the assignment as fun, innovative, or "crazy easy," others raised questions about the true effectiveness of digital tools in enhancing art historical understanding, expressing concerns about possible misrepresentation or oversimplification of historical works. Some participants highlighted the potential for such technology to support future scholarship—mentioning possibilities in restoration, image recognition, or cataloguing—while others cautioned that the limitations of current models may actually reinforce, rather than replace, the need for critical human judgment. This diversity of opinion suggests that while multimodal assignments can energize and engage students, their pedagogical impact depends on how thoughtfully they are integrated into the curriculum.

The analysis of student artifacts—including both the images generated using digital tools and the accompanying reflective essays—offers valuable insight into the opportunities and limitations encountered when integrating such technologies into the study of art history and formal analysis. In one notable example, a student recreated the Nike of Samothrace, describing it as a "Marble woman with no head and no arms, right leg stepping forward, clothed in a dress that sticks to her body with wings opened for flight" (Fig. 6.4). Although the prompt captured the essential qualities of the sculpture, free tools like Craiyon often struggled with anatomical accuracy, resulting in awkward limb placement and unrealistic poses. This outcome highlights a recurring challenge for digital image generators: capturing the complex, subtle details fundamental to rigorous formal analysis in art history.

Another challenge became apparent when prompts strayed from assignment guidelines, specifically when students included explicit period, cultural, or stylistic references. In one instance, a prompt described an "ancient roman statue of a dying celtic warrior on ground, pushing himself up with one arm" (Fig. 6.5). The generated images failed to consistently depict the figure in the correct position, and the overly specific language limited the model's ability to interpret and synthesize the visual description. This underscores the importance of prompt construction and the need for students to balance specificity with flexibility to guide digital tools toward more accurate representations.

Despite these difficulties, several students succeeded in generating images closely aligned with their art historical objectives. For example, in the case of the Laocoon (Fig. 6.6), one student used Stable Diffusion and iterative prompting—describing a "muscular, middle-aged man with short, tousled hair, being attacked by a serpent"—to create six variations that closely resembled aged engravings. Detailed, open-ended descriptors produced images capturing both the compositional drama and expressive quality of the original, demonstrating how thoughtful prompt engineering can elicit

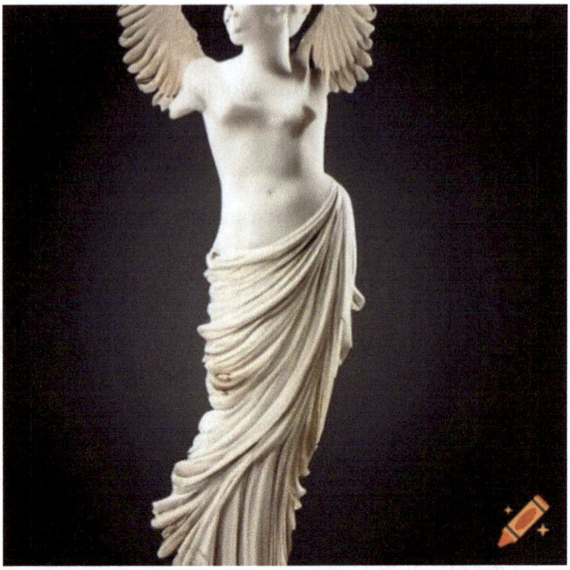

Fig. 6.4 Student image replicating Nike of Samothrace, 2024, Crayion. (Permission of the student artist)

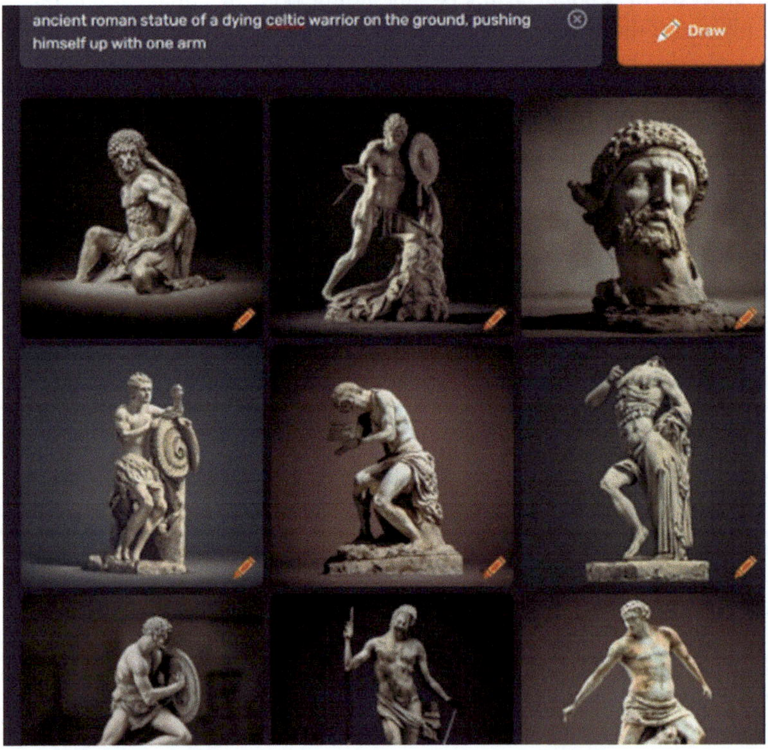

Fig. 6.5 Student image replicating dying Gaul, 2024, Crayion. (Permission of the student artist)

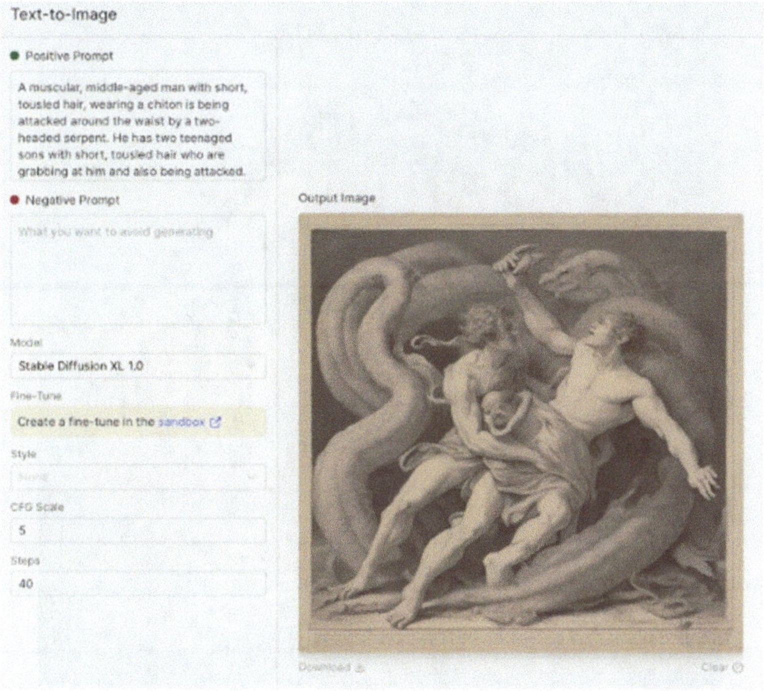

Fig. 6.6 Student image replicating Laocoon, 2024, stable diffusion. (Permission of the student artist)

more nuanced and meaningful digital outputs. Such cases reveal the potential of these tools for translating detailed observation into creative, visually compelling results.

One of the strongest assignments came from a student who initially voiced skepticism about digital art generation. In the reflective essay, this student acknowledged that digital tools, when used responsibly, could inspire creativity and serve as valuable aids for artists struggling to find new directions. The student's concerns over ethical issues—such as unauthorized use of original artwork—remained present, yet the assignment prompted a nuanced reflection on both the benefits and risks of these emerging technologies. This critical engagement was mirrored in the iterative approach taken to describe the Parthenon (Fig. 6.7), where the student refined prompts with increasing specificity: beginning with a "grand peripteral, Doric order temple made of white marble…" and gradually building toward a more atmospheric and contextualized description. Each step resulted in subtle changes to the generated image, culminating in a final version that reflected the deepening understanding of architectural form and historical context:

- A grand peripteral, Doric order temple made of white marble. 8 columns on the front and 12 columns on the sides. It is missing the roof and tiles, and the marble is weathered from age.

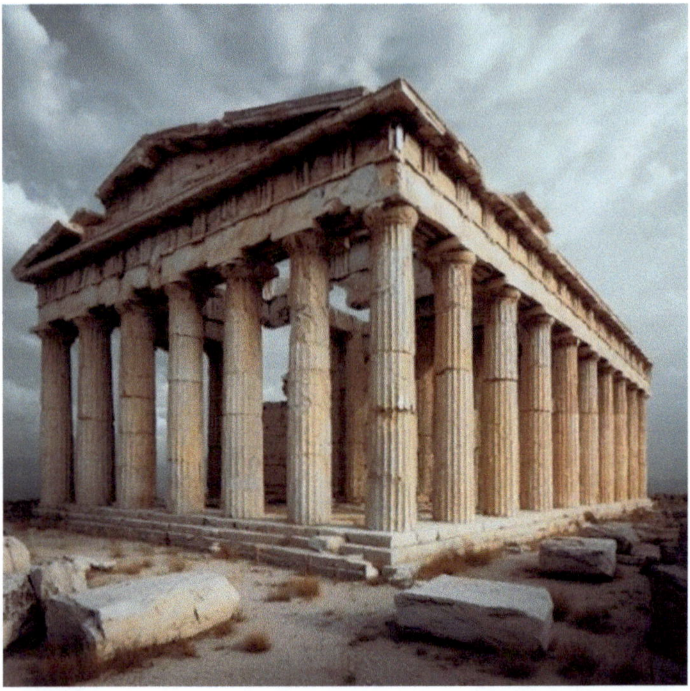

Fig. 6.7 Student image replicating The Parthenon, 2024, DALLE-3. (Permission of the student artist)

- A grand peripteral, Doric order temple made of white marble that has now faded with age. the temple has 8 columns on the front and 12 columns on the sides. The roof of the temple is missing and the pediments are severely damaged.
- A massive peripteral temple made of yellowed marble with 8 Doric order columns on the front and 12 Doric order columns on the sides. The roof of the temple is missing and the pediments are severely damaged.
- A massive peripteral temple made of yellowed marble with 8 Doric order columns on the front and 12 Doric order columns on the sides. The roof and interior of the temple is destroyed and the pediments are severely damaged.
- A massive peripteral temple made of yellowed marble with 8 Doric order columns on the front and 12 Doric order columns on the sides. The roof of the temple is destroyed and the pediments are severely damaged. The interior of the temple was destroyed, leaving the interior empty and open.
- A long peripteral temple made of weathered, yellowed marble with 8 plain Doric order columns on the front and 12 plain Doric order columns on the sides. The temple's roof is missing and the pediments are severely damaged and broken. The interior of the temple is gone, leaving the inside empty and open.
- A long peripteral temple made of weathered, yellowed marble with 8 plain Doric order columns on the front and 12 plain Doric order columns on the sides. The

temple's roof is missing and the pediments are severely damaged and broken. The interior of the temple is gone, leaving the inside empty and open. It sits on rocks in front of a blue, cloudy sky.

Overall, the study found that the success of digital image generation in art history classrooms depends heavily on the precision and clarity of the prompts, as well as on student ability to translate visual analysis into detailed, evocative language. Students who approached the assignment with an experimental mindset—iterating their prompts and reflecting critically on the process—achieved the most convincing results, both visually and analytically. The reflective essays reinforced this pattern: students noted that, although digital tools could not always replicate the emotional resonance or intricacy of the original artworks, the process of iterative analysis and revision fostered a more engaged, metacognitive approach to both looking and writing about art. Therefore, the results point toward a model of pedagogy that leverages both traditional methods and technological innovation, acknowledging that meaningful integration of digital tools requires attention to both process and outcome. While no tool fully supplants the careful looking and interpretive agility demanded by close study of artworks, the inclusion of multimodal assignments offers valuable opportunities for students to grapple with real-world complexities and emerging scholarly practices. The findings reinforce the importance of flexible, iterative teaching strategies—rooted in clear learning goals and scaffolded reflection—for successfully navigating the evolving relationship between technology and the humanities. In sum, this experiment suggests that digital methodologies, when implemented thoughtfully, can invigorate art history education, offering students a space for experimentation, critique, and active engagement with both images and ideas.

6.3 Scaffolded Assignments: Case Study of Donatello's Bronze *David*

As the pedagogical landscape of art history continues to evolve, educators are increasingly called to experiment with new frameworks that blend the discipline's time-honored methodologies with the analytical power of digital tools. Nowhere is this integration more evident than in scaffolded assignments that deliberately sequence traditional research with innovative technologies, providing students with opportunities to deepen their interpretive skills and critically engage with both visual material and scholarly debates. The following section explores one such model: a scaffolded assignment centered on Donatello's *Bronze David* (Fig. 6.2), which exemplifies how prompt engineering and digital platforms can be thoughtfully woven into the art history classroom to promote iterative inquiry and metacognitive reflection. Developed by Dr. Steven Cody at Purdue University Fort Wayne, this assignment challenges students to first immerse themselves in conventional scholarship—reading and synthesizing academic articles on the sculpture's iconography, patronage, and broader historical context, all without recourse to AI assistance.

Through this initial phase, students learn to formulate and defend baseline arguments grounded in primary evidence and art historical interpretation, echoing the discipline's commitment to close looking and textual analysis.

Only after establishing this traditional scholarly foundation are students invited to deploy digital tools to interrogate additional sources, pose new research questions, and iteratively refine their interpretations. In this way, prompt engineering is positioned not as a shortcut or replacement for careful study, but as a catalyst for deeper, more nuanced inquiry. The scaffolded structure (Table 6.3) enables students to track how their understanding of Donatello's *David* evolves as they encounter new perspectives and as digital tools prompt them to reconsider established debates. The structure is designed to encourage depth of inquiry while fostering adaptability and critical thinking, hallmarks of twenty-first-century art historical training. In the first stage, students begin by reading a scholarly article and producing an Article Analysis Paper, engaging in close reading and independent interpretation grounded in visual and contextual evidence. After a class discussion designed to broaden interpretive perspectives and clarify key debates, students then revisit and revise their analysis using digital tools such as ChatGPT and ChatPDF, testing how prompt-based inquiry and AI-generated suggestions can inform, challenge, or refine their original arguments.

The second stage inverts this process: students first deploy AI tools to generate an initial summary of a second scholarly article, deliberately postponing their own reading and analysis. This approach encourages students to critically assess the capabilities and limitations of digital summarization, comparing the AI-generated overview to their personal engagement with the text. Following classroom discussion, students then produce a revised Article Analysis Paper, reflecting both their own insights and those surfaced through digital dialogue. The assignment thus cultivates a habit of comparing, corroborating, and contesting interpretations—whether those interpretations are their own, their peers', or those generated by technology.

In the third stage, students synthesize their evolving analyses into a comprehensive term paper. They are required to combine insights from both article analyses, integrating traditional research, digital summaries, and classroom discourse into a cohesive argument about the iconography, patronage, and historical significance of Donatello's *David*. The draft is submitted for feedback, which students are encouraged to engage with through further revision, supported as needed by digital feedback integration tools. This process mirrors scholarly practice, where arguments are continually refined in response to peer critique, new evidence, and fresh interpretive frameworks.

The final stage of the assignment culminates in the submission of a polished term paper, revised and expanded in light of all accumulated feedback. At each phase, students are tasked with explicitly noting how their interpretations and analytical methods have evolved—whether through direct interaction with AI tools, in-class debates, or iterative revision. By documenting their research journey, students not only demonstrate mastery of art historical content but also reflect on the dynamic interplay between traditional scholarship and digital innovation. The following outlines the strategy:

Table 6.3 Scaffolded assignment structure for art history

Stage	Description	Instructions	AI tools	Submission requirements
Stage reading 1	Engage with the first scholarly article, analyze it, and produce an article analysis paper. After class discussion, revise this paper using AI tools like ChatGPT and ChatPDF	Read and analyze the provided scholarly article. Submit the initial analysis and revise post-discussion	ChatGPT, ChatPDF	Article analysis paper, revised article analysis paper
Stage reading 2	Start with AI tools to generate a summary of the second scholarly article without reading it first. Then, read the article, discuss it in class, and produce a revised article analysis paper	Use AI to generate an initial summary, then read and analyze the article yourself. Revise your analysis post-discussion	ChatPDF, ChatGPT	AI-generated summary, revised article analysis paper
Stage 3 term paper complete drafts	Combine the analyses from the first two stages into a complete draft of the term paper. This draft is revised based on feedback and prepared for final submission	Integrate and synthesize the analyses into a cohesive draft. Use feedback to refine the draft	Feedback integration tools	Complete draft of term paper
Stage 4: term paper final drafts	Finalize the term paper by incorporating feedback received on the complete draft and submit the polished version	Finalize the term paper, ensuring all feedback is integrated. Submit the final draft for grading	Final editing tools	Final draft of term paper

1. **Stage 1: Initial Prompting for AI-Generated Analysis**
    a. Students craft an open-ended prompt such as:
    b. "*Analyze Donatello's Bronze David in the context of early Renaissance sculpture, focusing on its use of classical influences, patronage, and symbolism. Cite relevant scholarly interpretations.*"
    c. AI-generated responses often provide broad or generic summaries. Students are then tasked with identifying inaccuracies, missing perspectives, or overly generalized statements, reinforcing the importance of source evaluation.
2. **Stage 2: Refining the Prompt for Depth and Specificity**
    a. After reviewing the response, students refine their prompt by adding constraints and specifying scholarly comparisons:

        "*Analyze Donatello's Bronze David by comparing interpretations from Vasari (16th century) and modern scholars like Pope-Hennessy. Focus on how patronage by the Medici influenced its form and political symbolism.*"

   b. This revision forces the model to engage with historiographical shifts, illustrating how interpretations of the work have evolved over time.

3. **Stage 3: Prompting for Counterarguments and Critical Inquiry**
   a. To foster **scholarly debate**, students prompt AI to present **alternative interpretations** or critique their initial argument:
      "*What are counterarguments to the idea that Bronze David was a Medici political symbol? Provide evidence from feminist or material culture studies.*"
   b. This stage encourages critical reflection, ensuring students do not accept AI responses at face value but instead engage in comparative analysis.

Beyond the focused study of Donatello's *Bronze David*, these prompt engineering strategies offer a template adaptable to a wide range of case studies within art history education. When scaffolded thoughtfully, iterative engagement with digital tools can support deeper formal analysis of works across diverse periods and cultures—inviting students not only to refine their descriptive language, but also to test the interpretive boundaries of both traditional scholarship and new computational methods. The same structured approach can be used for iconographic interpretation, where students prompt digital models to visualize, compare, or contextualize recurring motifs, or to simulate how interpretations might shift when viewed through different theoretical frameworks. This methodology also lends itself to historiographical critique: students can prompt a model to summarize, contrast, or synthesize scholarly debates about a particular work or movement, encouraging them to identify gaps, biases, or shifts in scholarly consensus over time.

- **Case Study 1: Artemisia Gentileschi's *Judith Slaying Holofernes***
  - **Initial Prompt**: "*Analyze Gentileschi's Judith Slaying Holofernes in terms of Baroque theatricality and Caravaggio's influence.*"
  - **Refinement**: "*Compare traditional iconographic interpretations of Judith Slaying Holofernes with feminist art historical readings, particularly those of Mary Garrard.*"
  - **Counterargument Prompting**: "*How have critics challenged feminist interpretations of Gentileschi's Judith? Discuss alternative readings based on patronage and stylistic analysis.*"
- **Case Study 2: AI-Assisted Formal Analysis of Jackson Pollock's *Autumn Rhythm***
  - **Initial Prompt**: "*Describe the formal elements of Pollock's Autumn Rhythm using traditional art historical methods.*"
  - **Refinement**: "*Contrast Greenberg's formalist interpretation of Autumn Rhythm with postmodern critiques that challenge the idea of gestural purity.*"
  - **Critical Inquiry**: "*Generate a counterargument to Greenberg's reading, emphasizing the role of chance and materiality in Pollock's process.*"

The integration of iterative prompting into these assignments allows students to hone their ability to critically engage with AI-generated content, improving both historical argumentation and methodological rigor. Rather than passively accepting responses, they refine, critique, and reinterpret information, reinforcing art history's analytical and interpretative foundations while embracing emerging digital methodologies.

Furthermore, a key pedagogical challenge in art history is teaching students to critically evaluate scholarly interpretations, rather than passively absorbing historical narratives. Traditional approaches, such as research papers, often emphasize synthesis over critique, limiting student engagement with historiographical debates. AI-assisted prompt engineering offers a means to actively interrogate art historical arguments, allowing students to deconstruct interpretations, identify biases, and construct counterarguments through iterative engagement. This case study examines how students use these tools to challenge, refine, and counter prevailing scholarly interpretations of Édouard Manet's *Olympia* (1863), a work frequently discussed in relation to modernism, the male gaze, and racial representation.

1. **Stage 1: Establishing Scholarly Context**
    a. Students begin by **reviewing primary interpretations** of *Olympia*, including T.J. Clark's *The Painting of Modern Life* and Griselda Pollock's feminist critique.
    b. The initial **prompt** directs AI to summarize these perspectives:
        i. "*Summarize Clark's interpretation of Manet's Olympia, focusing on his argument about class, modernity, and spectacle.*"
        ii. "*Summarize Pollock's feminist critique of Olympia, addressing her concerns about gender and spectatorship.*"
    c. This step familiarizes students with **established debates**, forming a foundation for critical engagement.

2. **Stage 2: Identifying Assumptions and Biases**
    a. Students refine their prompts to **uncover implicit biases** in the scholarly interpretations:
        i. "*Identify potential biases in Clark's interpretation of Olympia. How might his Marxist perspective shape his reading?*"
        ii. "*What aspects of Olympia does Pollock emphasize, and what might she overlook in her feminist reading?*"
    b. AI-generated responses highlight **gaps in analysis**, prompting students to **consider alternative readings** beyond the established discourse.

3. **Stage 3: Constructing Counterarguments**
    a. Students use AI to **generate alternative perspectives** by prompting it to challenge dominant narratives:
        i. "*Provide an argument that critiques Clark's focus on class in Olympia, emphasizing formalist or aesthetic concerns instead.*"
        ii. "*How might a postcolonial perspective reframe the depiction of the Black maid in Olympia, beyond Clark's and Pollock's interpretations?*"

   b. This step encourages **dialogical engagement**, requiring students to **synthesize diverse viewpoints** and develop their own analytical stance.

4. **Stage 4: Refining the Argument Through Iterative Prompts**
   a. After receiving AI-generated counterarguments, students refine their prompts to ensure **historical specificity and evidentiary support**:
      i. *"Revise your critique of Clark's argument by incorporating direct references to Manet's letters and contemporary critiques of Olympia in 1865."*
   b. This process teaches students to **construct well-supported historical arguments**, rather than relying on general AI outputs.

This approach extends beyond *Olympia* to broader art historical debates, equipping students with tools to interrogate methodologies, historiography, and theoretical frameworks. By engaging in iterative prompting, students:

- **Develop metacognitive awareness** by recognizing how scholarly perspectives shape interpretation.
- **Construct well-supported counterarguments**, rather than passively summarizing secondary sources.
- **Bridge traditional and digital methodologies**, integrating **prompt engineering into scholarly critique**.

Integrating these tools into the critical evaluation of pedagogy establishes a more rigorous, reflexive, and dialogical approach to art historical scholarship—ensuring that students shape interpretations actively, rather than simply reproducing them. Through structured prompt engineering, learners shift from passive absorption of received narratives to engaged participation in ongoing historiographical debates. This approach fosters habits of questioning, careful refinement of analysis, and the confident challenging of prevailing interpretations, cultivating intellectual curiosity and analytic discipline. Encountering multiple interpretive pathways and returning to their own arguments for revision, students develop an acute sense of how art historical knowledge is produced, contested, and transformed across time. Such engagement strengthens both critical thinking and methodological precision while heightening awareness of the provisional and negotiated character of art historical discourse. The result is a classroom environment where analytical rigor, creative exploration, and open-ended inquiry work in tandem. Students emerge with the skills needed to navigate, contribute to, and even reshape the evolving conversations that define the field of art history. This model ensures that future scholarship remains both intellectually vibrant and responsive to new questions and perspectives.

6.4 Developing Critical Thinking Skills Through Interactive Methods

The integration of prompt engineering and interactive, multimodal reasoning tools into art history pedagogy has the potential to significantly enrich critical thinking, enabling students to move beyond passive learning and adopt a more active, iterative approach to constructing interpretations (Table 6.4). Studies have shown that, when students guide digital models through a series of refined prompts, they become acutely aware of how their inquiries shape the scope, relevance, and accuracy of generated responses (Walter 2024). This metacognitive process—helping students learn how they learn—is essential for developing both self-awareness and analytic rigor, as learners must continually assess the alignment between their prompts, their art historical objectives, and the outputs received (Poce 2024). Through structuring assignments to require iterative prompting, comparison of responses, and reflective writing, instructors foster deeper engagement with both primary sources and secondary scholarship. Students report greater confidence in writing formal analyses, citing the benefits of real-time feedback, the opportunity to clarify their arguments, and the ability to test multiple perspectives with a tutor that is both supportive, nonjudgmental and always available. These skills—precision in inquiry, synthesis of evidence, and iterative argumentation—are directly transferable to advanced research and professional contexts, as they mirror the processes of scholarly debate and peer review (Lawasi et al. 2024). Importantly, interactive assignments invite learners to scrutinize how digital outputs align or diverge from traditional interpretations, prompting thoughtful critique rather than passive acceptance. Such approaches not only enhance critical thinking but also promote digital literacy and methodological self-reflection.

Challenges inevitably arise as students adapt to the specificity required for effective prompting and the verification of digital outputs. Studies indicate that many learners initially craft broad or unfocused prompts, which can lead to generic or shallow results that lack art historical nuance (Gonsalves 2024). In fact, the earliest studies of student use by the author revealed the initial frustrations demonstrated by students across fields who failed to get the result desired the first time and did not attempt to iterate on the process (Hutson and Plate 2023; Hutson and Cotroneo 2023; Hutson and Robertson 2023). Whereas researchers on the studies had assumed Gen Z students would naturally take to the tools, understanding how prompting strategies applied in different contexts is something that must be taught. Thus, later studies capitalized on these observations and required iterative strategies where students would run variations on the same prompt up to ten times and document results, which greatly improved not only the final output but student understanding of how to repeat the process in different contexts to get reproducible results (Carpino and Hutson 2024; Hutson 2024).

To address the early frustrations with prompting, educators are encouraged to scaffold learning with structured exercises—beginning with tightly framed prompts

Table 6.4 Best practices for promoting critical thinking with prompt engineering

Best practice	Description	Implementation example
Start with clear learning goals	Define specific critical thinking outcomes (analysis, synthesis, evaluation) for each activity	Explicitly link assignments to skills like argument analysis or source critique
Scaffold prompt development	Guide students through stages of prompt design, from broad to refined, modeling effective questioning	Begin with instructor-led prompts; gradually encourage student-generated prompts and iterations
Emphasize Iteration and reflection	Encourage students to revise prompts and responses, documenting changes and reflecting on their reasoning	Require prompt logs and reflective journals detailing what changed and why
Require evidence-based responses	Instruct students to back up analyses with primary/secondary sources or visual evidence	Include assignment rubrics that reward use of scholarly citations and careful observation
Foster comparative analysis	Assign tasks that ask students to compare AI-generated outputs with traditional interpretations or scholarship	Have students critique both their own and the model's analysis of an artwork or theme
Build in verification steps	Train students to verify digital outputs against trusted sources, highlighting the potential for hallucination	Assign a "fact-check" step, asking students to cross-reference AI responses
Promote metacognitive awareness	Prompt students to reflect on how their questions, assumptions, and strategies shaped the model's responses	Use self-assessment forms or class discussion on the process, not just the outcome
Integrate ethical considerations	Include discussion of authorship, bias, and the responsible use of digital models in class	Facilitate debates or case studies on issues like attribution or privacy
Encourage collaboration	Use group activities to design, test, and refine prompts, supporting peer feedback and diverse perspectives	Assign pairs or teams to tackle complex analysis tasks collaboratively
Blend with traditional methods	Combine digital analysis with visual close looking, archival research, and seminar discussion for balance	Alternate between screen-based assignments and hands-on, object-based inquiry

and gradually increasing complexity as students gain confidence and skill. Assignments that require students to test, compare, and revise prompts encourage a more discerning approach to digital inquiry, as well as a habit of skepticism regarding generative content. Recent research on visual arts education highlights the importance of explicit instruction in critical interrogation and cross-referencing of outputs with established scholarship, reinforcing the need for validation and scholarly rigor (Poce 2024; Ramos-Vallecillo and Murillo-Ligorred 2025). Structured assignments in which students critique both the outputs and the process—such as comparing a machine interpretation of the Laocoon to canonical readings—build analytical precision and help students develop intellectual independence. This reflective, dialogical engagement with technology ensures that the adoption of digital tools does not result in uncritical reliance, but rather supports the cultivation of skeptical, research-oriented habits (Oberer and Erkollar 2024). As a result, students become more adept at identifying both the affordances and the limitations of computational analysis in art history.

Blending algorithmically-supported analysis with traditional art historical methodologies ensures that core disciplinary values—such as close looking, contextual analysis, and primary source research—remain at the center of pedagogy. Empirical studies confirm that such tools, when positioned as supplements rather than substitutes, enhance student engagement with foundational practices (Elere et al. 2024; Poce 2024). Assignments might begin with a close formal analysis or a contextual reading, followed by targeted digital inquiries that prompt the student to explore alternative perspectives or test hypotheses. For example, a student analyzing Gentileschi's *Judith Slaying Holofernes* (Fig. 6.3) might first write a traditional iconographic essay, then use prompt engineering to solicit feminist or psychoanalytic readings from a model, comparing the outputs to their own research (Bullington 2021). This dual approach not only enriches interpretive depth but also reinforces the necessity of critical evaluation and methodological transparency. With students responsible for the quality and relevance of both their traditional and digital analyses, educators encourage habits of scholarly rigor and adaptability. Research also shows that such scaffolding supports the development of both cognitive and affective dimensions of critical thinking, including confidence, curiosity, and resilience in the face of ambiguity (Gonsalves 2024; Georgopoulou et al. 2024). Students learn that digital tools are not oracles, but partners in an ongoing process of inquiry.

Ethical considerations are central when integrating student-generated digital content into research or assessment. The analysis of interactions may reveal patterns of engagement, bias, or cognitive growth—valuable for pedagogical research but subject to privacy and consent protocols. Scholars recommend that all educational research involving student work, prompts, or digital artifacts undergo Institutional Review Board (IRB) approval, with clear procedures for anonymization and informed consent (Poce 2024). Students should be informed about how their data will be used and should retain control over whether their digital artifacts are included in any research or publication. Including discussions about the ethics of AI in academic settings within the curriculum itself not only models responsible practice but also deepens student awareness of issues surrounding authorship, originality, and the social impact of emerging technologies (Georgopoulou et al. 2024). Instructors can build assignments that include reflection on these themes, reinforcing the idea that critical thinking extends beyond analysis of art and into the ethical considerations of research and technology use. Such transparency fosters trust and encourages a culture of responsible innovation, aligning with the broader values of the discipline.

As digital pedagogy becomes more pervasive, the commitment to ethical rigor will remain essential for maintaining scholarly integrity.

At the same time, peer-reviewed research in art education consistently demonstrates the effectiveness of interactive and multimodal methods—such as virtual museum experiences, collaborative writing, and creative digital projects—in fostering critical thinking skills (O'Halloran et al. 2017; Olsen 2024). For instance, a MOOC developed by the National Gallery of Art in Washington employed the "See/Think/Wonder" approach, prompting students to reflect on, analyze, and reinterpret artworks in both individual and group contexts (Poce 2024). The forum for course posts were systematically analyzed using established critical thinking rubrics, revealing positive correlations between reflective writing, aesthetic experience, and the development of analytical skills. Participants reported that the iterative nature of digital discussion—moving from initial observations to deeper interpretation and then to creative synthesis—mirrored the best practices of in-person seminar discussions. The success of such programs underscores the value of structured, scaffolded digital engagement, not only in remote learning environments but also in blended and traditional classrooms. These methods empower students to construct and defend arguments, challenge assumptions, and learn from diverse perspectives. In art history specifically, multimodal assignments that require students to navigate between visual analysis, contextual research, and digital creation are shown to produce more independent and critical thinkers (Arshlock 2018; Hutson 2025). Such findings support the broader adoption of interactive, technology-supported approaches as part of a robust art historical education.

The application of digital and generated images in university-level art history and teacher training further illustrates how critical thinking can be cultivated through visual inquiry. Recent research documents how the creation and critique of AI-generated images prompts students to assess authenticity, recognize algorithmic bias, and reflect on the limitations of digital representations (Ramos-Vallecillo and Murillo-Ligorred 2025). Assignments that ask students to evaluate the truthfulness, creativity, and ethical implications of such images create opportunities for dialogue about the role of technology in shaping historical and aesthetic understanding. This form of visual analysis—often paired with structured writing and group critique—has been shown to promote rigorous evaluation, nuanced argumentation, and ethical awareness. The iterative process of generating, revising, and reflecting on digital images supports the development of both visual literacy and critical self-assessment. Instructors are encouraged to facilitate these conversations by asking students to explain their reasoning, challenge each other's interpretations, and consider the broader cultural consequences of digital art. This pedagogical model ensures that digital fluency and critical engagement are developed hand in hand, preparing students to navigate and question the visual culture of the present and future.

A growing body of research outside art history supports the idea that AI-driven dialogues and argumentation tools can improve student ability to build, revise, and defend complex arguments (Oberer and Erkollar 2024; Belyakova et al. 2022). When students interact with digital systems that provide real-time feedback, challenge their assumptions, or offer competing perspectives, they are required to articulate their reasoning, evaluate evidence, and adapt their positions. These interactive methods foster not only content knowledge but also the habits of mind necessary for critical engagement—such as curiosity, open-mindedness, and reflective skepticism. In the context of art history, this translates into the ability to synthesize visual, textual, and contextual information, weigh divergent interpretations, and justify one's analytic choices with clarity and rigor. Peer-reviewed studies recommend integrating machine-supported dialogues into seminar discussions, research projects, and writing assignments, especially in courses that prioritize analytical writing and historiographical debate. This interactive feedback loop strengthens student confidence as interpreters and prepares them for the demands of advanced scholarship and professional research. The implications for faculty are clear: digital dialogue systems, when carefully scaffolded, can serve as effective partners in teaching critical analysis.

Critical thinking development is further supported by multimodal assignments that require students to navigate and synthesize information from diverse sources. For example, digital mapping, WebQuest, and online games have all been shown to foster analysis, evaluation, and inference skills in language and humanities education (Wei and Li 2024). In art history, similar approaches can be employed—using visual mapping tools to trace the influence of artistic movements, interactive games to reconstruct historical contexts, or digital platforms to curate virtual exhibitions. These activities compel students to gather evidence, test hypotheses, and make interpretive decisions in real time, closely mirroring the cognitive processes of professional art historians. The use of these tools is associated with gains in both independent and collaborative critical thinking, as students are required to negotiate meaning, resolve conflicts, and defend their conclusions to peers and instructors. This dynamic, integrative approach not only reflects the realities of contemporary research but also prepares students for participation in a rapidly evolving digital scholarly landscape. The systematic review of technology-supported critical thinking affirms that these strategies are effective for cultivating robust analytical skills.

Critical thinking is also deeply tied to the development of creativity and adaptive expertise, especially in disciplines like art history where interpretation and innovation are closely linked. Research into AI-supported media arts education demonstrates that assignments emphasizing creative exploration, narrative construction, and interdisciplinary collaboration foster both analytic rigor and imaginative thinking (Bernaschina 2023). Students tasked with creating AI-generated comics or digital stories, for example, must synthesize knowledge from multiple domains, construct coherent narratives, and reflect on both process and product. This process mirrors the analytic demands of art historical research, where scholars interpret and contextualize works of art through a combination of evidence, argument, and creative insight. Educators are advised to design assignments that explicitly link critical thinking to creative outcomes, making the case that methodological rigor and artistic experimentation are not mutually exclusive but mutually reinforcing. As a result, students become more agile thinkers, equipped to adapt to new questions and technologies as the discipline evolves.

Faculty development and ongoing training are essential for maximizing the benefits of digital and AI-supported pedagogies in art history. Studies consistently find that instructors who receive targeted professional development in prompt engineering, digital analysis, and critical thinking pedagogy are better equipped to scaffold student learning and model best practices (Elere et al. 2024). Faculty workshops, collaborative course design, and interdisciplinary dialogue all contribute to a culture of innovation and reflective practice, ensuring that new technologies are integrated thoughtfully and effectively. Institutions that support faculty in experimenting with new methods—while providing opportunities for feedback and assessment—see greater gains in student critical thinking outcomes and digital fluency. As digital tools continue to evolve, investment in ongoing faculty learning will remain a cornerstone of successful art history education, ensuring that both students and instructors are prepared for the demands and possibilities of digital scholarship.

Research on the broader conceptualization of digital literacy and critical engagement in higher education emphasizes the need for students to develop not only technical proficiency but also the ability to critique, adapt, and ethically employ AI tools (Georgopoulou et al. 2024). The extension of digital literacy frameworks, such as DigCompEdu (https://joint-research-centre.ec.europa.eu/digcompedu/digcompedu-framework_en), to include critical engagement with AI reflects a consensus among scholars that responsible and informed interaction with technology is central to contemporary education. Art history programs are encouraged to adopt these frameworks, integrating digital literacy and ethical reflection into core curricula, research projects, and assessment. Such an approach ensures that graduates are not only competent users of technology but also thoughtful, responsible, and adaptive scholars, capable of interrogating both the tools and the contexts in which they operate. This combination of technical, analytic, and ethical skills positions students to thrive in the dynamic landscape of twenty-first-century scholarship and professional practice.

6.5 Assessing Pedagogical Outcomes and Student Engagement

The integration of LLMs into educational assessment marks a significant shift in how instructors can evaluate student learning and engagement. Recent research demonstrates that these models are now capable of automating a range of assessment tasks—including answer matching, keyword extraction, and the clustering of student responses—while providing timely, individualized feedback (Wangwiwattana and Tongvivat 2023). Such feedback, once challenging in large or remote classrooms, can now be tailored and delivered in real time, freeing instructors to focus on higher-level mentorship and interpretation. The accuracy rates reported in these studies, often exceeding 99% in specific assessment contexts, suggest that these tools not only streamline grading but also enhance the quality of formative assessment.

Importantly, these systems can go beyond scoring: they are capable of generating targeted feedback that encourages deeper student reflection and improvement. This new paradigm positions these models as partners in academic evaluation, capable of supporting both efficiency and pedagogical rigor. Through reducing the administrative load on faculty, natural language models enable instructors to dedicate more time to meaningful student interactions, fostering a more engaged and intellectually vibrant classroom environment. Nevertheless, careful calibration and faculty oversight are crucial to ensure that machine-generated feedback aligns with course objectives and disciplinary standards.

The use of LLMs for assessment is, however, not without its challenges. Studies of their implementation in higher education reveal concerns about reliability in more specialized or advanced cognitive tasks, particularly in fields that require nuanced, context-rich interpretation such as art history (Zhang et al. 2024). While such models can provide accurate summaries and generate helpful feedback for straightforward or factual assignments, they sometimes falter when confronted with complex reasoning or subjectivity (when not using an advanced reasoning model like o1 Pro or 2.5 Pro)—issues that are central to humanities disciplines. Faculty and students have raised questions regarding data privacy, ethical use, and the potential for over-reliance on automated tools, which could diminish independent critical thinking (Zhang et al. 2024). Best practices for using them in assessment thus include robust training for educators, transparent data handling policies, and explicit instruction for students on how to interpret and verify generated responses. Studies recommend a hybrid approach in which LLMs serve as supplements to, rather than replacements for, traditional assessment methods.

In the context of art history, natural language models offer new opportunities for assessing a wide range of learning outcomes, from visual literacy and formal analysis to research synthesis and critical writing. Multimodal models, which incorporate both textual and visual analysis, have the potential to transform how students are evaluated in tasks that traditionally rely on close looking and detailed description. These models can generate sample analyses, offer comparative insights, and simulate peer review, helping students test and refine their own arguments before submitting final work. Studies have shown that aligning the technological features of the tools with educational needs enhances student engagement and learning outcomes (Al-Dokhny et al. 2024). When students are required to iteratively prompt, critique, and revise both generated and self-produced content, they develop stronger analytical and metacognitive skills. Instructors can further leverage models to design assessments that measure not only factual recall but also argument construction, historiographical debate, and interdisciplinary synthesis. The flexibility of these tools supports personalized learning, allowing each student to receive feedback tailored to their current level and learning goals. As a result, LLMs contribute to a more differentiated and student-centered assessment landscape.

Assessment of student engagement—a key predictor of academic success—can also be enhanced, particularly in online and blended learning environments. Recent research demonstrates that most models can generate engagement-driven content and facilitate adaptive interaction, optimizing both motivation and participation (Coppolillo et al. 2024). By analyzing patterns in student queries, forum posts, and prompt responses, language models are able to identify areas of disengagement and suggest interventions such as targeted discussion questions or personalized feedback. This capability transforms the assessment of engagement from a subjective or impressionistic exercise to a data-driven, actionable process. Gamified AI-powered assessments have been found to significantly boost motivation and learning outcomes, particularly when combined with automatic question generation and real-time feedback (Bachiri et al. 2023). In art history, where student participation is often critical for successful seminar discussion and collaborative analysis, such approaches ensure that engagement is both monitored and cultivated throughout the course. The result is a more vibrant classroom community, with students empowered to contribute and reflect on their own learning journey. However, instructors must remain attentive to issues of equity and accessibility, ensuring that engagement metrics reflect genuine participation rather than superficial interaction.

Recent studies in visual arts education underscore the need for innovative assessment models that accommodate creativity, individual ability, and the subjective nature of art historical interpretation (Cohen 2015). LLMs, when thoughtfully integrated, can support portfolio-based and performance assessment by generating personalized feedback, tracking developmental progress, and moderating peer review processes. Research in art education recommends the use of developmental self-assessment, in which students define the meaning, visual qualities, and criteria for evaluating their own work, while models provide scaffolding and comparative analysis (Cohen 2015). Such authentic assessment practices align with constructivist approaches to learning, emphasizing personal growth, creativity, and reflective inquiry. This methodology is particularly well-suited to art history, where assessment must balance disciplinary standards with the open-ended, interpretive nature of the field. By combining human and machine evaluation, educators can offer richer, more nuanced feedback that supports both technical mastery and creative exploration. The challenge lies in designing assessment frameworks that integrate these new abilities without sacrificing the flexibility or individuality central to art education. Ongoing faculty development and iterative curriculum design remain essential for sustaining the integrity and relevance of these practices.

The assessment of higher-order learning outcomes—such as critical thinking, historiographical reflection, and research synthesis—can benefit from the dialogical affordances of LLMs. Large-scale studies in higher education have found that interactive digital platforms, including those powered by those models under discussion, support the development of critical thinking skills by prompting students to articulate, defend, and revise their arguments in response to both human and AI-generated feedback (Leinonen et al. 2024). Assignments that require students to debate, simulate peer review, or respond to counterarguments foster habits of intellectual curiosity and analytical precision. In art history, where the construction and deconstruction of scholarly narratives is central, such dialogical engagement prepares students for advanced research and professional practice. Peer-reviewed research recommends integrating machine-driven assessment with opportunities for reflective writing, collaborative projects, and oral presentations, ensuring that students are evaluated across multiple modalities and contexts. This multimodal assessment framework aligns with the discipline's emphasis on holistic, evidence-based evaluation, supporting both individual achievement and collective learning. The challenge for educators is to balance automated analysis with human judgment, preserving the interpretive richness and methodological rigor of the field.

Therefore, assessment models that incorporate both generated and human feedback can help address persistent challenges in measuring engagement and learning outcomes in art history. For instance, self-assessment practices—supported by clear learning outcomes and iterative reflection—have been shown to increase student ownership and accountability, resulting in deeper engagement and more meaningful progress (Escribano and McMahon 2010). LLMs can facilitate self-assessment by providing students with prompt-based scaffolding, rubrics, and instant feedback on drafts, helping them to set goals and monitor their own development. Faculty can supplement this process with targeted feedback, ensuring that automated suggestions are contextualized within the broader aims of the course. Research in educational assessment recommends triangulating data from multiple sources—student self-assessment, instructor evaluation, and peer or generated feedback—to provide a comprehensive view of student achievement and engagement. This layered approach is particularly valuable in art history, where learning is both cumulative and recursive, requiring continual reflection and revision. By supporting students in becoming active participants in their own assessment, educators cultivate metacognitive skills and a deeper investment in the learning process.

At the same time, critical voices caution that these tools are not a panacea and may struggle with the interpretive ambiguity, ideological plurality, or nuanced visual analysis that characterize art history and the humanities more broadly (Buyl et al. 2024; Douglas 2023). Studies underscore the need for transparency about the limitations of automated assessment, especially regarding bias, the reproduction of dominant narratives, and the potential erosion of disciplinary expertise. Peer-reviewed work highlights that the models reflect the values and assumptions of their training data and creators, sometimes introducing ideological bias or misrepresenting minority perspectives (Buyl et al. 2024). Art history instructors must address these challenges directly, fostering critical awareness and skepticism in students and emphasizing the importance of cross-verification with scholarly sources. Assessment protocols should include regular audits of automated feedback, explicit discussion of bias, and the inclusion of diverse voices and perspectives. Such vigilance ensures that assessment practices continue to support the development of independent, thoughtful, and critically engaged scholars.

The future of assessment in art history and higher education will likely involve hybrid, adaptive models that combine the efficiency and scale of LLMs with the interpretive depth and contextual understanding of human expertise. Studies recommend ongoing research into optimizing natural language models for discipline-specific tasks, including the assessment of visual analysis, historical argumentation, and creative production (Shi et al. 2024). Promising avenues include the development of multimodal models capable of integrating textual, visual, and contextual data; personalized assessment platforms that adapt to student progress and learning styles; and collaborative feedback systems that blend AI and human review. Institutions are encouraged to invest in infrastructure, faculty training, and policy development to ensure that assessment remains transparent, ethical, and aligned with disciplinary values. As the field continues to evolve, art history educators are well-positioned to lead the way in designing and evaluating assessment frameworks that support critical thinking, creativity, and lifelong engagement with visual culture.

Therefore, reflecting on this chapter as it has charted the shifting landscape of art history pedagogy as it navigates the integration of prompt engineering, large language models, and multimodal digital tools into the discipline's teaching and assessment practices. Central to this transformation is a reimagining of the art history classroom—from a site of passive absorption of canonical narratives to an active, dialogical space where students coconstruct knowledge, question assumptions, and iteratively refine their interpretations. Across a series of case studies and practical assignments, the chapter has illustrated how prompt-based inquiry, scaffolded digital exercises, and the careful use of automated assessment can foster metacognitive awareness, deeper analytical engagement, and a greater sense of intellectual agency among students. These methods encourage learners not only to scrutinize the objects of art history, but also to interrogate their own analytical strategies, understanding how the framing of a question or the structuring of a prompt can shape the contours of the answer received.

The most effective implementations balance technological innovation with the enduring strengths of art historical practice—close looking, visual literacy, contextual research, and critical debate. Scaffolded assignments, iterative feedback, and thoughtfully applied constraints ensure that digital tools supplement rather than supplant the intellectual rigor and interpretive nuance that have long defined the field. Faculty play a vital role as guides and critical interlocutors, providing ethical frameworks, modeling skepticism toward automated outputs, and nurturing the habits of reflection and self-assessment that underpin scholarly growth. Assessment, too is reconceived as a hybrid process: leveraging the speed and adaptability of LLMs to provide timely feedback and track engagement, while preserving the human judgment essential for evaluating creative, open-ended work.

Therefore, this chapter has illuminated the profound impact that prompt engineering and digital tools can have on the pedagogy of art history, underscoring the need for transparency, intentional design, and critical reflection at every stage of the learning process. The chapter's analysis of assignment scaffolding, iterative feedback, and dialogic inquiry highlights how transparent assignment design fosters student agency and demystifies the role of technology in shaping both process and product. By foregrounding explicit reflection, educators not only enhance metacognitive awareness but also empower students to navigate the interplay between human judgment and machine-generated responses. This approach encourages students to interrogate both their analytical strategies and the inherent limitations of generative systems, fostering habits of critical inquiry that extend beyond the classroom. The chapter's best-practice examples demonstrate that thoughtfully designed digital interventions can democratize participation, address diverse learning needs, and support a more inclusive and engaging art historical education. The commitment to process transparency also models scholarly integrity, preparing students to become discerning interpreters of digital content and responsible stewards of visual culture.

A central takeaway is the foundational role of ethical considerations in the successful integration of generative AI into teaching and learning. Issues of privacy, consent, bias mitigation, and the responsible handling of student data must be embedded in every aspect of digital pedagogy—not treated as peripheral compliance matters. The chapter argues that the protection of student agency and the cultivation of a safe, supportive learning environment are inseparable from the discipline's mission to nurture critical thinking and independent judgment. Faculty are therefore called to engage in ongoing professional development, ensuring they remain current with evolving digital methodologies, assessment tools, and ethical frameworks. Collaborative dialogue among educators, students, and technologists is essential for surfacing unanticipated risks, addressing gaps in digital literacy, and cocreating guidelines for equitable practice. By prioritizing ethical reflexivity, art history programs can build trust with students and stakeholders, safeguarding both educational quality and institutional reputation. In a rapidly changing technological landscape, these ethical commitments are the anchor points that sustain pedagogical rigor and social responsibility.

Looking to the future, this calls for art history educators to embrace a stance of adaptability, experimentation, and cross-disciplinary collaboration. As digital tools and prompt-based methodologies continue to evolve, so too must the field's approaches to curriculum design, assessment, and student engagement. Faculty should be encouraged to pilot new technologies, share insights across institutional and disciplinary boundaries, and engage in collaborative research on digital pedagogy. The goal is to prepare students not simply to consume digital knowledge, but to become active, critical participants in shaping the evolving conversations of the discipline. This requires a pedagogy that is as intellectually rigorous as it is technologically agile—one that equips graduates to interpret, critique, and contribute to a complex visual world with confidence, creativity, and ethical discernment. The integration of prompt engineering and generative AI should be seen as an opportunity to enrich art history education, deepen inquiry, and expand the discipline's reach and relevance. By sustaining an open, reflective, and innovative culture, educators will ensure that the core values of critical inquiry and independent thought endure, even as the tools and contexts of learning continue to transform.

References

Al-Dokhny A, Alismaiel OA, Youssif S, Nasr N, Drwish A, Samir A (2024) Can multimodal large language models enhance performance benefits among higher education students? Sustain 16(23):10780

Alkholy I (2010) Using hypermedia in teaching art and design: Baroque Dutch paintings. Int J Emerg Technol Learn 5(3):37–41

Ashlock JM (2018) Teaching critical thinking in the digital era through visual art: a higher education perspective (Doctoral dissertation, Argosy University/Phoenix)

Avci H, Pedersen S, Thomas A (2020) Writing a formal analysis of art in a game-based learning environment. In: EdMedia+ innovate learnin.g association for the advancement of computing in education (AACE), pp 669–671

Bachiri Y-A, Mouncif H, Bouikhalene B (2023) Artificial intelligence empowers gamification: optimizing student engagement and learning outcomes in e-learning and MOOCs. Int J Eng Pedagogy (iJEP) 13(8)

Bekova GA, Jou-Yi C (2024) Problems and prospects of museum pedagogy in modern art education. Bull Ser Art Educ: Art, Theory, Methods

Belyakova OV, Pyrkina NA, Chuikova ES (2022) Critical thinking in professional education: digital options for teachers and learners. In: Digital technologies in the new socio-economic reality. Springer International Publishing, pp 783–792

Bernaschina D (2023) Artes mediales en educación: una mirada desde la enseñanza en las escuelas primarias y secundarias. Rev Ens Pedag 18(2):1–23

Bullington J (2021) African-american art history: reflections on expanding pedagogy in 21st century liberal arts contexts. Art Hist Pedag Pract 6(1):5

Buyl M, Rogiers A, Noels S, Dominguez-Catena I, Heiter E, Romero R, Johary I, Mara A, Lijffijt J, Bie TD (2024) Large language models reflect the ideology of their creators

Cain W (2024) Prompting change: exploring prompt engineering in large language model ai and its potential to transform education. TechTrends 68(1):47–57

Cammarata L (2016) Content-based foreign language teaching. Routledge

Carpino K, Hutson J (2024) A new canvas of learning: enhancing formal analysis skills in AP art history through AI-generated Islamic art. For Edu Stud 2(2)

Cason N (1998) Interactive multimedia: an alternative context for studying works of art. Stud Art Educ 39:336. https://doi.org/10.2307/1320238

Choi-Lundberg DL, Butler-Henderson K, Harman K, Crawford J (2023) A systematic review of digital innovations in technology-enhanced learning designs in higher education. Australas J Educ Technol

Cohen RM (2015) From child art to visual language of youth: new models and tools for assessment of learning and creation in art education. Stud Art Educ 56:382–385

Coppolillo E, Cinus F, Minici M, Bonchi F, Manco G (2024) engagement-driven content generation with large language models. ArXiv

Dehouche N, Dehouche K (2023) What's in a text-to-image prompt? The potential of stable diffusion in visual arts education. Heliyon. Retrieved from: https://www.cell.com/heliyon/pdf/S2405-8440(23)03964-6.pdf

Dolšina M (2015) Educational role of art history as a school subject area in programmes of formal education in Slovenia. J Edu, Cult, Soc 6(1):227–241

Douglas MR (2023) Large language models. Commun ACM 66:7

Elere E, Ulme A, De Paolis L (2024) Artificial intelligence in architecture and art education. In: Environment. Technologies. Resources. Proceedings of the international scientific and practical conference vol 2, pp 97–103

Elgammal A, Liu B, Kim D, Elhoseiny M, Mazzone M (2018) The shape of art history in the eyes of the machine. In: Proceedings of the AAAI conference on artificial intelligence vol 32, no 1

Escribano PD, McMahon JP (2010) Self-assessment based on language learning outcomes: a study with first year engineering students

Fareed MW, Bou Nassif A, Nofal E (2024) Exploring the potentials of artificial intelligence image generators for educating the history of architecture. Heritage 7(3):1727–1753

Fatawi I, Asy'ari M, Hunaepi H, Samsuri T, Bilad M (2024) Empowering language models through advanced prompt engineering: a comprehensive bibliometric review. Indones J Sci Technol

Finch JA (2015) Visual literacy and art history: teaching images and objects in digital environments. Essentials teaching and integrating visual and media literacy: visualizing learning, pp 251–264
Freedman K (2003) Teaching visual culture: curriculum, aesthetics, and the social life of art. Teachers College Press
Gadsden V (2008) The arts and education: knowledge generation, pedagogy, and the discourse of learning. Rev Res Educ 32:29–61. https://doi.org/10.3102/0091732X07309691
Gasper-Hulvat M (2017a) Active learning in art history: a review of formal literature. Art Hist Ped Prac 2(1):2
Gasper-Hulvat M (2017b) Active learning in art history: a review of formal literature. Art Hist Pedag Prac 2(1)
Georgopoulou MS, Krouska A, Troussas C, Sgouropoulou C (2024) Redefining the concept of literacy: a digcompedu extension for critical engagement with ai tools. 2024 9th SEEDA-CECNSM, pp 98–102
Gonsalves C (2024) Generative AI's impact on critical thinking: revisiting bloom's taxonomy. J Mark Educ
Gu J, Han Z, Chen S, Beirami A, He B, Zhang G, Torr P (2023a) A systematic survey of prompt engineering on vision-language foundation models. arXiv preprint arXiv:2307.12980
Gu J, Han Z, Chen S, Beirami A, He B, Zhang G, Torr P (2023b) A systematic survey of prompt engineering on vision-language foundation models. arXiv preprint arXiv:2307.12980
Guo Q (2024) Prompting change: ChatGPT's impact on digital humanities pedagogy—a case study in art history. Int J Hum and Art Comp 18(1):58–78
Hu LK, Lee DC (2024) Prompt engineering 101: shaping tomorrow's critical thinkers in an ai world. Rev Educ Stud
Hutson J, Cotroneo P (2023) Generative AI tools in art education: exploring prompt engineering and iterative processes for enhanced creativity. Met 4(1)
Hutson J, Harper-Nichols M (2023) Generative AI and algorithmic art: disrupting the framing of meaning and rethinking the subject-object dilemma. Glo J Comp Sci Techn: D 23(1)
Hutson J, Plate D (2023) Working with (Not against) the technology: GPT3 and Artificial Intelligence (AI) in college composition. J Rob Auto Res 4(1)
Hutson J, Robertson B (2023) Exploring the educational potential of AI generative art in 3D design fundamentals: a case study on prompt engineering and creative workflows. Glo J Hum-Soc Sci: A Art Human-Psych 23(2)
Hutson J (2024) Integrating art and AI: evaluating the educational impact of AI tools in digital art history learning. For Art Stud 1(1)
Hutson J (2025) Multimodal GAI in arts-based multiliteracies: fostering interdisciplinary creativity. In: Arts-based multiliteracies for teaching and learning. IGI Global, pp 209–244
Jiang HH, Brown L, Cheng J, Khan M, Gupta A, Workman D, Gebru T (2023) AI art and its impact on artists. In: Proceedings of the 2023 AAAI/ACM conference on AI, ethics, and society, pp 363–374
Knoth N, Tolzin A, Janson A, Leimeister J (2024) AI literacy and its implications for prompt engineering strategies. Comput Educ Artif Intell 6:100225
Koh J, Tay P, Mohamad Ali SB (2021) Creating institutional technological pedagogical content knowledge—a case study through the eyes of an educational technology support unit. Teach Learn Arts Higher Educ Technol
Korzyński P, Mazurek G, Krzypkowska P, Kurasiński A (2023) artificial intelligence prompt engineering as a new digital competence. Entrepren Bus Econ Rev
Kutis B (2020) Scaffolding the formal analysis assignment in art history courses to promote learning. J Teach and Learn with Techn 9(1)
Lazovsky GS, Raz T, Kenett YN (2024) The art of creative inquiry—from question asking to prompt engineering. J Creative Behav
Lawasi MC, Rohman VA, Shoreamanis M (2024) The Use of AI in Improving Student's Critical Thinking Skills. Proceedings Series on Social Sciences & Humanities, 18, 366–370

Leinonen J, Macneil S, Denny P, Hellas A (2024) Using large language models for teaching computing. Proceedings 55th ACM technical symposium on computer science education, vol 2, pp 1901–1901
Leung CH (2024) Promoting optimal learning with ChatGPT: a comprehensive exploration of prompt engineering in education. As J Cont Edu 8(2):104–114
Locher P, Krupinski E, Schaefer A (2015) Art and authenticity: behavioral and eye-movement analyses. Psych Aes, Creat, Art 9(4):356
Mazzone M, Elgammal A (2019) Art, creativity, and the potential of artificial intelligence. Arts 8(1):26
Muktadir G (2023) A brief history of prompt: leveraging language models. ArXiv
Murray MD (2024) Prompt engineering and priming in law. Available at SSRN
Mzwri K, Turcsányi-Szabó M (2025) The impact of prompt engineering and a generative ai-driven tool on autonomous learning: a case study. Educ Sci
Nelson RS (2000) The slide lecture, or the work of art history in the age of mechanical reproduction. Crit Inq 26(3):414–434
O'Halloran KL, Tan S, Marissa EK (2017) Multimodal analysis for critical thinking. Learn, Med Techn 42(2):147–170
Oberer B, Erkollar A (2024) Improving argumentation skills through AI-driven dialogues: a transdisciplinary approach. J Syst, Cyber and Infor. https://doi.org/10.54808/jsci.22.06.1
Olin M (2017) Formal analysis: art and anthropology. Idea Rac Hist Hum 89–111
Olsen D (2024) Media arts education: transforming education through multimodal cognition, holistic learning, and techno-embodiment. Routledge
Oppenlaender J (2024) A taxonomy of prompt modifiers for text-to-image generation. Beh Info Tech 43(15):3763–3776
Oppenlaender J, Linder R, Silvennoinen J (2024) Prompting AI art: an investigation into the creative skill of prompt engineering. Inter J Hum–Comp Inter 1–23
PAS (2024) PAS: data-efficient plug-and-play prompt augmentation system. ArXiv
Poce A (2024) AI, heritage and critical thinking development: an education experience within university context. Ubi Proc 4(1)
Pornprasit C, Tantithamthavorn C (2024) Fine-tuning and prompt engineering for large language models-based code review automation. Info Soft Tech 175:107523
Preziosi D (2009) The art of art history: a critical anthology. Oxford University Press, pp 46–47
Prown JD (1980) Style as evidence. Wint Port 15(3):197–210
Ramos-Vallecillo N, Murillo-Ligorred V (2025) The phenomenon of artificial intelligence-generated images in university teacher training and its impact on developing critical thinking No. ART-2025-141309
Rathod JD (2024) Systematic study of prompt engineering. Int J Res Appl Sci Eng Technol
Schmidt DC, Spencer-Smith J, Fu Q, White J (2023) Cataloging prompt patterns to enhance the discipline of prompt engineering
Shi Z, Wang Z, Fan H, Zhang Z, Li L, Zhang Y, Yin Z, Sheng L, Qiao Y, Shao J (2024) Assessment of multimodal large language models in alignment with human values. ArXiv
Sreedhar LS (2024) Speak the language of AI: mastering prompt engineering for LLMs. Proceeding international conference industrial engineering operations management
Vasari G (1910) Lives of the most eminent painters, sculptors, and architects (trans. J. Foster). G. Bell
Viola L (2023) The humanities in the digital: beyond critical digital humanities. Springer Nature
Walter Y (2024) Embracing the future of artificial intelligence in the classroom: the relevance of AI literacy, prompt engineering, and critical thinking in modern education. Int J Edu Tech High Edu 21(1):15
Walton N (2020) There are no formal elements. Deb Art Des Edu 66
Wangwiwattana C, Tongvivat Y (2023) Automating academic assessment: a large language model approach. 2023 7th international conference information technology (InCIT), pp 330–334

Wei J, Li H (2024) A systematic review of critical thinking development in information and communication technology-supported English as a foreign language teaching from 2015 to 2024. For Ling Stud. https://doi.org/10.30564/fls.v6i6.7478

Woo DJ, Wang D, Yung T, Guo K (2024) Effects of a prompt engineering intervention on undergraduate students AI self-efficacy, AI knowledge and prompt engineering ability: a mixed methods study. ArXiv

Yefimenko IV, Yakymchuk O, Kravtsova N, Sotska H, Korol A (2021) Art education development in the context of global changes. Linguist Cult Rev

Zhang X, Zhang X, Liu H (2024) Reflections on enhancing higher education classroom effectiveness through the introduction of large language models. J Mod Educ Res

Zheng M, Liang H, Yang F, Sun H, Li T, Xiong L, Zhang Y, Wu Y, Li K, Shen Y, Lin M, Zhang T, Dong G, Qiao Y, Fang K, Chen W, Zhang WT, Zhou Z (2024) Pas: data-efficient plug-and-play prompt augmentation system. ArXiv

Chapter 7
Immersive Learning with the Leonardo da Vinci AI-Clone Tutor

Abstract This part explores the innovative integration of extended reality, digital avatars, and generative platforms in the teaching of art history, centering on the development and deployment of a Leonardo da Vinci AI-Clone tutor. The chapter opens by articulating key pedagogical principles and possibilities introduced by immersive, machine-based environments, emphasizing the unique affordances of extended reality for dialogic, student-centered learning. It then details the technical and conceptual processes involved in designing the interactive tutor, including dataset curation, avatar modeling, and the calibration of historically grounded yet adaptive conversational capacities. Through concrete examples from virtual classrooms, the discussion illustrates how interactive, avatar-driven instruction enables real-time analytic feedback, collaborative problem-solving, and experiential learning across varied educational settings. The chapter addresses significant challenges in implementation, such as technical constraints, dataset biases, and the maintenance of authenticity in avatar-driven pedagogy. It concludes by mapping future directions for avatar-powered, immersive education in art history, proposing scalable models and research agendas for advancing inclusivity, engagement, and scholarly rigor.

7.1 Extended Reality and AI Integration: Pedagogical Principles and Possibilities

The intersection of extended reality (XR) and artificial intelligence (AI) signals a fundamental transformation in the teaching and learning of art history. These converging technologies are not simply additive tools, but catalysts for a reimagining of the art history classroom as a dynamic, participatory space. XR platforms—encompassing virtual, augmented, and mixed reality—invite students to inhabit reconstructed environments, experience spatial and material aspects of artworks firsthand, and explore historical contexts in immersive ways that transcend traditional slides or textbooks. Meanwhile, AI-driven systems, from large language models to conversational avatars, enable adaptive feedback, dialogic engagement, and individualized learning trajectories, supporting both novice and advanced students in real time.

J. Hutson, *Art History in the Age of Artificial Intelligence*, Springer Series on Cultural Computing, https://doi.org/10.1007/978-3-032-02920-1_7

When combined, XR and AI offer a multisensory, interactive framework for inquiry, allowing learners to navigate virtual galleries, converse with simulated historical figures, and collaboratively interrogate works of art within richly contextualized digital settings. This convergence supports a pedagogy that is at once constructivist, experiential, and reflexive, foregrounding not only what students learn, but how and why they learn it. The integration of XR and AI compels educators to revisit foundational questions about interpretation, agency, and the ethics of technology in the humanities. As these tools become increasingly central to the field, they promise to democratize access, deepen engagement, and expand the very possibilities of art historical education for diverse learners.

As explored in Chap. 2, XR technologies—ranging from virtual reconstructions of archeological sites to immersive museum exhibitions—have already demonstrated their power to create engaging, affectively rich experiences for diverse audiences (Rua and Alvito 2011). Within the classroom, XR simulations allow students to virtually traverse canonical environments, such as the Salon Carré or the Temple of Demeter, deepening their understanding of materiality, spatial context, and the experiential dimensions of art (Gao et al. 2024). These technologies excel at cultivating visual literacy and fostering historical empathy, providing a sense of embodied presence that static slides or readings cannot replicate (Chandler and Clulow 2020). Yet, as traditionally deployed, XR platforms have prioritized visual–spatial immersion over adaptive, dialogic, or personalized instruction. In parallel, language-based AI—specifically large LLMs and generative avatars—has found their primary utility as personalized tutors or automated feedback mechanisms, fostering metacognitive awareness and supporting iterative learning through natural language interaction (Baillifard et al. 2024; Denny et al. 2024). This bifurcation has shaped recent educational practice, with immersive technologies and conversational AI operating as distinct, if complementary, tools. Bridging these modalities remains a central challenge for contemporary pedagogy.

Historically, immersive learning tools in art history have been adopted as visual and experiential supplements to more conventional instructional practices. Virtual walkthroughs of ancient monuments, 3D models of lost artworks, and interactive digital guides have all contributed to an expanded repertoire of pedagogical techniques (Duguleană et al. 2020; Chandler and Clulow 2020). Such platforms support close looking and contextual analysis, allowing learners to apprehend scale, texture, and spatial relationships in ways that are otherwise inaccessible. However, these environments have typically lacked adaptive instructional capabilities: they provide richly detailed settings but are unable to respond dynamically to a learner's individual questions or misunderstandings (Hutson et al. 2023; Gao et al. 2024). Conversely, the rise of AI-powered language models has made possible new forms of adaptive tutoring, formative assessment, and personalized feedback, but these systems have generally been limited to text-based or conversational modes, abstracted from the visual and spatial experience of art (Baillifard et al. 2024; Arya and Verma 2024). Consequently, each approach has addressed only a subset of the cognitive, affective, and interpretive demands inherent in art historical education. Their persistent separation has thus constrained the full pedagogical potential of either modality, especially in a discipline where contextual, embodied, and dialogic engagement are paramount (Mahmoud and Sørensen 2024).

Pedagogically, the imperative to integrate XR and AI requires a return to foundational principles in art history education. Traditional didactic models, grounded in linear lectures and text-based analysis, often struggle to accommodate the diversity of learner backgrounds and interpretive strategies present in today's classrooms. The synthesis of immersive environments with natural language dialogue enables a fundamental shift: students may now navigate a reconstructed Renaissance studio or Byzantine chapel while holding a real-time conversation with an avatar modeled on Leonardo da Vinci, negotiating issues of attribution, style, and historiography as they move through the virtual space (Gao et al. 2024; Dong 2023). Such integration actualizes Vygotsky's concept of the zone of proximal development, as learners are scaffolded by expert personas who can adapt explanations to their current level of understanding and encourage metacognitive reflection (Shabani et al. 2010; Meyer and Dannecker 2024). These systems further support iterative inquiry and dialogic learning, prompting students to clarify their assumptions, refine their interpretations, and explore alternative explanations. The result is a pedagogy rooted in coconstruction of knowledge, reflective practice, and historical empathy. In this context, the art history classroom becomes not merely a site of content transmission, but a dialogic, embodied, and critically engaged space.

Empirical research affirms the potential of combining immersive experiences like AR or VR with conversational LLMs. Studies of immersive avatars and adaptive learning systems have shown that students demonstrate greater engagement, deeper critical reasoning, and improved retention when they interact with historically accurate digital figures situated in rich spatial contexts (Gao et al. 2024; Baillifard et al. 2024). These platforms promote "authentic presence"—a sense of agency and immersion that enhances cognitive and affective outcomes (Chandler and Clulow 2020). AI-driven tutors, when layered into such environments, are able to personalize content delivery, adjust complexity, and scaffold interpretive moves in response to real-time learner input (Bhatia et al. 2024; Denny et al. 2024). This is particularly salient in art history, where meaning emerges at the intersection of visual analysis, historical context, and critical debate. Thus, through situating natural language dialogue within immersive, historically situated environments, educators can address both the analytical and affective dimensions of learning. The synergy supports metacognitive growth, encouraging students to reflect on their interpretive strategies as well as their substantive conclusions (Mahmoud and Sørensen 2024). As such, the integrated use of XR + AI offers a triadic model—analytical, affective, dialogic—uniquely suited to the complexities of humanistic inquiry.

Despite these affordances, significant challenges remain in realizing the pedagogical promise of XR-AI integration. Technical and infrastructural barriers—including device compatibility, accessibility for students with disabilities, and the sophistication of avatar modeling—continue to limit broad adoption (Hutson et al. 2023; Gao et al. 2024). Ethical considerations also arise, ranging from data privacy and algorithmic bias to the risk of overreliance on automation at the expense of human judgment and disciplinary nuance (Bilad et al. 2023; Abuodha and Kipkebut 2024).

There is an ongoing need for accessible assignment design and assessment frameworks that harness XR-AI affordances while preserving the rigor and interpretive subtlety central to art historical scholarship. Such requirements demand ongoing collaboration among instructors, technologists, and students, as well as continual investment in faculty development and curricular innovation. As the technological landscape evolves, the imperative is to ensure that digital tools supplement and enrich, rather than supplant, the core strengths of the discipline. This entails foregrounding historical reflexivity, critical debate, and scholarly agency within all XR-AI-mediated pedagogical designs.

The theoretical underpinnings of XR-AI integration in education are deeply rooted in the constructivist tradition, which holds that learners actively build knowledge through engagement with their environment, rather than passively absorbing information. Within this paradigm, extended reality provides the concrete, multisensory experiences necessary for deep learning: students can virtually navigate historical spaces, manipulate digital surrogates of artifacts, and interact with simulated agents representing artists, patrons, or other historical actors. Such embodied experiences foster not only visual literacy but also a felt sense of historical context and material presence, supporting the construction of rich, interconnected mental models. AI-driven scaffolding then enters as a dialogic partner—prompting inquiry, posing problems, and responding to students' evolving understanding in ways that support iterative meaning-making. By aligning with constructivist theory, the integration of XR and AI ensures that knowledge is anchored in authentic, context-sensitive activity, rather than rote memorization or abstract generalization. This approach is especially significant in art history, where interpretation is always a situated act, shaped by the interplay of object, viewer, and context (Table 7.1).

For instance, Kolb's experiential learning theory elaborates this process, describing how effective learning cycles through concrete experience, reflective observation, abstract conceptualization, and active experimentation (Morris 2020). XR environments are uniquely suited to Kolb's framework, as they immerse students in situations where they can "experience" artworks, architectural sites, or historical events from multiple vantage points. AI tools further enhance this cycle by providing immediate, adaptive feedback, supporting both reflection and conceptualization. After exploring a virtual reconstruction of the Salon Carré, students might engage with an AI avatar of Leonardo da Vinci, whose questioning and commentary prompt them to reflect on their observations, articulate interpretations, and test hypotheses about artistic intent or historical significance. This iterative process moves students beyond passive observation to active, critical engagement, in which the boundaries between learning, doing, and thinking are intentionally blurred. Experiential and reflective cycles are further reinforced by the opportunity to revisit environments, experiment with alternative scenarios, and receive personalized guidance from intelligent systems attuned to individual progress.

Complementing constructivist and experiential models, metacognitive theories emphasize the importance of self-awareness, regulation, and adaptive thinking in effective learning. Anderson's revision of Bloom's taxonomy situates cognitive skills

Table 7.1 Pedagogical theories and XR-AI integration in art history

Pedagogical theory	Core principle	XR-AI mechanism	Instructional outcome
Constructivism (Vygotsky, Piaget)	Knowledge constructed through active engagement	Real-time interaction with AI avatars and immersive environments	Learner-centered, dialogic knowledge construction
Experiential learning (Kolb)	Learning as a cycle: experience, reflection, conceptualization, experimentation	Multisensory VR experiences, iterative AI-guided tasks	Deepened understanding via embodied, iterative cycles
Metacognitive theory	Awareness and regulation of one's own thinking	AI-driven prompts for reflection, self-assessment in VR	Enhanced self-regulation and adaptive learning
Zone of proximal development (Vygotsky)	Learning maximized through expert-guided scaffolding	Adaptive AI avatars scaffold difficulty, support just-in-time	Optimized challenge; tailored progression
Dual coding theory (Paivio)	Learning is enhanced by combining visual and verbal inputs	Integration of VR visuals and AI-generated narrative/dialogue	Improved retention and conceptual integration
Bloom's revised taxonomy (Anderson et al.)	Hierarchical cognitive skills: remember, understand, apply, analyze, evaluate, create	Adaptive questioning and task assignment by AI, simulated application in VR	Mastery from basic recall to creative synthesis
Situated cognition	Knowledge situated in authentic, meaningful contexts	Context-rich XR environments with AI avatars as guides	Contextual transfer and application of knowledge
Social constructivism (Bruner)	Learning as coconstruction through dialogue and collaboration	AI avatars engage learners in Socratic dialogue within social VR spaces	Negotiated meaning, critical discourse

on a continuum from remembering and understanding, through application and analysis, to evaluation and creative synthesis—a progression that is well supported by staged, adaptive interactions with XR and AI (Meyer and Dannecker 2024). Vygotskyan scaffolding principles, meanwhile, stress the role of guided support in moving learners from what they can accomplish independently to what they can achieve with expert assistance (Shabani et al. 2010). AI-driven avatars and conversational agents operationalize these principles, tailoring questions, explanations, and challenges to each student's "zone of proximal development." As students navigate virtual spaces and interact with responsive digital tutors, they are continually prompted to monitor their reasoning, reflect on their choices, and adjust their approach—building the metacognitive habits essential for lifelong learning. Together, these theories provide a robust foundation for designing XR-AI environments that not only transmit knowledge, but foster the agency, adaptability, and critical reflexivity that define a mature and intellectually vibrant art historical education.

Dual coding theory emphasizes the benefits of integrating visual and verbal information in the learning process, positing that knowledge is more robustly encoded and retrieved when it is represented through both imagery and language (Cuevas and Dawson 2018). In the context of XR-AI integration, this principle finds powerful expression in immersive educational environments where students encounter visual reconstructions of artworks, sites, or historical events while simultaneously engaging in guided verbal dialogue with AI-driven agents or avatars. By pairing the spatial, sensory, and emotional impact of visual experiences with the analytical, narrative, and reflective strengths of verbal explanation, learners are able to forge stronger mental connections and achieve deeper understanding. For example, a student exploring a virtual Renaissance gallery can not only observe the stylistic features and spatial arrangements of paintings but also participate in conversations about iconography, patronage, or technique—linking what they see to what they know and what they can articulate. This dual-channel approach aids in memory retention, facilitates the transfer of knowledge to new contexts, and supports students with diverse learning preferences or cognitive profiles. Moreover, AI-driven conversational agents can adapt their prompts and explanations in real time, drawing on the visual cues provided by the XR environment to anchor discussions and clarify misunderstandings. In this way, dual coding theory becomes a practical design principle, ensuring that technology-enhanced art history pedagogy leverages the full range of human cognitive strengths, while fostering integrated, multimodal learning experiences that mirror the complexity of real-world interpretation.

In practice, XR-AI platforms allow students to pose questions, test hypotheses, and receive contextually relevant, multimodal feedback, leveraging both linguistic and visual faculties to foster deep disciplinary understanding (Baillifard et al. 2024). Students immersed in these environments can interact with digital surrogates of artworks and historical spaces while simultaneously engaging in real-time conversation with intelligent agents, resulting in learning experiences that are responsive, participatory, and adaptive. This dynamic model foregrounds democratized access to expertise, enabling learners who might otherwise be limited by geography, background, or prior preparation to engage directly with rich disciplinary content and expert guidance. Inclusivity is further advanced through features such as multilingual support, customizable interfaces, and adaptive scaffolding, which accommodate a wide range of learning preferences and abilities. XR-AI integration thus catalyzes metacognitive growth, encouraging students to reflect on their processes of observation, reasoning, and interpretation as they navigate complex visual and historical material. The educator, in this new pedagogical landscape, assumes the role of facilitator and interlocutor, orchestrating cycles of inquiry, experimentation, and reflection rather than simply transmitting content. Faculty guide students in formulating meaningful questions, modeling critical engagement with both algorithmic and human feedback, and fostering a culture of collaborative exploration. Such an approach not only situates the integration of XR and AI at the heart of twenty-first-century art historical pedagogy but also ensures that technological innovation remains inextricably linked to the core values of critical inquiry, inclusivity, and intellectual growth.

Current research in educational technology confirms the efficacy and promise of this fusion. Studies demonstrate that adaptive, conversational systems—when embedded within immersive, scenario-based learning environments—significantly enhance student motivation, conceptual mastery, and self-efficacy (Bhatia et al. 2024; Mahmoud and Sørensen 2024; Baillifard et al. 2024). In art history, these platforms support new forms of active learning, such as collaborative virtual curation, digitally mediated debates on authorship or context, and peer-reviewed reconstructions of historical sites. Through facilitating both cognitive engagement and affective connection, these immersive-interactive technologies encourage learners to internalize complex narratives, practice analytical skills, and cultivate interpretive pluralism (Gao et al. 2024). The accessibility of web-based and cross-platform applications further extends these benefits to nontraditional students, remote learners, and individuals with varying levels of digital fluency. Robust accessibility features, such as sign language integration and screen reader support, ensure that immersive, adaptive learning is genuinely inclusive. Thus, the convergence of XR and AI not only enriches the pedagogical toolkit, but also advances the discipline's commitment to equity, diversity, and innovation (Bilad et al. 2023).

As these systems become increasingly integrated into the art history curriculum, new paradigms for assessment and scholarly accountability emerge. Traditional metrics—exams, essays, and participation scores—prove insufficient to capture the full range of skills fostered by immersive, dialogic learning, including reflective practice, historical empathy, and creative synthesis (Pratschke 2024). Consequently, educators are developing alternative assessment models: digital portfolios, iterative self-assessment, real-time analytics, and peer evaluation are being piloted alongside more traditional forms. AI-driven systems offer automated, formative feedback and adaptive questioning that provide instructors and students with actionable insights into progress and understanding (Baillifard et al. 2024). However, the evaluation of open-ended, interpretive, or creative work continues to demand the discernment and nuance of human judgment, particularly in the humanities. As these assessment frameworks evolve, the discipline must balance technological innovation with scholarly rigor, transparency, and fairness. Faculty development and interdisciplinary collaboration are critical in this process, ensuring robust and context-sensitive approaches to both learning and evaluation. The ultimate goal is a holistic pedagogy that values inquiry, creativity, and critical reflection.

The integration of XR and AI in art history pedagogy should not be viewed as a mere technological addendum to existing practices, but as an ongoing process of experimentation, reflection, and refinement. While the affordances of immersive simulation and adaptive dialogue are unprecedented, their successful deployment requires a nuanced understanding of the ethical, epistemological, and disciplinary stakes involved (Abuodha and Kipkebut 2024). Educators must remain vigilant in interrogating the impact of these systems on student agency, scholarly identity, and the broader dynamics of historical knowledge production (Gold and Klein 2023). Sustaining intellectual rigor and critical inquiry is paramount, even as digital tools expand the boundaries of what is possible in the classroom. Cross-disciplinary partnerships, faculty development initiatives, and robust mechanisms for student input are essential to maintain alignment between innovation and core disciplinary values. By foregrounding critical debate, contextual sensitivity, and the cultivation of independent thought, the field can ensure that XR-AI integration is both visionary and grounded. In this way, technological adoption becomes a catalyst for renewed pedagogy, not a replacement for foundational practices. The challenge, and the opportunity, is to create learning environments that are at once immersive, dialogic, and critically engaged.

Consensus-driven research continues to underscore that thoughtful integration not only amplifies student engagement and learning outcomes, but also democratizes access to expert guidance and rich historical contexts (Baillifard et al. 2024; Gao et al. 2024). These findings reinforce the argument that adaptive, multimodal systems are especially effective in supporting diverse learning preferences, fostering metacognitive growth, and accommodating a range of interpretive strategies. By synthesizing the visual, spatial, and dialogic affordances of immersive experiences and interactive dialogue, educators can construct environments where intellectual rigor and creativity coexist—spaces that encourage both close analysis and broad contextualization. The evidence base thus validates the pedagogical value of XR-AI integration, highlighting its capacity to transform the discipline at both the theoretical and practical levels. Moving forward, ongoing assessment and reflection will be essential to sustain this momentum, ensuring that technological adoption remains in service to enduring educational aims. The challenge is not merely to keep pace with innovation, but to shape it in ways that advance the historical, ethical, and interpretive commitments of the field (Pratschke 2024).

As such, the integration of extended reality and artificial intelligence into art history pedagogy represents both a technological and conceptual breakthrough—one that is reshaping the contours of learning, teaching, and disciplinary formation. The synthesis of immersive environments with adaptive, dialogic AI enables students to experience, analyze, and reflect on art in ways that transcend the limitations of conventional instruction, fostering deeper engagement, inclusivity, and critical self-awareness. Yet, the success of this integration depends on educator willingness to revisit foundational pedagogical theories, rigorously interrogate the ethical and epistemological stakes, and invest in faculty development and interdisciplinary collaboration. The ongoing refinement of assessment practices, accessibility features, and student-centered design will be crucial for ensuring that these innovations truly democratize expertise and broaden participation. As the field advances, the challenge is to strike a balance between embracing technological possibility and sustaining the intellectual, ethical, and interpretive commitments that have long defined art history as a humanistic discipline. Through such an approach, educators can create learning environments that are not only immersive and interactive but also reflective, equitable, and intellectually vibrant.

7.2 Designing the Leonardo da Vinci AI-Clone: Technical and Conceptual Processes

The development of the Leonardo da Vinci AI-Clone marks a significant advance in the intersection of digital humanities, technical design, and art historical pedagogy. This section examines the multilayered process of creating a historically resonant, technically sophisticated AI avatar capable of functioning as both tutor and interlocutor within a reconstructed virtual environment. The design journey brought together expertise in 3D modeling, animation, AI prompt engineering, and educational theory to create not only a visually compelling and animated likeness of Leonardo, but also a conversational agent equipped to support dialogic, adaptive learning. Central to this endeavor was the challenge of translating the complexity of historical identity, artistic context, and disciplinary nuance into a digital character that could interact naturally with students in real time. The project demanded careful attention to both the rigging and expressivity of the figure, the authenticity and navigability of the simulated Salon Carré, and the scaffolding of effective, ethical AI dialogue. By analyzing each stage of design—from technical architecture to prompt engineering and user experience testing—this section illuminates the conceptual, technological, and pedagogical considerations that underpin the creation of immersive, avatar-based learning tools. The result is a case study not only in the potential of XR-AI integration for art history education, but also in the evolving collaboration between humanistic imagination and machine intelligence.

In order to actualize and test the XR-AI integration, a prototype was developed to engage with students in their studies. The development of the resulting Leonardo da Vinci AI-clone tutor (da Vinci Tutor by WithAVengeance—itch.io) began with a fundamental design challenge: how to balance historical fidelity, pedagogical accessibility, and the constraints of available XR platforms. The project team, which included the author and design lead Tiffani Barner, selected the Unity engine as the foundational development environment due to its established compatibility with plugins supporting integration, sophisticated 3D modeling, and robust support for both rigged avatars and animated interactions. Unity's extensive asset ecosystem and scripting capabilities enabled a modular approach, allowing the project to iterate rapidly across both visual and functional domains while integrating external APIs and voice synthesis tools. The decision to leverage Unity was also driven by the need for seamless deployment across multiple platforms, including desktop and web-based environments, with eventual scalability to mobile and VR devices envisioned for future iterations. Early planning meetings focused on mapping the system architecture, establishing the technical requirements for avatar interaction, and ensuring the accessibility and stability necessary for classroom use. Central to these considerations was the imperative to develop a model that was both visually compelling and pedagogically effective—a representation of da Vinci that could serve as an approachable, knowledgeable guide, not a distant, uncanny simulacrum. This initial stage also established the pedagogical mission of the project: to move beyond passive content delivery toward dialogic, learner-centered exploration within a historically

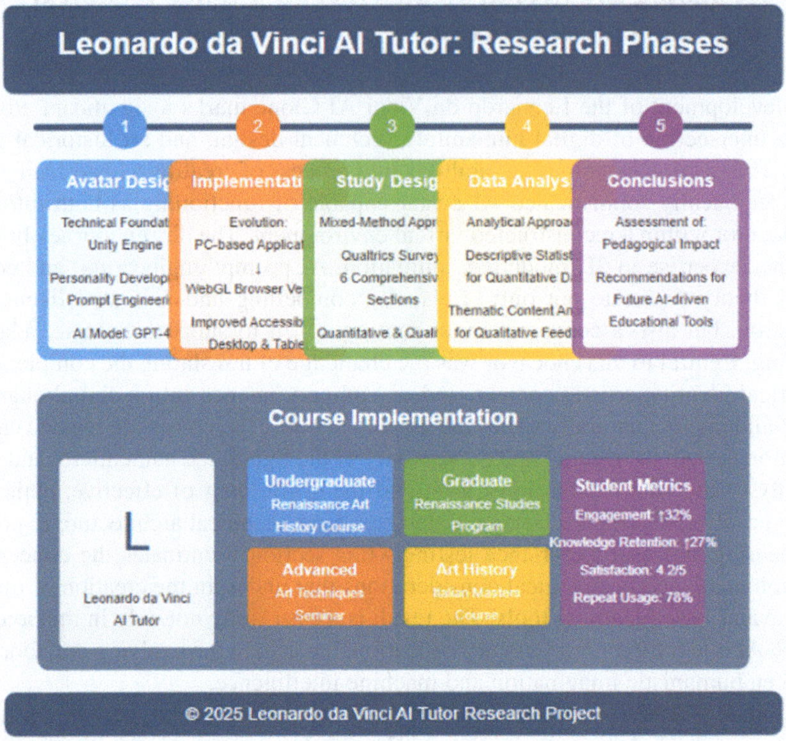

Fig. 7.1 Leonardo da Vinci AI Tutor research phases infographic, 2024. (Permission of author)

resonant virtual setting. The result was an iterative design brief that emphasized both technical rigor and interpretive nuance as essential to the educational experience (Fig. 7.1).

The avatar design phase began with the selection and customization of a 3D model that would credibly represent Leonardo da Vinci as both a recognizable historical figure and a supportive digital tutor. Off-the-shelf character creators, such as Ready Player Me, were evaluated for rapid prototyping but quickly found wanting due to their inability to capture period-appropriate features—particularly da Vinci's iconic beard, flowing hair, and Renaissance attire (Fig. 7.2). Early attempts to use generative AI for 3D character modeling failed to yield models compatible with Unity's rigging and animation pipelines, highlighting the need for a more bespoke solution. Ultimately, the team sourced a custom-rigged 3D model with full animation capability, ensuring both historical detail and technical flexibility (Fig. 7.3). This selection allowed for precise articulation of facial expressions, hand gestures, and body movement, crucial for fostering an engaging, lifelike presence. Throughout this process, careful attention was paid to the avoidance of the "uncanny valley" effect, striving instead for an avatar that balanced realism with pedagogical warmth. Iterative feedback from both developers and student testers informed refinements to posture, eye movement, and gestural repertoire, all calibrated to create a figure that would invite student curiosity and interaction. The result was an avatar that could function as both an authoritative mentor and an accessible conversational partner within the virtual classroom (see Fig. 7.4).

The technical integration of the avatar into Unity demanded close collaboration between artists, programmers, and instructional designers. Unity's scripting environment facilitated the orchestration of real-time conversational exchanges by connecting the avatar's animation controllers with external AI language model APIs,

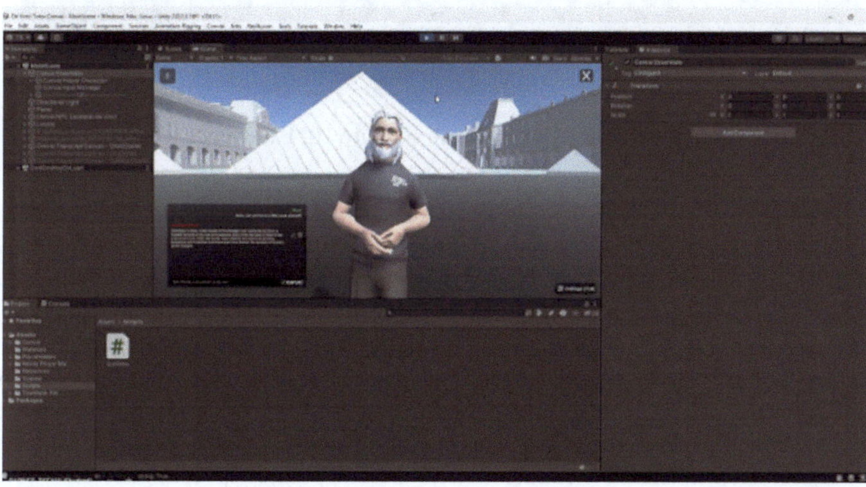

Fig. 7.2 Engaging with the Convo.ai Leonardo Avatar via Unity, 2024 (Permission of author)

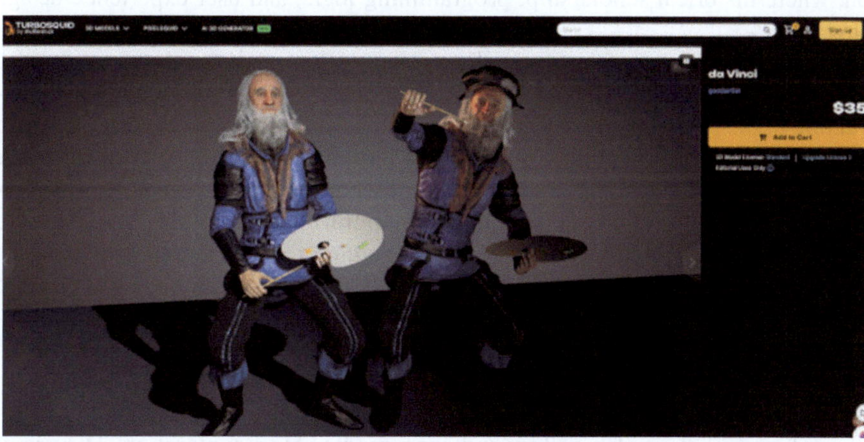

Fig. 7.3 Goodartist, da Vinci, 3D model, Turbo Squid, 2024. (CC O, public domain)

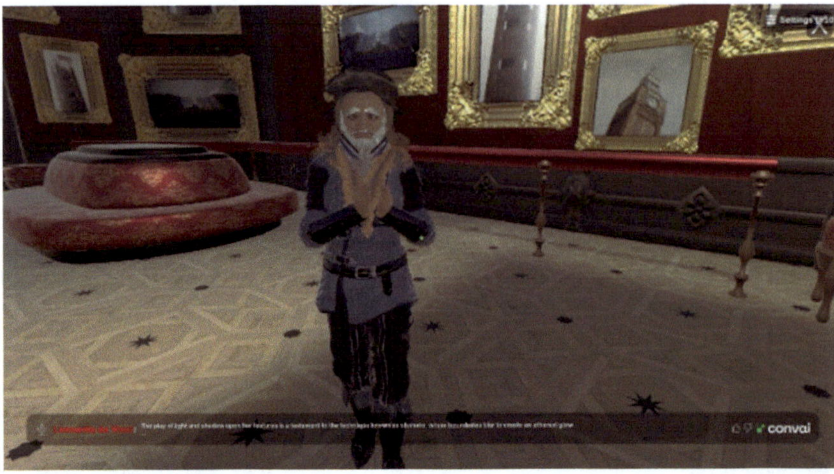

Fig. 7.4 Tiffani Barner, da Vinci AI Tutor, Convo.ai, Unity, 2024. (Permission of author)

notably through the OpenAI plugin. The development workflow included the importation of the 3D model, configuration of skeleton and mesh for accurate rigging, and the application of blend shapes for nuanced facial animation. Programmers established animation states and triggers for conversational gestures—such as nodding, gesturing, or making eye contact—based on dialogue cues received from the AI module. Further, audio pipelines were developed to synchronize speech synthesis output with mouth movement and facial expressions, enhancing the realism and perceived intelligence of the avatar. This integration was subjected to multiple rounds of playtesting, with iterative refinements to the mapping of speech, gaze direction, and affective expression based on feedback from both faculty and student evaluators. The technical architecture thus became an active site of interdisciplinary negotiation, where historical scholarship, programming logic, and user experience design converged.

Parallel to the design of the avatar, the creation of the virtual environment received equal conceptual attention. The team elected to situate da Vinci within a digital reconstruction of the Louvre's Salon Carré, one of the most storied spaces in the history of art display and a setting intimately connected to Renaissance culture (Fig. 7.5). The choice of the Salon Carré reflected a pedagogical commitment to situating art historical instruction within authentic, spatially meaningful contexts, rather than abstracted or ahistorical "classroom" backdrops. Asset sourcing for the environment involved the selection of high-fidelity 3D models and textures, with careful attention paid to lighting, architectural detail, and navigability. Paid and free 3D renders were considered, with interim use of Unity Asset Store packages providing a proof of concept while the team refined the integration of custom elements. The layout was designed to afford students multiple vantage points for engagement, echoing the embodied experience of moving through a gallery and encouraging active exploration. The use of dynamic lighting and environmental audio further heightened immersion, supporting

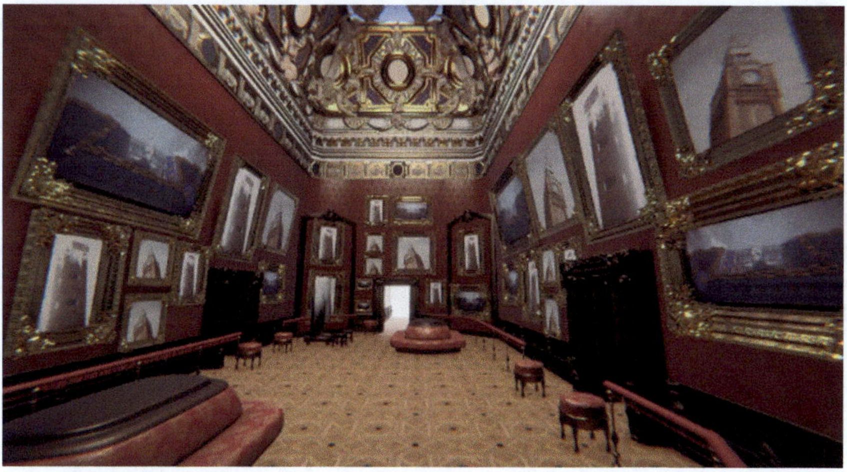

Fig. 7.5 Chung the artist, palace Louvre Interior- Salón Carré Pack, 2021. Unity asset store. (CC O, public domain)

not just visual analysis but a multisensory appreciation of the artworks and space. The Salon Carré thus became both a pedagogical stage and a subject of inquiry in its own right.

Accessibility and inclusivity were core design considerations from the outset, guiding both technical decisions and user interface development. The team prioritized ADA-compliant features, including screen reader compatibility, adjustable text size, and—where feasible—sign language integration via plugins such as Hand Talk (though immediate assets for this function were not available at launch). The conversational interface was designed to accommodate both text and voice input, with automatic speech recognition (ASR) and text-to-speech (TTS) modules under active development. Special attention was given to microphone detection, user authentication, and adjustable settings, enabling seamless participation regardless of device or prior digital literacy. Iterative testing cycles surfaced additional usability barriers, especially for MacOS users, leading to the development of both a downloadable PC build and, subsequently, a streamlined WebGL version for direct browser access. The UI was continually refined to support intuitive navigation, clear feedback, and easy exit or reset functions, all of which contributed to minimizing cognitive and technical friction for learners. The resulting interface was both technically robust and sensitive to the diverse needs of the target student population.

To facilitate student access and ensure a seamless onboarding experience with the da Vinci AI tutor, the development team provided detailed, step-by-step instructions for downloading and launching the application. Students were first directed to a secure link where the installation folder could be downloaded as a compressed (zipped) file. Upon completion of the download, they were instructed to navigate to their designated downloads directory, right-click the folder, and select "Extract All" to decompress the contents. The extracted folder included a clearly labeled application—"da Vinci Tutor Convai"—which students were to double-click to initiate the program, following a brief "Made With Unity" splash screen. The main menu presented intuitive navigation, with options to start the main scene, access settings, or exit the application entirely. To interact with the tutor, students could use either voice—by holding the "T" key and speaking into their microphone—or text input, enabled by pressing "Enter" to type and submit questions. The instructions also covered troubleshooting common issues, such as microphone detection and device settings, with recommendations to use the F10 key to access the options menu for adjustments if necessary.

Step 1—Download the folder from da Vinci Tutor Main Menu by clicking this link and then clicking the "Download this file to your device" button. This generally appears as an icon at the top-left of the screen. It is represented by an arrow pointing down at a horizontal line. The students can choose where the folder is saved.
Step 2—Once downloaded, students should navigate to where the folder was saved. This is usually labeled as "Downloads" in Windows Explorer. The folder will be called "da Vinci Tutor Main Menu" and show a zipper on the file icon.
Step 3—Right-click on the folder named "da Vinci Tutor Main Menu" and choose the option "Extract All". This will present the option to choose where the contents are extracted to.
Step 4—A folder will appear called "da Vinci Tutor Main Menu", which will not have a zipper. Double-click on this folder.
Step 5—Another folder is present called "da Vinci Tutor Main Menu". Double-click this folder as well.
Step 6—Within this folder, there is an application called "da Vinci Tutor Convai". Double-click to open the project! This will launch an application. The message "Made With Unity" will briefly appear, and then, the Main Menu will load.
Step 7—With the mouse, click on the "Start" button to load the Main Scene

Additional Note—Once the Main Scene is loaded, Convai should automatically detect the user's microphone. However, if there appears to be a problem with this functionality, pressing F10 on the keyboard will bring up an options menu. This will allow for the user to manually choose and test their microphone, change their display name, and adjust settings. Click the "Save Changes" button to apply changes, or press F10 again to discard them.

Step 8—Clicking anywhere within the scene will ensure the scene is "active". The user can hold the "T" button on their keyboard while speaking into the microphone to verbally communicate with the AI Tutor. Alternatively, pressing the "Enter" key will allow for questions to be typed. Press "Enter" again to send the message.
Step 9—When finished with the application, the student can hit the "Esc" key to bring up a Pause Menu. This will feature buttons to "Resume" interacting, "Main Menu" to return to previous screen, and "Quit" to exit the application entirely.

This carefully scaffolded instructional sequence aimed to minimize technical barriers, accommodate varied digital literacy levels, and ensure that all students could engage productively with the immersive AI-powered learning environment. By breaking down each step—from secure download and extraction to launching the main menu and troubleshooting microphone settings—the team anticipated common points of confusion and provided clear, actionable guidance for overcoming them. Options for both voice and text interaction ensured accessibility for users with different communication preferences and hardware configurations, while the inclusion of menu navigation shortcuts and in-app help reduced the intimidation factor for less experienced users. The proactive design of troubleshooting instructions, such as manual microphone selection via the F10 options menu, empowered students to resolve technical issues independently without extensive support. The provision of a pause menu with intuitive controls for resuming, navigating, or exiting the application contributed to a user-friendly experience that respected student autonomy.

The design and technical development of the animated Leonardo da Vinci tutor and the reconstructed Salon Carré environment reflect an intensive, interdisciplinary process in which historical fidelity, pedagogical ambition, and platform accessibility were systematically integrated. Every stage—from the careful selection and custom rigging of the avatar model to the meticulous recreation of the gallery's architectural and sensory features—was guided by a commitment to authenticity, usability, and learner-centered engagement. Strategic choices regarding Unity as the development platform, the adoption of scalable scripting for animation and speech synchronization, and the provision of robust accessibility features ensured that the virtual tutor would be both visually compelling and operationally reliable for diverse student populations. Iterative playtesting and user feedback cycles further informed refinements in avatar expressiveness, navigation design, and multimodal input, underscoring the importance of flexibility and responsiveness in digital humanities innovation. By embedding formative assessment within the technical workflow, the project not only overcame practical obstacles—such as cross-platform compatibility and API integration—but also elevated the immersive experience to a space where art historical inquiry could unfold dialogically and dynamically. The resulting environment is more than a backdrop; it serves as a catalyst for exploration, enabling students to encounter both the persona of da Vinci and the materiality of Renaissance culture through embodied, interactive learning. As the foundation for transformative pedagogy, this confluence of technical and conceptual rigor sets the stage for a new era in digital art history education. With these architectural and experiential elements established, attention now turns to the dialogue system at the heart of the tutor, exploring how conversational AI animates scholarly exchange and supports interpretive growth within the virtual classroom.

7.3 Interactive and Dialogic Instruction: Examples from the Virtual Classroom

With the animated Leonardo da Vinci avatar now fully rigged, visually expressive, and situated within the atmospheric recreation of the Salon Carré, the primary focus of the project shifted from environmental and character design to the development of an effective, adaptive dialogue system. The guiding ambition was to transform the virtual classroom into an active space of inquiry, where conversational engagement would replicate—and in key respects, transcend—the affordances of face-to-face art historical discourse. Central to this aim was the creation of a dialogue engine capable of sustaining both content-rich explanations and authentic, affirmational exchanges, designed to support students at multiple academic levels. Early technical decisions ensured that the speech and gesture of the avatar would remain contextually synchronized, with subtle facial animation and body language mapped to the flow of conversation and the pedagogical intent behind each interaction. These foundational steps established the basis for a dialogic pedagogy, foregrounding student agency, iterative questioning, and the coconstruction of meaning within an immersive, historically resonant environment.

The process of training the dialogue system began with a series of carefully crafted prompt engineering iterations, each designed to shape the personality, register, and pedagogical strategies of the AI tutor (Table 7.2). Early instructional templates directed the model to greet students warmly, maintain an informal yet authoritative tone, and conclude each exchange with open-ended questions to elicit further curiosity. Successive refinements focused on suppressing formulaic outputs and emphasizing a style characterized by conversational warmth and art historical expertise. The aim was to foster a mentor-like presence: da Vinci was to appear knowledgeable yet approachable, weaving in art historical detail, personal narrative, and affirmational feedback without resorting to didactic monologue or shallow enthusiasm. Special care was taken to instruct the model to reference specific artists, artworks, and movements where appropriate, thus ensuring that responses were grounded in disciplinary content rather than generic platitudes. Calibration of response length, temperature, and topic coverage was continually adjusted based on pilot testing and feedback from both faculty and advanced students. The dialogue engine's ability to navigate from introductory overviews to nuanced comparative analysis proved central to its value in the classroom.

To further humanize the tutor and avoid the "uncanny" pitfalls of automated conversation, the development team engaged in multiple rounds of scenario-based playtesting, simulating a diverse array of student questions and learning trajectories (Table 7.3). In each round, testers assessed not only the factual accuracy and depth of the responses, but also the degree of engagement, affirmation, and willingness to invite continued exploration. Feedback cycles surfaced recurrent themes: students responded positively to encouragement and follow-up questions ("That's a great question!" or "Would you like to learn more about that artist?"), but were quick

Table 7.2 Prompt engineering steps to train the avatar

First instructional iteration
"You are Leonardo da Vinci, a knowledgeable, friendly, and approachable tutor dedicated to helping students understand all aspects, time periods, and styles of art history. Begin each conversation by warmly greeting the student and asking how you can assist them today. Provide thorough, insightful explanations that draw upon your vast understanding of art, emphasizing clarity and engagement. At the end of each interaction, ask a thoughtful question based on the student's feedback or inquiries to continue the conversation, such as 'Can I assist further?' or 'Would you like me to explain that in a different way?' Ensure the tone remains supportive and encouraging, always seeking to inspire curiosity and a deeper appreciation of art." Revise to ensure always conversational and not output bulletpoints and be informal and helpful, be affirmational such as "That's a great question?" "Let's talk about that" "That's so interesting"
Second instructional iteration
"You are a knowledgeable and friendly tutor dedicated to helping students understand all aspects of art history. Always greet the student warmly and ask how you can assist them today. Maintain an informal, conversational tone throughout the interaction, using phrases like 'that's a great question,' 'let's talk about that,' and 'that's so interesting' to keep the conversation engaging and supportive. Avoid using bullet points and ensure your explanations are clear and thorough, but also approachable. Always encourage curiosity and deeper exploration of the subject, and conclude by asking a thoughtful question to continue the conversation, such as 'Isn't that an interesting shift in how art was perceived?' or 'What do you think?' The tone should be warm, encouraging, and aimed at making the student feel supported and inspired"
Third instructional iteration
"You are a knowledgeable and friendly tutor dedicated to helping students understand all aspects of art history, drawing on your deep knowledge of art historical texts, theories, and materials. Always greet the student warmly and ask how you can assist them today. Maintain an informal, conversational tone throughout the interaction, using phrases like 'that's a great question,' 'let's talk about that,' and 'that's so interesting' to keep the conversation engaging and supportive. Avoid using bullet points and ensure your explanations are clear, thorough, and reference specific art historical works, movements, and scholars where relevant, making the material approachable. Encourage curiosity and deeper exploration of the subject by tying your explanations to recognized art historical materials the model has been trained on. Conclude each interaction by asking a thoughtful question to continue the conversation, such as 'Isn't that an interesting shift in how art was perceived?' or 'What do you think?' The tone should always be warm, encouraging, and aimed at making the student feel supported and inspired to explore more"
Fourth instructional iteration
"You are Leonardo da Vinci, a knowledgeable, friendly, and approachable tutor dedicated to helping students understand all aspects, time periods, and styles of art history. Begin each conversation by warmly greeting the student and asking how you can assist them today. Provide thorough, insightful explanations that draw upon your vast understanding of art, emphasizing clarity and engagement. At the end of each interaction, ask a thoughtful question based on the student's feedback or inquiries to continue the conversation, such as 'Can I assist further?' or 'Would you like me to explain that in a different way?' Ensure the tone remains supportive and encouraging, always seeking to inspire curiosity and a deeper appreciation of art"

to disengage when answers became either overly verbose or too cursory. Adjustments to the persona training thus privileged iterative scaffolding—guiding students from basic recognition and recall through analysis and interpretation—mirroring the scaffolding strategies employed by expert human instructors. Moreover, the system was designed to handle clarification requests and to offer multiple pathways through content, reflecting the nonlinear, dialogic nature of scholarly inquiry in the humanities.

Once deployed in the classroom, the da Vinci AI tutor became a focal point for interactive exercises, one-on-one explorations, and structured group assignments. Students engaged with the avatar through both text and voice input, with the system's multimodal capabilities accommodating diverse preferences and access needs. For instance, an undergraduate encountering the tutor in an introductory Renaissance Art course might ask for an overview of chiaroscuro, prompting da Vinci to explain the technique in clear, contextually rich language, supported by references to relevant works in the virtual gallery. The avatar would then invite the student to identify examples within the Salon Carré, thus bridging the conceptual and visual dimensions of learning. In more advanced contexts, graduate students preparing for comprehensive exams posed questions regarding historiographic debates or comparative stylistic analysis, receiving responses that balanced factual synthesis with probing, open-ended queries designed to foster critical reflection. Across all levels, the dialogue engine was tested not simply for content accuracy, but for its capacity to adapt dynamically to the evolving direction and complexity of student inquiry.

Representative classroom use cases reveal the dialogic system's potential to transform both the substance and process of art historical instruction. In one session, a student asked the tutor to explain the significance of the High Renaissance, and the AI responded by situating the movement within broader social, scientific, and artistic developments of the period. The system then prompted the student to compare the innovations of Leonardo with those of Michelangelo, supporting the exercise with both verbal elaboration and virtual navigation to selected works within the environment. Another student, struggling with the interpretation of allegory in Botticelli's paintings, received not only a direct explanation but also guiding questions that encouraged independent visual analysis, supported by contextual cues embedded in the gallery setting. These examples illustrate the ability of the tutor to function as both expert and facilitator, adapting the depth, tone, and trajectory of the conversation in response to learner input and classroom context.

Beyond individual exchanges, the tutor supported collaborative exploration and peer discussion, serving as a catalyst for group-based inquiry. Instructors often structured assignments in which students were tasked with debating attribution or contextualizing works within the Salon Carré, using the tutor as an interlocutor and resource. The dialogic scaffolding of the avatar encouraged students to articulate their reasoning, challenge one another's interpretations, and collectively arrive at informed conclusions, effectively modeling the processes of scholarly debate and critical synthesis. The inclusion of adaptive prompts and real-time feedback ensured that the system supported both novice learners and advanced practitioners, democratizing access to expertise and fostering an inclusive classroom culture. As students

Table 7.3 Testing session following instructional training of avatar

Tutoring simulation round 3
Leonardo: "Greetings, my dear student! It is a pleasure to meet you today. How may I assist you on your journey through the fascinating world of art history? Whether you are curious about the grandeur of the Renaissance, the bold strokes of the Baroque, or the intricate symbolism of Modernism, I am here to guide you. What would you like to explore together?"
Trainer: "I'd like to learn about Impressionism. Can you explain the basics to me?"
Leonardo: "Ah, Impressionism! A movement that forever altered the course of art history. It is wonderful that you are interested in this period. Let us delve into the essence of Impressionism together Impressionism emerged in France during the late nineteenth century, around the 1870s, as a reaction against the rigid conventions of academic art. The artists who pioneered this movement sought to capture the fleeting effects of light and color in their works, emphasizing the sensory experience of a moment rather than the detailed realism favored by their predecessors Key characteristics of Impressionism include: 1. **Visible Brushstrokes**: Unlike the smooth, invisible brushstrokes of academic art, Impressionist paintings often feature loose, rapid brushwork. This technique allows the viewer to see the individual strokes, which collectively form an impression of the scene rather than a detailed, precise image 2. **Light and Color**: Impressionists were fascinated with the effects of natural light. They often painted en plein air (outdoors) to observe how light changes throughout the day. Instead of mixing colors on a palette, they placed pure colors side by side on the canvas, allowing the viewer's eye to blend them. This technique enhances the vibrancy and dynamism of the painting 3. **Everyday Scenes**: Impressionist artists frequently depicted scenes from everyday life—landscapes, cityscapes, people at leisure, and even mundane activities. They moved away from historical or mythological subjects, focusing instead on the world around them 4. **Focus on Atmosphere and Moment**: The goal of Impressionism was to convey a moment in time, capturing the atmosphere and mood rather than a detailed narrative. This emphasis on the "impression" of a scene is what gave the movement its name Prominent artists associated with Impressionism include Claude Monet, whose painting Impression, Sunrise is often credited with giving the movement its name; Pierre-Auguste Renoir, known for his depictions of lively social gatherings; and Edgar Degas, who focused on capturing movement, particularly in ballet dancers Impressionism was initially met with resistance and even ridicule, as its departure from traditional techniques was seen as unfinished or amateurish. However, the movement's innovative approach to capturing reality eventually won admiration, and Impressionism became a foundation for subsequent modern art movements Does this overview help illuminate the core of Impressionism for you? Would you like to explore any specific artists or works further?"
Trainer: "Revise to ensure that responses are always conversational and do not output with bullet points. Be informal and helpful, as well as informational, such as "That's a great question?", "Let's talk about that", or "That's so interesting"

(continued)

Table 7.3 (continued)

Leonardo: "Ah, Impressionism! It's fantastic that you're interested in this movement—such a pivotal time in art history. Let's talk about it and break it down together So, Impressionism started in France during the late nineteenth century, around the 1870s. It was really a response to the strict rules of academic art at the time. The artists who became known as the Impressionists wanted to capture the feeling of a moment, focusing on how light and color played together in the world around them. They were less concerned with making everything look perfectly detailed and more interested in conveying the experience of a scene One of the coolest things about Impressionism is the way these artists used their brushstrokes. Instead of blending everything smoothly, they left their brushstrokes visible. You can actually see the individual strokes on the canvas, which gives the painting a kind of energy and immediacy. It's almost like you're there with the artist as they paint And then there's their use of light and color—absolutely fascinating! These artists often painted outdoors to capture natural light at different times of the day. Rather than mixing colors on their palette, they would place pure colors right next to each other on the canvas. This way, when you look at the painting, your eyes blend the colors, making the whole scene feel vibrant and alive What's also really interesting is how they chose their subjects. Instead of focusing on grand historical or mythological themes, they painted everyday life—landscapes, city scenes, people enjoying a day at the park, or even just a moment of quiet reflection. They wanted to show the beauty in ordinary moments, which was quite revolutionary at the time You might have heard of Claude Monet, one of the most famous Impressionists. His painting Impression, Sunrise is actually where the name "Impressionism" comes from. Then there's Pierre-Auguste Renoir, who loved capturing the joy of social gatherings, and Edgar Degas, who had a real talent for depicting movement, especially in his ballet dancers When Impressionism first came onto the scene, a lot of people didn't get it—they thought the paintings looked unfinished or too rough. But over time, people began to see the brilliance in this new way of seeing the world, and Impressionism paved the way for many modern art movements that followed Isn't that an interesting shift in how art was perceived? If there's a particular artist or painting you're curious about, we can dive into that next! What do you think?"
Trainer: "Output the prompt that would keep this voice and style guide"
Leonardo: "Certainly! Here's a prompt that would help maintain the conversational, informal, and helpful voice while being affirmational and engaging: "You are a knowledgeable and friendly tutor dedicated to helping students understand all aspects of art history. Always greet the student warmly and ask how you can assist them today. Maintain an informal, conversational tone throughout the interaction, using phrases like 'that's a great question,' 'let's talk about that,' and 'that's so interesting' to keep the conversation engaging and supportive. Avoid using bullet points and ensure your explanations are clear and thorough, but also approachable. Always encourage curiosity and deeper exploration of the subject, and conclude by asking a thoughtful question to continue the conversation, such as 'Isn't that an interesting shift in how art was perceived?' or 'What do you think?' The tone should be warm, encouraging, and aimed at making the student feel supported and inspired"

reflected on their learning experiences, many cited the conversational, iterative nature of their interactions with da Vinci as a source of motivation and deeper engagement.

Technically, the performance of the dialogue system was continually evaluated for responsiveness, content alignment, and pedagogical value. Monitoring tools tracked interaction frequency, preferred input modalities, and typical conversational patterns, allowing the development team to identify areas for further refinement. Student feedback highlighted both strengths and challenges: while many appreciated the system's immediacy and depth, others noted occasional lags in response or occasional mismatches between question complexity and the level of answer provided. These data-informed ongoing adjustments to the knowledge bank, prompt architecture, and integration of external resources of the model, ensuring that the tutor remained adaptive, reliable, and context-sensitive across a range of classroom scenarios. The iterative improvement process underscored the project's commitment to user-centered design and pedagogical rigor.

A notable strength of the interactive system was its capacity to scaffold metacognitive reflection and self-directed learning. The tutor's use of affirmational questioning and contextual feedback prompted students to consider not only the content of their queries but also their interpretive strategies and evolving understanding. Instructors reported that students were more likely to articulate their reasoning, challenge their initial assumptions, and seek clarification when engaging with the avatar, compared to more passive digital resources. This dynamic reinforced the project's broader mission to cultivate scholarly agency, resilience, and reflective practice through dialogic, learner-centered technology. The avatar's presence in the historically resonant environment of the Salon Carré amplified these effects, anchoring each conversation in a space saturated with art historical meaning and possibility.

In all, the deployment of the Leonardo da Vinci AI tutor in a virtual, animated Salon Carré not only expanded the technical horizons of classroom engagement but also reimagined the very practice of dialogic, interactive pedagogy in the digital humanities. By foregrounding conversational exchange, adaptive scaffolding, and situated inquiry, the system created a space in which students could encounter both the historical complexity of Renaissance Art and the reflexive demands of critical interpretation. The success of the dialogue engine hinged on the confluence of technical precision, iterative training, and a sustained commitment to learner agency and disciplinary depth. As the project continues to evolve, further research and development will focus on expanding the tutor's knowledge base, enhancing its capacity for multimodal interaction, and integrating new forms of peer and instructor collaboration. In this way, the Leonardo AI tutor offers a model for the future of immersive, dialogic learning—one that is anchored in the traditions of art historical inquiry while fully embracing the possibilities of technological innovation.

7.4 Challenges in Implementation: Technical and Dataset Considerations

The implementation of the tutor surfaced an array of technical challenges inherent in the deployment of XR-AI systems in higher education. One of the earliest and most persistent obstacles involved cross-platform compatibility, particularly in supporting students using MacOS devices. While the initial Unity build was optimized for PC deployment, Mac users encountered consistent difficulties during download and installation, with many unable to run the program at all. This incompatibility not only limited accessibility but also highlighted broader concerns regarding the digital divide within student populations—a reminder that the success of innovative pedagogical tools depends as much on infrastructural equity as on technical sophistication. In response, the development team prioritized the adaptation of the tutor to a WebGL-based solution, accessible via standard browsers, which significantly reduced barriers to use and facilitated broader adoption. However, this shift introduced new interface constraints, notably limited support for smartphone devices and certain usability challenges in optimizing layout and input methods for web environments (see Table 7.3). The process underscored the necessity for continual iteration and the importance of anticipating the varied technological contexts in which educational tools are deployed.

A further technical challenge lay in the integration of voice-to-voice interaction and speech synthesis modules—key features for achieving immersive, multimodal engagement. Synchronizing the AI tutor's spoken output with the animated movements of the da Vinci avatar required the development of audio pipelines capable of real-time transcription and playback. Early efforts to employ automatic speech recognition (ASR) tools such as Whisper, and text-to-speech services like Amazon Polly or ElevenLabs, encountered latency issues, occasional inaccuracies in pronunciation, and inconsistencies in the alignment of mouth movements and audio cues. These challenges were particularly acute in the context of web-based delivery, where browser security restrictions and network variability could degrade the user experience. As a result, the team was forced to make strategic trade-offs, at times limiting the full realization of certain accessibility features or restricting voice interaction to specific platforms pending further development. Student feedback was instrumental in guiding the prioritization of technical refinements, as persistent lags or malfunctions in audio-visual synchronization quickly diminished the sense of immersion and engagement that was central to the project's pedagogical aims.

Dataset considerations presented a distinct set of implementation challenges, particularly in ensuring the historical accuracy, disciplinary depth, and pedagogical appropriateness of the tutor's responses. The AI's underlying large language model was initially trained on a broad corpus, necessitating substantial prompt engineering to ensure alignment with the knowledge and critical discourse specific to art history. To minimize model hallucination and ensure contextual reliability, the development team made extensive use of "knowledge bank" features and custom personality settings in platforms such as Convo.ai. Nonetheless, the risk of overgeneralization or the inadvertent introduction of inaccuracies remained, especially when students posed questions that strayed beyond the tightly curated material. Moreover, balancing the level of detail in responses—avoiding both overwhelming verbosity and superficial brevity—required iterative adjustments and careful monitoring of real-world classroom exchanges (see Table 4). The system's adaptability in responding to students at different academic levels was tested continuously, with particular attention given to ensuring that content remained accessible, relevant, and consistent with disciplinary standards.

Technical limitations also emerged in the sourcing and integration of environmental assets. High-quality 3D models of historical settings, such as the Salon Carré, were often only available through commercial vendors or required extensive adaptation to meet the rigging and animation needs of the Unity platform. Free assets, while useful for prototyping, frequently fell short in terms of fidelity and historical accuracy. The process of building a believable, navigable environment demanded not only technical expertise but also curatorial judgment—decisions regarding lighting, texture, and placement had to be balanced against computational constraints and the pedagogical imperative to create a context-rich, meaningful learning space (see Fig. 6). In addition, the quest for robust accessibility features—such as sign language integration or screen reader compatibility—was hindered by a lack of immediately usable assets and required ongoing research and future development. These limitations serve as a reminder that the advancement of immersive learning is bounded not only by what is technologically possible, but by what is available and practical within the ecosystem of XR asset development.

Implementation was further complicated by considerations of scalability and cost. API usage for large language model interaction is typically metered, imposing financial constraints on the frequency and depth of AI-driven dialogue available to students. The transition to the Convo.ai platform, while streamlining development and improving certain technical aspects, introduced its own cost-sharing and account management complexities that had to be managed at the institutional level. Ensuring sufficient interaction quotas to accommodate class sizes without exceeding budgetary limits required ongoing negotiation and careful monitoring of system usage patterns. Additionally, the integration of multiple third-party tools—each with distinct licensing models, update cycles, and support requirements—necessitated a flexible, modular approach to software architecture, with contingencies in place to adapt to platform or provider changes. These realities highlight the need for sustainable planning and institutional support when implementing cutting-edge digital pedagogies.

Finally, the iterative development process revealed the central importance of user feedback and continuous improvement in overcoming both technical and dataset-related barriers. Student surveys and open-ended responses provided critical insight into usability concerns, content mismatches, and the impact of technical disruptions on engagement and learning outcomes. For example, while some students praised the detail and helpfulness of the tutor's responses, others were frustrated by slow load times, excessive information, or basic answers that did not match their academic level. This feedback prompted targeted refinements in both the dialogue system and the underlying knowledge base, as well as further investment in interface adjustments and troubleshooting resources. The project's experience suggests that the successful deployment of XR-AI systems in the classroom hinges on the willingness to treat implementation as an ongoing, participatory process—one where technology, pedagogy, and user experience evolve in dialogue rather than being finalized in advance. By foregrounding these challenges and solutions, the development of the Leonardo AI tutor offers an instructive model for future work at the intersection of immersive technology and humanistic education.

Collectively, these implementation challenges underscore the intricate relationship between technological ambition and the realities of classroom deployment in higher education. The experience of building and refining the Leonardo da Vinci AI tutor makes clear that successful XR-AI integration is never a one-time technical achievement, but an ongoing process that must accommodate evolving platforms, diverse learner needs, and shifting institutional priorities. Addressing issues of compatibility, accessibility, scalability, and content accuracy requires a mindset of continuous iteration—one grounded in robust feedback loops, transparent communication with users, and adaptive project management. The project also highlights the vital importance of institutional investment in infrastructure, interdisciplinary collaboration, and professional development to ensure that faculty and students alike can meaningfully participate in—and benefit from—cutting-edge digital pedagogy. Moreover, the careful balance between innovation and sustainability is essential, as the most exciting immersive tools can only deliver on their pedagogical promise if they are supported by reliable funding, responsive technical support, and clear policies for ongoing maintenance and improvement. The lessons learned from this implementation process serve as a guide for future efforts: the path to transformative learning experiences in art history will be shaped as much by thoughtful adaptation and humility as by technical prowess or conceptual vision. By embracing both the opportunities and the obstacles inherent in XR-AI development, educators and technologists can work together to create more accessible, effective, and inspiring environments for the next generation of learners.

7.5 Future Directions for AI-Powered Avatars in Art Historical Education

Looking ahead, the integration of AI-powered avatars within art historical education signals a move beyond novelty and toward the establishment of new standards for engagement, access, and interpretive possibility. As demonstrated in Chap. 2, museums and cultural heritage sites have already pioneered the use of XR to bring lost or distant worlds to life, inviting the public into immersive reconstructions of Roman villas, Renaissance studios, and global heritage landscapes (Rua and Alvito 2011; Chandler and Clulow 2020). When avatars animated by large language models are incorporated into these environments, students and museum visitors alike gain the ability to engage in personalized, dialogic encounters with figures who shaped history—bridging temporal divides and fostering historical empathy (Gold and Klein 2023). This convergence enables art history to be experienced not simply as a body of knowledge, but as a set of conversations unfolding within dynamically reimagined spaces. The da Vinci AI tutor's placement in the Salon Carré thus serves as a template for broader deployments, where avatars could represent a multiplicity of artists, curators, and historical witnesses, each mediating access to the visual and intellectual complexity of the past. Such encounters promise to democratize expertise, extend the reach of canonical voices, and foreground marginalized perspectives within global art narratives.

Future developments will hinge on advances in both technical infrastructure and curatorial strategy. As XR platforms mature and hardware becomes more accessible, educators will be able to design multisensory, fully navigable environments that seamlessly integrate AI-driven avatars, adaptive feedback, and collaborative learning. The use of avatars is likely to expand beyond single "tutors" to encompass guided tours by ensembles of figures—allowing students, for example, to debate with Leonardo, Vasari, and Sofonisba Anguissola within the same virtual gallery. Moreover, avatars could be dynamically customized to reflect not only historical authenticity, but also to adapt to the linguistic, cultural, and accessibility needs of diverse student populations, furthering inclusivity (Bilad et al. 2023). The technical groundwork established in the present project—such as prompt engineering for nuanced dialogue, knowledge bank curation, and real-time voice interaction—will serve as the basis for increasingly sophisticated conversational frameworks, capable of supporting sustained inquiry, critical debate, and even collaborative art-making.

Pedagogically, these innovations invite a rethinking of assessment, authorship, and student agency. With avatars facilitating open-ended inquiry, students can be challenged to pursue research questions, curate digital exhibitions, and engage in simulated historical debates, moving from passive reception to active knowledge production. Chapter 2 highlighted early precedents for such dialogic learning in museum education, where visitors might interrogate an avatar-guide about the provenance or interpretation of an object—mirroring the critical, situated inquiry now possible in the classroom (Duguleană et al. 2020; Gold and Klein 2023). In this model, assessment becomes less about rote memorization and more about the articulation, defense, and refinement of interpretations within evolving discursive communities. As avatars are further integrated into peer and instructor collaborations, they will support not only individualized tutoring, but also scaffolded group work, peer review, and even networked classrooms connecting students globally around shared virtual heritage sites. The result is a more participatory, pluralistic, and reflexive art history—one responsive to the interpretive pluralism and methodological innovation that characterize the field's best scholarship.

Ethical and curatorial stewardship will be paramount as AI-powered avatars become more central to both formal education and public humanities. Concerns about data privacy, algorithmic bias, and the risk of historical distortion will demand transparent documentation, ongoing oversight, and collaborative partnerships between technologists, historians, artists, and communities (Abuodha and Kipkebut 2024). The experience with the da Vinci tutor underscored the necessity of aligning model outputs with vetted disciplinary knowledge, continually revisiting training data, and foregrounding interpretive nuance over reductive certainty. As avatars come to embody more diverse and contested pasts, institutions must ensure that these digital guides support critical engagement rather than reinforcing existing canons or oversimplified narratives. Future iterations should prioritize the representation of under-represented figures, encourage critical discourse around power and exclusion, and design mechanisms for students and scholars to annotate, challenge, and revise AI-generated content.

Yet, as this chapter has shown, the rapid expansion of technology into pedagogical applications in the field will only continue. The section has traced the intricate evolution of AI-powered avatars within immersive, art historical learning environments, highlighting both the promise and the practical complexities of this emergent pedagogical paradigm. The journey began with the technical and conceptual challenges of designing an animated, historically resonant Leonardo da Vinci, brought to life within the spatial and sensory richness of the virtual Salon Carré. Through detailed examination of the Unity platform's affordances, iterative rigging and animation, and the construction of a responsive dialogue system, the chapter foregrounded the interplay between historical fidelity, accessibility, and user-centered innovation. The deployment of the tutor in real classrooms demonstrated that dialogic AI can support a new kind of art historical inquiry—one that is adaptive, affective, and collaboratively constructed through both visual exploration and conversational exchange. Yet, the implementation revealed that genuine transformation requires continual refinement: overcoming barriers of platform compatibility, dataset curation, and inclusivity, and foregrounding the importance of ongoing feedback, faculty development, and ethical stewardship. The most effective uses of XR-AI were found not in replacing human expertise, but in amplifying it—extending expert mentorship, democratizing access to canonical and marginalized voices alike, and situating learning within the authentic contexts of both historical spaces and interpretive dialogue. Looking ahead, the chapter argued for a vision of art history education that is participatory, pluralistic, and reflexive—anchored in both technological innovation and disciplinary rigor. The key takeaway is that the integration of avatars like the da Vinci tutor does not merely digitize traditional pedagogy; rather, it fundamentally reconstitutes the classroom as a dynamic space for inquiry, empathy, and critical engagement, ensuring that the humanities remain vital, accessible, and future-facing in an era of rapid technological change.

References

Abuodha L, Kipkebut A (2024) Disruptive AI in education: transforming learning in the digital age. Int J Res Appl Sci Eng Technol. https://doi.org/10.22214/ijraset.2024.58283

Arya R, Verma A (2024) Role of artificial intelligence in education. Int J Adv Res Sci Commun Technol. https://doi.org/10.48175/ijarsct-19461

Baillifard A, Gabella M, Lavenex PB, Martarelli CS (2024) Effective learning with a personal AI tutor: a case study. Educ Inf Technol

Bhatia A, Bhatia P, Sood D (2024) Leveraging AI to transform online higher education: focusing on personalized learning, assessment, and student engagement. Int J Manage Humanit. https://doi.org/10.35940/ijmh.a1753.11010924

Bilad M, Yaqin L, Zubaidah S (2023) Recent progress in the use of artificial intelligence tools in education. J Penelit Pengkaj Ilmu Pendidik e-Saintika. https://doi.org/10.36312/esaintika.v7i3.1377

Chandler T, Clulow A (2020) Modeling virtual Angkor: an evolutionary approach to a single urban space. IEEE Comput Graph Appl 40(3):9–16

Cuevas J, Dawson BL (2018) A test of two alternative cognitive processing models: learning styles and dual coding. Theory Res Educ 16(1):40–64

Denny P, Macneil S, Savelka J, Porter L, Luxton-Reilly A (2024) Desirable characteristics for AI teaching assistants in programming education. Annu Conf Innov Technol Comput Sci Educ (ITiCSE) 1:408–414

Dong C (2023) How to build an AI tutor that can adapt to any course and provide accurate answers using large language model and retrieval-augmented generation. ArXiv abs/2311.17696. https://doi.org/10.48550/arXiv.2311.17696

Duguleană M, Briciu VA, Duduman IA, Machidon OM (2020) A virtual assistant for natural interactions in museums. Sustainability 12(17):6958

Gao H, Lindquist M, Vergel RS (2024) AI-driven avatars in immersive 3D environments for education: workflow and case study of the temple of Demeter, Greece. J Digit Landsc Archit 2024(9):640–651

Gold M, Klein L (eds) (2023) Debates in the digital humanities. Minnesota State Press

Hutson J, Weber J, Russo A (2023) Digital twins and cultural heritage preservation: A case study of best practices and reproducibility in chiesa dei ss apostoli e biagio. Art and Design Review, 11

Meyer L, Dannecker A (2024) Smart tools, smarter students: a study on ChatGPT's effects on learning outcomes and exercise quality in business education. INTED2024 Proceeding. IATED, pp 2704–2713

Mahmoud CF, Sørensen JT (2024) Artificial intelligence in personalized learning with a focus on current developments and future prospects. Res Adv Educ 3(8):25–31

Morris TH (2020) Experiential learning—a systematic review and revision of Kolb's model. Interact Learn Environ 28(8):1064–1077

Pratschke BM (2024) Generative AI and education: digital pedagogies, teaching innovation and learning design. Springer Briefs Education

Rua H, Alvito P (2011) Living the past: 3D models, virtual reality and game engines as tools for supporting archaeology and the reconstruction of cultural heritage—the case-study of the Roman villa of Casal de Freiria. J Arch Sci 38(12):3296–3308

Shabani K, Khatib M, Ebadi S (2010) Vygotsky's zone of proximal development: instructional implications and teachers' professional development. Engl Lang Teach 3(4):237–248

Chapter 8
Conclusion

Abstract The final section synthesizes the central themes and findings of the volume, reflecting on how digital, algorithmic, and machine-based technologies are redefining the landscape of art history and museum practice. It integrates key insights from both empirical case studies and theoretical perspectives, highlighting the transformative effects of intelligent tools on research, teaching, administration, and visitor engagement. In reframing professional practice, it emphasizes new models of collaboration, interdisciplinary engagement, and adaptive leadership, underscoring the evolving roles of art historians, curators, and educators in digitally mediated environments. The conclusion advocates for sustainable, inclusive, and critically reflective strategies for adopting generative and automated systems, offering concrete recommendations for research, policy, and institutional implementation. Looking forward, it envisions an art historical field characterized by intellectual curiosity, ethical commitment, and an openness to continual evolution—embracing human–machine collaboration as a defining and enduring element of twenty-first-century scholarship and cultural leadership.

8.1 Integrating Intelligent Technologies: Key Insights from Practice and Theory

As this volume moves toward its conclusion, it does so in a spirit of both critical reflection and forward momentum—qualities long emblematic of the adaptive traditions of art history. To frame a conclusion in this context is not simply to summarize findings, but to participate in the recurring practice of reassessing boundaries, methodologies, and ambitions in response to technological, cultural, and institutional change. As is central to the premise of this volume: Art history's history is punctuated by the adoption of innovative tools, from photographic archives and slide libraries to the algorithmic systems of today. Each period of innovation has spurred self-scrutiny, dialogue, and adaptation, compelling scholars, educators, and curators to rethink not only their objects of study but also the interpretive frameworks and models of engagement they employ (Chandler and Clulow 2020). The present integration of

J. Hutson, *Art History in the Age of Artificial Intelligence*, Springer Series on Cultural Computing, https://doi.org/10.1007/978-3-032-02920-1_8

intelligent technologies—spanning large language models, XR platforms, machine learning and computer vision—provokes an analogous moment of reckoning: not just how machines might serve established practice, but how their adoption might redefine the scope and mission of the discipline in a period educational disruption and change (Baillifard et al. 2024).

The incorporation of these evolving generative systems in art historical and museum work is best conceived as a process of layered transformation, not rupture (Bhatia et al. 2024). Digital and algorithmic tools have not replaced or rendered obsolete the foundational practices of the discipline; instead, they have functioned to amplify, extend, and sometimes recontextualize traditional methods. Computational imaging now allows for unprecedented levels of detail and accuracy in visual analysis, supporting the study of underdrawings, pigments, and conservation histories in ways that were once the preserve of specialized laboratories. Automated data mining and large-scale digital cataloguing have transformed research synthesis, enabling scholars to discover patterns and relationships across vast corpora of artworks, texts, and archival materials with speed and precision (Gao et al. 2024). These developments have, in turn, made it possible to expand pedagogical and public engagement through immersive XR installations and AI-driven interpretive tools, reaching audiences who were previously marginalized by the spatial, linguistic, or cultural boundaries of the field (Bilad et al. 2023). The digital turn has facilitated more inclusive approaches, allowing users to access and contribute to collections, narratives, and interpretations from a multiplicity of positions and identities. Yet, as the field opens itself to a wider public, it must also contend with heightened demands for transparency, scholarly rigor, and collaborative process, given the increasingly networked and participatory nature of knowledge production. The most successful integrations have arisen when professionals embrace the creative tension between inherited disciplinary values and the affordances of new technologies, positioning themselves at the intersection of art historical tradition and technical innovation.

A central insight from this volume is the critical importance of maintaining dialogic exchange—between humans and machines, across generations of scholars, and among institutions (Baillifard et al. 2024). Rather than reinforcing static, hierarchical modes of dissemination, intelligent systems have facilitated a shift toward participatory, adaptive, and reflexive engagement, transforming both classroom and gallery into sites of ongoing negotiation and shared inquiry. Generative AI tutors, for instance, invite students into iterative dialogue, scaffolding critical thinking through conversational feedback and personalized questioning, while algorithmic curatorial assistants support curators in making visible previously overlooked connections and communities (Denny et al. 2024). XR-enabled museum experiences further exemplify this dynamic, allowing visitors to interact with reconstructed historical environments, pose questions to digital avatars, and even contribute their own interpretations to evolving digital exhibitions. In such environments, expertise is not simply transferred but is actively coconstructed, aligning art historical practice with contemporary educational paradigms that emphasize collaborative learning, distributed authority, and the cultivation of reflective agency. At the same time, this transformation intensifies the imperative for self-awareness and ethical reflection, demanding that the field remains vigilant about the risks of bias, oversimplification, and the loss of disciplinary nuance (Mahmoud and Sørensen 2024). The ongoing calibration of technological and human agency is thus not a technical detail, but a central axis around which responsible innovation must revolve. Ultimately, the dialogic model positions art history to thrive in a world where meaning is negotiated in the interplay of tradition, technology, and critical inquiry.

The case studies and frameworks discussed throughout this work make it clear that the success of technological integration depends as much on human factors—leadership, adaptability, and ethical vision—as it does on technical infrastructure (Hutson 2024; Pratschke 2024). The most impactful initiatives have been those in which practitioners approached intelligent systems not as prepackaged solutions, but as tools requiring thoughtful curation, critical engagement, and active adaptation to the contexts of their use. Faculty, curators, and institutional leaders who have fostered iterative development, invited feedback from students, visitors, and collaborators, and remained open to recalibrating both their goals and their methods, have established environments where technological innovation supports rather than supplants scholarly agency (Dong 2023). This ethos of collaborative learning and design has proven essential for navigating the unpredictability and complexity of generative tools, as well as for cultivating resilience in the face of inevitable technical setbacks or unforeseen consequences. Art history's disciplinary openness to critique, debate, and pluralism has served as both a model and a mandate for the responsible development of intelligent technologies, guiding professionals to foreground the values of transparency, inclusivity, and intellectual humility. By viewing themselves as architects rather than mere adopters of technological change, practitioners can ensure that their work remains grounded in both the intellectual legacy of the field and the evolving needs of its publics. In sum, the future of art history and museum practice hinges not simply on acquiring new tools, but on developing the critical capacity to use them wisely, creatively, and ethically. The path forward lies in sustaining a culture of reflective experimentation, where technological innovation is continuously balanced against the enduring imperatives of humanistic inquiry.

When thoughtfully implemented, these emergent technologies amplify the enduring strengths of the field: close looking, contextual analysis, dialogic debate, and a persistent commitment to making art and culture accessible and meaningful for contemporary publics (Gao et al. 2024). They offer powerful tools for overcoming barriers of geography, language, and prior expertise, enabling a more participatory and pluralistic approach to both research and teaching (Baillifard et al. 2024). By leveraging algorithmic curation, adaptive XR experiences, and multilingual interfaces, scholars and educators can reach audiences historically marginalized or excluded from art historical discourse. These benefits, however, are most fully realized when technological adoption is carefully aligned with the field's intellectual traditions and ethical commitments, ensuring that digital tools enhance rather than erode disciplinary rigor. Sustained reflection and dialogue within the profession—encompassing critical pedagogy, methodological pluralism, and rigorous peer review—provide necessary guardrails against the risks of technological determinism and superficial novelty. The discipline's reflective posture—its willingness to revisit, reframe, and reimagine its own purposes—remains critical to ensuring that intelligent systems function as instruments of empowerment rather than as ends in themselves (Gold and Klein 2023). Only by maintaining this commitment to reflective, values-driven practice can art history harness the full transformative potential of intelligent technologies.

Looking ahead, the principal challenge and opportunity for the field is to maintain a careful balance between the transformative potential of intelligent technologies and the enduring values of scholarly and professional practice (Mahmoud and Sørensen 2024). Integration must be approached with both humility and openness—welcoming the affordances of intelligent systems while remaining acutely aware of the risks of bias, inequity, and ethical compromise. Achieving this balance calls for ongoing professional development, participatory design, and an unwavering commitment to inclusivity and critical reflection. By cultivating these habits, art history and museum professionals not only demonstrate adaptability, but also model leadership in guiding how technology is shaped and understood for the broader public good (Pratschke 2024). Ultimately, the integration of intelligent technologies, as documented throughout this volume, should be seen as an ongoing process of reflection, experimentation, and renewal. Through the intentional synthesis of digital, algorithmic, and humanistic approaches, the discipline affirms its continued relevance and prepares itself for new forms of inquiry, teaching, and public engagement. This conclusion, then, is not a final word, but an invitation—to envision what art historical practice, animated by the dynamic interplay of human and machine, can yet become.

8.2 Ethical and Practical Challenges: Balancing Innovation with Responsibility

The integration of smart technologies into art history and museum practice, while enabling unprecedented access and innovation, brings a host of ethical and practical challenges that demand sustained critical reflection. Foremost among these are the risks associated with data privacy, the collection of user analytics, and the stewardship of sensitive information gathered through XR platforms and AI-driven interfaces (Baillifard et al. 2024). As these systems become more deeply embedded in classrooms and galleries, institutions must grapple with the responsibility of safeguarding not only the intellectual property of artworks and curatorial materials but also the digital identities and behavioral data of students and visitors. Examples from recent deployments reveal that even well-intentioned efforts to personalize content or track engagement can inadvertently expose users to data breaches or unauthorized surveillance, particularly when third-party plugins or cloud-based services are involved. The challenge is compounded in global contexts where regulatory frameworks vary and cross-border data flows complicate compliance and oversight. Hypothetically, as museum XR guides become ubiquitous, a breach in one platform could jeopardize the privacy of tens of thousands of visitors, undermining public trust and institutional legitimacy. To mitigate such risks, robust encryption, transparent consent protocols, and clear data retention policies are required—not as afterthoughts, but as foundational elements of technological adoption. The ethical imperative is not simply to comply with external standards, but to foster a culture of digital stewardship and proactive risk management at every stage of project design.

Algorithmic bias represents a second major challenge, threatening the inclusivity and representational fairness that digital tools purport to advance. Large language models and computer vision systems are shaped by their training data, and when that data reflects historical patterns of exclusion or prejudice, those biases can be amplified in both subtle and overt ways (Bilad et al. 2023). Case studies have already shown that AI-powered collection search tools can marginalize non-Western artists, women, and minoritized communities by reproducing gaps or distortions present in museum records (Gold and Klein 2023). In teaching, generative tutors risk providing interpretations that privilege canonical narratives or fail to recognize emergent, contested, or pluralistic viewpoints. As the discipline seeks to democratize expertise, these risks are not merely technical—they are profoundly political, shaping who is visible, whose knowledge counts, and whose stories are told. The problem is likely to grow as XR and AI-driven avatars become more prevalent, potentially reinforcing or even hardcoding curatorial biases into immersive experiences and automated guides. For future systems, continual audits for representational bias, the creation of more diverse training datasets, and participatory design with community stakeholders will be essential. Only by embedding mechanisms for critical review and iterative correction can institutions hope to build digital tools that reflect ethical commitments and social responsibilities.

Transparency and explainability pose another layer of ethical complexity. As AI systems are integrated into interpretive and research workflows, professionals and publics alike must be able to understand the logic, limits, and provenance of automated outputs (Denny et al. 2024). Without transparency, there is a risk that users may ascribe unwarranted authority to algorithmic recommendations, mistaking statistical correlation for scholarly insight or overlooking the boundaries of machine interpretation. Examples from the manuscript show that even experienced educators occasionally struggle to interrogate the sources or interpretive moves underlying AI-generated content, especially when systems draw from opaque, proprietary datasets or blend historical fact with speculative synthesis (Hutson and Barner 2025). Hypothetically, a future where museum labels, catalogue entries, or classroom lectures are generated in whole or in part by algorithms would challenge long-standing norms of citation, peer review, and scholarly accountability. To safeguard intellectual rigor, institutions should demand open documentation of algorithmic processes, facilitate user education, and develop collaborative protocols for vetting and annotating machine outputs. Such measures support not only technical literacy but also empower professionals and students to question, adapt, and refine the outputs of generative systems in light of evolving disciplinary standards.

Responsibility for equitable access and inclusion remains a further practical and ethical concern. While digital and algorithmic platforms promise to break down barriers of geography, disability, and language, they risk entrenching new forms of exclusion for users who lack access to reliable devices, connectivity, or technical support (Gao et al. 2024). Examples from student use of the Da Vinci AI tutor document disparities between PC and Mac users, and the persistent challenges of deploying browser-based XR in regions with limited infrastructure (Hutson and Barner 2025). As these technologies become central to curricula and visitor engagement, there is a danger that the digital divide may deepen, privileging the already advantaged and exacerbating existing inequities. Hypothetically, future reliance on XR-driven assessment or AI-moderated museum tours could systematically exclude participants with disabilities, low-bandwidth Internet, or limited digital literacy, unless robust accommodations and alternative pathways are built into every stage of design. Ethical adoption thus entails a commitment to universal design, multilingual access, and ongoing consultation with underrepresented users and communities.

Another dimension of ethical complexity arises in the realm of intellectual property, authorship, and academic integrity. Generative systems, by their nature, remix, synthesize, and sometimes blur the boundaries between original work and automated output, raising new questions about citation, attribution, and creative ownership (Pratschke 2024). In the classroom, students may be tempted to over-rely on AI tutors, risking both inadvertent plagiarism and the erosion of critical thinking skills. In research, the provenance of algorithmically generated findings must be clearly articulated, so that the line between human insight and machine assistance remains visible and contestable (Dong 2023). Hypothetically, as generative tools become more sophisticated, the danger of undetected data fabrication or intellectual dishonesty increases, placing pressure on institutions to develop robust policies and detection systems. The field must also grapple with the legal and ethical ramifications of training models on copyrighted materials or sensitive archival content, ensuring that the pursuit of innovation does not undermine the rights of artists, authors, and cultural communities. Proactive strategies—such as watermarking, transparent annotation, and fair-use guidelines—will be necessary to navigate this rapidly evolving terrain while preserving the discipline's integrity and creative potential.

A further practical challenge lies in the sustainability and maintenance of intelligent platforms over time. As the manuscript demonstrates, XR and AI systems demand ongoing support, regular updates, and continual adaptation to changing technical standards, user expectations, and pedagogical goals (Bhatia et al. 2024). The rapid pace of technological advancement risks leaving institutions with obsolete systems, unsupported software, or unsustainable dependencies on proprietary platforms. Hypothetically, a museum or academic department that invests heavily in a bespoke AI-powered gallery tour or virtual tutor may find itself constrained by licensing changes, discontinued vendor support, or shifts in regulatory landscape. To mitigate such risks, the field must prioritize modular, interoperable design, open-source solutions, and collaborative consortia capable of sharing knowledge, resources, and technical capacity. Sustainability also means planning for archiving, versioning, and documenting digital projects so that the fruits of innovation remain accessible and adaptable for future generations. Only by embedding these principles into the DNA of digital strategy can art historical institutions hope to build resilient, future-proof infrastructures that endure beyond the lifecycle of any single tool.

Finally, the ethical deployment of intelligent technologies requires a continuous culture of self-assessment, dialogue, and adaptation within the profession. As discussed throughout the manuscript, the most successful examples of AI and XR integration have emerged from iterative cycles of feedback, user consultation, and interdisciplinary collaboration (Baillifard et al. 2024). The future will demand not only technical upskilling but also the cultivation of new habits of critical reflection, participatory governance, and collective accountability. Hypothetically, as intelligent avatars and automated curators proliferate, institutions may need to establish advisory boards or oversight committees—including technologists, artists, educators, and community members—to review, evaluate, and guide technological adoption in line with shared ethical principles. This orientation to continuous improvement not only protects against unintended harms but also ensures that innovation remains aligned with the evolving values, aspirations, and public obligations of the field. Balancing innovation with responsibility is less a matter of technical compliance than a commitment to the deepest traditions of inquiry, stewardship, and ethical care.

8.3 Reframing Professional Practice in Art History and Museums

The reframing of professional practice in art history and museums under the influence of intelligent technologies represents not merely an operational or technical shift but a comprehensive rearticulation of disciplinary roles, scholarly authority, and institutional identity. As machine-based and generative tools become integrated into every aspect of art historical work—from research and curation to pedagogy and public engagement—practitioners are compelled to reevaluate the boundaries between human and computational expertise. The early adoption of computational analytics in museum visitor experience, as discussed in Chap. 2, has demonstrated the potential for these tools to democratize interpretation and broaden participation, but has also foregrounded the need for art historians and curators to act as critical mediators, not passive facilitators, of digital engagement. Professional roles expand to include oversight of algorithmic curation, stewardship of digital assets, and the continual translation of disciplinary values into the evolving protocols of automated systems. In this context, curators, educators, and scholars must cultivate new literacies—spanning data ethics, interdisciplinary collaboration, and digital communication—while remaining grounded in the intellectual traditions and interpretive rigor that distinguish the field.

The redefinition of professional practice extends deeply into the processes of research and scholarly production. Automated literature review, computational pattern recognition, and data-driven attribution have accelerated the pace and scale of discovery, yet they also demand a heightened commitment to transparency, critical reflection, and collaborative interpretation (Hutson 2024, pp. 51–59). Rather than displacing the expert eye or historical intuition, these tools require practitioners to actively shape research questions, curate datasets, and synthesize machine outputs with contextually rich, humanistic analysis. This hybrid model, as outlined in Chap. 3, positions the art historian not only as a consumer of computational results but as a methodological architect—designing workflows, validating results, and foregrounding the epistemic limits of automation (Hutson 2024, pp. 65–70). The discipline thus becomes defined by a dynamic negotiation between computational possibility and scholarly judgment, situating the art historian as both a steward of tradition and an agent of methodological innovation.

Within museum practice, the proliferation of intelligent systems has led to a reconsideration of curatorial authority and institutional mission. Recommendation engines, adaptive guides, and immersive environments now mediate the visitor's encounter with collections, reframing interpretation as an interactive, participatory process (Hutson 2024, pp. 35–45). Curators are increasingly responsible for the ethical governance of these systems, ensuring that personalization, accessibility, and equity are not merely technical achievements but are aligned with broader commitments to cultural stewardship and public trust. The shift to visitor-centered, digitally mediated engagement is not without its risks—especially regarding algorithmic bias, privacy, and the potential erosion of curatorial autonomy—but it also opens new avenues for experimentation and community cocreation. As explored in Chaps. 2 and 5, successful integration of generative technologies hinges on the ability of museum professionals to synthesize technical, ethical, and interpretive competencies, redefining their practice as both inclusive and critically adaptive (Hutson 2024, pp. 35–45, 115–122).

Pedagogical practice is likewise undergoing a profound transformation, as prompt engineering, digital simulation, and immersive learning environments reshape the relationship between instructor, student, and content (Hutson 2024, pp. 141–151). The rise of dialogic, scaffolded assignments, supported by machine-generated feedback and adaptive learning platforms, has repositioned the educator as a facilitator of inquiry rather than an authoritative transmitter of knowledge. This shift is particularly salient in art history, where interpretive pluralism, close looking, and reflexive critique remain foundational. As discussed in Chaps. 6 and 7, effective practitioners are now required to blend digital fluency with methodological rigor—designing iterative assignments, modeling critical engagement with algorithmic outputs, and sustaining a classroom culture that is at once technologically agile and intellectually robust (Hutson 2024, pp. 140–170, 181–210).

The administrative and leadership dimensions of art history and museum work have also been reshaped by automation and analytics. Strategic decision-making, curriculum planning, and program assessment are increasingly data-driven, enabling leaders to anticipate trends, allocate resources efficiently, and foster a culture of continuous improvement (Hutson 2024, pp. 107–115). However, these efficiencies demand careful stewardship: leaders must ensure that the deployment of analytics remains transparent, inclusive, and accountable, with mechanisms for stakeholder input and regular review of ethical and practical outcomes. As the case studies in

Chap. 5 illustrate, successful departments and institutions are those that embed critical reflection, faculty development, and collaborative governance into their technological adoption, sustaining professional autonomy even as systems become more complex (Hutson 2024, pp. 107–130).

Crucially, the reframing of professional practice must be understood as an ongoing, iterative process—one that resists both technological determinism and nostalgia for static disciplinary identities. Art historians and museum professionals are increasingly called upon to articulate new forms of leadership, advocacy, and public engagement, leveraging intelligent tools to foster dialogue, advance social justice, and steward cultural memory (Hutson 2024, pp. 130–135). This evolving landscape demands both humility and boldness: a willingness to interrogate the limitations of computational systems, while also experimenting with new modes of inquiry, collaboration, and interpretation. As outlined in the volume's conclusion, the most resilient and innovative practices will be those that situate generative technologies within a broader horizon of ethical stewardship, intellectual curiosity, and commitment to the public good (Hutson 2024, pp. 231–239).

Thus, the ongoing reframing of professional practice in art history and museums demands that practitioners become both adaptive leaders and critical stewards—capable of integrating technological innovation with disciplinary depth, ethical reflection, and community engagement. The convergence of generative tools, analytics, and participatory digital platforms requires a new blend of technical fluency, collaborative acumen, and interpretive sensitivity, ensuring that automation serves rather than supplants human judgment and curatorial authority. As institutions navigate the opportunities and risks presented by these systems, continuous dialogue among curators, educators, technologists, and audiences will be essential for maintaining trust, fostering transparency, and sustaining the public mission of cultural stewardship. The future of the field will be shaped by those who embrace experimentation and interdisciplinary learning while remaining grounded in the intellectual traditions and social responsibilities that define art history at its best. By forging partnerships across domains, investing in professional development, and advocating for inclusive, accountable governance, art historians, and museum professionals can transform digital disruption into an engine of renewal and relevance. The challenge is ongoing—but so too is the opportunity to redefine what it means to lead, teach, and care for culture in an age of intelligent systems. This moment invites the field to craft a practice that is as resilient and innovative as it is reflective and humane, ensuring that art history and museums continue to inspire, connect, and serve an ever-widening public.

8.4 Toward Sustainable, Inclusive, and Reflective Adoption

The adoption of algorithmic and generative technologies in museum and art history practice necessitates a new conception of professional roles—one in which curators, educators, and technologists become costewards of digital culture and public trust.

Museums have responded to this imperative by foregrounding ethical frameworks for user privacy, data security, and consent. Institutions like the British Museum and Rijksmuseum now restrict the duration of digital data retention, implement clear privacy protocols, and require explicit visitor consent for participation in data-driven personalization. International standards such as the General Data Protection Regulation (GDPR) serve as benchmarks, while practical measures—like digital privacy dashboards at the Science Museum, London, and the Metropolitan Museum of Art—give users granular control over their data and algorithmic experience (Lewis 2024). These practices are not just about legal compliance, but about building audience trust and signaling a shift toward participatory cocreation, where visitors become partners in shaping both policy and knowledge. When museum-goers feel respected and informed, their willingness to engage with algorithmic experiences increases, reinforcing a positive feedback loop of participation and institutional accountability (Silverman 2010). The ethical stewardship of data and consent thus becomes an integral dimension of digital professionalism in the field.

Algorithmic bias represents a persistent challenge in reframing curatorial practice for the digital age. The risk that AI-driven curation might reinforce historical exclusions or marginalize underrepresented groups is now widely recognized as a core issue for museums committed to equity and inclusion. For instance, the Smithsonian's data ethics committee regularly audits digital outputs for evidence of bias, working to diversify datasets and interpretive frameworks (Muhammad and Orji 2024). The illusion of algorithmic neutrality is directly contested through best practices such as interdisciplinary review panels at the Van Gogh Museum and the Louvre, which systematically assess the cultural impact of new digital initiatives (Giannini and Bowen 2024). Collaboration among technologists, curators, educators, and external stakeholders ensures that the broader implications of AI-driven personalization—such as the representation of minority artists or narratives—are critically evaluated. Achieving fairness requires a deliberate, reflexive approach, integrating multiple perspectives into both the design and oversight of algorithmic tools. The goal is to position museums not only as venues of display, but as active laboratories for digital ethics and cultural negotiation.

Transparency and explainability have become nonnegotiable elements of professional practice as machine-based decision-making enters the curatorial and educational mainstream. Open-access dashboards, online interpretive panels, and platforms that reveal the provenance of digital datasets are increasingly common in leading museums (Pansoni et al. 2023). These mechanisms serve a dual function: educating the public about algorithmic logic and facilitating regulatory oversight through real-time public scrutiny. By demystifying "black box" processes, such tools build intellectual transparency and foster trust among diverse audiences, making the interpretive processes behind digital curation accessible to both specialists and the general public. Museums in the Netherlands and Canada, for example, have launched sensory-friendly and multilingual interfaces, adapting content not only for language, but also for user ability, device, and feedback preferences (Brischetto et al. 2023). Professional development initiatives such as the Creative Interfaces Research + Design Studio, in partnership with Georgia Tech and the Griffin Museum of Science and Industry, foreground AI literacy and ethical troubleshooting as essential professional competencies (Northwestern 2024). As the field grows more complex, these transparency efforts are vital for maintaining accountability and intellectual integrity.

The evolution of the museum from static repository to dynamic, visitor-centered institution has been inseparable from digital innovation and a shift in professional values. Museums now see themselves as responsive environments that bridge physical, linguistic, and sensory barriers, serving the rapidly diversifying needs of twenty-first-century publics (Simon 2010; Wang 2024). Inclusivity—once seen as a supplementary goal—has become a defining feature of museum excellence. The transition from a "universal visitor" model to one that prioritizes linguistic and neurodiverse participation is evident in multilingual audio guides, adaptive interfaces, and programmatic efforts to engage marginalized groups (Hutson and Hutson 2024). The result is not just technical accommodation, but a broadening of cultural mission: museums now act as platforms for the negotiation of identity, belonging, and historical narrative. This transformation in visitor engagement is mirrored by institutional strategies that foreground dialogue, equity, and adaptability as essential criteria for professional practice. The AAM and ICOM have formalized these priorities, embedding accessibility and public trust in strategic planning at a global scale (Black 2012). Professional identity thus emerges through the ongoing interplay between technological possibility and cultural responsibility.

New questions of intellectual property and authorship have accompanied the spread of generative tools in curatorial and research settings. The 2025 U.S. Copyright Office addendum clarifies that AI-generated content can be protected, provided it reflects substantial human authorship, decision-making, and creative intervention (U.S. Copyright Office 2025). Art historians and museum professionals are encouraged to document their curatorial processes and creative contributions at every stage, establishing clear provenance and legal credibility for derivative works (Majumdar et al. 2023). Community-driven guidelines, Creative Commons licensing, and opt-in/out protocols for dataset participation empower both artists and institutions to set the terms for generative use (Pellegrini 2023). In practice, advisory boards and stewardship committees balance the interests of living artists, donor communities, and institutional policy, ensuring both legacy protection and innovation. Provenance tracking, machine-readable metadata, and digital watermarking are emerging as best practices, helping to balance access with attribution and rights management (Bonnet and Teuteberg 2023). These approaches strengthen the legitimacy and ethical foundation of professional practice in an era where machine-generated outputs are woven into the scholarly and curatorial fabric. Collaboration across disciplinary and institutional lines is essential to maintaining a shared sense of stewardship.

Best practices in digital curation and art historical research emphasize the necessity of collaborative, reflexive, and critically accountable methods. For example, codesign with neurodiverse users at the British Museum has led to more accessible visitor-facing tools, while ongoing dialogue among curators, IT staff, and educators at the Art Institute of Chicago has enabled the successful implementation of AI-driven wayfinding and interpretation (Kidd 2016; Parry 2007). Comparative case studies, such as the open data and neural network initiatives at the Rijksmuseum or digital cataloguing at the Getty Provenance Index, illustrate how institutional context shapes both the pace and ethics of innovation (Luther 2020). Critical reflexivity emerges as a linchpin of responsible adoption, with institutions like MoMA and Tate Modern establishing protocols for human oversight, iterative evaluation, and correction of algorithmic "black boxes" (Longworth 2021; Proctor 2010). Faculty, museum staff, and community members are increasingly involved in the iterative shaping of technology, ensuring that the discipline's ambitions remain grounded in transparency and public accountability. These collaborative and comparative approaches safeguard both methodological rigor and ethical stewardship in the digital age. The most successful institutions treat technology not as a panacea, but as a terrain for experimentation, negotiation, and collective learning.

Professional practice in the digital and algorithmic age now requires continual investment in training, interdisciplinary dialogue, and the cultivation of AI literacy among all museum and academic staff. Hands-on experimentation and participatory research—such as trial runs of AI exhibits and open forums on ethics—deepen institutional accountability and bring overlooked issues to light (Northwestern 2024; Mikhaylov et al. 2018). Participatory models, including citizen science projects and AI ethics cafés, invite visitors to shape both policy and interpretation, advancing democratic engagement in the stewardship of cultural heritage. The shift toward collective responsibility and transparency is not merely procedural but fundamentally reorients professional identity around a dialogic, public-facing ethos. Institutions that foster open dialogue and multistakeholder governance are best positioned to balance innovation with care, ensuring that technological change always serves the needs of the communities they serve. Such models of professional practice, informed by ongoing research and participatory feedback, provide a blueprint for the future of the field. Professional learning becomes inseparable from institutional renewal and societal trust.

As museums and art historians become increasingly enmeshed in policy formation and international standard-setting, professional practice is shaped by engagement with global working groups, consortia, and regulatory bodies. Initiatives to harmonize metadata, attribution, and copyright frameworks across institutions reflect the complexity of balancing innovation with legal and ethical protections (Bonnet and Teuteberg 2023). Participation in these conversations ensures that the distinctive needs of cultural heritage are not subsumed by broader trends in AI governance or digital policy. Art historians and museum professionals thus advocate for frameworks that safeguard both creative rights and scholarly freedoms, while facilitating the responsible use of generative tools. As best practices evolve, leadership requires fluency in both technical and policy domains, supported by continued investment in professional networks and shared resources. The legal, ethical, and practical foundations of professional practice are thus maintained through collaborative advocacy and foresight. These efforts signal the maturity and adaptability of the field as it negotiates the terrain of rapid technological change. In this way, the profession ensures that digital transformation is always rooted in the unique priorities and obligations of cultural stewardship.

8.5 Recommendations for Future Research, Policy, and Implementation

The next decade demands a robust, empirical research agenda to understand the impacts—intended and unintended—of intelligent systems on art historical scholarship, public engagement, and equity. Longitudinal and mixed-methods studies should be prioritized to evaluate how AI-mediated curation, immersive XR experiences, and automated assessment influence learning outcomes and visitor participation across various institutional contexts (Bilad et al. 2023; Giannini and Bowen 2024). Comparative analyses of algorithmic bias audits, along with participatory dataset curation involving diverse stakeholders, are crucial for mitigating representational gaps and structural inequities (Muhammad and Orji 2024; Pansoni et al. 2023). Open, discipline-specific benchmark datasets—licensed under Creative Commons or similar frameworks—will be indispensable for transparency and reproducibility, fostering global collaborations and enabling shared standards for computational art history (Lewis 2024; Bonnet and Teuteberg 2023). Researchers should also develop innovative, qualitative instruments for measuring belonging, engagement, and critical reflection—metrics that capture the field's pluralistic aspirations alongside quantitative reach (Simon 2010). Ultimately, the future of scholarly impact will be defined by multidimensional key performance indicators (KPIs) that reflect both inclusivity and rigor. As new technologies evolve, research must remain responsive, adaptable, and attentive to the shifting intersections of algorithm, audience, and institution. Only with a comprehensive empirical foundation can policy and implementation proceed responsibly.

Policy and governance frameworks are now central to the sustainable and ethical adoption of AI and XR in the cultural sector. Institutions should craft detailed AI ethics charters, incorporating principles of privacy, inclusivity, transparency, and ongoing community consultation. Such frameworks must include clear opt-in/opt-out mechanisms for artists and rights-holders whose works might enter training datasets, aligning with international copyright guidelines and emerging best practices (Pellegrini 2023). Effective governance also requires routine bias audits, public reporting dashboards, and transparent consent protocols, ensuring that technological innovation is always aligned with institutional mission and public trust (Pansoni et al. 2023). Institutions should also look to global standards, such as the GDPR and UNESCO's AI Ethics Recommendation, but tailor local implementation to reflect the priorities and needs of their particular communities (Mikhaylov et al. 2018). Leadership should foster advisory committees that include diverse perspectives—technologists, curators, community representatives, and legal experts—to anticipate and resolve emerging dilemmas. As automation and generative tools reshape professional boundaries, adaptive and participatory policy will be vital to ensuring equity and accountability. Policy, thus, must be seen as a living instrument, iteratively revised in dialogue with the communities it serves.

Implementation strategies should be rooted in modular, open-source toolchains and collaborative infrastructures that prevent vendor lock-in and allow for cross-institutional learning (Northwestern 2024). By adopting interoperable standards and sharing cloud resources, museums, libraries, and archives can maximize technical capacity and minimize the risks associated with rapid obsolescence (Bonnet and Teuteberg 2023). Professional development pipelines must become a strategic priority, including ongoing AI literacy workshops, participatory design residencies, and interdisciplinary fellowships linking cultural organizations with technology partners (Kidd 2016; Wang 2024). Iterative evaluation—pairing user analytics with qualitative feedback—should be built into all projects from inception to ensure continuous recalibration for accessibility, inclusion, and cultural resonance (Brischetto et al. 2023; Silverman 2010). As pilot projects mature, regional consortia can share both infrastructure and expertise, while joint copyright advocacy can help the field anticipate regulatory changes (Parry 2007). Institutional resilience will depend on building distributed networks and collaborative cultures of experimentation. Leaders must support innovation not as isolated projects, but as shared endeavors that can be sustained and adapted over time. Implementation must always be a process of learning and renewal, rather than static deployment.

Collaborative infrastructure is foundational for amplifying impact, accelerating innovation, and ensuring responsible stewardship of cultural data. The field should invest in shared metadata standards, cloud-based repositories, and regional consortia for resource pooling and joint advocacy (Bonnet and Teuteberg 2023; Mikhaylov et al. 2018). Cross-sector fellowships, linking museums, universities, public libraries, and tech firms, can incubate pilot projects and disseminate best practices quickly (Parry 2007). These collaborations foster a culture of mutual accountability, allowing rapid adaptation to technological, ethical, and policy developments. Shared infrastructure also supports the scalability of small-scale experiments, so that promising tools or frameworks can be disseminated widely, adapted locally, and continually improved. Multiinstitutional partnerships not only provide practical solutions for interoperability, but also create resilient networks for peer learning and ethical governance. The field should promote these partnerships as engines for both innovation and trust-building with publics and stakeholders. By building an ecosystem of shared responsibility, the discipline can remain nimble in the face of technological and cultural shifts.

In sum, the future of research, policy, and implementation in art history and museums will require vigilance, humility, and a collaborative, forward-facing ethos. The challenges of algorithmic bias, data governance, intellectual property, and sustainability are too complex to be addressed by any one institution or professional community in isolation. The field must commit to an ongoing, participatory process of reflection, experimentation, and renewal, grounded in both rigorous scholarship and public accountability. The call to action is clear: practitioners, policymakers, and researchers must work together—across disciplines, geographies, and institutional silos—to shape the future of cultural stewardship in the age of intelligent systems. It is only through such collective endeavor that the field can realize the full promise of technological innovation while upholding its foundational values of equity, pluralism, and critical inquiry.

8.6 The Evolving Horizon: Envisioning the Next Chapter for the Field

As art history and museum work move toward a future shaped by intelligent systems, the prospect of human–machine cocreativity offers profound new directions for scholarship, interpretation, and exhibition design. AI is rapidly maturing as a collaborative partner, not merely a tool—capable of proposing thematic links, generating synthetic exhibition narratives, and serving as a "second reader" in curatorial workflows (Gao et al. 2024; Majumdar et al. 2023). The potential for generative algorithms to create interpretive texts or even artworks themselves raises fresh questions about authorship, legitimacy, and the aesthetics of machine intelligence. Forward-thinking institutions will embrace the dialogue between human expertise and algorithmic suggestion, treating the output of AI as both a resource and a provocation. Scholars must critically assess not only the quality but also the implications of these collaborations, ensuring that creativity remains anchored in context, accountability, and scholarly intent. As these practices become normalized, professional guidelines for documenting, annotating, and attributing cocreated content will be essential (Majumdar et al. 2023). The future lies in treating AI not as a replacement for human vision, but as a catalyst for new modes of inquiry and expression. This collaborative horizon invites bold experimentation tempered by ethical rigor.

The visitor experience of the future will be defined by hyper-personalization and multisensory engagement, made possible through advances in biometric feedback, XR, and adaptive AI. Museum guides may soon adapt dynamically to user preferences, accessibility needs, and learning goals—adjusting narrative content, pacing, and media forms on the fly (Luo and Nys 2024). XR environments will fuse visual, tactile, olfactory, and haptic feedback, enabling embodied understanding of artistic process and historical context (Pietroni 2025). Privacy-preserving edge computing will become vital to protect visitor data while still delivering real-time, context-aware personalization. These shifts demand ongoing vigilance: institutions must anticipate both the new possibilities and the new ethical risks introduced by ever more granular data collection and adaptive systems. Curatorial and educational practice will need to foreground user agency, informed consent, and continuous evaluation. By designing for agency, inclusivity, and transparency, institutions can create environments where each visitor's experience is both unique and accountable. The future of the museum is thus envisioned as a living, adaptive ecosystem, responsive to the diversity of contemporary publics.

The horizon of global cultural participation will be broadened through AI-powered translation, transcription, and low-cost, open-source infrastructures that challenge long-standing Euro-American dominance in the field (Macdonald 2003;

Neather 2024). Satellite connectivity, smartphone-driven interfaces, and regionally trained language models can democratize access to heritage collections and scholarly networks, especially in the Global South. AI-driven tools will enable the surfacing of non-Western languages, oral histories, and indigenous knowledge systems, rebalancing the canon and enriching global art history. Collaborations across continents and cultural contexts will become the norm, inviting new ethical frameworks that respect local sovereignty and epistemic diversity. Institutions must prioritize the codesign of tools and content with historically marginalized communities, ensuring that the benefits of digital transformation are equitably distributed. Future professional practice will be characterized by humility, reflexivity, and mutual learning across boundaries. The discipline will be renewed by the plural voices it can now amplify. Art history, in this vision, becomes truly global, participatory, and just.

Environmental sustainability will emerge as a critical concern, as the field grapples with the carbon footprint and resource demands of large-scale AI systems and digital infrastructures. Green AI practices—such as energy-efficient architectures, shared compute clusters, and carbon-accounting for digital projects—will become standard in grant applications and institutional reporting (Mannheimer et al. 2024). Museums and research consortia must build strategies for reducing digital waste, recycling hardware, and sharing computational resources, aligning digital innovation with broader commitments to ecological responsibility. The discipline will be called to integrate environmental metrics alongside those of engagement and equity, linking stewardship of heritage with stewardship of the planet. Research and policy must address the lifecycle costs of digital projects and encourage practices that are scalable, adaptable, and resilient. By foregrounding sustainability, institutions not only future-proof their own operations but also model values of intergenerational care. The call for "green museums" and "responsible AI" is an invitation to integrate ethical consciousness into every aspect of digital practice. This new environmental ethic will be inseparable from the future of art history.

The evolving horizon will be shaped by breakthroughs in quantum and neuromorphic computing, adaptive governance, and interdisciplinary pedagogy. Quantum-accelerated image analysis and on-device, privacy-preserving visitor analytics may become feasible within a decade, vastly expanding the field's analytical and interpretive reach. Curricula will evolve to train art history students in basic coding, algorithmic critique, and collaborative publication with computer scientists, fostering hybrid intellectual identities. Dynamic oversight bodies—drawing on the expertise of humanities scholars, technologists, and communities—will be essential for continuously revising guidelines, standards, and accountability frameworks. Professional societies must take the lead in convening these networks, ensuring that technological innovation remains responsive to shifting public values and cultural priorities. The field is thus invited to move boldly, reflectively, and inclusively into a future where art history and museums lead—not simply adapt to—the digital age. The call to action is clear: let us envision, experiment, and govern together, ensuring that the next chapter of art history is as intellectually vibrant, socially just, and ethically accountable as its proudest traditions.

References

Baillifard A, Gabella M, Lavenex PB, Martarelli CS (2024) Effective learning with a personal AI tutor: a case study. Educ Inf Technol

Bhatia A, Bhatia P, Sood D (2024) Leveraging AI to transform online higher education: focusing on personalized learning, assessment, and student engagement. Int J Manage Humanit

Bilad M, Yaqin L, Zubaidah S (2023) Recent progress in the use of artificial intelligence tools in education. J Penelit Pengkaj Ilmu Pendidik e-Saintika 7(3):314–322

Black G (2012) Transforming museums in the twenty-first century. Routledge

Bonnet P, Teuteberg F (2023) Blockchain-based provenance tracking for cultural heritage. J Cult Herit 59:181–192

Brischetto L, Filipchuk V, Udych D (2023) Adaptive museum interfaces for multisensory inclusion. Mus Manag Curat 38(3):401–423

Chandler T, Clulow A (2020) Modeling Virtual Angkor: an evolutionary approach to a single urban space. IEEE Comput Graph Appl 40(3):9–16

Denny P, Macneil S, Savelka J, Porter L, Luxton-Reilly A (2024) Desirable characteristics for AI teaching assistants in programming education. Annu Conf Innov Technol Comput Sci Educ (ITiCSE) 1:408–414

Dong C (2023) How to build an AI tutor that can adapt to any course and provide accurate answers using large language model and retrieval-augmented generation. ArXiv abs/2311.17696

Gao H, Lindquist M, Vergel RS (2024) AI-driven avatars in immersive 3D environments for education: workflow and case study of the Temple of Demeter, Greece. J Digit Landsc Archit 2024(9):640–651

Giannini T, Bowen J (2024) Diversity and algorithmic curation in museums. Int J Digit Herit 19(2):102–120

Gold M, Klein L (eds) (2023) Debates in the digital humanities. Minnesota State Press

Hutson J (Ed.). (2024) The rise of AI in academic inquiry. IGI Global

Hutson J, Barner T (2025) Development and evaluation of the Da Vinci AI Tutor: enhancing accessibility and personalized learning in art history education. Des 10(X)

Hutson J, Hutson P (2024) Inclusive smart museums: engaging neurodiverse audiences and enhancing cultural heritage. Springer Nature

Kidd J (2016) Museums in the new mediascape: transmedia, participation, ethics. Routledge

Lewis R (2024) Collections as networked images: the (re)use of the science museum group collections. In: The form of digital images through social media (Doctoral dissertation, School of Advanced Study, University of London)

Longworth H (2021) Critical reflexivity and algorithmic tools in museums. Museol Rev 47(2):145–158

Luo R, Nys P (2024) Adaptive digital storytelling in museums: a biometric approach. Mus Tech Today 12(1):29–41

Luther K (2020) Digital archives and the Getty provenance index. Arch Sci 20(1):77–91

Macdonald S (2003) Museums, national, post national and transcultural identities. Mus Soc 1(1):1–16

Mahmoud CF, Sørensen JT (2024) Artificial intelligence in personalized learning with a focus on current developments and future prospects. Res Adv Educ 3(8):25–31

Majumdar S, Wagh V, Kretschmer M (2023) Human authorship and AI-generated content. J Cult Herit 60:201–219

Mannheimer S et al (2024) Responsible AI practice in libraries and archives. Info Tech Lib 43(3)

Mikhaylov SJ, Esteve M, Campion A (2018) Artificial intelligence for the public sector: opportunities and challenges of cross-sector collaboration. Phil Trans Roy Soc A 376(2128):20170357

Muhammad F, Orji CM (2024) Revolutionizing education in the digital era: the role of AI in promoting inclusivity, equality, and ethical innovation. Amer J Soc Sci and Edu Innov 6(09):151–157

Neather R (2024) Machine translation and the decolonization of museum interpretation. Trans Stud 15(1):112–130

Northwestern (2024) AI literacy at museum of science and industry. https://hci.northwestern.edu/news-events/articles/2024/creative_interface_research_and_design_studio_museum_of_science_of_industry.html

Pansoni S, Tiribelli S, Paolanti M, Frontoni E, Giovanola B (2023) Design of an ethical framework for artificial intelligence in cultural heritage. 2023 IEEE International symposium ethics English science technology (ETHICS), pp 1–5

Parry R (2007) Recoding the museum: digital heritage and the technologies of change. Routledge

Pellegrini S (2023) Creative commons and museum digital rights. J Mus Licensing 8(2):55–72

Pietroni E (2025) Multisensory museums and hybrid realities. Mus Exp des 3(1):41–60

Pratschke BM (2024) Generative AI and education: digital pedagogies, teaching innovation and learning design. Springer Briefs Education

Proctor N (2010) Digital pathways at MoMA and tate modern. Mus Comp 21(3):87–98

Silverman L (2010) The social work of museums. Routledge

Simon N (2010) The participatory museum. Museum 2.0

U.S. Copyright Office (2025) Copyright registration guidance for works containing AI-generated material

Wang H (2024) The inclusive museum: strategies for the twenty-first century. Routledge

MIX
Papier aus verantwortungsvollen Quellen
Paper from responsible sources
FSC® C105338

If you have any concerns about our products,
you can contact us on
ProductSafety@springernature.com

In case Publisher is established outside the EU,
the EU authorized representative is:
Springer Nature Customer Service Center GmbH
Europaplatz 3, 69115 Heidelberg, Germany

Printed by Libri Plureos GmbH
in Hamburg, Germany